★ NEW ENGLAND STUDIES ★

Edited by John Putnam Demos, David Hackett Fischer,
and Robert A. Gross

THE

Economic & Social Transformation of Rural Rhode Island, 1780–1850

Daniel P. Jones

Northeastern University Press

BOSTON

Northeastern University Press

Library of Congress Cataloging-in-Publication Data

Jones, Daniel P., 1954–
The economic and social transformation of rural Rhode Island,
1780–1850 / Daniel P. Jones.
     p. cm. — (New England studies)
  Includes bibliographical references and index.
  ISBN 1-55553-121-0 (acid-free paper)
  1. Rural development — Rhode Island — History.   2.   Rhode Island —
Social conditions.   3.   Rhode Island — Economic conditions.   4.   Rhode
Island — History — 1775–1865.   I. Title.   II.   Series.
HN79.R43C65   1992   91-30487
307.1'412'09745 — dc20

Designed by Richard C. Bartlett and Ann Twombly

This book was composed in Ehrhardt by Coghill Composition Company in
Richmond, Virginia. It was printed and bound by McNaughton & Gunn, Inc., in
Saline, Michigan. The paper is Glatfelter, an acid-free sheet.

MANUFACTURED IN THE UNITED STATES OF AMERICA
96 95 94 93 92   5 4 3 2 1

To my parents, Howard E. and Harriet Gallup Jones,
and to my brothers, Edmund and Kenneth Jones

Contents

Figures

Preface

ALTHOUGH the federal Constitution of 1787 created a unified national government, American society itself remained divided among myriad regions, subregions, and particularistic locales. The cosmopolitan gentry who framed the new government shared a common elite education and many gentlemanly assumptions, but beneath them socially lay a sprawling, disparate collection of unique communities. Besides the most obvious differences between the slave South and a largely free North, Americans were separated by religious affiliation, national origin, and, perhaps most important, their relative proximity to commercial markets. Whereas in the Middle Atlantic states, and even the South, ethnic identities and religious traditions were crucial in creating local cultures, in New England demographic homogeneity meant that relative commercialization would above all help to define the nature of various locales.

Throughout the early Republic, and especially in New England, Americans who lived in backcountry areas exhibited a collection of values and behavior patterns that contrasted, often sharply, with those of their fellow citizens in more commercialized, coastal locales. Backcountry societies were characterized first by their remoteness from Western capitalist markets. To be sure, they traded frequently with commercial ports, exchanging small agricultural surpluses for industrial products made of pottery and iron, and nonessential tropical foods such as rum, chocolate, and tea. But these exchanges were chiefly controlled and operated not by the local yeomanry themselves, but rather by the resident gentry or leading farmers, or even by the agents or factors of distant urban merchants. Trade for most backcountry farmers meant not long-distance commerce with socially superior mercantile grandees, but rather local exchange with relative equals. Different moral principles and customs, moreover, governed these two semiseparate trading spheres. International merchants insisted on the sanctity of abstract, legal contracts, such as large speculative land sales and definitive credit arrangements. Backcountry settlers operated by a more flexible set of rules, based on actual land usage, the preservation of household independence, and the need for community stability. They certainly believed in repaying debts and honoring land boundaries, but not at the expense of the practical need for providing for their families and their sons' inheritances. Backcountry economies were not only less wealthy and less commercialized than coastal ones, they were also more loosely governed by the tenets of international commercial capitalism.[1]

It is perhaps no coincidence that interior American societies were at the same time developing their own distinctive religious cultures. In the South, beginning in the mid–1700s, Baptists and Methodist revivalists began to supplant the traditional Anglican establishment. This process was hastened by the arrival of Germans, Scotch, and Scotch-Irish immigrants, who contributed their own dissenting religious persuasions to both southern and mid-Atlantic backcountry regions. Farther north, through a more complicated process that began with the First Great Awakening, Baptist sectarians emerged in southern New England, splintering the power of the Puritan established order. A few decades later, the Congregational Standing Order came under more thorough assault in northern New England, as entirely new sects emerged from backcountry conditions in New Hampshire, Vermont, and the district of Maine. Alternative rural religions developed most strikingly in areas such as the southern piedmont and hill country of New England, where established churches existed but were weakened by their isolation from cosmopolitan society. But everywhere in backcountry America, the yeomanry tended to prefer religions that emphasized communal intimacy and personal piety over either the hierarchical formalism of Anglicanism or the abstruse theology of New England Calvinism.[2]

Although most backcountry residents remained apolitical through the colonial era, they were increasingly radicalized by the American Revolution, and by the disruptions caused by a commercializing Western economy. Imbibing revolutionary concepts of crowd action, popular sovereignty, and republican equality, hill-country farmers began to resist the imposition of cosmopolitan notions of political economy and religious decorum. In a series of well-known eruptions, backwoods yeomanry throughout the United States impeded tax collection, creditors' suits, and land ejectments. Resorting to violent threats, riots, and even armed rebellion, farmers organized into groups as geographically varied as the North Carolina Regulators, the Pennsylvania Whisky Rebels, the Massachusetts Shaysites, and the antilandlord rioters of Maine and Vermont.[3] In the meantime, new and still more stridently antielitist religious sects emerged, powered by continuing "frontier" revivals. Calling themselves variously Christians, Universalists, and Freewill Baptists, they not only established their own independent modes of worship but also actively denounced the influence of gentlemanly respectability and elite power over America's religious faiths.[4] The revolutionary era witnessed widespread political and cultural rebellions by a variety of backcountry societies, most of which had long remained politically quiescent during the colonial era.

Yet by the second quarter of the nineteenth century, conflicts between agrarian and commercial centers had largely withered throughout most of the United States. And here our historical knowledge remains rather incomplete. We know much about the eruptions of backcountry rebellions and their immediate defeats, either through military repression or political cooptation. But we remain ignorant of the process by which once-alienated settlers were reintegrated—economically, socially, and culturally—into the nation. In this book I seek to explore not only the building but also the waning of this kind of interregional antagonism—by examining in depth the rural society of northwestern Rhode Island.

Early Rhode Island had long been viewed by contemporaries—and later by historians—as an exceptional, even bizarre locale, the Baptist–Quaker colony of early Puritan nightmares, and the rogue agrarian state of later Federalist contempt.[5] But Rhode Island experienced many of the same backcountry-coast conflicts that stirred Americans to disorder throughout the early Republic. Its merchants and coastal farmers were every bit as commercialized as their like elsewhere in New England; and its backwoods farmers, although scarcely twenty miles from the nearest port, generally shared the relative economic and social isolation of their neighbors in central Massachusetts and eastern Connecticut.

What distinguished Rhode Island from the other states was the ability of its agrarian leaders to retain considerable influence over the central government until the 1790s, because of the state's long-standing tradition of upholding individual liberty and local autonomy. Elsewhere in the United States, with the exception of Vermont, cosmopolitan elites mounted successful counter-revolutions against the relatively leveling agrarian regimes that had been installed—in many states—at the height of the American Revolution. As a result, issues concerning taxes, debt payment, and land tenure, which led to riot and rebellion throughout the revolutionary era, were resolved on terms favorable to the backwoodsmen themselves. Conflicts between backcountry yeomen and the commercial gentry centered instead on the latter's attempts to promote and direct the growth of a regional market economy through the imposition of turnpike roads, ecologically destructive cotton-mill dams, and tax-supported schools. Backcountry farmers may have opposed these innovations elsewhere in the early Republic, but they were more fully occupied (like later historians) by the more pressing and explosive features of backcountry turbulence.

Finally, rural Rhode Island featured an intense contest between backcountry and cosmopolitan religious persuasions, a conflict obscured elsewhere by the strength of established churches and educated cultural elites. Backwoods religious preferences crystallized earliest and most clearly in Rhode Island, where an avowedly anticosmopolitan sect, the Six-Principle Baptists, evolved independently from, and in contradistinction to the churches of commercialized Rhode Island.

Of course, backcountry social and cultural features, aside from the remnants of a few Six-Principle churches, have long since vanished from Rhode Island, as they have from rural areas throughout the United States. From the vantage point of postindustrial United States, the triumph of commercial civilization and its values seems to have been inevitable. Such hindsight, however, was not available to those interior yeomanry who struggled, for a few crucial decades at the turn of the eighteenth century, to maintain their social independence and cultural identity. Although their efforts generally failed, they nevertheless forced their cosmopolitan antagonists to alter the course of cultural progress and commercial growth. And in a larger sense, if the values of antielitism and democratic localism have survived in the late twentieth century, they can trace their origins in part to the persistent strivings of the backcountry yeomen.

I have labored on this work for many years now—too many, in fact, to detail without embarrassment; and in that time I have profited from the advice and assistance of a large number of people. First on my list are the many individuals in northwestern Rhode Island who opened their records, and often their homes, to me, an otherwise unknown, young scholar. Margery I. Matthews introduced herself to me when we met as researchers in the Foster Town Clerk's Office and subsequently invited me to her home to examine important private manuscripts and town tax lists. She also provided me with leads to several other local record holders, including Audrey Hall, clerk of the Rice City Christian Church, Ernest Nye of the Foster Center Baptist Church, and Byron Waterman of the North Foster Baptist Church. They all cheerfully let me peruse their institutions' records. Also extremely helpful was Edna Kent of Chepachet, who photocopied for me her typescript copy of Hiram Salisbury's diary. She also put me on the trail of the Glocester Heritage Society, whose proprietors let me examine some important local account books, and of Mr. and Mrs. Clifford Brown, possessors of the Glocester Freewill Baptist Church records.

Most of the research, of course, took place in the more familiar institutional world of archives and manuscript repositories. Harold Kemble and Cynthia Bendroth were able and helpful guides to the riches of the Rhode Island Historical Society's manuscript collections, as was Phyllis Silva to the Rhode Island State Archives. I was also helped by the research library staff of the American Baptist Historical Society, Old Sturbridge Village, and the New York Historical Society. Special thanks go to the town hall staffs of the five municipalities that make up the northwest: they were always helpful and often charming in their kindliness.

When I first began to write this book, in its early incarnation as a Brown University dissertation, I was ably assisted by Naomi Lamoureax, who helped bridge the many lacunae in my knowledge of economic history. John L. Thomas was a wonderfully intelligent and enthusiastic commentator on the dissertation's initial drafts. The dissertation would not have been possible, of course, without the help of my advisor, Gordon S. Wood, who supported me all along, even though he often disagreed philosophically with some of my conclusions. Offering both moral and intellectual support during my graduate years and beyond were my friends Shank Gilkeson and Drew and Mary Cayton.

My work has been immeasurably improved, however, by the process of preparing it for publication at Northeastern University Press. Gregory Nobles, Robert Gross, and Alan Taylor read my initial draft in its entirety and offered many detailed and constructive suggestions for its improvement. They were all extremely supportive in their efforts to ensure that I strengthened interpretative failings, eliminated excessive detail, and recast inappropriate rhetoric. My editors at Northeastern, Deborah Kops and Emily McKeigue, steered me with a steady hand through the publication process. I should also thank the director of the Philadelphia Center for Early American History, Richard Dunn, for providing a base for my scholarly activities, and to the center's participants, who read and offered helpful comments on a paper distilled from a portion of Chapter Three. An earlier version of Chapter Two appeared as an article in *Rhode Island History*.

I must also thank, at least in a general way, my friends in New Jersey and Pennsylvania who have supported and humored me ever since I came to the area ten years ago to work at the New Jersey State Archives. I owe a special debt of gratitude to my supervisor at the archives, Karl J. Niederer, who twice granted me a leave of absence when I was beginning to despair of ever actually finishing. Outside of work, more people than I can list here helped me in a variety of ways: lending their library cards, loaning me their word-processing facilities, and cheering me up on countless occasions.

I dedicate this book to my parents, Howard and Harriet Jones, and to my brothers, Ed and Ken Jones, for the love and encouragement they have given throughout my young scholarly career. This book is about them, too, in that they are all descendants of backcountry New England farmers.

THE ECONOMIC AND SOCIAL
TRANSFORMATION OF RURAL
RHODE ISLAND, 1780–1850

MASSACHUSETTS

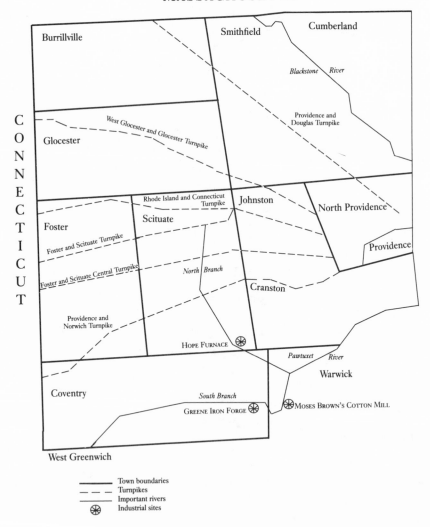

Figure 1. Northwestern Rhode Island: Early Turnpikes and Industrial Sites.

CHAPTER ONE

Rhode Island and the Rural Northwest
The Colonial and Revolutionary Heritage

▼ ▼

THROUGHOUT the colonial period, Rhode Island had always been viewed with scorn and derision by its neighbors in the other twelve colonies. They considered its religion to be an irresponsible blend of indifference and enthusiasm, and its government to be a chaotic mixture of democracy and anarchy. And as merchants and traders, Rhode Islanders were considered an unscrupulous and self-serving lot. To be sure, Rhode Island was hardly a monolithic community. The society and culture of the rural northwest differed considerably from that of the port towns that ringed Narragansett Bay; and it is partly the task of this book to examine and dramatize these differences. But during the colonial period, the differences that separated Rhode Islanders were underlain by those that differentiated all Rhode Islanders from British colonists elsewhere. Understanding the rural northwest, therefore, first requires a brief examination of the special peculiarities that distinguished Rhode Island as a whole.

Of all of Rhode Island's neighboring colonists, the orthodox leaders of Massachusetts and Connecticut particularly were appalled to find a neighboring government run by Baptists and Quakers, and one which accordingly lacked an established church. In a celebrated case in 1658, the Boston authorities had even executed two Rhode Island Quakers who had insisted on spreading the news of their divine inspiration to the heart of Puritan orthodoxy. By the middle of the eighteenth century, the imposition of religious tolerance and growing latitudinarianism had long since put an end to such repressive measures; yet Puritan New England continued to view its wayward

3

sister colony as a moral "sewer," whose policy of religious freedom attracted "all the cranks of New England."[1]

The political system developed by this motley collection of Quakers and Baptists was also quite naturally criticized by neighboring colonists; for it was a highly localistic form of government, reflecting in political form the religious beliefs of a people who preferred congregational autonomy and local liberties to the power of a centrally established church. Under the royal charter of 1663, provincial authority was thoroughly concentrated in the colony's legislature, which in turn was closely controlled by the individual towns. Laws passed by the General Assembly could be neither vetoed by the governor nor disallowed by the crown. The assembly also appointed all provincial officials, including judges, sheriffs, customs officials, and tax collectors. More important, the legislators were themselves carefully watched over by the towns they represented. Although members of the upper house of the assembly were elected at large, deputies of the more powerful lower house represented individual towns and were chosen semiannually by the town meeting. Town meetings exerted continual control over the deputies; they frequently gave them binding "instructions" on how to vote and often reviewed pending legislation before allowing final passage by the assembly as a whole. The towns also reserved the right to nullify legislative acts on occasion, especially when an enactment appeared to threaten local authority. In 1785, for example, when the legislature ordered smallpox inoculations for the populace, several towns refused to comply: the New Shoreham Town Meeting defiantly voted "not . . . to admit of Inoculation being brought in said Town."[2]

The towns succeeded in extracting from the legislature an unusual degree of authority over local affairs. In addition to control over highways and poor relief, traditionally wielded by New England towns, Rhode Island municipalities often exercised responsibility for local military defense. In 1776, when Newport's town meeting voted for local defense measures against British attack, the legislature approved this unusual aggrandizement of authority by a local government: in sweeping terms, it declared that all towns "were sufficiently authorized to make and ordain acts, orders and regulations, binding upon their respective inhabitants, in all cases whatever, for their advantage and safety." It is not surprising that Rhode Island's more conventional neighbors frequently denounced this highly localistic political system. One observer from Massachusetts referred to it as a "Quaker mob government," thus neatly combining in one term the colony's related evils of heretical religion and anarchical government.[3]

Finally, Rhode Island's numerous detractors were greatly annoyed and even disgusted by the economic policies pursued by the colony's government—or lack thereof. Some of the basic elements of civilized political economy, such as uniform road-building regulations and a standard system of measures and weights, were enacted belatedly in Rhode Island.[4] Where they existed at all, economic regulations and programs were either weakly enforced or designed simply to please the largest possible number of constituents. Customs and trade laws were ignored to such an extent that even during the French and Indian War the colony's merchants traded openly with the enemy.[5]

Most offensive of all was the colony's profligate paper-money policy, which was deliberately designed to give local merchants access to the trade controlled by their rivals in Massachusetts and Connecticut. Royal review of laws prevented neighboring colonies from issuing paper money, except in times of war. But in Rhode Island, with its omnipotent legislature, bills of credit were issued continually until 1741, when they were outlawed by an act of Parliament. When Rhode Island bills flooded into credit-starved Massachusetts, Boston merchants were forced, however reluctantly, to accept them, and thus they provided Rhode Islanders with an entry into their lucrative carrying trade. To their neighbors elsewhere in New England, Rhode Islanders appeared to have obtained wealth not through the virtues of hard work and steady application, but rather from the devious expedient of paper money, which when depreciated, simply defrauded creditors of their honestly earned wealth.[6]

American hostility toward Rhode Island's seemingly self-serving and overly popular economic policies rose to a peak during the Revolution, particularly during the controversy over the federal impost of 1781. When Congress sought to improve the credit of the new nation by amending the Articles of Confederation to permit collection of a 5 percent import duty, Rhode Islanders alone of all the thirteen states refused ratification and thus effectively vetoed the proposed tax. Asserting states' rights over the "tyranny" of an enlarged federal government, the General Assembly unanimously rejected the import tariff as an unfair burden for a state that depended heavily, as Rhode Island did, on foreign trade. The U.S. Continental Congress responded by rigorously denouncing the state, declaring that, in the words of Pennsylvania's John Montgomery, "the cursed state ought to be erased out of the Confederation, and I was going to say out of the earth, if any worse place could be found for them." Rhode Island's rejection of the impost of 1781 was the culmination of a long tradition of what its neighbors saw as a narrowly provincial, flagrantly immoral, and overly democratic political and religious culture.[7]

However, by the 1780s, forces were also at work that would soon end the unanimity with which Rhode Islanders reacted to and were judged by the outside world. Throughout the eighteenth century, the growing commercialization of the eastern half of the colony bordering along Narragansett Bay was giving rise to a division of interests within the colony. Increasingly, the commercial east shed the provincial and sectarian ways of Rhode Island's past and sought respectability by following the mores and traditions of its neighbors in the other colonies or states. After traveling through Rhode Island at the turn of the eighteenth century, Timothy Dwight observed that "the morals of Providence," which was by then the state's leading commercial center, "are probably superior to those of any other town in this State. The usual order of things, with respect to morality, seem here to be inverted. In most other States the country is more virtuous than the city. Here [in Providence] a general, and honourable regard to morality, and a general performance of its duties . . . appears to prevail." Dwight particularly admired the "spirit of industry, enterprise and perseverance" which he believed was responsible for Providence's commercial success. In the rural west, on the other hand, "everything indicates a want of energy; a destitution of all views, and efforts towards improvement."[8] Although couched in moralistic terms, Dwight's observations accurately reflect the cultural and economic differences that were growing between eastern and western Rhode Island. By the fourth quarter of the eighteenth century, while the commercial east was becoming socially more conventional, the west remained a relatively isolated region, characterized economically by semisubsistence agriculture, and culturally by adherence to a highly rustic and communalistic religious sect called the Six-Principle Baptists.

The Economy of a Backcountry Community

Although culturally and politically distinct from the rest of southern New England, Rhode Island in the eighteenth century was evolving economically in much the same way as its more orthodox neighbors. Just as was happening in Connecticut, Massachusetts, and New Hampshire, in Rhode Island a growing gap was emerging between the coastal ports and adjacent commercial farming areas and the largely subsistence farming areas in the interior part of the state. Of all the commercial areas, Newport was the first to emerge as a major colonial port by the early eighteenth century and at the time of the Revolution was in turn overtaken by Providence as Rhode Island's leading entrepôt. Bristol, a smaller port, developed into an important slave-trading center. Leading mercantile families, such as the Lopezes and Cranstons of Newport, the Browns and Russells of Providence, and the DeWolfs of Bristol, quickly developed a reputation for their shrewd and hardheaded business practices. We have already seen how zeal for profit led Rhode Island merchants to trade with the French during the Seven Years' War. Pecuniary motives also led the infamous John Brown to charge the revolutionary army the exorbitant price of six shillings per pound for gun powder, which he sold in November 1775.[9]

Attached to and sharing in the interests of the merchants were the commercial farmers, artisans, manufacturers, and lawyers who flourished in the towns along Narragansett Bay. Among the many agricultural goods exported by the merchants were cheese and beef from Aquidneck Island, onions from Bristol, tobacco from the vicinity of Providence, and the famous Narragansett pacers of North and South Kingston. Travelers throughout coastal Rhode Island often remarked that local farmers tended "well cultivated," "wonderfully luxuriant" fields, whose fertility showed that "they fertilize and prepare the earth to a superlative degree." Although farms along most of the coast were generally only middling in size, the Narragansett country quickly developed into a plantation-style economy, with some estates holding as many as fifty slaves. The Narragansett planters also tended to intermarry with the Newport merchant elite.[10]

The merchants' commercial network included manufacturers, mainly distillers, like Providence's Daniel Tillinghast, who converted West Indian molasses into rum for sale to Africa and the colonial hinterland; Daniel's mercantile connections were social as well as financial, for he was a brother of Joseph Tillinghast, another important Providence merchant.[11] Attorneys also participated in Rhode Island's emerging commercial political economy; lawyers like David Howell and Theodore Foster represented the merchants' interests in court and in the new United States Congress.[12] Finally, the numerous artisans and shopkeepers of Newport, Providence, and Bristol frequently exchanged goods and services with the mercantile elite. United by trade, family, and patronage ties, these groups usually favored the same economic policies, and as we shall see, shared many of the same political and religious convictions.

In contrast to the complex and far-reaching commercial web of eastern Rhode Island, economic transactions in northwestern Rhode Island seldom led its inhabitants beyond their immediate locality. For one thing, geographic conditions hindered the development of a significant external trade. The northwest corner of the state is dominated by rough, hilly terrain, varying in elevation from about 140 feet in eastern Coventry to 812-foot Jerimoth Hill in northern Foster. Two small river systems drain the waters of the region: the Chepachet and Clear rivers, tributaries of the Blackstone, flow north from the towns of Glocester and Burrillville; the Pawtuxet River and its various tributaries flow south and east from Foster, Scituate, and Coventry. These streams would later furnish sites for several cotton mills, but they were much too narrow and meandering to service the needs of commerce. Finally, the soil of northwest Rhode Island, like that of much of the New England upland, is stony and infertile. Grain production, which flourished in the Connecticut River valley and in parts of the Middle Atlantic states, would make little headway in this little corner of the state.

The farmers of the northwest, or "yeomen," to use a possibly more appropriate term, thus lacked easy transport to the nearest sizeable market, Providence, as well as the produce to constitute a sizeable trade. Agriculture was largely pastoral and semisubsistence: in 1778 a median-size Glocester household owned only three cows and two heifers,[13] six sheep, and two or three pigs, supporting them on about nine acres of meadowland and seven of pasture. This livestock would have yielded annually about 380 pounds of beef, 300 gallons of milk or dairy equivalent, 20 pounds of wool, and perhaps 180 pounds of pork. In addition, the typical household planted three or four acres of land with grain, generally corn and rye, yielding about forty bushels. A garden plot for growing potatoes, beans, and turnips and a small orchard, yielding about three barrels of cider, rounded out the family's agricultural holdings and production.[14]

Given a median-size family of six children and adults, such produce would yield only a small surplus beyond satisfying their own basic needs. Supposing that Glocester families partook of a typical diet of a main meal of meat and vegetables, sandwiched between breakfasts and suppers of bread and milk, their daily consumption would probably average about 1.5 pounds of beef or pork, five pounds of vegetables, five pounds of flour, and eight cups of milk (or other dairy equivalent). Together with necessary feed for livestock, this hypothetical diet would consume all of a typical household's orchard and garden products, nearly all of its yearly grain supply, and most of its livestock production. A family's marketable surpluses, if any, would most likely come in the form of a few pounds per year of beef, cheese, and butter, yielding at best a few dollars in income.[15]

All told, this "typical" Glocester farm differed little from its counterparts elsewhere in the hill country of New England. A median-size farm in contemporary Massachusetts held an almost identical number of cattle and improved land—three and twenty acres, respectively, and produced only slightly more grain—about forty-five bushels. A relatively young town by southern New England standards, having been founded in 1731, Glocester tended to share the traits of other more recently settled areas. Its farms were still relatively undeveloped: almost two-thirds of their land was called "waste," or unused, land, much more than the two-fifths proportion found in older seventeenth-century towns, like Concord, Massachusetts. Glocester farms were more likely than older settlements to hold pigs and sheep, both of which were cheaper and better suited to uncleared grazing land than those finicky and relatively expensive creatures called cattle. Farming in the northwest approximated patterns found across the border in Worcester County, Massachusetts, more than those experienced by the older towns of southern New England. Still, aside from these small differences, the typical Glocester household, like those found throughout most of New England, produced only slightly more food than it consumed.[16]

Of course, this tale of the typical household's lot obscures considerable variation in the size of local farm operations. Although landlessness and tenancy were much lower in northwestern Rhode Island than in the more commercialized mid-Atlantic region, a large number of families owned precious little land or farm resources. About a quarter produced no grain and over a third owned fewer than two cows. Households like these relied on either artisanal skills or agricultural labor for their livelihood and often rented their homes from their more substantial neighbors. The Peleg Shaw family of the nearby town of Warwick, for example, rented a small house with pasture and orchard privileges on the property of Nehemiah Atwood, paying for it with three months of agriculture labor and unspecified tailoring services.[17] Fortunately, most of these lesser households would eventually become more prosperous through inheritance and gradual accumulation: all but one-sixth of Glocester's landless households were newlyweds or young families, for whom poverty was a temporary, albeit difficult, stage in their life cycle.

At the other end of the local social hierarchy, a small minority of households were clearly selling foodstuffs on the market. About one-sixth owned seven or more cows and produced upwards of 100 bushels of grain, more than enough to feed all but the largest families. Although much of this surplus merely supplied their poorer neighbors and tenants, some farmers did export produce all the way to Providence. The papers of the Brown mercantile firm, the largest in that city, reveal a few scattered instances of trade with the interior of Rhode Island. During the 1760s and 1770s, the Browns purchased butter, pork, and beef from Israel Arnold and Thomas and Solomon Owen, who headed three of the wealthiest families in the town of Glocester. In general, this commercial one-sixth of all households owned about thirty times more taxable property than the bottom one-quarter.[18] For about one-third of this group, commercial farming was merely a temporary function of household maturity: for a brief period in their family history they would be blessed with enough grown children to produce sizeable surpluses for the market. But most of the commercial elite appeared destined for prosperity by luck of inheritance. Some were active commercially even as young adults: about one-fifth of all young couples owned four or more cows and produced over fifty bushels of grain, much more than they needed to feed their small families. By the time they matured, this fortunate one-fifth would most likely boast a farm operation with over a dozen cows and an annual grain production upwards of 120 bushels, enough to allow them to sell and buy fairly regularly through the Providence market. Families in this class distinguished themselves by the quality as well as the quantity of their market purchases. About a tenth of all households owned relatively extravagant luxuries such as clocks and silverware.

Rounding out the northwest's economic hierarchy was a sizeable class of middling farms. About half of all the youngest farmers owned three to five cows and heifers and produced ten to fifty bushels of grain, thus allowing a comfortable subsistence for their still small families. Their margin of comfort probably declined somewhat over the next ten years of household life, as increases in family size surpassed gains in farm production. Only in their mature years would this middling half of the population own enough cattle and harvest sufficient corn to market a sizeable surplus. They used the resulting income to pay yearly taxes and to purchase a few basic imported goods, such as linen sheets, brass cookware, and pewter plates. But they could spend little on such "luxuries," concentrating instead on raising capital for the purchase of farms and dowries for their maturing children.[19]

The yeomanry also exported a few nonfood items, including lumber, although only the wealthy few could engage in this trade on an ongoing basis. Almost every farm had a few acres of "wood and waste land," at least some of which must have been covered over by forests. But marketing a bulky commodity like timber required access to both sawmills and substantial wagons, both of which were held disproportionately by the local economic elite. In 1778 four of the town of Glocester's eight mills were owned by the wealthiest one-fifth of all taxpayers. Even more important, probate records suggest that less than 5 percent of all households owned wagons, which, unlike the less substantial carts, were necessary for transporting heavy lumber to the Providence market.[20] It is not surprising that only the wealthiest northwesterners show up in the records as steady exporters of timber. The papers of the Brown family merchants, for example, reveal purchases only from the prominent Greene family of Coventry and the Owens of Glocester.[21]

The last potential export item was iron, manufactured in both pig and bar forms; but here the economic structure of this industry demonstrates how greatly the commercial stature of the northwesterners paled in comparison to the townspeople of eastern Rhode Island. Hope Furnace, the area's largest iron-producing enterprise, was owned largely by those ubiquitous Providence merchants, the Browns. Much of the income from this venture therefore never benefited the farmers of the northwest, although a few were employed by the Browns to cut down, chop, and cart lumber from their lands for use as fuel at the furnace. The northwest also contained three iron forges owned by the Owens of Glocester, the Greenes of Coventry, and the Scituate family of John Barden. These were used to refine pig iron, usually purchased from the Hope Furnace, into bar iron, part of which was then sold back to the Browns. With the exception of the Greenes' forge, which manufactured anchors for nearby shipyards, much of the remaining iron making was no doubt for local needs— horseshoes, cooking utensils, nails, and so forth. In practical terms, iron was more of an import than an export for northwestern Rhode Islanders. Controlled principally by outside investors, the iron trade provided few avenues through which northwesterners could enter the wider colonial commercial network.[22]

Finally, for the few households fortunate enough to produce a marketable surplus, there were additional obstacles to participation in a commercial economy. When Thomas and Solomon Owen offered to pay for iron from the Hope Furnace with a combination of lumber, cash, and food products, they had to ask that the Browns grant them six months' credit before charging interest. The Owens explained, "its being late in the year, we cannot Expect to do much towards Collecting Either of those goods towards making Remittances." Seasonal changes also adversely affected the farmers' ability to transport goods to market. In March 1771, after receiving a request from the Browns for floorboards, Nathaniel Greene, Jr., responded that transportation may be unavailable, since "it's a season of the year when every Body is useing their Teams."[23] Local road conditions, moreover, were terrible no matter what the season. When James Aldrich, a prominent dairy farmer, moved from Smithfield to Scituate in the late eighteenth century, he and his "family travelled on horseback, that being the usual mode of conveyance," since the roads were too poor for the use of "carriages."[24]

It is doubtful, then, that more than a fraction of northwest Rhode Islanders participated regularly in a long-distance market economy during the eighteenth century. The typical rock-hard soils of up-country New England would only support a simple pastoral form of agriculture. The pigs, sheep, and cattle owned by most households furnished only a comfortable subsistence: food enough for all, plus a few dollars a year from the sale of livestock products. Only a few families produced enough cheese, beef, and pork to provide enough surplus during all phases of their life cycle. An equally small number, having easy access to sawmills and wagons, were able to export lumber products. Finally, primitive credit and transportation facilities hindered even the most prosperous in trading with the commercial centers of Narragansett Bay.

Numerous physical obstacles thus made it difficult for the farmers of hinterland Rhode Island to engage in a commercial economy; but there were perhaps more significant cultural and psychological obstacles. Instead of seeking material and capital accumulation, most farmers sought only a simple subsistence. And instead of trying to exploit their communities as potential commercial markets, they preferred to trade with their neighbors in a simple, barterlike system of exchange in which prices are established as much by community custom as by impersonal market forces. In sum, the values of commercial capitalism were fundamentally at odds with the limited aspirations of the typical backcountry household.[25]

First of all, a closer look at tax valuation data reveals that farmers' agricultural production was limited not simply by nature, but also by conscious intent. The farmers seemed generally uninterested in exploiting the full potential of their holdings. A typical household owned fifty-five acres of land yet devoted only about twenty acres to tillage, meadow, pasture, or orchard land. The remainder—almost two-thirds of the typical landholding—remained as waste land.[26] Of course, parts of almost every farm were unsuitable for improvement, being either too hilly or too wet; and each farmer needed to set aside acreage as woodland for supplying the household with fuel. But poor as the land may have been, it strains credulity to suggest that only one-third of each farm could be cultivated. As has been noted, farmers in older hill-country regions left only two-fifths of their acreage in waste, thus suggesting that population density, rather than soil quality, dictated land usage. Farmers everywhere in backcountry New England tended to improve an average of only twenty acres, regardless of the total size of their holdings. This remarkable constancy indicates that most farmers sought to cultivate only the minimum required to support their families.

Indeed, in Glocester, this may have been a bare minimum at best. Although the town's farmers typically owned five cattle, the tax assessors computed that the median pasture holding of seven acres would only be enough to "keep" two or three. Since little grain was left over from human consumption, the typical farm household probably forced its pigs, sheep, and cattle to forage in the nearby marshes and woods, or waste land. This primitive form of agriculture certainly would not have provided the farmers with marketable beasts, since brush- and marsh-fed animals were no doubt a skinny and undelectable lot. But for the yeoman who sought a relatively easy subsistence, without a life of backbreaking labor spent plowing and clearing fields, open grazing must have been a perfectly acceptable agricultural technique.[27]

Like other recently settled areas in New England with a weak—or nonexistent—established church, northwestern Rhode Island had a relatively slovenly and wasteful style of agriculture. Contemporary travelers almost always invidiously compared northwestern farmers with their more orderly neighbors in Connecticut. The Connecticut Federalist Theodore Dwight observed that whereas northwesterners lived in "very poor and ill-repaired houses" and cultivated the land with "very few proofs either of skill or success," residents in nearby Connecticut enjoyed "comfortable dwellings" and the fruits of "better agriculture." Significantly, Dwight's observations were echoed by other, less biased observers. Elias Boudinot, on traveling from his native New Jersey in 1809, compared "the high state of Cultivation prevailing" in Connecticut, with the "poor appearance of farm Houses" that "was immediately discoverable" upon entering Rhode Island. Even an English traveler, Sir Augustus John Foster, remarked that "the farmhouses of the state of Rhode Island appear to great disadvantage on leaving Connecticut, being as dirty in appearance as the inmates are grossly ignorant." Conditions improved, on the other hand, upon reaching the outskirts of Providence. As one traveler noticed, "six miles before reaching Providence there suddenly appears a region which is open, fertile and cheerful, and in place of the stones we have seen hitherto there are green meadows and fertile fields." Living in a still sparsely populated area, and lacking the college-educated clergy who helped set standards for order and diligence in the countryside, rural Rhode Islanders settled for a livelihood that emphasized the attainment of bare necessities, rather than the achievement of bounty and refinement.[28]

The northwestern farmers seem to have purposely limited their agricultural output to accord with the particular needs of their families. Livestock numbers and grain production varied directly with family size and food consumption. Large families of ten or more members usually owned four times the cattle and harvested three times the grain of households with only two members; and they produced twice as much food as families of four or five. Of course, part of this correlation stems from the tendency of farms to grow in size as families matured, increasing their holdings through inheritance and steady accumulation. But even among families who shared the same life-cycle stage, production clearly varied according to size. For example, among middle-stage households—families who had both young and adolescent children—those with ten or more members owned an average of ten cattle and produced over eighty bushels of corn; comparable figures for middle-stage households with four or five members were four cattle and fifty bushels of grain.[29] Instead of keeping production up in order to create a surplus, the small households simply produced less. In general, it appears that a simple subsistence, not production for a market, was the goal of hinterland farmers when administering their agricultural holdings.

Of course, it would be a mistake to suggest that each household was a completely self-sufficient economic unit. No single household carried on all the trades, owned all the implements, or produced all the food necessary for a modest subsistence. Instead, they sold and purchased a variety of goods and services from their neighbors, ranging from a relatively expensive service such as grinding grain at a gristmill to a lowly trade such as shoemaking, or even a simple sale of corn to a food-deficient household. A survey of 112 probate inventories from the 1780s reveals the existence of eleven blacksmiths, six shoemakers, a dozen carpenters, a saddler, a physician, and a potash kiln owner, all of whom doubled as farmers. Their wives contributed their own services to local trade networks, spinning yarn from wool or flax, churning butter, and midwifing births.[30]

Yet these exchanges, however frequent, were governed only partially by the logic of commercial capitalism, that is, by a system of exchange in which prices are established by impersonal market forces, rather than by custom or community norm. Commodity prices, for example, had only recently begun to follow trends established in nearby urban markets. In the colonial era, trends in food prices throughout rural New England bore little resemblance to the vagaries of urban demand. This began to change during the revolutionary war, when enhanced demand for backcountry food products created a semblance of synchronicity between rural and urban prices for basic agricultural commodities. But even as late as the 1780s and 1790s, prices recorded in northwest Rhode Island only vaguely followed the market patterns of the great urban entrepôts of New York and Philadelphia. Prices set by probate appraisers for corn, rye, pork, and butter usually lagged behind urban trends by about a year. More important, local prices were generally less volatile than urban prices: they rarely met or exceeded the highs and lows experienced in large towns. Indeed, prices in the northwest for corn, butter, and pork often remained unchanged for months on end, so much so that one suspects that customary constraints must have played a role in mitigating market forces.[31]

Market forces played an even more tangential role in establishing prices for capital, that is, interest rates. Although a capital market may have begun to form in rural New England by the 1780s, evidence for its existence in northwestern Rhode Island remains extremely weak. Most local transactions were entirely devoid of usury charges. Sales were usually made by means of ac-

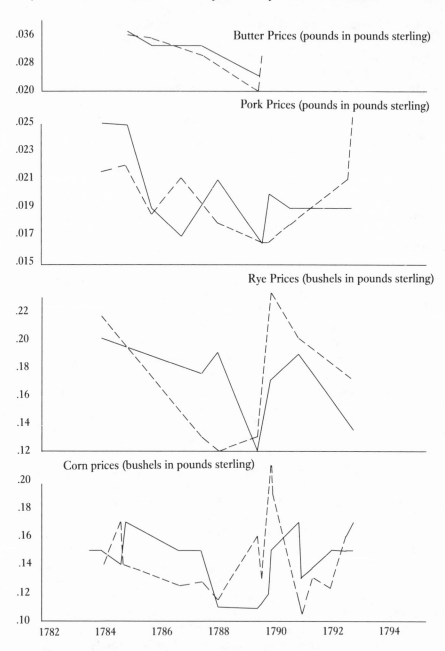

Figure 2. Prices in Northwestern Rhode Island and Philadelphia. Sources: For Glocester, Town probate inventories; for Philadelphia, Bezanson et al., Wholesale Prices in Philadelphia, 1784–1861.

count-book credit, in which a seller simply kept a running total of the value of each customer's purchases. Since payment never occurred immediately, each purchase was in effect a debt owed by the purchaser to the vendor. Every year or so, each pair of trading partners would compare their credits and debits and "settle" their accounts by a small exchange of cash. But interest was never charged on what was effectively a months-old debt. Indeed, book-account systems of purchase and credit were so informal that it would have been difficult, even if desired, to assess interest accurately; for although the Rhode Island yeomanry regularly used their account books to record sales or credits, they rarely bothered to record purchases or debits, thus making impossible an exact accounting of net debt or credit. Instead, they trusted the veracity of their debtors' own bookkeeping to ensure that all accounts were accurately balanced. In general, account-book transactions in rural Rhode Island relied on the premodern traditions of informal accounting and community trust, rather than on the capitalist innovation of precisely accounted debts and credits, with interest unerringly charged on the balance.[32]

In some cases, goods and services were paid for by notes of hand, a somewhat more formal arrangement than book accounts. But even these seldom charged interest. Of the sixty-two probate inventories containing notes of hand, only fifteen mentioned the accrual of interest to those notes; and in eight of the fifteen, some of the notes were held interest-free. Because of the informal and haphazard way in which notes were recorded, it is difficult to tell why they were treated inconsistently; but in general, only those notes that were over a year old, or that were valued at more than five pounds, were ever paid with interest, and even these debts more often than not were recorded without trace of a usury charge.[33] Moreover, in some cases notes called for paying debts in kind, thus rendering absurd the accurate calculation of interest. When Glocester yeoman Peregreene Mathewson died in 1789, his estate inventory listed twenty-one notes due to him, but four of the notes explicitly called for payment in kind, including one note "for 2½ Bus. rye, payable after next rye harvest." Between 1784 and 1791, of all the inventories that listed notes of hand, 27 percent included notes written in such a style. The actual percentage was probably higher, since many inventories did not list individual notes but rather lumped them all together informally as "private securities for money." At any rate, payment by note, especially an interest-bearing note, occurred much less often than by book account or by a simple unrecorded barter: of all 112 men and women appearing in the 1780s probate inventory file, only 46 percent died with "notes of hand" in their possession.[34] Within the local economy of northwestern Rhode Island, farmers incurred credits and debts largely as a means for facilitating local trade, not as an avenue for capital accumulation through the practice of usury.

By contrast, credit transactions in the mercantile port of Providence were constructed much more formally. The account books of Cyrus Butler, merchant, and Theodore Foster, a local lawyer, meticulously recorded both their credits and their debits. Foster, for example, regularly balanced his account books every three or four months; if he still owed or was owed money at the end of each period, he or his debtor would issue a "note for the balance." Moreover, northwestern farmers who traded long-distance with Providence merchants soon found that they had to conduct business according to mercantile rules, rather than their own, more informal ones. When the Owens bought iron from the Browns in the 1770s, they had to ask formally for six months' credit, free of interest. In the northwest, such a request would have been unnecessary, given its tradition of informal and largely interest-free credit arrangements.[35]

Finally, the rural northwest had yet to develop a commercial market for labor, one in which laborers freely circulated from farm to farm and were paid precisely according to a market rate. The supply of labor, for one thing, remained limited in the late 1700s. Although about one-quarter of all young couples and families produced no grain, and therefore must have worked for others for their living, almost all mature families owned enough resources to maintain an independent livelihood. Instead of hiring laborers during times of peak planting and harvesting, most farmers were simply forced to exchange labor with each other. Indeed, farm account books typically listed labor services alongside commodity sales, thus blurring the distinction between laborer and producer. Between 1788 and 1792, Nehemiah Atwood, for example, recorded the sale of cider-pressing and lumber-sawing services to Anthony Rice, alongside sales of corn, rum, and iron. A few years earlier, in nearby Mendon, Massachusetts, Samuel Smith plowed Seth Killey's land and sawed his lumber and also sold him apples.[36]

Even for landless laborers, the market remained constrained by custom and ties to the land. In the case of Peleg Shaw's labor agreement with Nehemiah Atwood, some wages were precisely enumerated—three shillings per day for mowing and six dollars per month for planting; but blurring this precision was Atwood's concession that Shaw could have a "privilige in the orchard for apples to use for his famely." Indeed, as reported by British travelers, American laborers generally believed that they had a "customary" right to pick "a little fruit" from their neighbors' trees.[37] Prices for labor, as was the case with foodstuffs and capital, were therefore determined as much by a sense of custom and common rights as they were by impersonal market forces.

At the time of the American Revolution, most northwestern households thus remained rather insulated from the conditions and values of long-range market transactions. Except for a relatively wealthy minority, most farmers appear to have deliberately limited their production, providing for only a small marketable surplus, and using the resulting income to pay their annual taxes and to purchase a few basic imported goods. But most exchanges took place not within a larger regional economy, but rather within a series of relatively self-sufficient local communities in which the power of market forces was tempered by custom and informal community obligations. The language and prices of local economic exchange, of account books and probate inventories, reveals a social structure and cultural ethos of independent householders who were nevertheless interdependent within their community. The nature of this society helps explain why in the 1770s rural Rhode Islanders, like their counterparts throughout New England, wholeheartedly embraced republicanism and the revolutionary cause. It also helps explain why in the 1780s and 1790s they viewed the efforts of Providence merchants to commercialize the area as a threat to both their individual independence as semisubsistence households and the political independence of their local communities.

Religion in Backcountry Rhode Island

The religious ethos of northwestern Rhode Island closely reflected the needs and aspirations of a society composed of interdependent, semi–self-sufficient yeomen farmers. Dominated by the Baptists, and more especially by the General Six-Principle sect, rural Rhode Islanders were religiously a rustic and provincial lot, egalitarian and obscurantist in their customs and highly suspicious of outsiders. They were particularly troubled by religious developments in the eastern, commercial half of the colony, where the emerging merchant elite sought to make more respectable their own forms of worship by eliminating unorthodox and colloquial practices. In Rhode Island, where the absence of an established church no doubt encouraged the growth of religious heterogeneity,[38] uneven rates of social and economic development by the 1780s were polarizing religious life between the commercial and noncommercial parts of the state. The social significance of backcountry religion therefore emerges most clearly when it is studied not only on its own terms, but also as a product of a dialectical relationship between opposing rural and urban cultures.

Throughout the colonial period, religious liberty in Rhode Island had made it a magnet for nonconformists of all stripes and colors, and this was especially true of the rural northwest. Surviving records indicate that Baptists and Quakers of various persuasions managed to form congregations in this part of the colony. Of these, the Six-Principle Baptists were by far the most numerous. Distinguished by their insistence on the "laying on of hands" as a requirement for membership—the "sixth principle"—and by their belief in a "general" atonement, this particular sect made up about two-thirds of the area's church members. The remaining members were split fairly evenly between Six-Principle Calvinist Baptists, Five-Principle Calvinist Baptists, and the Quakers.

The great majority of rural folk—perhaps 90 percent of all inhabitants over age fifteen—belonged to no church at all; nevertheless, it would be a mistake to characterize northwestern Rhode Island as religiously indifferent. Indeed, a 10 percent church membership compares rather favorably with that of either orthodox New England or upstate New York.[39] Although the New England Congregational establishment consistently portrayed Rhode Island as a cesspool of immorality and irreligion, religious liberty did not in fact produce religious indifference; what it produced instead was a genuine folk religion, characterized most typically by the practices and beliefs of the General Six-Principle Baptists.

Although nurtured by the particular conditions of colonial Rhode Island, this folk religion had important historical roots in the English Reformation. Arising during the first decade of the seventeenth century, the English General Baptists were strongly influenced by the continental Anabaptists, and in particular, the Mennonites. From the Mennonites these first English Baptists inherited the Arminian belief in "general" redemption (as opposed to the Calvinist belief that only a "particular" few would be saved), as well as certain unusual sectlike traits. In this latter respect, they pushed the Reformation belief in scriptural authority to extreme limits, adhering resolutely to the most minute biblical injunctions, while rejecting as worldly any rites not specifically sanctioned by the Bible. Thus, they read in Paul's mention of "the doctrine . . . of laying on of hands" (Hebrews, vi. 2) an injunction whereby admission to communion required that the pastor lay his hands on the heads of each candidate immediately after performing the act of baptism.[40] The General Baptists also believed in various other unusual rites, such as washing the saints' feet and anointing the sick with oil, although these were not practiced as universally as the laying on of hands.

Conversely, these Baptists rejected as unscriptural any practice that was even remotely suggestive of hierarchical, high-church ornamentation. They opposed congregational singing, preferring to hear only single voices at one time; and they refused to waste either education or salary money on their pastors (whom they deliberately referred to as "elders"), since that would only dampen the simple spirituality of their leaders. Finally, they also eschewed contact with other religious groups who were compromising enough to engage in these worldly customs. Until 1774, if a member married outside of the General Baptist sect, he or she was summarily excommunicated. The spiritual world of the General Baptists was a closed and communal one: they exercised rigorous discipline over their members; and they deliberately kept their congregations small, in order to promote the development of close, face-to-face relationships.

Finally, these beliefs and practices reflected the radical, leveling spirit engendered in England by the revolution of the 1640s and 1650s. Their insistence on general redemption of all through Christ often tended toward a radical embrace of human perfectability. Furthermore, by requiring new members to submit to the "laying on of hands," in addition to adult baptism, the General Baptists heightened their sense of separation from the evil worldliness of England's stratified social order. As rituals, both "hands" and the washing of the saints' feet also acted as leveling agents, placing all members regardless of their economic status on the same spiritual level.

Although they emerged a full generation before the rival and more doctrinally conservative Particular Baptists (who were an offshoot of the 1630s from Puritan nonconformity), the General Baptist sect quickly fell behind in strength and numbers. Their stricter injunctions against paid and trained ministers, as well as against associating with others, hampered their ability to recruit able leaders and proselytize among nonbelievers. Isolated and generally confined to poor, rural communities, the General Baptists declined throughout the eighteenth century. Eventually they split into two groups: one followed the logic of general redemption to an almost Unitarian form of Arianism; the other caught hold of the Methodist stir and evolved from Reformation-era Arminianism to an evangelical belief in freedom of the will.[41]

Returning again to the Rhode Island Baptists, it should first be emphasized that, at least after the Restoration, they were only loosely connected to their General Baptist brethren in England. When originally founded in the 1630s by Roger Williams and his fellow refugees from orthodox Massachusetts, the First Baptist Church of Providence had actually been Calvinist in doctrine, reflecting the remaining influence of their Puritan origins. Buoyed perhaps by an influx of more radical Baptists from abroad, during the height of the English revolution, the church gradually swung toward Six-Principle, General beliefs, until in 1652 a schism resulted in the departure of a weak and dwindling minority of Five-Principle Calvinist Baptists.[42] The Providence church retained its Six-Principle, Arminian orientation for the next 118 years and during that time spawned a number of like-minded congregations throughout northern Rhode Island. Still, with the waning of English radicalism and westward migration after 1660, Baptism in Rhode Island increasingly evolved independently of its overseas doctrinal brethren. Although the "Old Baptists" in England continued to define themselves most thoroughly by their Arminian beliefs, the Providence church and its rural offspring increasingly singled out the sixth principle—the laying on of hands—as the sine qua non of their sectarian identity.[43]

The relative importance of the sixth principle was further strengthened by the Great Awakening of the 1740s. Within New England, the awakening stirred most strongly in eastern Connecticut and south-central Massachusetts, areas bordering on Rhode Island. Although the awakening aroused little enthusiasm among the state's existing Baptist churches, owing to their natural suspicion of anything originating from the hated land of Puritanism, it did spill over into the general population of the border towns of northwestern Rhode Island. Influenced by both Puritan and local Baptist traditions, the local inhabitants of the border region developed their own hybrid "Six-Principle Calvinist" sect, embracing both Calvinism and an insistence on the laying on of hands. By the 1750s, two such churches had formed in the northwest and, together with several others across the border in Connecticut and Massachusetts, organized their own denominational association. Thus, by the middle of the eighteenth century, Six-Principle Baptism, whether of the Calvinist or Arminian persuasion, had become by far the most dominant religious doctrine of northwestern Rhode Island.[44]

Like their English forebears, Rhode Island rural Baptists adhered to a series of beliefs and rituals that reflected a strict interpretation of the scriptures as well as a propensity toward socially leveling patterns of behavior. In addition to holding fast to "hands," they rejected modern congregational singing as an unnecessary ornamentation that only obscured the pure message of the scriptures. Although they did not go so far as to insist on singing only by solo voices, they declined to use the harmonized, prepackaged hymns that were then being distributed by colonial publishers. Instead, they merely sang psalms line by line; as each line was read aloud by a church deacon, the congregation responded, drawing on their memories for the melody deemed appropriate by folk tradition.[45]

The Six-Principle Baptists also opposed the "modern" and potentially hierarchical imposition of a paid and educated ministry. As reported by Ezra Stiles, then the Congregational minister of Newport, the "elders . . . are not Men of College Education, know nothing of the learned Languages, or Ecclesiastical History, or Systematical Divinity." Although he recognized that "they are well read in the Bible," Stiles reported that "some Tracts and a few Sermons make all their Reading."[46] The rural Baptists preferred the simple Word of God to the complications of contemporary theology. Even the very names that they gave to some of their churches—Stony Lane, Maple Root, Wood River—evoke a kind of simple and folksy rusticity.[47] Plain and unpretentious, much like their everyday life, the Sunday meetings of the rural Baptists reflected a rich treasure of local tradition and community folkways.

Perhaps more important, the language and practice of the Six-Principle Baptists suggest a spirit of communalism reminiscent of their English forebears. The Baptists of northwestern Rhode Island also preferred small churches in order to foster a strong and intimate sense of religious community. True, some churches had close to one hundred or more members at a time, but these figures distort the actual nature of their religious experience; for each elder rarely met two Sundays in a row at the same place with the same members. Instead, as Ezra Stiles relates, "in Scituate they have 3 or 4 baptist Meeting houses which they preach in, in Circulation in Summer, but leave in Winter & hold Lordsday Meetings in private houses in different vicinities." He observed further that "this is the common practice thro' the Counties of Providence and Kent in the back Towns." Meeting in this way must have fostered a strong sense of attachment to the local community and an almost familial sense of mutual togetherness. The rural Baptists spoke of the need to develop a sense of being in "a measure of peace" with each other, or in "love and unity," phrases that they repeated ad infinitum in their church meeting minute books.[48]

A strong attachment to community oneness is also apt to produce a repressive desire to preserve the local order from disrupting influences. Each church observed a strict watch over its members, warning and rebuking the disorderly and sinful, sending committees to reason with the stubborn, and excommunicating the absolutely recalcitrant. The General Six-Principle Baptist Church of Scituate suspended its own clerk, Richard Knight, for keeping "a house of merriment and friendship with the Vain & worldly People allowing them in fidling and Dancing and Some Kind of Gaming."[49] Churches would even act occasionally as unofficial law courts in seeking to reconcile individual differences and thus promote community order. For example, in 1769 mediators appointed by the Smithfield and Glocester Baptist meeting ruled that church member Samuel Winsor owed the heirs of Elisha Baker £182.8 in payment for a farm.[50]

Like the English Baptists, the rural Baptists of Rhode Island actively discouraged relations with other religious groups. Letters of recommendation granted to departing members were specifically addressed only "to our Sister Churches who maintain by faith and practices the six principles of the Doctrine of Christ." When Mary Ann Wait of the West Greenwich church "Transgressed our Laws by Embodying herself with a Nother church oute of [our] faith and order," the church "Voted that she be Excommunicated." Similarly, the Six-Principle General Assembly forbade individual churches to admit individuals to communion "without a letter of commendation" from a "sister" church. Although no evidence exists of anything as harsh as the English Baptists' ban on marriage to outsiders, the Rhode Islanders were apparently a rather strict and intolerant lot. They jealously guarded their local congregations against corrupting influences from both within and without, in order to preserve a sense of communitarian order.[51]

Symbolically embodying all of the rural Baptists' main tendencies—their communalism, their sometimes harsh emphasis on repressing individual freedom, and their radical rejection of religious orthodoxy—was the central rite of the laying on of hands. The ceremony of the "hands" heightened the communal quality of the rural Baptists' religious experience because it served to "comfort, confirm and strengthen true believers" as well as to erase divisions based on social distinctions. The sixth principle symbolized as well the repressive side of Baptist communalism; for in submitting to the rite, new members were said to have "made an offering . . . of themselves . . . to the[ir] church." Some observers even likened the elders' act of laying hands on initiates to the ancient Hebraic practice of placing "their hands on the head of their [animal] offerings" prior to sacrifice. Finally, and perhaps most important, in requiring all members to submit to the laying on of hands prior to and in addition to baptism, the Six-Principlists emphasized their radical rejection of the Puritan pedobaptist order; for just as baptism symbolized the ending of one life, through submission to a "watery grave," the laying on of hands represented "a beginning of a new life [as] we are . . . made partakers of the Holy Ghost."[52] Their devotion to the sixth principle thus served to exaggerate the usual Baptist sense of separation from the rest of the world. It is not surprising, then, as will soon be demonstrated, that the rural Baptists viewed a threat to the "hands" requirement as a direct attack on the very nature of their religious identity.

Thanks to the existence of religious liberty in Rhode Island, the northwestern yeomanry developed a form of Protestant religion that helped fulfill their particular cultural needs. In social background the Six-Principlists mirrored the residence and wealth patterns of the surrounding rural population: they included both the poor and the rich, as well as the middling in means. As typical residents of a society based on relatively equal, independent households, they were naturally attracted to some of the more symbolically egalitarian practices within the Protestant tradition, such as the laying on of hands and washing the saints' feet. At the same time, their economic interdependence within each local community went hand in hand with a religion of communal sharing and self-discipline. Religious liberty allowed the rural Baptists to develop their own colorful, local idiosyncrasies, as they were able to evade the centralizing and homogenizing influences of learned religious elites. In rural Rhode Island, an authentic folk religion was able to emerge which in neighboring colonies was often smothered and obscured by the Puritan established church.[53]

In the meantime, a very different religious ethos was emerging in the commercial, eastern half of Rhode Island. By the middle of the eighteenth century, the communities ringing Narragansett Bay had begun that transformation from low-church simplicity to high-church formality that so often accompanies the rise of commercial civilization and the accumulation of wealth.[54] There were already four Anglican churches: one each in Newport, Providence, Bristol, and the Narragansett country. Meanwhile, Congregationalists founded two churches each in Newport and Providence, and one in Narragansett. To these were added the Puritan orthodox churches of Cumberland, Barrington, Bristol, Tiverton, and Little Compton, when those towns were ceded by Massachusetts to Rhode Island.[55]

Even the Baptists were caught up in this general drift toward stateliness and respectability; and it is here that a conflict emerged most clearly between competing rural and urban visions of the proper religious order. In an effort to improve the quality of their pastors, the Baptists of Newport, Bristol, and other commercial centers established in 1765 the College of Rhode Island, located in the small Narragansett port of Warren. (The college would soon be moved to Providence and later have its name changed to Brown University.) The more cosmopolitan Rhode Islanders were aided and encouraged in this endeavor by the Philadelphia Baptist Association, which sent the college its first president, James Manning. They were supported as well by Isaac Backus, who sought an educational center for his own Separate-Baptists.[56]

The rural Baptists reacted with suspicion and fear to this unwanted innovation on the simple Word of God. The new college seemed to be too much the project of outsiders from beyond the colony. Moreover, in James Manning, Rhode Island's first college-educated Baptist minister, the rural Baptists saw a fearful portent of what was soon to come. As Ezra Stiles summarized, repeating the fears, as well as the grammatical errors, of a typical backwoods preacher, "Elder Young is illiterate—don't like the College—says when the old Ministers die off he foresees a new Succession of Scholar Ministers: that it has got so far already as scarcely to do for a common Illiterate Minister to preach in the baptist meeting at Providence." Fearful of a new breed of learned preachers who would pollute the pure word of the scriptures, and to whom they were intellectually helpless to respond, the rural elders and their flocks bitterly opposed the founding of Rhode Island's first college.[57]

As for Elder Young's fears for the church in Providence, events would soon prove his prediction remarkably astute. By 1770, the conflict between rural and commercial Baptists came to center in that town's first and only Baptist church. A single incident involving James Manning suddenly crystallized the differences between two competing versions of Baptist faith: an urban and commercial version that stressed the need for rational, formal, and respectable religious worship; and a rural version that emphasized adherence to egalitarian rituals, local custom, and ancient tradition. In this particular incident a controversy emerged over the practice of the sixth principle and congregational singing. As its upshot, the rural Baptists lost control of the town's church and retreated to form a new church in the hinterlands.

As may be recalled, during the late seventeenth century, the Providence church had adopted Six-Principle and Arminian doctrinal views. Providence was then still overwhelmingly a farming community, and many of the church's members were farmers who resided in the adjacent agricultural towns of Johnston and North Providence. It is not surprising that the church in Providence also took on many of the other traits characteristic of Rhode Island's rural Baptists. Church members refused to practice congregational hymn singing; and they met in a simple forty-by-forty-foot building, sitting mostly on crude benches because the church had only a handful of pews. The elders, generally farmers themselves, were unpaid as well as uneducated.[58] Ironically, three of the elders who served in the colonial period were ancestors of the well-known Brown family merchants. When the issue of laying on of hands was the center of a brief controversy in 1732, the merchants' grandfather, Elder James Brown, delivered a sermon in support of the sixth principle: he compared believing in only five principles to paying a carpenter to put six windows in a room and finding that only five were actually constructed.[59]

By the 1770s, however, Elder Brown's grandsons and their mercantile associates had already transformed Providence into a sizeable commercial center, a place where Six-Principle Baptists, and Elder James's rustic artisanal metaphors, would increasingly seem out of place. Local merchants turned a backwater agricultural village into an important regional port. Between 1755 and 1774 its population jumped from 3,169 to 4,321, in spite of losing 1,861 persons when the new towns of Johnston and North Providence were set apart. Wharves and shops spread out along the banks of the Providence River as the center of the town's population moved south, away from the gristmill around which the old agricultural community had gathered. By 1750, the merchants had already achieved political control of the town: in an important test of strength, they successfully proposed the building of Benefit Street, a key thoroughfare bitterly opposed by the farmers because it would separate their home lots from their fields.[60] In the 1770s, the Browns and other mercantile families, such as the Jenckes and the Tillinghasts, would seek to exercise their influence over the town's religious life as well.

By this time the Providence merchants had already demonstrated a keen regard for increasing the respectability and urbanity of Rhode Island Baptism. Nicholas Brown and Daniel Jenckes were both original incorporators of the College of Rhode Island; and in 1769, they and their local allies succeeded in relocating the college from Warren to their own town of Providence.[61] The Providence Baptist church was still led by a traditional rural preacher, the Elder Samuel Winsor, an unlettered farmer who held firmly to the laying on of hands as a requirement for membership. But President Manning had moved to Providence with the college, and so it was only natural that the church would soon invite him to preach on occasion. As Ezra Stiles reported, this set the stage for "the Browns and the Jenckes . . . to turn off Elder Winsor and put [in] President Manning for their Minister."[62]

Manning first preached at the church in May 1770 and immediately drew a hostile response from the congregation's rural members. They opposed sharing communion with Manning because he did not hold the laying on of hands to be a requirement for membership: that is, he was a Five-Principle instead of a Six-Principle Baptist. They also resented Manning because he introduced singing to public worship, a practice "which was highly disgustful [in particular] to Mr. Winsor." When the backcountry members failed in their efforts to have Manning denied communion, they simply withdrew from the church and formed under Winsor's leadership a new and purely Six-Principle congregation, to the west of Providence in the town of Johnston. According to church records, "April 18, 1771, being a church meeting, Mr. Winsor appeared and produced a paper signed by a number of members living out of town, [which stated that] we must in conscience withdraw ourselves from all who do not hold strictly to the Six Principles of the doctrine of Christ, as laid down in Hebrews vi. 1 and 2." With Winsor now out of the way, the remaining church members in Providence quickly ordained Manning as their pastor, thus fulfilling the strategem of the Providence mercantile elite.[63]

For the Browns, the Jenckes, and their clerical allies, the issues involved in this schism, although seemingly petty, were crucial to their vision of the proper religious order. As Rhode Island's first educated Baptist minister, and as an emissary from Philadelphia, the Reverend James Manning symbolized for the Providence merchants many of the superior qualities of the new Baptist order: he was learned, relatively cosmopolitan, and perhaps most important, not a farmer but a gentleman of considerable respect. As for the congregational hymn singing reviled by Winsor, it appealed to the emerging commercial classes because of its emphasis on orderly, rationally composed harmonies and uniformity of practice.[64] Finally, rigid adherence to the laying on of hands, central to the rural Baptists' religious experience, was for the merchants merely embarrassing. Opponents of "hands" claimed that the rite originated not from Early Christian tradition, but rather from "the elements of the Jews' religion," particularly the Old Testament practice of laying "hands on the head[s] of" sacrificial offerings.[65] For the merchants, the sixth principle thus smacked of both Hebraic exclusivity and ancient blood barbarism, qualities that insulted their aspirations to cosmopolitan social standing. Even if interpreted symbolically, as an "offering" of oneself to God, the laying on of hands connoted a leveling form of religious obeisance that would have offended the increasingly self-confident leaders of Providence society. Opponents of the sixth principle further charged that the Old Baptists' insistence on "hands" came at the expense of "the daily practice of devotion and piety." As Isaac Backus, the principal spokesman for New England Five-Principle Baptists, once concluded, the Six-Principlists often "neglect to keep the Lordsday holy, are slack in attending public worship and have little or nothing of religious worship in their families."[66] The rural Baptists' idiosyncratic attachment to "hands" thus militated against the achievement of a sabbatarian regularity and household social order, crucial aims in the merchants' vision of a rational commercial order.

The changes wrought by Manning, the Browns, and others must have struck a responsive chord within Providence's society. A revival occurred in 1774–1775, adding 110 new members to the congregation. Over the next two decades the church continued to eliminate obscure old customs while taking on further trappings of respectability. A new meeting house was built in 1775, which, unlike its crude and unpretentious predecessor, boasted a full set of pews and a soaring and elegant steeple. The church soon began paying its pastor a salary of £50 per annum, which was raised to £150 by 1788. In 1782 it joined the Warren Association of Five-Principle Calvinist Baptist churches, an organization that Manning himself had created in order to promote order and respectability among New England Baptists. Finally, in 1791 the laying on of hands, which had been only loosely enforced since the beginning of Manning's tenure, was officially revoked as a requirement for church membership. Thus, the church cast off forever the principle that most clearly symbolized the differences between rural obscurantism and urban respectability, and which henceforth would be the distinguishing mark and namesake of Rhode Island's backcountry Baptists.[67]

Elsewhere in Rhode Island's commercial towns, traditional Baptists were powerless to stop a general drift toward formality and respectability. In 1728, when Newport was emerging as a major port, its Baptist church experienced a schism similar to the Providence church controversy. Out of disagreement with the church elder's belief in the sixth principle, "two of the most powerful members" of the congregation forced him to resign, whereupon he and his followers withdrew to form the Second Baptist Church of Newport. But these Six-Principle adherents also began to drift away from the rural model of Rhode Island Baptism: in 1759 congregational singing was introduced into the services, in spite of the protests of the few remaining traditionalists.[68]

Even in their own Rhode Island Six-Principle Baptist Association, which had been in existence since at least the 1720s, the rural Baptists were unable to control crucial policy-making decisions. By the 1760s, the association consisted of nine churches, only three of which, Providence, Newport, and Tiverton, were located in commercial areas; but this minority nevertheless exerted a disproportionate influence over the association's deliberations. In 1765, when James Manning first came to Rhode Island to preach at the Baptist Church in Warren, the association initially invited his church to join its ranks, even though "none of [its] members were under the laying on of hands." It was not until a year later, at the next annual meeting, that the traditionalists were able to reverse the association's original decision and reject Manning's church for failing to comply with Six-Principle doctrines.[69]

Five years later, when the Providence schism once again raised the issue of church membership credentials, the rural Baptists were no longer able to preserve the association's Six-Principle purity. When representatives from each congregation gathered for the annual meeting of 1771, the question was raised as to which church to recognize: "the Baptist Church of Providence which meet together to worship in the Town or Those which meet together to Worship God out of Town." The former prevailed. Although the association's minutes do not reveal exactly how this decision was reached, it appears that the rural Baptists were simply overawed by the social prominence of their adversaries from the towns. The church "in the town" was represented by Daniel Jenckes, the third wealthiest merchant in Providence, and by Manning himself, whose education and urbanity greatly surpassed the rest of the delegates. The delegates, moreover, were hardly meeting on neutral ground, since, as was often the case, the Providence meeting, the "mother church" of Rhode Island Baptism, hosted the yearly meeting. With the odds so stacked against the rural true-believers, the Rehoboth delegates apparently saw the handwriting on the wall and "withdrew from the association" immediately before this crucial vote was taken. The remaining rural delegates quietly acquiesced in the association's decision to recognize Manning's church, instead of the orthodox believers who had gathered around Samuel Winsor outside of town.[70]

The rural Baptists reacted to this defeat just as Elder Winsor's followers had the year before: they withdrew into the countryside. Within the next four years, the backcountry churches all followed Rehoboth's example and resigned from the existing Six-Principle association, leaving the Providence and Newport churches as the sole members of an organization that would soon become extinct. In 1774 the rural Baptists established a new association, composed of churches in Johnston, Smithfield, Scituate, Richmond, and Cumberland, Rhode Island, as well as in nearby Rehoboth, Massachusetts. Appropriately enough, they met for the first time at the Johnston meetinghouse to which Elder Winsor's supporters had retreated the year before.

The Six-Principle General Baptists soon reversed their fortunes. Although encroachment of religious urbanity led to their expulsion from Providence, it also may have pressured the existing rural churches into rallying to the new Six-Principle association. Between 1783 and 1791, several Six-Principle General churches that had existed independently for decades suddenly joined the yearly meeting.[71] By century's end, the association had grown from the original six to twelve churches, including new arrivals in Coventry, Foster, Glocester, East Greenwich, and North Kingstown, Rhode Island, and Swanzey, Massachusetts. With the exception of the Swanzey, East Greenwich, and North Kingston congregations, none of which were ever very large, these twelve churches were all located in backcountry towns.

In the meantime, the Six-Principle General sect solidified its religious ascendancy over the rural northwest, as the more minor variations in rural Baptism gradually died out. Pressured to take sides in the struggle over the laying on of hands, the pastors of the local Six-Principle Calvinist churches were gradually persuaded by Isaac Backus and other orthodox Calvinist Baptists into abandoning their insistence on the "hands" requirement. But as a result, they appear to have alienated their own parishioners: the Six-Principle Calvinist church of Glocester weakened toward the end of the 1780s, until it became defunct in 1802, as did a similar church in Foster, in 1805.[72] As for the Five-Principle Calvinists, they were hurt by both Shaysite political conflicts and westward immigration.[73] By 1800 the Six-Principle General Baptists had become overwhelmingly the largest denomination in rural Rhode Island and were particularly strong in the upland northwestern part of the state. By now firmly conscious of their differences with the Baptists of eastern Rhode Island, the Six-Principle Baptists succeeded in rebounding in strength and in establishing their own identity as the religion of a backcountry, yeomen social order.[74]

The Radicalization of the Backcountry Yeomen

The political culture of northwestern Rhode Islanders, like their religious culture, was both similar to and different from that of their agrarian neighbors in other New England colonies. Like the farmers of Puritan Connecticut and Massachusetts, in the colonial period the residents of upland Rhode Island generally deferred to men of prominence, both within town meetings and on a wider level in provincial government. But just as the absence of an established church had permitted Rhode Island's religion to evolve localistically, in a similar way, the absence of a royal or proprietary charter, together with English indifference to the fate of such a tiny colony, allowed for the development of a highly decentralized form of government. For rural Rhode Islanders, the town, not the colony, was the principal seat of political authority. The farmers' strong attachment to local independence helps explain their unique response to the deflationary economic crisis of the 1780s.

Although remarkably free from the constraints of imperial rule, the towns of northwestern Rhode Island were hardly preserves of democratic government. Like their counterparts in Massachusetts and Connecticut, Rhode Island farmers habitually chose from among the town's wealthier men in electing their more important local officers. About 75 percent of all town councilmen (Rhode Island's version of selectmen) ranked in the top quarter of local tax lists, a figure similar to the pattern of office holding found elsewhere in New England.[75] Of course, the focus of local authority resided in the town meeting, in which every freeman was allowed to participate, but here actual political participation reflected the reality of economic inequality. The moderators chosen to run each meeting were usually more prominent than the average town councilmen; and although almost two-thirds of all adult males could qualify for freemanship, only about half of those eligible bothered to vote at all, and even fewer attended the typical town meeting.[76] For the average farmer, politics was something best left to those with greater social prominence.

In a corresponding way, on the level of provincial government, the backcountry towns deferred to the leadership of coastal elites. Here again the Rhode Island farmers behaved much like their counterparts in Massachusetts, who with a few exceptions ceded control of provincial offices to Boston-area families like the Hancocks and Adamses. In the case of Rhode Island, Newport mercantile families—the Cranstons, Wards, and Wantons—monopolized the governorship and other important governmental posts until the 1750s, when they began to be successfully challenged by the merchant leadership of Providence. The typical farmer had neither the time nor the resources to participate in colonial government and would have been socially overawed by easterners of vastly greater wealth. Moreover, contemporary issues rarely interested most yeomen, since they dealt principally with the colony's participation in overseas trade, a commercial network that only tangentially affected their everyday lives.[77]

In the rare instances when a rural leader became prominent in provincial politics, he inevitably wound up moving to Providence or Newport to better pursue his career. Early in the century, when Providence was still a backwater community, the election of one of its freemen, Joseph Jenckes, as governor resulted in his immediate removal to Newport. Later on, Providence itself would attract rural leaders on the rise; Stephen Hopkins, for example, moved from Scituate in 1742, well before being eventually elected governor for the first time in 1763. The transplantation of local leaders also served to create ties between rural towns and the commercial centers to which they politically deferred. When Stephen Hopkins moved to Providence, he left behind kinship and neighborhood ties that would develop into political and commercial connections: Hopkins's son Rufus remained in Scituate, where he served as manager of the Brown family furnaces, as well as a town representative in the General Assembly.[78]

Deferential relations between the colonial elite and backcountry towns were also mediated by a scattering of patron–client relationships involving coastal merchants and their customers in the interior. When the Providence elite began to challenge the Newport merchants for control of provincial government, they enlisted the aid of their local contacts in the northwest. The Browns relied on local leaders, such as the Arnolds and Owens of Glocester, not only for supplying lumber and dairy products, but also for securing the votes of the neighboring yeomanry. On April 15, 1763, just a few months after concluding a butter deal with the Browns, Israel Arnold wrote to them about the recent triumph of the Providence faction in the spring legislative elections. Expressing satisfaction at the "change of the Legislative Powers in this Government," Arnold signed the letter, appropriately enough, "with Profound Deference to you." Arnold had probably been well rewarded for his political loyalty; for the Browns had raised over £5,000 as an election war chest, a good deal of which had been spent on bribing for the votes of Arnold's poorer neighbors with handouts of free rum, fish, and corn. Serving as the Browns' local conduit, Arnold exported votes as well as foodstuffs, in exchange for the merchants' good credit.[79] Based on traditional habits of deference, and tied together loosely by occasional kinship and commercial connections, political relations between Providence and the northwest would remain closely allied, as long as their economic interests did not diverge.

The American Revolution itself, if narrowly defined as the imperial crisis, had no discernible effect on this existing colonial political structure. More than any other colony, Rhode Island united wholeheartedly behind the independence movement. This is hardly surprising, when one considers that the colony was practically an independent state to begin with and was certainly viewed as such by Rhode Islanders themselves: one political correspondent even referred to the colony as a "republick." Independence for Rhode Islanders was hardly a sudden break from the past and thus did not threaten the existing leadership classes. As a result, with the possible exception of wealthy Newport, the Revolution hardly disturbed the structure of local political leadership. Town councilmen in the northwest continued to serve an average of four to five consecutive yearly terms, as had been typical of the colonial era; there were no loyalists or weak-hearted patriots to turn out of office. And on the provincial level, the northwestern farmers continued to follow the lead of the Providence merchants in loyally supporting the independence movement.[80]

It was the economic crisis of the 1780s that overturned the existing political order and severed the political alliances that had existed between Rhode Island's commercial ports and hill-country towns. As occurred elsewhere in the country, postwar deflation and high taxes levied to pay for revolutionary debts hit hardest on the state's rural population. Lacking much by way of exportable surpluses, farmers were hard-pressed to repay their debts. The era's tax load angered farmers even more because the personal property of urban centers was consistently underassessed.[81]

Protests and extralegal actions soon followed. In 1786 the Six-Principle Baptists of Glocester petitioned for a public lottery to assist in the construction of a meetinghouse. As the principal justification for their request, they pointed to the "taxes which takes our money As fast As we can Raise Produce to turn off to Collect it." So intense was indignation over high taxes that farmers actually fled the state to avoid their oppressive financial burden. An English traveler in frontier New York stumbled upon two families of ex–Rhode Islanders who had recently left the state "on account of the legislature having made a capitation tax which is considered above the ability of the common people to pay." When he asked one of the family members, "a young and handsome woman," why they had moved to such a "remote" location, "she replied with eagerness and warmth that sooner than be subjected to the tyranny of others she would undergo every hardship that she might be liable to from the change." Rural Rhode Islanders reacted bitterly to the imposition of taxes that were levied as a means of paying for wartime expenditures.[82]

By early 1783 farmers were mobilizing to obstruct the collection of taxes. The village of Pascoag in Glocester was the scene of a particularly violent altercation. When local officials began seizing cattle for nonpayment of taxes, a mob quickly formed and proceeded to overpower the tax collectors and forcibly repossess the cattle. Efforts to imprison the ringleaders were to no avail; the crowd simply broke open the jails. Further violence was averted only when the governor offered amnesty to all who would cease acting in disorderly fashion.[83]

To ease their financial woes the farmers began to agitate for a legislative remedy that would place them at odds with the state's commercial leaders: an inflationary paper-money system coupled with strict legal tender laws. In the northwest, the towns of Coventry, Foster, and Glocester all petitioned the legislature for paper money with which to pay their taxes and debts. The merchants of Providence and Newport strenuously objected. They had already engrossed a large proportion of the state's debt and were loath to have it repaid in depreciated currency. Legal tender laws would in turn allow their debtors to force them to accept paper money in return for canceling their outstanding accounts. More fundamentally, they viewed paper money as an essentially cheap and fraudulent panacea, incompatible with their carefully cultivated image as respectable gentlemen. In their own towns, the merchants were able to use their prominent social standing, as well as their myriad ties with local shopkeepers and manufacturers, to sway public support against the farmers' petitions. But out in the countryside the fragile set of connections that the merchants had established with local leaders could not span the gap between divergent economic interests. By the spring of 1786, like their neighbors who erupted into rebellion in Massachusetts, the farmers of backcountry Rhode Island were irreconcilably opposed to the state's traditional merchant leaders.[84]

But unlike the farmers in Massachusetts, those of Rhode Island eventually avoided rebellion and further violent protests because they captured control of state government. Organizing in a new "Country party," they swept into power in the elections of April 1786, winning by majorities of over 90 percent in the hill-country towns of Coventry, Foster, and West Greenwich. Glocester's own Daniel Owen, Thomas's son and heir to his forge business, was elected lieutenant governor. Never before had anyone from the northwest served in so high an office. The farmer-controlled legislature quickly printed 100,000 pounds in paper currency, which it lent to the state's citizens in return for mortgages on real estate. More important, the value of currency was enforced by a legal tender statute of unprecedented severity: creditors who refused to accept paper money from debtors would in effect forfeit the entire principal of their original loan; by a subsequent statutory provision, they could even be fined £100 for each refusal. Although five other states emitted paper currency in the 1780s, their legal tender laws at most allowed debtors to suspend interest payments to a uncooperator creditor. The Country party was defeated only in its most radical schemes, which included a proposal to assume state control of foreign trade. By 1789 it had succeeded in its principal aim: the liquidation of the state's internal debt.[85]

The question remains as to why Rhode Island's farmers triumphed so thoroughly while their counterparts elsewhere, especially in nearby New England, were either compromised politically or crushed militarily. For one thing, and perhaps most important from a politically strategic point of view, Rhode Island's gentry class entered the 1780s in a weak and divided state. This division was of crucial importance, because elsewhere in New England the gentry served as a bulwark against demands for inflationary currency.

Historically, Rhode Island's upper classes lacked the cohesive sense of unity that in much of Puritan New England had been engendered by the established church. As contemporary observers realized, the docile and orderly behavior of Connecticut's citizens resulted from the fact that "the minister, with two or three principal characters, were supreme in each town. Hence the body of the clergy, with a few families of distinction, between whom there was ever a most intimate connection, in effect, ruled the whole state." The clergy of orthodox New England were bound together by kinship ties as well as by the shared experience of education at Harvard or Yale. They were therefore able to promote social order and stability by linking together the leading families of economically and socially disparate communities. In Rhode Island, the lack of a clerical establishment meant the absence of religious ties needed to supplement weak commercial links between the coastal and backcountry elites.[86]

The economic crisis of the 1780s, moreover, left Rhode Island's gentry in a particularly divided condition. Indeed, unlike the commercial farmers of Essex County, Massachusetts, and the Connecticut River valley, the planters of Rhode Island's coastal areas actively supported inflationary currency schemes. During the 1770s and 1780s, these planters experienced considerable economic and social distress. Opposition to slavery and constant subdivision of estates threatened to ruin the once-great fortunes of the Narragansett planters. The coastal areas of southern Rhode Island had also been thoroughly ravaged by the revolutionary war; the British had occupied Newport and from that position had mounted raids on the other towns that ringed Narragansett Bay. In southern, coastal Rhode Island, farmers were desperate for a solution to severe economic disorder, perhaps more so than in any other commercial farming area in the country. Rhode Island also had a long history of enacting land banks; as a result, groups that elsewhere would have blanched at the thought of paper money may have been more willing to accept the Country party's plans. It is not surprising, then, that prominent landowners, such as Joseph Stanton of Charlestown, Job Comstock of East Greenwich, and Nicholas Easton of Newport, all supported the Country party and served as its leaders in the state legislature. Even a few lesser merchants, like Providence's Arthur Fenner, Jr., and Newport's John Collins, joined with the farmers; for they shared their economic distress and their resentment of the grander merchants: the Browns, the Nightingales, and the Jenckes.[87]

Assisted by such influential allies, backcountry farmers were able to face down their social superiors among the merchants, despite the scorn heaped upon them by respectable gentlemen both within the state and abroad.[88] As the experience of the Six-Principle Baptists had demonstrated, the rural yeomanry could sometimes be easily overawed by their adversaries within the merchant community. Gentry support for paper-money policies may have been crucial in determining the success of the farmers and the Country party.

Nevertheless, the farmers also had to thank the fierceness of their own resolve for their success in the face of a heated and powerful opposition. The debate over ratifying the U.S. Constitution, which developed out of the politics of paper money, helps to illustrate and explain the strength of yeomanry devotion to the Country party's positions. The Constitution threatened the farmers' paper-money system because it forbade the states to issue coin or currency. More important, the farmers feared that their precious tradition of local autonomy would be overturned by a new and vastly stronger federal government. Only after a bitter three-year struggle, further described below, did the state's Federalists muster enough support for ratification to defeat the back-country opposition. The yeomanry reacted bitterly to this defeat. When Obadiah Fenner, a prominent farmer and one of the few Foster freemen to support the Constitution, dared to travel to Providence to attend an ox-roast in celebration of ratification, he was greeted by an armed mob of hundreds of men, declaring it not "proper" to rejoice "at our liberties being taken from us." These men knew that Madisonian Federalism flew in the face of Rhode Island's tradition of an omnipotent legislature closely controlled by town meetings.[89]

Although Obadiah Fenner eventually passed through the mob unharmed, his experience speaks well of the yeomanry's ability to assert themselves in the face of gentlemanly prestige. Comments from travelers at the turn of the century suggest that Rhode Island was developing a pattern of relatively egalitarian social behavior. The English traveler Sir Augustus John Foster, staying at a tavern in Bristol, expressed shock: "I had not only the company of my host, who was a farmer, at table, but that of the coach driver, who to my astonishment sat himself down very unceremoniously alongside me, and the hostler of the tavern." After observing that "this was all new [to me]," Foster reported finding "the same complete easiness of manner and practical equality in the other parts of this state." A few years later, another British traveler, Henry Bradshaw Fearon, was surprised by the lack of servility displayed by Rhode Island workers toward their social superiors. When a female textile weaver addressed her Providence supplier with an "independent (although not impudent) air . . . : 'I want work, Boss, I guess for Harriet Angel,' " the supplier replied that he would "attend to you directly."[90] Reared in a tradition of religious liberty and political localism, to which had recently been added the fervor of revolutionary unrest, Rhode Islanders in the early republican period exhibited a lack of deferential behavior to a degree that astonished contemporary observers.

This aspect of Rhode Island's political culture played a key role in the state's fervent espousal of paper money and Anti-Federalist policies. It should be pointed out that the farmers subscribed to paper money not only as a panacea for their economic woes, but also as a way to insult the superior status of their merchant antagonists. Put more simply, the farmers were really more socially audacious than they were politically radical. They knew that the merchants of Providence owned a large portion of the state's revolutionary debt, and they bitterly resented the merchants' attempts to profit therefrom by imposing a policy of monetary deflation. John Brown's family, for example, owned about 20 percent of the state's debt. As one memoir relates, when Brown passed by a cooper's shop one day in a shiny new carriage, a workman called out scornfully, "Soldiers' blood makes good varnish."[91] Of course, a cooper's helper, if he could vote at all, would have been subtly swayed to ballot for the merchants' interests during the crucial elections of 1786–1789. But in the backcountry towns, where commercial links were few and scattered, and where the clerical establishment, if it existed at all, was hostile to the urban ministry, the farmers were relatively free to vote on the basis of their economic needs and social resentments. The economic crisis of the 1780s brought to the fore a nascent tradition of rural social independence that during the colonial period had been obscured by the more "normal" pattern of political deference.

In the meantime, however, the new nation's inexorable drive to ratify the Constitution eventually resulted in the collapse of the Country party, and with that the withdrawal of northwestern farmers from state party politics. Although rural opposition to the Constitution prevented serious consideration of ratification until 1790, the pressures brought to bear on Rhode Island as a now outcast state soon began to erode the unanimity of rural opinion. By 1790, the new federal government was threatening to cut off trade with the state; and within Rhode Island, Federalist Providence and Newport were speaking openly of seceding from the state to join with Massachusetts. These threats scarcely fazed most backcountry yeomen, relatively isolated as they were from the workings of national commerce and statewide politics. But the local economic and political elite could hardly feel so sanguine about the loss of the Providence market as a source of commerce and patronage. At a ratification election held in early 1790, a small number of the area's wealthier inhabitants actually supported the Constitution. These included Obadiah Fenner, the Foster grandee whose journey to Providence to celebrate ratification was so rudely impeded by a mob of armed men. Obadiah, interestingly enough, was a nephew of Country party leader Arthur Fenner. In Glocester, only ten out of 237 voters supported ratification in 1790, but those ten included Thomas Owen, the father of the Country party's lieutenant governor.[92]

Even those leaders who publicly opposed ratification seem to have done so somewhat reluctantly, out of a need to satisfy the demands of an aroused constituency. In their public pronouncements, Arthur Fenner and Daniel Owen continued steadfastly to oppose the ratification of the Constitution, thus placing themselves seemingly at odds with their kinsmen Obadiah Fenner and Thomas Owen. But Thomas and his son Daniel, and Arthur and nephew Obadiah, probably differed not so much over the actual issue of ratification as they did over tactical questions concerning the proper way to handle the Anti-Federalist passions of their constituents. Although Arthur Fenner, Jr., was re-elected governor in 1790 on a strict antiratification, Country party ticket, he privately acquiesced to the pressures successfully brought on the state by an increasingly hostile federal government. In the meantime Owen was elected by the Country party majority to chair the Rhode Island ratifying convention of May 1790. As one of the town of Glocester's representatives, he dutifully followed the town meeting's instructions, casting his vote against ratification; but as chairman, he acted in subtle ways to ensure that the Constitution would finally be approved. By this time, most of the state's commercial farming towns had joined the Federalist faction in the state's port communities, thus producing a bare majority in favor of ratification. Through a critical procedural ruling, Owen helped defeat one of the backcountry loyalists' last attempts to derail the ratification process, thereby paving the way for the Constitution's final acceptance by a narrow vote of thirty-four to thirty-two.[93]

With the state now rejoined to the union, Governor Fenner soon realized that the realities of federal government authority and patronage practices required him to expand his power base beyond the old Country party. Although his principal constituency lay with the leaders of northwestern towns, with whom he was socially and commercially connected, he soon began seeking allies among Providence Federalists, including his brother-in-law Theodore Foster, whom he supported for the U.S. Senate, and Samuel J. Potter, a wealthy Narragansett planter and lawyer. Foster was elected, and Potter replaced Thomas Owen as lieutenant governor. Fenner was generally able to ignore the backcountry yeomanry because, in the absence of important issues, they simply ceased participating in partisan politics. In the town of Foster, for example, voter turnout collapsed, falling from a peak of 185 in 1786 to only 62 in 1794. As happened elsewhere in the North, the freemen of rural Rhode Island ceded control of the emerging Republican party to a coalition of lesser merchants and coastal planters.[94]

Nevertheless, by the 1790s, the northwestern yeomanry had all the ingredients necessary to sustain an opposition culture: a set of beliefs and behavior patterns that were fundamentally at odds with the commercial civilization of Narragansett Bay. Economically, they were relatively isolated and independent; the northwest was essentially a collection of communities that traded and cooperated internally while seeking out the marketplace for only basic essentials that could not be furnished at home. Religiously, although many enjoyed the fruits of liberty, preferring indifference, a key minority of the farmers actively embraced a variety of Baptism that was self-consciously opposed to the growing cosmopolitanism and respectability of mercantile culture. Finally, the farmers had developed a fierce tradition of localistic politics and democratic behavior, which had been case-hardened in the fires of the economic crisis and political upheaval of the 1780s. Although political cooptation resulted in their withdrawal from state party politics, on the local level, northwestern farmers would continue to resist the encroachment of commercial interests and cosmopolitan culture.

CHAPTER TWO

Rural Resistance to Economic and Cultural Improvements: The 1790s

LIKE MOST enterprising merchants of the early American Republic, the commercial leaders of Providence sought to take advantage of the economic resources of the city's surrounding hinterland. In the colonial period, Providence merchants had already tried to exploit this rural marketplace, although with limited success, owing to the semisubsistence nature of the region's economy. After the Revolution and the economic crisis of the 1780s, renewed prosperity led the city's elite to redouble efforts to capture the countryside's economic, if not its political, allegiance. British occupation during the war had devastated the city of Newport, and Providence's merchants quickly took advantage of its rival's demise to become the state's leading port, and indeed, the second largest in New England. They reacted to the end of imperial mercantilist restrictions by charting new trade routes to Europe, Latin America, and the Far East. Total tonnage doubled between 1790 and 1820, as did Providence's population. Although the city's carriage trade comprised most of this commerce, Providence's merchants looked to the surrounding countryside as an additional market for imported goods, as well as a source of food and lumber for the urban populace. Exploiting this market, however, required improved transportation. Beginning in the 1790s, the merchants would play a leading role in constructing a series of turnpike roads radiating north and west from the city through the Rhode Island countryside toward adjacent Connecticut and Massachusetts. Partly as a result of these enterprising schemes, the Browns and their fellow merchants, as Timothy Dwight ad-

miringly observed in 1810, had "engrossed, to a considerable extent, the custom, and produce, of the neighboring regions of Massachusetts and
Connecticut."[1]

An even more enterprising form of hinterland exploitation were the local
elite's investments in cotton manufacturing. The rugged terrain surrounding
Providence may have made farming and navigation difficult, but it was perfect
for the construction of water-powered mills. Indeed, the industrial revolution
in America began along the banks of the Blackstone and Pawtuxet rivers and
their tributaries. Beginning in 1790 with Samuel Slater's spinning mill in
North Providence, the first to be built in the New World, construction of
cotton factories proceeded slowly at first, before accelerating rapidly when the
embargo of 1807 and the War of 1812 isolated the country from the competition of British manufacturers. By 1815 the state's one hundred mills were
operating over 75,000 spindles. Providence's merchants contributed most of
the investment capital and financial management required for operating these
factories, and they hired English-trained mechanics to provide technical expertise. Moses Brown, the driving force behind Samuel Slater's mill, was soon
joined by his brother's company, Brown & Ives, and by other merchants, such
as Edward Carrington, Richard Jackson, and Amasa Mason, in building textile
factories throughout northern Rhode Island. Although they often relied on
local mechanics and millwrights in constructing the mills, the merchants
themselves were the major impetus behind the creation of factories in rural
valleys. Although the return of peace in 1815 caused a temporary setback,
merchant investment in textiles continued to expand after 1820. By the 1830s
it had replaced the re-export trade as Providence's principal business.[2]

The merchant community also sought to improve the state's cultural and
financial infrastructure as a way to support its various commercial and industrial enterprises. They established banks, beginning with the Providence Bank
in 1792, the nation's fifth such institution. By 1800, the city had four banks,
comprising 60 percent of the state's banking capital. Insurance companies
soon followed, including the Providence Insurance Company (1799) and the
Washington Insurance Company (1800). Finally, acting in alliance with the
city's major artisanal shopkeepers, who were organized in the Providence
Association of Mechanics and Manufacturers, the merchants provided major
support for the enactment of the state's first public school system in 1799.
The merchants and their mechanic allies believed that public education would
help create a population of skilled and enlightened citizens, an essential ingredient in building a secure Republic and a strong commercial and industrial
economy.[3]

For the farmers of Rhode Island's northwest, these new developments
threatened the traditional social and economic fabric of their communities.
Although most of the textile factories were located outside the area, many were
built along the same streams that drained the northwest and therefore vitally
affected the interests of the area's farmers. Factory dams blocked the normal

flow of water, flooding fields and preventing anadromous fish from swimming upstream. The new turnpike roads imposed an irritating new toll on land travelers, most of whom lacked interest in—or the resources needed to benefit from—the improvements that presumably resulted thereby. Public education, a goal of limited usefulness for a society of semisubsistence farmers, required taxing the already limited liquid resources of the rural population.

Perhaps more importantly, the merchants' innovations not only impinged on the farmers' economic interests; they also threatened the traditional structure and cultural outlook of rural society. Cotton-mill dams and turnpikes violated certain long-held common rights, either to fish in unimpeded waters or to travel freely on public highways. These were built with an eye toward regional marketing and individual remuneration, values that flew in the face of the yeomanry's traditions of social independence and local community interchange and cooperation. The flow of capital into the northwest also threatened to upset the traditional power structure; no rural leader could match the social status of a Moses Brown. On a statewide level, bank charters symbolized the accumulation of special privileges by a wealthy elite. Finally, turnpikes, cotton mills, and public schools all undermined the localistic nature of Rhode Island's political system; for by their creation, they all received powers from the state legislature that had traditionally belonged to the towns alone.

The northwest's farmers opposed these economic and cultural innovations with a variety of political, legal, and extralegal means. They petitioned the legislature for redress of grievances. They publicly opposed the adoption of offensive legislation. They harassed outside entrepreneurs with discriminatory taxes and local regulations. And occasionally they went beyond the law by destroying the property of foreign capitalist interests and even threatening their local agents with bodily harm.

Fishway Rights versus Textile-Mill Dams

Cotton mills were the most innovative of all the devices developed by Providence's merchants to exploit the rural hinterland; perhaps for that reason the struggles that erupted between farmers and mill owners over fishing rights reveal most clearly their diverging views on political economy. The first protest by northwestern farmers against cotton-mill dams occurred in 1799: a large number of farmers living in the Pawtuxet River valley petitioned the legislature to force open dams that blocked fish from migrating up the south branch of the river. They received support from the Coventry Town Meeting, which instructed the town's representatives to seek necessary legislation at the next session of the General Assembly. Seven years earlier farmers from the northeastern part of the state had protested against Moses Brown's cotton-mill dam in North Providence, which was located on the Blackstone River. But in that case the issues were complicated by the presence of a preexisting community of mill operators who out of jealousy sided with the farmers against the new and powerful interlopers, Moses Brown and Samuel Slater. In 1799, the Coventry farmers would take on the mill owners by themselves.[4]

For the up-country farmers, the ability to catch migrating fish was an important traditional right. Herring, or alewives as they were called then, would swim upstream every year in the springtime. Spring was the season when farmers needed fish the most, both to replenish the previous year's harvest and to fertilize the new year's crops. The arrival of the fish therefore nicely corresponded with the needs of the northwest's semisubsistence economy.[5] The farmers' rights, moreover, were supported by the principles of English common law, under which any obstruction of a waterway could be prosecuted as a public nuisance. Offended parties could even physically remove or destroy a dam or other obstruction without fear of legal reprisal.[6]

Nevertheless, by the middle of the eighteenth century, gristmills, sawmills, and other water-powered artisanal enterprises had proliferated in the Rhode Island countryside, and legal rights had been altered to account for their importance. This development occurred largely without heated controversy. For one thing, rural industries did not need to be in operation all year round. Rural artisanal production was generally a sporadic activity; gristmills, in particular, were busy only during fall harvest seasons. Especially in the spring, when the fish were heading upstream, it would not trouble mill owners to open their dams at least partially, because in that season the water supply was usually ample. Besides, mills were essential to the local economy: towns often offered bounties and other inducements to encourage their construction and continued operation. Perhaps more to the point, the mill owners were all farmers themselves. They were seen as an integral part of the community, not as intruding outsiders or a hostile or alien class.

Legal developments reflected this commonality of farmer and mill owner interests. In the colonial period the legislature passed a series of laws that provided for the water-power needs of mills while preserving the fishing rights of local farmers. An act passed in 1719 gave towns the right to regulate and if necessary remove dams that obstructed the passage of fish. Another act in 1735 further specified that fishways be opened in dams between April 18 and May 20, when the alewives were making their annual run. Legislation also limited the use of seines, or fishing nets, to four days a week during the spring run of fish. In general, these statutes helped preserve the migration of certain fish while allowing for the necessary operation of local mills. Equally important, the legislation preserved local autonomy by entrusting each town with authority over its own streams and rivers.[7]

Conflicts over fishing rights occurred only rarely among Rhode Island's rural residents. In the period between 1765 and 1790, rivalry broke out between residents of the upper and lower portions of the Pawtuxet River valley. In 1767 residents of the upper valley succeeded in obtaining passage of an act that prohibited entirely the springtime use of seines below the Pawtuxet River falls.[8] They had complained that those who lived below the falls were trapping fish at the expense of those who lived upstream. In 1784 they returned to the legislature to seek further protection for "their inalienable Right [to fish], as Transmitted to us by our fore-Fathers." Complaining that dams and nets located on the river "entirely prevented" the migration of fish, they requested statutory revisions "so that all Obstructions Relating the Fishery in said River . . . may be thereby removed."[9]

But this time the upper-valley residents provoked a successful opposition by their downstream neighbors, chiefly from the towns of Warwick and Cranston, who responded by defending their own right to fish at the mouth or cove of the Pawtuxet River. Invoking the sanctity of tradition, just as their antagonists had done, they claimed that it had "been a long custom for the People in the Country to cume to Pawtuxet [a village at the river's mouth, to purchase] fish . . . Cominly thirty or forty in a day; most of them must be wholly dissapinted and return without any fish if it was not for Catchen them with Seines." The assembly decided the issue by passing laws in 1786 and 1788 that again allowed the use of seines four days a week, while leaving dam and fishway regulations essentially unchanged.[10] As one of the only known examples of disagreement among the rural yeomanry,[11] the Pawtuxet River valley is the exception that proves the rule concerning fishing rights in colonial Rhode Island; conflict, when it existed, tended to occur between different rural communities, rather than within a single locale.

The only major threat to this general harmony of interests was the introduction to the region of iron-working furnaces and forges. The water power required by this industry varied considerably. Iron furnaces, like the one operated by the Browns in Scituate, needed a constant supply of water throughout the duration of each "blast" for the bellows, which operated night and day, often for several months at a time. Since neither winter ice nor summer heat was conducive to iron working, furnaces would inevitably be in use during the spring, the season for the spawning of fish. Forges, on the other hand, did not necessarily come into conflict with the interests of the farmer–fishermen. They did not have to run continuously, and they only required water power when their trip-hammers were in operation. Since forges did not require as many workers or as much capital investment as furnaces, their owners could tolerate temporary work stoppages more easily.[12] Furnaces stood apart from the local agricultural community, exporting their products far afield, their operation conflicting with the normal, seasonal ebb and flow of rural life. Forges more often resembled gristmills or sawmills since the refined iron they produced was distributed mostly to local blacksmiths.

The historical record in Rhode Island reflects the varying levels of conflict produced by different kinds of ironworks. In 1748 local opposition to the "Furnace Unity" on the Blackstone River resulted in a favorable court decision, which implemented common-law remedies, ordering that the dam be broken open. The mill owners, who were Boston merchants, responded by successfully petitioning the legislature to overturn the justices' decision. The Brown brothers resorted to a similar recourse when they began operating their Hope Furnace in the 1760s. In August 1765 they and their partners petitioned the assembly for an exemption to the 1735 act requiring fishways in dams. There is no direct evidence of local conflict, but the petitioners must have met with opposition in the legislature; for it was not until four years later that their wishes were fully granted: the legislature exempted from fishway requirements all dams on the north branch of the Pawtuxet River that were located above the Hope Furnace.[13] As with the Furnace Unity, it was probably only the social prominence of the owners that allowed their interests to prevail in the provincial government.

Relations between forge owners and the local community were generally more harmonious. No records exist, unfortunately, for the Owens' forge in Glocester; but since the owners never petitioned the legislature for a statutory exemption, their operations were presumably not hindered by the requirement for fishways. The Greene family operation on the Pawtuxet River in Coventry was much larger, employing upwards of one hundred men. Perhaps for that reason the Greenes felt that they could not operate profitably without a continuous supply of water. In 1740 they petitioned the assembly for an exemption to the act of 1735. In this case, the owners were probably supported by their neighbors; after all, unlike the Browns in Scituate, they were local residents themselves, and they were producing refined iron needed by the immediate community. Their petition met with no known opposition; and one year later, the legislature exempted all dams on the south branch of the Pawtuxet River from fulfilling fishway requirements; this exemption was reconfirmed in 1770.[14] (See Figure 1 for locations of the Hope Furnace and the Greene forge.)

At any rate, by the 1780s, whatever conflict had existed between farmers and iron manufacturers was lessening considerably. Local iron production was simply withering away as a result of competition with the superior quality ores of the Middle Atlantic states. During the revolutionary war demand for cannon did cause a spurt of business, but activity at the Hope Furnace declined rapidly thereafter. The Greenes' forge, moreover, was destroyed by fire on August 17, 1772, and since its production was geared partly toward the manufacture of ship anchors, business did not fully recover until the end of the British wartime blockade of Narragansett Bay.[15] The issue of fishing rights became moot, because no dams were operating frequently enough to impede the annual run of the alewives. Nevertheless, the experience of the ironworks, as the area's first large-scale manufacturing operations, would serve as a prelude to the more dramatic conflicts that would soon emerge over the creation of cotton mills.

After its beginnings in 1790, with the Brown–Slater mill in North Providence, the industrial revolution spread to the Pawtuxet River valley. In 1794 a small cotton mill was opened on the river's south branch in the village of Centreville in Warwick, just a few miles downstream from the Coventry town border. The mill was initially owned by John Allen, a local millwright, two members of the prominent Greene family, James and Job, and William Potter, a Providence merchant. However, the mill was poorly operated from the beginning; its machinery was old and dilapidated, and none of the owners had the technical experience that Samuel Slater had contributed to the factory he and Moses Brown operated on the Blackstone. Perhaps for this reason, the mill and its dam did not pose a threat to the fishing rights of area farmers; for the first five years of the factory's operation, the local yeomanry kept silent about its effect on the migration of herring.

A complete turnabout in this situation came after August 31, 1799, when Moses Brown and his son-in-law William Olney purchased a 50 percent share in the value of the mill. Using their superior financial and technical resources, the new owners immediately began to transform the ailing factory into a productive and expanded enterprise. By December 1799, James Greene was already expecting the imminent arrival of new "machinery" to replace his malfunctioning equipment; and in the following winter, the new team of partners contacted mill owners throughout New England in search of additional spinning machinery. They also boasted of plans to expand factory employment from twenty to one hundred hands. What had once been a failed example of early industrialization now looked like a viable and growing operation.[16]

The farmers who lived upstream from the revitalized mill acted swiftly to meet this threat. They undoubtedly were familiar with Moses Brown's earlier success on the Blackstone River, both technically in creating a successful operation and politically in gaining a statutory exemption for his dam from the usual fishway requirements. Unfortunately for the farmers, since the south branch of the Pawtuxet was still exempt from fishway requirements, they could not sue the new dam owners for damages and therefore had to seek legislative repeal of the existing exemption. In September 1799, 235 inhabitants of the Pawtuxet River valley petitioned the legislature complaining about "Dams across the south Branch of the Pawtuxet River which Prevent the Fish from coming up said River" to their spawning grounds, located in "several large Ponds In the towns of Coventry and West Greenwich." They asked that all dams be opened during the spring migrating season. Invoking traditional notions of a moral economy, they noted that opening the dams "would be Very Beneficial to . . . the People in General and especially to the Poorer sort of the People." For the petitioners, the subsistence rights of a traditional economy took precedence over a new and productive form of manufacturing.[17]

This defense of customary rights received widespread support among the local yeomanry. Over one-fifth of all adult males in the town of Coventry signed the petition for fishways, together with about one-tenth of the men of nearby Scituate and West Greenwich. More significant, five of the petitioners identified themselves as "dam owners," thus reaffirming the traditional harmony of interests that existed between farmers and mill owners in rural Rhode Island. It is not surprising, then, that the fishing-rights advocates obtained the support of the Coventry Town Meeting, which voted on September 28 to instruct its assembly representatives to seek a legislative mandate for opening fishways in dams.

As evidenced by the semiliterate scrawl in which they wrote their protest and signed their names, the petitioners were typical of Rhode Island's backcountry farmers. The 108 petitioners who appeared on the Coventry tax list of 1798 paid a median tax of $.78, a trifle more than the town median of $.77. In fact, the petitioners were even more "average" economically than the town as a whole. Only 29 percent of them were listed in either the top or bottom quintiles of the town's tax list. The defense of traditional fishing rights thus involved neither the poor nor the town elite, but rather the mass of middling farmers. When the petitioners spoke of the needs of "the poorer sort of people," they did so not out of a pragmatic attention to their own interests, but rather out of a rhetorical need to assert the ascendance of moral claims on the economy over the efficiency concerns of entrepreneurs.[18]

Moses Brown and his manufacturing associates responded with a petition of their own, which in both style and ideological substance contrasted sharply with the farmers' protest. The manufacturers based their arguments on an entirely different notion of what constitutes the "publick good." They admitted the validity of "the principle . . . that private Interest and conveniences must give place to the publick good"; but they denied that fishing for herring outweighed cotton manufacture in overall utility. For these nascent capitalists, leaving dams open for migratory fish would only accommodate "a few Individuals with an opportunity of spending their time in the fruitless pursuit after a few scattering Herring." The public benefits of cotton manufacture would be much greater; instead of aiding just a few local fishermen, it would help the entire country, freeing the United States from "dependence on the Industry of other nations." The manufacturers measured the "publick good" in terms of an abstract appreciation of the entire national economy; the farmers were more concerned with the immediate and practical needs of the local community.

Even in style the two petitions differed markedly from each other. Written in immaculate and almost ornate handwriting, the manufacturers' petition must have been crafted by a hired clerk, not scribbled by semiliterate farmers. Moreover, the manufacturers' rhetorical style reveals the contempt with which they viewed the needs and beliefs of backwoods farmers. While the farmers' petition was supplicating in tone, Moses Brown and his partners' comments on the farmers' arguments were fraught with condescension and scarcely veiled sarcasm. Referring to herring fishing as a mere "recreation and useless diversion," the textile industrialists doubted that the "opportunities" for idle pursuits "were so scarce as to require the aid of [a] Legislative provision."[19]

Although the main response to the farmers' protest came from Brown and his immediate partners, the nascent industrialists succeeded in securing the support of a large number of other commercially minded men. Attached to their petition was a supporting document, signed by almost four hundred men, mostly from the port of Providence. As usual, the list was headed by some of the town's most prominent citizens, all of whom lived in Providence's eastern half, where the wealthiest merchants kept their wharves and warehouses. But a still larger proportion of the signers resided in the western part of Providence, the center of the city's artisanal, or petty manufacturing trades. Although modest in their financial circumstances, many would eventually rise through manufacturing success to rank with the city's wealthiest citizens.[20] Eighty-one of these middling-class petitioners also belonged to the recently formed Providence Association of Mechanics and Manufacturers, representing about 30 percent of the membership. Composed of a great variety of skilled tradesmen, the mechanics' society sought to promote economic and civic improvement. Far from fearing economic development, the mechanics welcomed the opportunity for technological advancement. As the vanguard of Providence's emerging entrepreneurial classes, the mechanics naturally rejected the farmers' efforts to impede technological advances in the Pawtuxet River valley.[21] Together with the city's merchant elite, they served as formidable allies for the interests of the cotton manufacturers.

The cotton manufacturers also obtained a modicum of support from the mill area's local community. By the 1790s, the Greenes' iron forge was back in operation, and its owners were loathe to relinquish the statutory exemption to fishway requirements that the family had enjoyed for over fifty years. They responded to the farmers' attack on this privilege with their own petition of sixty-three names. Like the cotton manufacturers, they adopted a view of the "public weal" that denigrated the needs of local independent households in favor of the requirements of industrial production. Boasting that their enterprise was "one of the most extensive and flourishing Forges and Anchor Manufacturers in New-England," they claimed that only "a very inconsiderable number [of fish] was taken" by the local population during the preceding year.

Perhaps more important, the Greene family entrepreneurs were disturbed by the way that fishing—as a traditional custom—adversely affected labor force discipline. As their petition observed, the previous year's fishing had only resulted in the "Diversion of a great number of Hands from employments [at the cotton mill] more profitable to themselves and more beneficial to the public."[22] Unaccustomed to the regimen of modern factory life, the cotton-mill operatives had apparently responded to the spring run of migrating alewives by simply skipping out from work. As either farmers or mill operatives (a distinction that at this point did not really exist), the local population's fishing habits contrasted sharply with the values and interests of both the iron and the cotton manufacturers. The cultural expectations and consumption needs of a community of semisubsistence households were in some ways diametrically opposed to the disciplined and productive enterprises envisioned by an emerging entrepreneurial class.

Still, in spite of the Greenes' support for dam owners' rights, one should not overemphasize the divisive impact of the fishing-rights controversy on the community of Coventry and its environs. The great majority of the petitioners actually lived in Warwick, rather than Coventry. A somewhat more commercialized town, owing to its border on Narragansett Bay, Warwick was also home to a second forge owned by the Greenes, located near the coast at Potowumut.[23] And, of course, since most of Warwick's population lived downstream from the controversial cotton mill, their fishing interests would not have been directly affected by the dam's hindrance to migratory alewives. The nine petitioners who did live in Coventry consisted of a peculiar socioeconomic mix. Unlike the advocates of traditional rights, who were solidly average in wealth, their local opponents came from either extreme. Three of the nine Coventry petitioners ranked near the top of the town's tax list, including Jacob Greene, the owner of the forge and the town's second-wealthiest citizen. Three others placed near the bottom, including two who paid only a poll tax. The Greene family supporters were thus anomalies in a relatively egalitarian society of independent households. As a small coterie of employers and their dependents/employees, they were unable to significantly weaken the town's unified support for customary fishing rights.[24]

But however unified the local community may have been, the farmers failed in their attempt to repeal the Greenes' old exemption from fishing requirements. As had happened in the case of an earlier controversy over his original mill on the Pawtuxet River, Moses Brown was able to use his considerable influence to defeat the interests of the rural community. He could draw on the support of the harmony of interests that in this case prevailed among merchants and artisans in Providence. The Greenes themselves were prominent in state and national affairs and could thus appeal over the heads of the local community. On February 6, 1800, the assembly dismissed the farmers' petition.[25]

Public Roads versus Private Turnpikes

Although investment in cotton mills was the most dramatic example of the business activity of the Providence elite, at the turn of the century commerce was still far and away the leading interest of the city's merchant community. The Brown brothers and others searched for new markets in China, Latin America, and Europe, while seeking to develop the commercial potential of their own backyard. The population of the rural hinterland continued to grow after the Revolution: in northwestern Rhode Island alone it jumped by over a third between 1782 and 1800, reaching a total of about 11,400; growth was even more rapid in the adjacent communities of eastern Connecticut and central Massachusetts.[26] To help tap this growing market, the merchants of Providence, like their counterparts elsewhere in the country, began rebuilding major roads by means of turnpike companies. (See Figure 1 for locations of turnpikes in northwestern Rhode Island.) The first major turnpike company, the Providence and Norwich Turnpike Society, was chartered in 1794 as a cooperative effort by the mercantile communities of the two cities aimed at linking themselves to each other and to their respective hinterlands. The result was a ten-year running battle with the yeomanry of Rhode Island who lived along the highway's path, and for whom the turnpike was an affront to their traditional liberties and local rights.

The merchants of Providence resorted to turnpike improvements largely because the existing system for building highways was inadequate for the needs of a modern commercial economy. As was the case with much of eighteenth-century America, statutory provisions for road repair represented a triumph for the localistic concerns over the needs of regional commerce. State road regulations divided each town into upwards of twenty districts for the purpose of repairing all public highways. An overseer of the highways, elected annually by the town meeting, was responsible for the proper condition of the roads in his district. Once or twice each year, he was authorized to call forth the labor of all the men necessary for repairing the district's highways, with each man required to work a full day or two every year, or pay an equivalent amount in taxes.

In theory, since a fair proportion of the labor force was thereby reserved for road repair, the highways should have been kept in good condition; but in practice it was exceedingly difficult to enforce the provisions of the law. Like most local officials, highway overseers served without remuneration and therefore had little incentive, beyond their own economic interests and sense of social standing, to fulfill the dictates of the law. Fines were instituted for nonperformance of duties, but as everywhere in local government, their collection depended on the energies and concerns of private individuals; there were no attorneys general or other local officials responsible for suing negligent officers of the highways.[27]

Even if roads were repaired, they may not have fulfilled the needs of long-distance commercial travel. Since road repair was organized on the level of tiny individual districts, its progress was dictated by the needs of the local citizenry, not the cosmopolitan concerns of seaport merchants. In northwestern Rhode Island, roads that led to the local mill or meeting house may have taken precedence over those that headed straight to more distant marketplaces. And in any case, subdivision of road authority meant that the repair of major highways would be highly uncoordinated and uneven. The result was a patchwork system of highways, with countless bends and twists to suit local needs, rather than the efficiency concerns of regional commerce.[28]

To remedy this unsatisfactory situation, Rhode Island merchants, like those elsewhere in the country, adopted the English innovation of a chartered turnpike company. As in the case of other early American corporations, such as banks and insurance companies, turnpike companies were created by petitioning the state legislature for permission to form a joint stock corporation. The typical turnpike charter—they varied little from case to case—allowed investors to pool their resources through the purchase of stock certificates, and then to expend them in repairing and straightening an existing road. The company was given the right of eminent domain for purchasing extra parcels of land where necessary, and, of course, the right to charge a toll at gates erected approximately ten miles apart. Tolls generally ranged from one cent for cattle to six cents for a horse cart, and to upwards of fifteen cents for a relatively heavy vehicle such as a wagon or chaise; but they were not chargeable to local travelers on their way to church, a neighbor's field, or the nearby mill. Finally, all turnpikes were required to revert to being public roads as soon as the stockholders earned a 12 percent return on investment. Although the companies' rights and powers were thus narrowly restricted in some ways, merchants all along the Atlantic seaboard quickly seized on what appeared to be a sure method for engrossing the trade of their respective hinterlands.[29] In New England, 33 charters were issued in the 1790s, with over 130 to follow in the next ten years.[30]

Unfortunately for the merchants, the farmers through whose lands the new roads were being cut did not share their entrepreneurial enthusiasm. Since they were only loosely connected to a market economy, most New England farmers had little need for the improvements necessary to serve the long-distance transportation needs of coastal merchants. One of their principal exports was cattle, which could be easily transported in herds over the poorest of roads. The fall harvest season, moreover, was soon followed by winter snows, which allowed for much easier transport by means of sleds.[31] Although the farmers' trips were short and subject to lesser tolls, they were also more frequent than those of merchants, whose large and heavy wagons were the vehicles that most required improved highways.[32] The farmers were thus effectively subsidizing the creation of roads for which they had little use. At the very least, turnpikes were an irksome nuisance for a rural population that had little cash to spare for passage through tollgates.

More fundamentally, farmers resented the turnpikes as an invasion of their traditional rights and liberties. In a traditional culture that associated rights with long-held customs, the erection of tollgates onto formerly public highways was seen as a tyrannical affront to common liberties. Turnpikes and other private roads may have existed in Europe for decades or even centuries, but in the New England of the 1790s they intruded on a system of free roads that had existed since earliest settlement.[33] Farmers also disliked the assumption by the turnpike companies of the right of eminent domain, a right that had formerly resided with local town government. Earlier in the century, the Greene and Brown family iron manufacturers had obtained needed exemptions from local fishway regulators by appealing over their heads to the colonial or state legislature. Now the merchants were following a similar route in gaining control over the upkeep of local highways. The farmers were all the more annoyed because turnpike charters replaced local authorities with private, profit-making corporations and thus violated the farmers' own traditions of neighborhood interchange and cooperation. All over New England, and perhaps especially in Rhode Island, the backwoods yeomanry reacted to the loss of local rights and authority with a variety of legal, quasi-legal, and sometimes violently illegal forms of protest.[34]

As was the case with fishing rights, rural Rhode Islanders were never unanimous in their defense of local customs at the expense of commercial progress. Indeed, the first turnpike company in Rhode Island was formed by a group of men who lived along the road from Providence to Killingly, Connecticut, on both sides of the Connecticut state line. In February 1794, the legislature chartered the Glocester Turnpike Society, allowing it to improve that portion of the Killingly road that extended westward from the village of Chepachet to the state line. Since the charter restricted the placement of tollgates to within four miles of the state line—a sparsely populated area—its inconvenience was not serious enough to warrant opposition by the Glocester Town Meeting.[35] Nevertheless, the company's experience suggests that it was a decidedly unpopular institution.

The townspeople demonstrated their hostility toward the turnpike builders by adopting a policy of noncooperation and financial harassment. As soon as the turnpike was completed in 1798, the town meeting directed that local inhabitants "work out the Whole of their taxes on other roads," rather than on the turnpike itself, thus depriving the corporation of the benefits of traditional highway regulations.[36] The town also resorted to the quasi-legal practice of double taxation. In 1798 the company's directors complained to the legislature that the town was assessing individual shareholders and the corporation itself for the value of its capital stock. The directors asked the legislature for exemption from taxes on both their physical property and their capital stock. The town responded with a spirited reply, instructing its representatives "to oppose Every Paragraph of said Petition." The assembly resolved the disagreement by rejecting the town's claimed right to double taxation of turnpike stock: given the political influences wielded by coastal merchants, who wished to protect their own interests in bank and turnpike stock, it was inconceivable that the legislature would decide to the contrary. But the assembly also denied the company's request for exemption from local property taxes. A compromise was thus fashioned, thereby ending the bitter dispute.[37]

Finally, the town successfully rejected efforts to turnpike the remainder of the Providence–Killingly road. In 1799, twenty-four inhabitants of the towns of Glocester, Scituate, and Johnston petitioned the legislature for a turnpike charter to cover that part of the road "lying between Tripptown bridge [near Providence] and Cepatchet [*sic*] Bridge." The petitioners included some of the most prominent members of each town, including the iron masters Daniel and Thomas Owen and Daniel Manton, Johnston's wealthiest resident. But in spite of the social prominence of the turnpike advocates, the Glocester Town Meeting voted to oppose altogether their request for a new and expanded charter. On this occasion, the legislature acceded completely to the town's request and dismissed the petition for turnpike privilege in June of the following year.[38]

In the case of the Providence and Norwich Turnpike Society, the yeomanry were not as successful in thwarting the turnpikers' aims, although they nevertheless struggled tenaciously to impede the company's efforts every step of the way. In October 1794, the assembly chartered the turnpike company after receiving petitions from inhabitants of Rhode Island and eastern Connecticut. Most of the fifteen Rhode Island petitioners were members of the Providence merchant elite, including John Innes Clarke and Nicholas and John Brown, the town's three wealthiest men. The charter granted the company the right to turnpike the existing post road to Norwich, which ran from Providence along the path of the present route 14, passing southwest through Cranston, Johnston, Scituate, Foster, and the northwest corner of Coventry, before entering Connecticut to link up with a turnpike sponsored by that state's mercantile community. The charter allowed the company to raise $6,000 in capital stock, and to receive a return on investment by establishing a tollgate within nine miles of the Connecticut border, thus placing it somewhere in the town of Scituate.

Included among the original petitioners were John Waterman of Johnston and William Battey of Scituate, two of the wealthier members of their respective towns; but Waterman's and Battey's support for the new turnpike was obviously not shared by the great majority of their neighbors. In the spring of the following year the town meetings of Coventry, Scituate, and Foster instructed their deputies to seek the complete repeal of the company's charter. But since the political influence of the Providence elite undoubtedly exceeded that of the backcountry farmers, the legislature dismissed the towns' request without further comment.[39]

Having failed to stop the turnpike in the legislature, the towns along its path resorted to the same tactics of noncooperation and harassment used earlier by the town of Glocester. On June 12, 1797, the Foster town meeting voted to "apportion the two Districts that have heretofore bin on the Post road among the other districts in Said town." On some occasions, jealousy over the loss of their traditional authority led towns and local highway supervisors to actually obstruct the work of the turnpike company. In 1799 the turnpike company wrote to the Coventry town council, accusing Philip Bowen, an overseer of the highways, of having damaged their road. But instead of chastising the obstreperous overseer, the council voted on July 1 to "protect the said Philip Bowen in the Lawfull Discharge of his Duty as an officer of the Town of Coventry."[40]

Finally, the town's residents did their best to evade payment of turnpike tolls, occasionally resorting to violence and intimidation. Charles Angell, the turnpike's tollkeeper, was in a decidedly unenviable position, having to balance company loyalty against the practical necessity of mollifying the enraged local citizenry. In July 1801 Angell admitted to the company that "I have not charged any toles to any persons that I should be afraid to trust with my Property for them sums." In other words, Angell was afraid that charging tolls might result in the destruction of his tollgate and house by disgruntled local travelers. Eventually, the company adopted a lenient policy toward toll collection, out of a desire "to conciliate the minds of the Neighbors." The company directors would occasionally order that the tollgate be opened during the spring, when weather conditions made roads everywhere nearly impassable. The company also allowed the tollkeeper to let "the people of the Neighborhood . . . pass, when it was not convenient [for them] to pay on credit." Unfortunately for the company, the local yeomanry, ever eager to turn a temporary policy into a customary right, only reacted all the more vehemently when the gates were once again closed. This misunderstanding, as the company reported in 1807, "has lately brot on some altercations at the gates." Collecting turnpike tolls from Rhode Island farmers was certainly a hazardous occupation.[41]

In the midst of all this contention, the company was able to make very little progress in actually improving the road. Partly because of local tollgate evasions, the company's receipts always fell far short of its expenditures in making improvements. More important, constructing a superior road simply cost much more than the corporation had ever anticipated. By 1797 the turnpike company had already spent at least $7,500 on construction costs, well over the original $6,000 raised by the sale of stock.[42]

In order to salvage their investment, the turnpikers introduced into the legislature a variety of cost-saving or revenue-enhancing schemes, almost all of which were successfully opposed by Rhode Island's northwestern farmers. The turnpike society attempted twice to amend its charter provisions in order to increase tollgate receipts. In 1795, it successfully petitioned the legislature for the right to move its tollgate from nine to eleven miles from the Connecticut border. But when the company returned four years later, asking that its gate be moved three miles closer to Providence, the rural towns mounted a successful opposition. In their own counterpetition to the legislature, signed by 218 residents of Foster and Scituate, the farmers complained of being "very much Burdened . . . By reason of having our Post road stopped up By a turnpike Gate." Should the toll be moved still closer to Providence, they feared that "instead of public highways open and free for the accommodation of the good Citizens of this State. . . . [the highways] may and will be connected to the purpose of private gain and emolument." The legislature agreed with the counterpetition and dismissed the company's request in June 1799.

In 1801 the company again asked for financial relief from the legislature, on this occasion simply by requesting whatever the legislature "sees fit." In response, the assembly appointed an investigative committee whose report severely criticized the company. Noting that the turnpike road is "in a bad state and wanting great repairs," the committee concluded that "the said Company have [*sic*] no prospect of ever realizing any profit on the capital by them extended." According to the committee report, which the assembly fully accepted, "any further priviledges extended to said company . . . would be an injury to [the nearby] inhabitants." In spite of the considerable political influence of the company's stockholders, it was thus unable to significantly amend the financial provisions of its original charter.[43]

Having failed to increase its revenues, the turnpike company turned to statutory amendments aimed at reducing its costs. The company began advocating, ironically, a return to the traditional method for repairing highways: using the labor power of local inhabitants. In 1797 Col. John Waterman, a charter member of the turnpike society and one of its rural agents, circulated a petition among those farmers who lived along the path of the Providence to Norwich road. The petition requested that the legislature pass an act that would require the rural towns to expend highway taxes and labor on the turnpike road, just as had been the tradition before the road was turnpiked. As an inducement to sign the petition, Col. Waterman promised that all who "did their duty on the turnpike Road as they formerly did should be Exempt from paying pikedge [*sic*]." As presented to the legislature, the petition contained signatures only from residents of Johnston and Cranston. When originally written, the document included the more western towns of Scituate, Foster, and Coventry; but the names of those towns were later crossed out, suggesting that Waterman had failed to gather support from their citizens. At any rate, the legislature passed the requested act three years later, over the protests of the Johnston Town Meeting.[44]

The company's strategy was in some ways clever, for it succeeded in weakening the rural opposition by dividing it between the turnpike's immediate neighbors on the one hand and the remainder of the local population on the other. However, the company soon overplayed its hand when it deviously misinterpreted the new law to its advantage. The statute called for "the Town-Council and Surveyors of the towns of Johnston and Cranston . . . to cause a just proportion of highway taxes and highway labour to be expended and done in and upon the said turnpike road, by the inhabitants living upon or near the same who usually paid taxes or laboured upon the said road before the charter of incorporation was granted to the turnpike company." If interpreted at all literally, the statute's language essentially directed a return to local provision for, and control of repairs along the turnpike highway. But instead of trusting the "Town-Council and Surveyors" to supervise repair work, as the act directed, the turnpike society employed Col. Waterman as its local foreman, who proceeded to order local residents to work for him alone. Even more sinisterly, the company may have also reneged on its promise of pikage exemption for those who lived near the road. As it was passed, the legislative act made absolutely no mention of granting free access to the turnpike.[45] Although in the short run the company would gain some free repair work from its misapplication of the statute's provisions, in the long run an angry rural reaction to the turnpikers' duplicity would lead them to regret their clever machinations.

The turnpike company did not foresee the heated reaction of one Barzillai Knight, a Cranston cooper who had signed Col. Waterman's petition, and who as a local highway overseer was especially offended by the company's actions. By this time, the merchants who ran the company must have been impressed by the stubbornness and irrascibility of the rural opposition; but Barzillai Knight was an unusually cantankerous sort, even when judged by the standards of his neighbors. Like many others in northwestern Rhode Island, he had belonged to the Six-Principle Baptist sect, having joined the Johnston church in 1780; but he was dismissed by the church three years later for "his ongospel [sic] conduct." Also like many of his neighbors, Knight's business contacts with the merchants of Providence, although perhaps infrequent, tended to be decidedly unpleasant. Twice during the 1790s he was sued for debts by his Providence creditors, one of whom was John Innes Clark, the town's second leading merchant, and a charter member of the turnpike society. In sum, Barzillai Knight was no friend to the Providence gentry, and he was, moreover, a prickly man to cross.[46]

Having been tricked into a bargain with the company, whose end was never held up, Knight was doubly offended. In his capacity as a private citizen, he was, of course, angered by a promise broken; and as a local highway official, he resented having his authority circumvented by the company's local agent, Col. John Waterman. Knight quickly used this second capacity as highway surveyor to exact a sort of petty revenge on the turnpike's promoters. It so happened that Col. Waterman owned land along the highway's path, as did Jabez Bowen, Providence's wealthiest doctor and another charter member of the turnpike society. As local landowners, Waterman and Bowen were thus required, under the provisions of preexisting highway regulations, to either work on the nearby roads or hire laborers in their stead. As the highway surveyor for the turnpike district, Barzillai Knight ignored the recently passed legislative act and ordered Bowen, Waterman, and other local residents to work not on the turnpike road, but on an altogether different piece of highway. Bowen and Waterman, along with a few other neighbors, defied his order, choosing instead to work on the turnpike, where Waterman was the foreman. Knight responded by turning to the town authorities, who issued "warrants of distress" to seize "their goods and chattels." No doubt to their astonishment and outrage, these two worthy gentlemen thus found their property threatened by a rural artisan of only mediocre social standing.[47]

In the meantime, the towns of Johnston and Cranston renewed their opposition to the turnpike company's new statutory privilege, complaining to the legislature that it is "a heavy grievance to them that any Individuals thereof should be compelled to expend their proportion of the Highway Taxes or Labour upon said Road and thereby take so much money or labour from the Funds or general property of said Towns and place it in the funds and to the profits of said Turnpike Company."[48] The statute's provisions thus violated the towns' rural traditions of local autonomy and neighborhood cooperation. For the citizens of Cranston and Johnston, the repair of highways, like so many other aspects of their culture, should have depended upon a system of local interchange and cooperation, mediated by a traditional framework of laws and customs. The turnpike company's new privileges, on the other hand, represented a threatening innovation, replacing local authority and community involvement with outside control and private pecuniary gain.

More on the individual level, Caleb Remington, Barzillai Knight's counterpart in Johnston as the turnpike road's highway surveyor, was deeply offended by the turnpike company's usurpation of his local authority. As he complained in his semiliterate prose: "It was out of My power to git any worke from the Men it was porpotioned to . . . thea [they] Told me the Turnpike Company Tolde them if thea would work on that Rode [i.e., the Turnpike] thea would Bare them Harmlyss and therefore thea should not work under Me." The local highway workers apparently believed that the turnpike company, using its statutory privileges and considerable wealth and prestige, could offer legal protection to keep them "Harmlyss" from the penalties of local highway regulations. (They obviously had not anticipated the spirited response in Cranston of Barzillai Knight.) After all, in terms of social standing, Caleb Remington, a farmer of only average wealth, was no match for his rival supervisor, Col. Waterman, the town's wealthiest citizen. In his crude attempt at written communication, Remington was thus voicing the resentment of a rural people whose social order and traditional freedoms were being undermined by a powerful set of commercially minded men.[49]

As the upshot of this bitterly fought dispute, the turnpike company directors lost everything they had temporarily gained through their tactical cleverness and social prominence. In February 1801, only one year after their enactment, the company's offensive privileges were completely repealed by the legislature.[50] In the case of Barzillai Knight's particular conflict with turnpike officials, Jabez Bowen petitioned the legislature to seek relief from prosecution for back payment of highway taxes by the town of Cranston. But the legislature, by this time weary of the company's endless financial troubles and political schemes, offered him little support. Bowen instead was forced to settle the matter out of court; in return for a payment of twenty-five dollars, the town agreed to drop its suit for taxes "assessed on the Inhabitants that live on the Turnpike Road."[51] To balance the score, Barzillai Knight's creditors may have had the final revenge. At least ten times within the next eight years he was hauled into court for nonpayment of debts, until in 1809 he was forced to petition the legislature for relief as an insolvent debtor.[52] Otherwise, the only thing gained by the turnpike company as a result of this sorry affair was the continued ill will of the state's rural population.

At the turn of the eighteenth century, the struggle between turnpikers and the rural northwest reached a stalemate. Except in the case of the politically powerful Providence and Norwich Turnpike Society, the farmers were able to defeat petitions for turnpike charters that threatened to close long sections of public highways. The Glocester turnpike, running between Chepachet and Connecticut, was too short to be particularly troublesome; the local population was therefore content merely to protest its operation through occasional acts of harassment. Turnpike advocates were not, of course, devoid of rural allies. As the Glocester turnpike case demonstrated, together with Col. Waterman's loyal service to his Providence connections, there were already a few local inhabitants wealthy enough to see the advantages of promoting commercial expansion. But in spite of their social prominence, these turnpike advocates, like those who supported the rights of dam owners, were consistently overruled at local town meetings.

The two turnpikes that obtained charters were able to preserve their original privileges; but they soon ran into financial difficulties, thanks in part to the intransigence of a hostile local population. The turnpike companies resorted to a variety of schemes, ranging from moving tollgates to more lucrative sites to further circumventing the authority of local highway officials. They were usually defeated in this regard, partly because of the turnpike companies' own arrogance and incompetence, but more often because of the stubborn resourcefulness of the rural opposition.

Indeed, although turnpike development sparked rural resistance throughout New England, opposition appears to have been particularly fierce among Rhode Island's backcountry farmers. In Connecticut, controversies over turnpikes centered largely on the issue of responsibility for bridge construction and repair. Most turnpike charters issued in that state actually required that the individual towns bear the responsibility for the upkeep of bridges along the highway's path. But while the towns frequently objected to having to share the turnpike's burdens, opposition to turnpikes per se was not particularly widespread.[53] In Rhode Island it was inconceivable that a legislative charter would foist the onerous task of bridge construction onto the shoulders of an already angered rural population.

Contemporary travelers also noted the particular vehemence with which Rhode Island's rural yeomanry resisted the intrusion of corporate turnpiking. While passing in 1819 through the town of Scituate, the British observer Henry Bradshaw Fearon observed to a local laborer that the area's "roads were bad." The Rhode Islander responded that "roads, I guess, are unpopular in this State: we think . . . that they are invasions of our liberties: we were mightily roiled when they [the turnpikes] were first cut, and we always spoiled them in the night." Rhode Islanders did not stop short of vandalism in their attacks on this perceived threat to their freedom. Timothy Dwight also noted the abysmal condition of northwestern Rhode Island's roads, and he elaborated on the interrelationship, expressed by the Scituate laborer, between turnpikes and popular liberty. Dwight was traveling through Rhode Island just as the Providence and Norwich Turnpike Society was unsuccessfully petitioning the legislature for various forms of financial aid. According to Dwight, the society's legislative opponents rejected its request, because, in their view, "turnpikes, and the establishment of religious worship, had their origin in Great Britain: the government of which was a monarchy, and the inhabitants slaves . . . the people of Massachusetts and Connecticut were obliged by law to support ministers and pay the fare of turnpikes, and were therefore slaves also." Therefore, "free born Rhode-Islanders," the turnpike opponents concluded, "ought never to submit to be priest-ridden, nor to pay for the privileges of travelling on the highway."[54]

This analogy between religion and highways highlights a crucial element in the culture and political economy of rural Rhode Island. Turnpikes and established churches are indeed similar, in that they both seek to promote social interconnections through legal coercion, thus threatening local autonomy and freedom. Rhode Islanders knew that the establishment of religion in neighboring states had already compromised the independence of their local communities. The omnipresence of Harvard- and Yale-educated clergymen, together with a creeping trend toward Presbyterianism, were creating binding ties between orthodox New England's rural communities and its urban, educated, and commercial elites. Rhode Islanders called their neighbors to the north and west "slaves" for having relinquished local freedom and autonomy under the guidance of an educated clergy.

In their own state, on the other hand, an autonomous rural culture was able to develop in the absence of overarching and homogenizing central institutions. Largely inert and unreflective for most of the eighteenth century, northwestern Rhode Islanders were suddenly made aware of the distinctly localistic nature of their culture by the economic, political, and religious conflicts of the revolutionary era. It was this self-conscious commitment to the preservation of local autonomy that fueled the tenacious response by the rural northwest to the ambitions of the Providence and Norwich Turnpike Society.

The Yeomanry versus Public Schools

The final issue over which farmers and merchants locked horns was the Free School Act of 1800. Passed as a result of a political alliance between Providence merchants and mechanics, the Free School Act required for the first time in Rhode Island that each town establish a rudimentary system of grammar schools. Unfortunately for its proponents, the act was short-lived. Its passage prompted an enormous outpouring of hostility from the state's backwoodsmen, and it was repealed only three years later. Nevertheless, rural opposition to this cultural improvement was less widespread than it was in the case of cotton-mill dams and turnpikes. An important minority within the rural northwest appears to have supported the creation of public schools. Although unsuccessful on this occasion, the modernizing aspirations of this minority would serve as an important harbinger for later developments.

For several decades prior to 1800 the merchants of Providence had sought to establish a public school system, at least within their own community, if not within the state as a whole. On a practical level, they needed schools in their community in order to supply their commercial operations with trained and orderly personnel. But perhaps more important, the merchants saw public education as a necessary ingredient in the formation of a respectable and civilized society. Neighboring Massachusetts and Connecticut had long since established their own public school systems, a fact which made Rhode Island's educational inadequacies seem all the more embarrassing for the Providence civic elite. In the 1760s and 1770s the merchants had sought to make their religion more respectable by providing college training for the ministry, and by ridding their First Baptist Church of rural obscurantisms. The first attempt to establish schools in Providence came at about the same time, in 1769. In that year a public schools ordinance was proposed by the Browns, the Jenckes, the Bowens, and several other prominent mercantile families. However, it was defeated in town meeting by the "poorer" members of the town, a class probably composed principally of the town's artisans and outlying farmers.[55]

Artisanal opposition soon faded in the wake of the Revolution and the return of prosperity in the 1790s. Under the leadership of the Providence Association of Mechanics and Manufacturers, the city's shopkeepers soon joined the merchants in advocating public schooling, just as earlier they had supported Moses Brown in defending the rights of dam owners. The association's members welcomed economic growth and technological innovation. At the same time they expressed concern that without proper education, their children would be unable to prosper in an increasingly dynamic economy. The establishment of republican governments in the wake of the Revolution added a note of urgency to appeals by both merchants and artisans for public schooling. "Under a Republican form of government," the school advocates claimed, "liberty and security . . . depends [*sic*] on a general diffusion of Knowledge among the people"; an ignorant people could only too easily be swayed by the charms of an ambitious despot.[56] The result of these hopes and concerns was a drive for a system of public schooling not only for Providence, but for the entire state. The city's school advocates knew that the efficacy of a local school system would be greatly improved if they were backed by the legal and financial support of the state government. In February 1799 the Providence Association of Mechanics and Manufacturers petitioned the legislature for a state-funded system of public schools.

The state's farmers, on the other hand, and especially those from hill-country areas, had little reason to favor public schooling. Subsistence farmers needed only the bare rudiments of an education, mainly for keeping account books and writing wills. Farmers might even have resented schools for removing their children from the family economy, especially during the crucial spring-planting and fall-harvesting seasons. Besides, at the bottom line financially, cash-poor subsistence farmers would resist any new government program that resulted in increased taxes.

But a more fundamental fear lay at the heart of rural opposition to public education. Essentially, the farmers identified education not with hope for a better life, but rather with the powers and privileges of their enemies and economic superiors. It was the well-educated James Manning, after all, who replaced Elder Winsor as the pastor of Providence's Baptist church. Lawyers, another breed of educated men, stirred even more anger and resentment among farmers, especially during the credit crisis of the 1780s, when many a farmer was sued in court for nonpayment of debts. In 1786 the town of Foster even resolved that "no sworn attorney be for the future chosen a Member of the upper or Lower House of Assembly." Antilawyer and antipedagogical feelings by rural Rhode Islanders were perhaps best expressed by a fellow backwoodsman from Pennsylvania who opposed financial support for Dickinson College, stating that "this College has 'sent forward' a parcel of fellows, lawyers to prey upon the public. I hate the lawyers, and learned men, Mr. Speaker, they are an evil to the community."[57] Backwoods farmers identified schools with the production of powerful men who would threaten the order of their local communities. Of course, yeomen farmers did not oppose all forms of education. A scattering of schools already existed in most of Rhode Island's rural towns, and about 75 percent of all adult males could at least sign their name. But backcountry farmers generally insisted that schools be established on the basis of local initiative, rather than as a mandate from the central state government.[58]

In spite of this general rural hostility to public schools, the mechanics' petition was favorably received by the assembly. Supporters managed to have the petition reviewed by a committee of three assemblymen, all of whom were likely to issue a commendatory report: James Burrill, the mechanics' association's president; Richard Jackson, a leading Providence merchant; and Moses Lippitt, a wealthy Warwick landowner and future cotton-mill owner.[59] As was still often the case with important legislation, the bill reported by the committee was referred to local town meetings for the purpose of issuing proper "instructions" to their deputies. In the rural northwest, the results of these meetings were mixed. An influential minority in each town apparently supported the Free School Act, and in some cases this minority was able to take advantage of low voter turnout in order to secure the passage of a positive set of instructions. In the western town of Foster, which was perhaps the least commercialized town in the state, school advocates were defeated in town meeting by a vote of eighty-four to forty-three. But in Glocester the committee's school bill was approved, although by an unknown margin. Receiving support from coastal ports and even a few hill-country towns, the school bill sailed through the legislature three sessions later and was signed into law in February 1800.[60]

In its final form, the "Act to Establish Free Schools" consisted of a mixture of requirements and inducements, all aimed at encouraging towns to satisfactorily establish their own school systems. As was the case with Massachusetts' and Connecticut's early colonial school acts, each town was required to establish a certain number of schools, depending on its population. These schools were to provide for instructing "all the white inhabitants of said towns between the ages of six and twenty years, in reading, writing and common arithmetic." The act also established a statewide system for financing local schools, much like a similar provision passed into law in New York in 1795. To induce compliance with school requirements, the Rhode Island act provided that each town that established proper schools would receive an educational subsidy equal to 20 percent of its yearly tax quota. Finally, in keeping with the state's strong localistic traditions, the authors of the act wisely yielded control over the building and regulation of schools to individual town districts and delegated overall supervision of the districts to the town council. The act was singularly lacking in any kind of enforcement or inspection provisions; towns could qualify for a state refund by simply having the appropriate officers sign a certificate. Put simply, it purposely required only the rudiments of a public school system, in hopes of securing a modicum of support from a possibly hostile population.[61]

Unfortunately, much to the chagrin of the school advocates, the backwoods farmers acted quickly to nullify the new act. A brief struggle ensued within the town governments of northwestern Rhode Island. The town deputies who had supported the school bill in assembly were the first to feel the effects of the farmers' aroused anger. In the election of May 1800, which immediately followed passage of the school act, the town of Glocester's two deputies, who were originally "instructed" to support the bill, were turned out of office, never to serve in the assembly again. A similar turnover occurred in all the other northwestern towns, except for Foster, whose deputies had been instructed to oppose the bill in the first place.[62]

The farmers then acted to nullify the effects of the school act. They simply refused to appropriate expenditures from their respective town treasuries; and on the statewide level, they quickly pressured the assembly into suspending the act's educational subsidies, which could only be raised by an increase in overall state taxes. The assembly passed temporary suspension clauses in June 1801 and again in June 1802.[63]

Actual repeal of the unfortunate act was achieved with greater difficulty. The issue caused considerable political disorder within the town of Glocester. Knowing that theirs was a minority view, public-school advocates tried to discourage political debate on the issue by voting at a special meeting "that Whoever signs a Request to Call a Town Meeting for the purpose of abolishing the free Schools shall pay [for] . . . the Whole expence of said Meeting." The school advocates took advantage of the fact that few local yeomen farmers could afford to pay for the cost of a town meeting. Nevertheless, opposition continued to mount, until on November 1, 1802, the town meeting voted down a local school tax "by a large Majority" and then instructed the town's deputies "to act against the School Bill."[64]

Elsewhere in backcountry Rhode Island the opponents of public schools eventually prevailed. In Smithfield, a town adjacent to Glocester on the east, school proponents passed a $1,000 appropriation for local schools in 1800 and 1801; but in a special town meeting held in September 1802, funds were rescinded, "by the votes of the backwoodsmen." Even many coastal farm communities refused to comply with the bill's provisions. In addition to Smithfield, only Providence, Bristol, and Middletown are known to have established public schools in accordance with the school act's regulations.[65] In February 1803 the entire act was repealed.

The bill's original proponents in Providence reacted bitterly to this defeat. They cried: "Alas for insulted Rhode Island! How long will ignorance be for us the order of the day?" And in a letter that perhaps unconsciously revealed their true opinion of the backwoods illiterates, they claimed that "in a civilized country, the man who is destitute of education is not much superior . . . to savages." The city of Providence would continue to maintain its own public schools, in spite of the repeal of the Free School Act. But in the state as a whole, the issue would remain dead for the next twenty years.[66]

By the end of the eighteenth century, the northwestern yeomanry and their commercial antagonists had reached a stalemate. As in most other states, the Rhode Island coastal elite were a politically powerful group, especially when supported by commercial farmers and urban mechanics. But more than in any other state, Rhode Island's hill-country farmers had developed highly localistic social and political traditions that led them to bitterly resent the intrusion of capitalist innovations and cultural improvements as a threat to their special liberties. The northwestern farmers had also developed a uniquely autonomous culture, which gave them a remarkable degree of unity and social courage and thereby allowed them to stand up to and defeat the innovations favored by their commercial antagonists.

During the 1790s, the Providence merchants largely failed in their attempts to commercialize and industrialize the northwest's economy and society. They succeeded only when their plans did not necessitate significant statutory changes, or when they did not need to rely on the farmers for cooperation and assistance. Thus, Moses Brown and his associates were able to build cotton-mill dams on the south branch of the Pawtuxet River because there was a preexisting exemption to customary fishway requirements. The Providence and Norwich Turnpike Society succeeded in obtaining rudimentary charter privileges, but it failed when it sought further statutory assistance. Capitalistic endeavors that required active participation and cooperation by the back-woodsmen were equally unsuccessful. When the Providence and Norwich Turnpike Society tried to enlist turnpike residents in the task of repairing their failed "improvements," it provoked an angry and successful opposition. Similarly, the Free School Act was quickly doomed to failure, because the pied-mont farmers simply refused to enforce its provisions. In the face of a hostile and united rural opposition, the merchants made little headway in their plans to colonialize the northwestern economy.

Nevertheless, while unsuccessful in the short run, the merchants' initiatives disrupted to some extent the harmony of interests that had earlier prevailed in the northwestern society. When Moses Brown established the first viable cotton factory in the Pawtuxet River valley, he succeeded not only in antagonizing the local population, but also in aggravating relations between farmers and an indigenous iron-manufacturing operation. Until the 1790s, the Greene family had managed its forge establishments without provoking local opposition; but the intrusion of cotton manufacturing into the area forced the Greenes to support Brown's defense of dam-owner rights, thereby placing themselves at odds with their yeomen neighbors. The introduction of turnpikes into the northwest also produced a few divisions within an otherwise unified rural society. While most backcountry farmers opposed the new roads, a few of their wealthier and more enterprising neighbors began to see advantages in improved land transportation. The turnpike proposal by Daniel Owen and associates was rejected by the Glocester Town Meeting in 1799; but their initiative was far from over. Finally, the passage of the Free School Act produced a lively struggle within the northwest, as school proponents fought for three years to retain control of local town meetings, before being finally overwhelmed by the backwoods opposition. In the next two decades, when social and economic conditions began to change in the northwest, sometimes in troubling directions, it would become increasingly tempting for more farmers to favor economic and social improvements as both an opportunity for private gain and a panacea for public ills.

CHAPTER THREE

The Struggle within the Northwest

Customary Rights versus Commercial and Entrepreneurial Improvements

⊤ ⊤

BY THE TURN of the nineteenth century, economic and demographic growth in northwestern Rhode Island began to alter significantly the balance of power between opponents and advocates of private, entrepreneurial development and government-sponsored improvement. On the positive side, growth led a significant minority of northwesterners into becoming increasingly interested in commercializing their rural communities. While most northwesterners in the revolutionary era were incapable of participating extensively in a commercial market, a small fraction—about one-fifth of all households—were able to produce a significant surplus of marketable goods. Moreover, incentives to trade in the regional rather than local market were increasing considerably by the start of the 1800s. The town of Providence emerged from the postwar depression of the 1780s in booming fashion. Its enterprising merchants opened new trading routes to China and Latin America and profited from the lucrative if risky neutral carriage trade occasioned by the Napoleonic Wars. Providence's population grew by almost half between 1782 and 1800, and by another third in the following decade. An enticing market developed in the sale of farm products and the purchase of a wider array of imported consumer goods, at least for those northwesterners who were viable and enterprising enough to take advantage of this new opportunity.[1] Partly as a result, by the turn of the century, a well-defined economic and political elite began initiating plans for exploiting and further increasing this trade through the creation of turnpikes, banks, and other private corporations.

At the same time, the negative consequences of population growth and market cycles impelled northwesterners of all kinds into reconsidering the values of the traditional economic and social order. Although economic and demographic growth enlarged commercial avenues for some, it also led to a new and pressing set of social problems. Population density in the northwest had been low in the eighteenth century relative to the rest of southern New England, but it climbed rapidly following the revolutionary war. The area's population rose by a third between 1774 and 1800, and by another 7 percent in the next decade. Average farm holdings dropped below fifty acres by 1810, leaving many households struggling at a bare level of subsistence.[2] In the meantime, although long-term trends pointed toward increasing commercialization, short-term market disturbances caused considerable economic dislocation. The embargo of 1808, the War of 1812, and the panic of 1819 disrupted and distorted demand for local products. These twin problems of overpopulation and market instability led to the growth of excessive household indebtedness and outright poverty. As local residents grappled with these problems, they were eventually drawn into rejecting an older, semisubsistence way of life in favor of an improved local infrastructure and enhanced market conditions. Thus, a troubling collection of public problems together with the private visions of a prospering elite combined to pull the northwest gradually into a new commercializing order.

The Emergence of a Commercializing Elite

By around 1800, a significant number of northwestern Rhode Islanders were actively interested in expanding the commercial development of their rural communities. Within the northwest, this enterprising minority seemed to center in an area that began in northern Scituate and stretched north and west through Glocester to the vicinity of the village of Chepachet. Here originated most of the northwest's early attempts to mimic the modernizing improvements that were first introduced into Rhode Island by the merchants of Providence: banks, turnpikes, schools, and cotton mills.[3] Among the leading innovators from the town of Glocester were the venerable Owen family; the Smith family of Daniel, Mowry, and Simon; Daniel Tourtellot; Timothy Willmarth; and Samuel Winsor. These men ranked in the top 10 percent of the town's tax list of 1822. Mowry Smith's taxable wealth ranked him in the middle of this group. When he died in 1829 he left a personal estate valued at over $1,800, including twenty-one cattle, three horses, and a sizeable inventory of imported luxuries: silver spoons, mahogany furniture, and a brass clock.[4] In Scituate, the leading commercializers included such prosperous farmers as Elisha Mathewson of the Moswansicutt Pond area, and John Harris and James Aldrich in the town's northwestern corner. The mill-owning family of Dean and Joshua Kimball, whose properties stretched from eastern Scituate to the adjacent town of Johnston, were also active proponents of turnpikes and other modernizing institutions. Rounding off the list of local innovators was Charles Angell, a lawyer and tavern keeper whose home and establishment stood astride the infamous Providence and Norwich Turnpike road. He served for several years as the company's tollgate keeper, a position that gave him considerable practice in the art of upholding the needs of turnpike progress while also attempting to conciliate angry local citizens.[5] Angell and the town's other leading modernizing innovators had already revealed an interest in cultural improvements when in 1796 they helped incorporate the Scituate Library Company, the northwest's first chartered institution.[6] Together with their associates in nearby Glocester, these men were the driving force behind the first bank and the first two turnpikes to be founded and built largely by native northwesterners.

Of course, turnpikes and banks could only be established upon receipt of a legislative charter; it therefore comes as no surprise that these individuals were linked together by a common political agenda. They had served as leaders of the old Country party, and after that party's demise, remained active as a major faction within Rhode Island's growing Republican party. Under the leadership of their chief ally in Providence, Governor Arthur Fenner, the old Country party leaders of the northwest continued to meet to form political strategy. Fenner referred to his contacts there as "our Friends in the Country." Among the more prominent members of this faction were Daniel Owen, who had served as lieutenant governor during the Country party's reign in 1780s, and Elisha Mathewson, who would serve for a short while in the U.S. Senate, between 1807 and 1811. Also active were John Harris, who held a judgeship for several years on the Providence County Court of Common Pleas, and James Aldrich, who frequently hosted political meetings at his home in Scituate.[7]

But for all its contacts with the leading men in state politics, the country faction continued to depend for its success on at least a modicum of local popular support. During the ratification crisis of the late 1780s the backcountry leaders had to play their cards carefully as they sought to mediate between popular Anti-Federalism and their own political and economic goals. In the next two decades, however, popular pressures eased, giving local leaders more room to maneuver. The return of voter apathy allowed the northwestern elite to cooperate with Governor Arthur Fenner while the latter, pursuing the politics of realism, formed an uneasy coalition with the Federalists.

The rural leadership still needed to act carefully lest they arouse local unrest. Elite support for the unpopular Free School Act had resulted in the dismissal at the polls of several of the area's deputies to the General Assembly. Fortunately for the backcountry Republicans, the excesses of the Federalists were at the same time helping to strengthen their bonds with the local yeomanry. The hated land tax of 1798 was principally responsible for the over-whelming success of Arthur Fenner and the Republican party in the election of 1800. During the 1790s, the rural leaders generally supported the local population in resisting the turnpiking and manufacturing schemes of a common enemy: the Providence mercantile and Federalist elite. As important pillars within the resurgent Republican party of the 1800s, they would be less vulnerable than the Federalists to popular opposition when they began to pursue their own plans for modernizing the rural northwest.

Finally, the rural leadership acquired an important ally of sorts. In 1803 Senator Theodore Foster retired with his long-time friend, Dr. Solomon Drowne, to Foster, the town named for him at its formation in 1782. In social stature, Foster and Drowne stood head and shoulders above the Owens, Aldriches, and Smiths of northwestern Rhode Island. Born and bred as gentlemen, they both graduated from Brown University before becoming locally prominent in their respective fields of law and medicine. Although Drowne always led a fairly private life, his friend Foster pursued a successful political career that culminated in serving as U.S. Senator for Rhode Island between 1791 and 1803. In politics, Foster always maintained a studied pose of moderation. Although in the 1780s he supported ratification of the Constitution, and was later loosely affiliated with the Federalist party, he retained close ties with his friend and kin, Governor Arthur Fenner, and eventually broke ranks with the Federalists around 1798 out of opposition to the land tax and the undeclared war with France. By 1803 he had wearied of partisan strife and decided to join his friend Drowne in moving to the quieter locale of Foster, Rhode Island. Although their contemporaries expressed "astonishment" that they should move to "so rough and so uncultivated a part of country—so destitute of privileges," they were both drawn to the area out of a kind of neoclassical love for a natural world that, although uncultivated, was at least well removed from savagery and barbarism. They settled close to the town's northern border, near a large hill, which Drowne hopefully—and typically—renamed Mount Hygeia, after the classical Greek goddess of health.[8]

Drowne and Foster brought to this new land their own particular plans for civilizing and modernizing the environs. As classically educated products of the American Enlightenment, they sought improvements that, considering the rusticity of the setting, were rather on the cerebral and ornamental side. Because both were gentlemen farmers, their interests were considerably less pragmatic than even their most prosperous neighbors. In 1806, Foster and Drowne succeeded in convincing some of the townspeople to join them in founding the "Foster Social Library," to which Foster contributed "the larger part of [his own] pretty large library"; but they were disappointed by the library's failure to charge its members fees. As Foster commented to a local leader, while enclosing a draft of the library's corporate charter, "there is no provision for yearly payments, for increasing and preserving the library, a mea-

Figure 3. Solomon Drowne House (1807–1808), an example of Federal-style architecture that contrasted sharply with the simpler, vernacular architecture of his neighbors in Foster. Courtesy of Rhode Island Historical Preservation Commission.

sure which I regret was not agreed to by the proprietors of our library." The local farmers were no doubt happy to help form a library, as long as their two new gentlemen neighbors were willing to supply most of the reading materials; but since they had struggled in the 1780s to keep their taxes low, they could hardly be expected to tax themselves again for something as frivolous as a collection of books.[9]

Some of Foster's and Drowne's plans were downright visionary. They hoped that the Social Library would form the nucleus of a college, to be founded some day amid the rocks of northern Foster. Even more grandiose were their plans for building a turnpike road from the small port of Westerly, Rhode Island, clear across New England to the Canadian border. The northwestern Rhode Island portion of this dream road was incorporated in 1815 as the "Foster and Glocester Appian Way Society," but actual construction of the highway never began. It is hard to imagine why anyone would want to pay for the privilege of traveling from the wilds of central New England to an obscure market town like Westerly. Foster and Drowne may have been an intelligent and learned pair, but they were certainly not businessmen.[10]

In the absence of written records, it is difficult to gauge the reaction of the native population to this intrusion of classical allusions and enlightenment fantasies into the rough-hewn world of backwoods Rhode Island. Their actions nevertheless suggest that the typical backwoodsman viewed Foster and Drowne with unease and suspicion, tempered by the happy knowledge that some of the two gentlemen's wealth would eventually be spread around the neighborhood. Eight years would pass before the once politically active Foster would be elected to town office. Of course, Foster may have preferred to remain politically retired; but his neighbors were probably in no hurry to have him elected. After all, in 1786, during the height of the furor over debts and paper money, the town meeting had voted "that no sworn attorney be for the future chosen a Member of the upper or Lower House of Assembly." As a lawyer and former Federalist, Foster must have aroused a few bitter memories of recent struggles with the eastern mercantile elite.[11] The area's more commercial and "progressive" farmers were more likely to welcome Foster's support for modernizing institutions; but while their association with him would soon bear fruit, they would have to exercise care in cooperating with this visionary and slightly unpopular new neighbor.

The Triumph of the Turnpiking

The opening of the nineteenth century witnessed a revival of the turnpike movement in Rhode Island, a movement that a few years earlier had seemed on the verge of collapse amidst the devious tactics of turnpike promoters and the heated reaction of local opponents. In 1803 and 1804 two new turnpikes were chartered through northwestern Rhode Island: the Rhode Island and Connecticut Turnpike and the Glocester Turnpike Society. (See Figure 1 for turnpike locations.) Each of these turnpikes was designed to lead from Providence through the northwest to the Connecticut hinterland, and each was sponsored at least in part by native northwesterners. The turnpikes' proponents could not succeed, however, until they overcame significant local opposition. The northwest's modernizing leadership used a variety of tactics in dealing with their opponents, ranging from threats and coercion to offering rewards and special benefits to area residents. The story of these two turnpikes reveals, in different ways, a good deal about the nature of the rural commercializers and their backcountry opponents.

The first turnpike incorporated by northwestern Rhode Islanders, the Rhode Island and Connecticut Turnpike, resulted largely from the cooperative efforts of Theodore Foster and some of the area's native leaders. The original impetus for this improvement appears to have come from Foster himself. Foster and his friend Solomon Drowne may have moved to the northwest to avoid the hustle and bustle of city life, but they certainly did not plan on divorcing themselves from all of the benefits of urban civilization. The life of a gentleman farmer would require frequent trips to Providence for those provisions that could not be stocked by the country stores of rural Rhode Island. Also, Drowne continued to frequent Brown University, where he occasionally lectured and spent time planning the college's botanical garden. In the meantime, Foster maintained a semblance of his old law practice and eventually returned to Providence permanently in 1820. As Drowne revealed, the charm of rural Foster lay partly in its proximity to urban life: "Here you can enjoy thrice happy leisure . . . you can be sometimes in the country, sometimes in the city, and oftener in the fields."[12]

Foster had begun to lay plans for the turnpike even before he actually moved to the northwest. In December 1801, while still a senator in Washington, he pressed his thoughts upon Drowne: "Let us . . . endeavour to obtain a *Turnpike Road*, by our Temple [?] from Hartford to Providence, to facilitate the intercourse between those rapidly flourishing towns; a direct line between which will pass very near the Hill which we have chosen to improve."[13] Foster soon found local support for his turnpike project, especially among leaders in the northern Scituate–eastern Glocester area. In May 1802, John Harris, Dean and Joshua Kimball of Scituate, and John Colwell and Elisha Aldrich of Glocester petitioned the legislature for turnpike charter privileges. The road that they proposed would lead west from Providence and traverse the northern edge of Johnston, Scituate, and Foster on the way to the Connecticut border. They were joined in the petition by several residents of eastern Connecticut, who sought a Rhode Island link for a turnpike that they had chartered from Hartford to the state line. Their combined efforts were rewarded in February 1803, when the legislature chartered the Rhode Island and Connecticut Turnpike Society.[14]

The new turnpike society's charter differed from its predecessors in Rhode Island in two important respects. Unlike the earlier Providence and Norwich Turnpike Society, which was chartered to improve an existing highway, this company planned to create an almost completely new road. The reasons why the promoters chose such an ambitious project remain unclear, although Foster's fondness for visionary schemes was no doubt a contributing factor. At any rate, no existing east–west roads traversed the beloved "hill" called Mount Hygeia, which Foster and Drowne planned to "improve," so only a new road would suit their purposes.[15] The turnpike charter was also unusually generous in its provisions for the company's investors. Perhaps because the company was especially ambitious in its plans, the legislature rewarded it with the right to erect two tollgates along its nineteen-mile length, one of which was to be within six miles of the Connecticut border, the other no farther than six miles from Providence. The longer Providence and Norwich pike had been granted but one tollgate.[16] These two unique features of the Rhode Island and Connecticut Turnpike charter would significantly affect the company's own plans, as well as the nature of the local resistance that it soon would face.

Although the turnpike advocates received a prompt and generous response from the Republican-controlled legislature, they still had to contend with significant local opposition. On June 17, 1802, 161 inhabitants of northern Foster and northwestern Scituate petitioned the legislature to limit the charter privileges of the newly proposed turnpike company. After referring to an earlier petition that opposed the turnpike altogether in favor of a "free road" (this petition has since been lost), the petitioners requested "that in Case Your Honors should grant the petition for A pike Road," only a single gate should be permitted, to be erected at least "eleven miles from Providence."[17] Most of them, it turns out, lived close to a preexisting road that ran nearly parallel to the proposed turnpike until it intersected it in the middle of northern Scituate, about ten miles from Providence. These petitioners knew that if the turnpike's tollgate had to be erected farther than eleven miles from the city, they could simply bypass the tollgate altogether. The petitioners' support was both widespread, representing about half the adult male population of northern Foster, and powerful, since half of them ranked in the top 40 percent of local tax lists. But unlike earlier antiturnpike petitions, these claimants did not oppose the principle of turnpiking altogether; rather, they simply sought to avoid for themselves the onus of paying tolls.[18]

Although the legislature apparently denied the petitioners' request, since the company's charter allowed one tollgate to be placed within six miles of Providence, the turnpike's promoters may well have taken careful note of the petitioners' qualitative and quantitative support within the area; for the promoters continually displayed a willingness, and even eagerness, to consult the opinion of the local population. This trait proved useful at one point when they encountered brief but heated opposition from local farmers over the purchase of land for the road. The company's charter gave it the right of eminent domain, with the actual amount of financial compensation to be set by legislative committee. Unfortunately, five farmers from Foster and Scituate reacted angrily when they learned of the committee's proposal for fair purchase prices. They petitioned the governor and state senate in October 1804 "to object against Said new High Way Being Established Except the individual owners of the Lands . . . are first Setteled [sic] with to their Satisfaction." More fundamentally, the petitioners claimed that their "Rights and Liberties [under] the Constitution" protected them as individual property owners against the arbitrary demands of a private corporation. Challenging the legislature to uphold this essential element of republican liberty, they asked its members to "think of the Dear Bought and grately . . . vallued Rights and privileges of the Sons of Liberty in amearaca [sic] and [do] not in and [sic] tributary Tyrannical manner Injure your memoritest."[19]

The turnpike promoters moved quickly but dexterously to dissipate this opposition. They agreed to revise the legislative committee's membership to make it more amenable to the locals' point of view, replacing two Providence representatives with deputies from Johnston and Scituate. Now controlled by representatives of the northwest itself, the new committee greatly increased the original committee's assessment of compensation due to all local property owners. The five farmers who complained were particularly well rewarded: their total compensation was increased by 78 percent, as opposed to an average 31 percent increase for the others. Apparently pleased by the committee's deliberate attempt to satisfy their sense of republican justice, the farmers accepted the new awards for property damage; actual construction of the turnpike began in the following spring.[20]

The promoters also showed care in devising a road construction plan that seemed to be deliberately aimed at mollifying the local citizenry. The plan was formally authored by a four-man committee: two each from Rhode Island and Connecticut, with Theodore Foster and John Harris representing Rhode Island. Judging by the prevalence of classical allusions and idealistic principles, Foster alone was probably responsible for most of the writing. The proposal called for dividing the major part of the road's length into two hundred 450-foot "located" shares. Local residents would then be invited to subscribe to the particular share that ran through their land. Each subscriber would be responsible for "making and maintaining" their own section of the turnpike, in return for which they would be rewarded with a share of the company's stock and "1/200th of all tolls collected," less incidental expenses. Once subscribed, each share would became a part of the owner's freeholding, to be alienated or sold when the land itself was so disposed of. Finally, a portion of the road's length, consisting chiefly of parts running through swamp, rivers, and other rough terrain, would not be available for purchase by local residents. Instead, "unlocated" shares of turnpike stock would be sold for $75 cash, the proceeds of which would be spent on building the highway in these difficult and sparsely populated areas.[21]

Practical considerations mixed with a few philosophical ideals to form the basis of this ingenious proposal. The company's charter required that it spend $15,000 on the road before the turnpike could begin charging tolls. Since the directors were mostly farmers themselves, they realized that they could never raise such a large sum of money on their own. They therefore solicited the labor and resources of the area's residents as a means of "spending" the equivalent of $15,000 in wages and material. But the directors also knew that no turnpike could be successful unless it first obtained the moral support of the local community. Having witnessed the failed schemes of the Providence and Norwich Turnpike Company, they believed that local support could only be obtained by involving the community in the ownership and maintenance of the road. As the turnpike committee summarized, local stock ownership "is indeed the only proper foundation of every turnpike establishment. Without it there naturally arises a competition between the interests of the inhabitants on the road, and the interests of the owners of the turnpike who live at a distance from it. This creates a disaffection, on the part of the inhabitants, to any improvements on the road . . . owing to a jealousy that the money, collected by the turnpike, is not duly appropriated."[22] In the previous year, 161 local inhabitants, most of whom were relatively wealthy and influential, had petitioned the legislature to express their reluctance to pay tolls in return for highway improvements. The turnpike's promoters hoped to mollify this sentiment by making the farmers themselves the ultimate collectors of tollgate receipts.

Moreover, the construction plan was deliberately designed to maximize local participation in the ownership of turnpike stock. The meetings at which the company offered road subscriptions were advertised well in advance in local newspapers.[23] The plan also dictated that during the first two hours of each meeting "no person shall subscribe for more than one located share." Even after the two hours had expired, purchase of shares was limited to those that adjoin the owner's own land. In this way local inhabitants would be given every opportunity to become shareholders; purchase by speculators or nonresidents was discouraged or even forbidden. Limited evidence suggests that the plan was indeed a success: the turnpikers finished their road by 1809, prior to the completion of the highway's western extension among the supposedly more sober and hardworking people of Connecticut; and by 1832, its route was prominently displayed on local maps.[24]

By deliberately democratizing the ownership of company stock, the turnpike promoters were not only motivated by the practical goal of building a new highway; they were also guided, perhaps unconsciously, by some of the key ideals and motifs of the emerging Republican party. In his correspondence with Theodore Foster, Arthur Fenner revealed a concern for soliciting backwoods opinion, while at the same time he forged ahead in state government with his own political agenda. More generally, Republican leaders throughout the nation sought to develop in farmers the commercial habits of hard work and sobriety, without spoiling with luxuries the yeomenry's natural honesty and simplicity. Put more simply, they wanted to refine the character of rural society without undermining its traditional virtues.[25] In a corresponding way, through its ingenious construction plan, the turnpike company sought to intermix the yeoman tradition of local control with the relatively modern innovation of a joint-stock corporation. By dividing the road into many small sections, each to be maintained by local inhabitants, the construction plan emulated the highway districts of traditional road-building regulations. At the same time, however, the erection of a joint-stock company gave the promoters ultimate control over the turnpike's construction and maintenance, including the power to fine subscribers who failed to maintain their sections of the highway. This would help ensure that the road was properly constructed, thereby avoiding the evils of the old, unenforceable, highway regulations. Finally, the construction regulations appear to have been aimed at cultivating the participation of a particular class of farmers. Ownership of stock would be relatively widespread yet limited nevertheless to those wealthy enough to clear and maintain a 450-foot section of highway. Indeed, this consideration seems to have eventually forced the turnpike directors to waive their restrictions against multiple ownership of shares. As one example, when Henry Jones of Foster died in 1830, his probate inventory revealed that he held 13 ¾ shares of the turnpike company's stock.[26] The company's regulations thus restricted ownership and control of the turnpike to a fairly small segment of rural society, thereby excluding men like that obstreperous and propertyless cooper Barzillai Knight from a role in maintaining a vital commercial thoroughfare. Maintenance of the Rhode Island and Connecticut Turnpike would therefore depend not on the cooperative participation of an entire community, but rather on the individual aspiration of a class of substantial freeholders, a class that by 1800 was capable of carrying on a significant amount of trade with the growing port city of Providence.

The plan for the turnpike thus stood ingeniously on a middle ground between the cooperative and participatory tradition of local highway law and the coercive and corporate methods used by the Providence and Norwich Turnpike Society. The new road would be owned neither by an outside corporation nor by the local towns themselves, but rather by a large group of the area's more substantial freeholders. Construction labor would be performed neither by turnpike company hirelings, nor by the local people en masse (as in the case of traditional highway regulations), but rather by this same group of substantial freeholders (and perhaps their own hired laborers). Finally, ultimate control over construction and maintenance decisions would be exercised neither by an alien group of merchants nor by a locally elected set of public officials, but rather by a small set of native promoters and entrepreneurs. The Rhode Island and Connecticut Turnpike Society would be neither a coercive corporation run by Federalist merchants nor an example of localist mediocrity; instead, it would be a Republican turnpike.[27]

In the meantime, another group of turnpike promoters began seeking to improve a more northerly route through Rhode Island's northwest: the Providence to Chepachet highway, a road commonly called the Killingly or "Great Road" by contemporaries, which today is more prosaically named route 44. Like the founders of the Rhode Island and Connecticut Turnpike Society, the promoters of this "Glocester Turnpike" sought to improve transportation between the port of Providence and the Connecticut border, in order to exploit the market of northwestern Rhode Island and the hinterland beyond. Moreover, the two groups had one individual in common: Judge John Harris, the Scituate politician and farmer who seemed to have a stake in nearly every local modernizing enterprise. In other respects, however, the two projects were rather different. Unlike the ambitious and visionary Theodore Foster, the Glocester Turnpike promoters sought not to build a completely new road, but rather to improve the preexisting "North Road." More important, while Foster and his associates carefully tried to mollify the local population, and even sought to include them in the ownership and construction of the highway, the Glocester turnpikers dealt with their opponents by simply over-whelming them politically. As a result, in the case of the Glocester Turnpike, the lines of opposition were more sharply drawn and thus reveal more clearly the nature of the commercializing impulse in northwestern Rhode Island.

The Glocester Turnpike Company received its legislative charter only after spending five years overcoming a strong and persistent rural opposition. As may be recalled, a petition to turnpike the Chepachet road had been originally filed in 1798 by twenty-two of the wealthier inhabitants of Glocester, Johnston, and Scituate; but this request was successfully opposed in the Glocester Town Meeting, as well as in the General Assembly. Three years later, some of these same individuals renewed this initiative, and they were joined by a strong body of supporters from outside the community. The local petitioners included, as usual, several of the Owen family members, along with Timothy and Joseph Willmarth, and Mowry and Simon Smith, also of the town of Glocester.

The outside supporters consisted of merchants who lived at either end of the proposed turnpike. On the western end, these included men from as far away as Woodstock and Pomfret, Connecticut; Holland and Amherst in cen-tral Massachusetts; and even Pittstown in New York. Representing the road's eastern terminus were several merchants living in Providence who expressed frustration over the poor quality of Rhode Island's roads, as a result of which "people in the interior carry their produce to market and supply themselves with imported goods at Boston, Norwich, Hartford, New Haven, even New York [instead of at the ports of the Narragansett Bay]." But unlike the foun-ders of the original westward turnpike company, the Providence and Norwich, these newer turnpike promoters did not include the great mercantile families of Providence—the Browns, the Nightingales, and the Bowens. Instead, they consisted of lesser merchants like William Valentine, Stephen Ammidon, and Amasa Mason, and even more noteworthy, two of the leaders of Providence's growing Republican party: Henry Smith and Wheeler Martin. As lesser eco-nomic and political leaders they were envious, perhaps, of the power and riches of the great Federalist merchants. Now that their own party controlled the state legislature, they wanted a turnpike of their own, in order to open new trade routes and sources of wealth. Thus, by the end of 1802, when their petitions were descending on the state assembly, a powerful coalition of wealthy northwestern farmers, out-of-state merchants, and aspiring Provi-dence Republicans had gathered in favor of turnpiking the road to Che-pachet.[28]

Even so, a large number of the northwest's farmers rallied to oppose this latest affront to the freedom of the roads, and they successfully delayed the passage of the turnpike company's charter for almost two more years. In Feb-ruary 1803, 117 inhabitants of the towns of Glocester, Johnston, and North

Providence petitioned the legislature against the proposed Glocester turnpike charter. Typically, the turnpike opponents phrased their arguments in terms of a localist defense of the community's needs, pitting themselves against the selfish interests of uncooperative neighbors and untrustworthy outsiders. The petitioners stated emphatically that "the Public will always act for their own good and will have the sd. road in good repair under the Existant Laws, and regulations, if Left to their own way." It was only the trepidations of a selfish few that prevented the road to Chepachet from being repaired by the means of traditional highway regulations; according to the opponents' petition, part of the "money assigned for said road was . . . appropriated [instead] to small cross roads" in "some" of the local highway "Districts," thereby preventing the Chepachet highway from being properly repaired.

More important, the petitioners opposed the turnpike because its promoters did not represent the great mass of local yeomen of middling wealth. Instead, "a great number of them [are] Transcent persons and foreigners that Seldom pass Sd. Roads, and a great number more that do not keep a horse or team." The farmers viewed the turnpike promoters as a coalition of selfish outsiders and uncooperative, worthless locals, who were either "transcent" or too poor to own "horse or team." Such a coalition threatened the traditional control of town government by those farmers, who, if not wealthy, at least had a substantial stake in local society.[29]

In some ways, the turnpike opponents were remarkably accurate in their characterization of the social and geographic background of the highway's promoters. Many of the turnpike advocates were indeed "foreigners," in the sense that they lived outside of northwestern Rhode Island. About one-fifth of the petitioners who supported the turnpike lived in Providence, and another 18 percent lived outside of Rhode Island altogether. There was also an element of truth to the opponents' remark that "a great number" of their antagonists "do not keep a horse or team." True, of the seventy-two turnpike proponents who lived locally, the great majority came, of course, from some of the area's wealthiest families: the Owens, the Smiths, and the Tourtellots, to name a few examples. Almost half of the proponents ranked in the top fifth of their town's tax list, and another quarter ranked in the second fifth. But a significant portion—about one-sixth—of those who signed the turnpike petition actually were among the poorest residents of the northwest. Ranking in the bottom quintile of the tax list, these signers undoubtedly did not own a "horse or team." Conspicuously absent from the profile of turnpike supporters were men who typified the average local farmer. Only 13 percent of the proponents ranked in the middle and lower-middle tax quintiles.[30]

The economic profile of the turnpike proponents therefore closely resembles, although on an enlarged scale, the pattern found among the Greene family iron-forge faction that petitioned the legislature in 1800 in support of Moses Brown and the rights of dam owners.[31] In both cases, the advocates of economic modernization and entrepreneurial rights came from the poorest and wealthiest extremes of the local community. The wealthiest farmers supported the turnpike because they were economically positioned to profit from improved access to the Providence market. A handful of the area's poorest citizens added their signatures in support, perhaps in response to the blandishments and offers of gainful employment of their more influential neighbors, and perhaps because as farmers without "horses or teams," they would not be bothered by tollgates, anyway.

In contrast, the turnpike opponents more evenly represented the northwest's distribution of wealth. If anything, they were an especially "average" lot: fully one-third of them ranked within the middle fifth of local taxpayers. The rest of the 110 men who petitioned against the Glocester turnpike were distributed fairly equally among the area's poorer and wealthier citizens. In terms of wealth, the turnpike proponents were an anomalous group, standing apart from local society; their opponents, on the other hand, were more like a microcosm of Rhode Island's rural society.[32]

Where wealth does not explain the farmers' position on turnpiking, geography does. Local supporters of the turnpike tended to live in the more enterprising southeastern corner of the town, congregated around the village of Chepachet, and along main roads leading to Massachusetts and Connecticut. Opponents, on the other hand, resided in the town's hilly regions and northern and western fringes. The majority lived in the upland locales of Pine Hill, Snake Hill, and Tourtellot Hill, while another fifth or so resided in the northern half of Glocester, in what became the town of Burrillville in 1807.[33]

The opponents' geographical relationship with the turnpike promoters was analogous, therefore, to the relationship of the northwest as a whole, in the 1790s, to the port of Providence. In both cases, the residents of a poorer, peripheral area came into conflict with their wealthier, more market-oriented neighbors. Located closer to Providence, and along major commercial routes or in important trading villages, the wealthier residents of southeastern Glocester had developed, by the early 1800s, an attachment to the Providence market as a means of furthering their prosperity. Support for a new turnpike therefore came naturally from the market-oriented residents of that particular corner of the town. For the farmers on the poorer periphery, access to the market was not a goal to be yearned for, but rather a threat to their already weakening status within town society. In their protest to the legislature, the turnpike opponents couched their objections in the language of traditional fulminations against transients and foreigners; but what they really feared was a new class of commercializing farmers bent on exploiting their superior access to the Providence market.[34]

So divided were local residents over the turnpike proposal that the town meeting was unable to take a formal position. For nearly two years after the turnpike bill was first introduced, the meeting was conspicuously silent on the

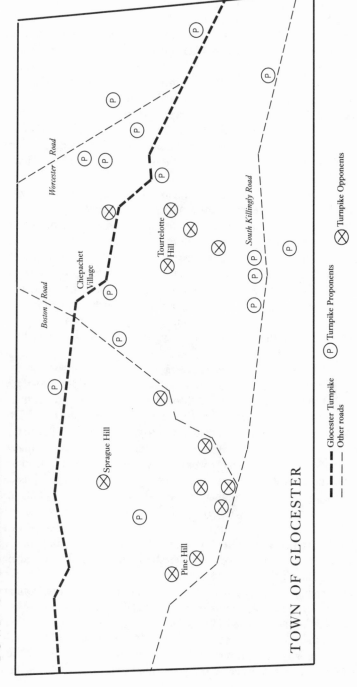

Figure 4. Residence of Proponents and Opponents of Glocester Turnpike. Source: Arthur C. Cole, Map of Glocester, R.I., as it was in 1790 (1963).

entire subject. Then on June 4, 1804, the issue apparently came to a head, and it was "voted that there should be a Turnpike granted," as the matter was tersely recorded by the town clerk. However, the brevity of the clerk's remarks conceal the bitterness with which this issue was contested. Using devious tactics on the night of the June 4 meeting, the opponents tried to reverse the town's decision, by bringing it to a vote once more, after most of "the Freemen were chiefly gone home." As the town moderator later recorded: "it being at a late hour of the day there was a vote called to known [*sic*] whether the Freemen would wish to have a Turn Pike road through the Town of Glocester . . . there were fourteen votes against it and none in favour . . . and I believe that there was not more than seven or eight Free holders in the House more than what voted."[35]

Unfortunately for the turnpike opponents, their deception was to no avail. Although somewhat unrepresentative of the town as a whole, the proponents were nevertheless a numerous and powerful collection of men. Four of the proponents had served for Glocester in the General Assembly in the previous two decades; and in 1804 they were represented by town deputy Solomon Owen. The late-evening quasi-legal vote against the turnpike was never recorded in the town minutes. This piece of trickery was, however, reported dutifully to the legislature by the town moderator, Elijah Armstrong, who was himself a turnpike supporter. In the same month of June 1804, the Glocester Turnpike bill passed through the senate, and the company was officially incorporated.[36]

After the defeat of the Glocester Turnpike opponents, opposition to turnpiking gradually faded in northwestern Rhode Island. In the next ten years, four more turnpikes were chartered through parts of the five towns that comprise that corner of the state. (See Figure 1.) The Providence and Douglas Turnpike, chartered without opposition in 1805, ran from Providence through the northeast corner of Burrillville, on its way to Worcester, Massachusetts. In 1812 and 1813, two more pikes were created to run from the Connecticut border to the Providence market: the Foster and Scituate, and Foster and Scituate Central Turnpike companies. Sponsored largely by residents of Foster, these two pikes ran generally parallel and to the south of the existing Rhode Island and Connecticut Turnpike. Support for these two pikes again came largely from the wealthier members of the local community; but unlike the earlier Glocester Turnpike, they were both chartered without facing any known opposition.[37]

When turnpike charters did arouse opposition, it resulted not from antagonism to the principle of turnpiking per se, but from local jealousy, as competing groups of commercializing farmers struggled to control and improve the roads in their particular neighborhoods. When the John and Philip Brown Turnpike Company was chartered in 1806 to turnpike a route from Glocester to the Massachusetts border, it provoked opposition not from the mass of middling farmers, but rather from a small group of wealthy men who had already improved the road by means of a public lottery. In their petition to the legislature, they proposed instead that the company improve a more southerly and sparsely populated portion of the road where "there is not but four men to mend sd. road."[38] Similarly particularistic concerns motivated opposition in 1814 to an extension of the Foster and Scituate Turnpike. When originally chartered in 1813, the eastward boundary of the turnpike was limited to Hopkins Mills, in northeast Foster, because of opposition by the powerful Rhode Island and Connecticut Turnpike Company, which feared that the new line would drain off passengers from its own operation. But within a year, the company withdrew this opposition, thereby prompting forty-two men from Foster and western Scituate to petition for an eastward extension and an additional tollgate. Their petition was resisted by fifty inhabitants of Scituate and Johnston, who lived in the area through which the extension would run. But unlike earlier turnpike opponents, these adversaries were hardly middling-class agrarian localists. Indeed, they were actually somewhat wealthier as a whole than the extension's proponents. The assembly resolved the dispute by simply compromising on the location of the extension's tollgate, placing it "westward of . . . the House of Richard Rhodes in Scituate," where it would not trouble the complaining parties.[39]

Even the once-reviled Providence and Norwich Turnpike Society benefited from a gradual diminution in organized opposition to turnpiking by backcountry yeomen. In March 1805, in response to a company petition, new legislation granted it the right to erect two additional half-fare tollgates, provided that the turnpike spend an additional $5,200 in highway repairs. The legislation also stipulated that the road pass inspection by local justices of the peace before the new gates could commence operation. In spite of these restrictions, the legislature's willingness to assist the once-reviled corporation suggests that much had changed in its attitudes since 1800, when it had summarily rejected the company's previous request for assistance. As for local inhabitants, they remained silent about the entire subject, which in view of their earlier boisterous objections to the turnpike's privileges, suggests that they were at least beginning to acquiesce to the coming of the turnpike era.[40]

Of course, the farmers of northwestern Rhode Island continued to complain sporadically about the turnpikes and their tolls; but increasingly, after the first few years of the nineteenth century, these complaints centered not on the actual principle and privileges associated with turnpiking, but rather on particular issues regarding the quality of the roads and the placement of tollgates.[41] Farmers also continued to resist turnpiking through individual acts of vandalism and intimidation. As late as 1807, the Providence and Norwich Company continued to report on outbreaks of violence between local travelers and the company's tollkeeper; and by 1810 turnpike charters regularly included a provision for fining individuals convicted of toll evasion or vandalism.[42] But these appear to have been isolated acts committed by disgruntled individuals, rather than an organized protest movement. Rural resistance to turnpiking continued throughout the second decade of the nineteenth century; but increasingly, the farmers expressed their opposition through particularistic complaints and random acts of violence, rather than through sustained community opposition.

When the turnpike movement first came to northwestern Rhode Island in 1794 it was greeted with a storm of local outrage; but after ten years of heated controversy, and another decade in which opposition gradually diminished, turnpikes finally became legitimized as an important part of the local transportation network. The turnpike opponents, it seems, were burdened with several political weaknesses. Although usually large in numbers, they were often divided among each other. For the mass of middling farmers, turnpikes were an unnecessary affront to local liberties and the spirit of community cooperation. Only loosely connected to a market economy, they were perfectly content to rely on continued use of traditional highway regulations. The area's wealthier and more enterprising farmers, on the other hand, saw much more value in an improved system of land transportation. In the 1790s, they joined their more modest neighbors in opposing the Federalist Providence and Norwich Turnpike Society, partly out of a sense of political rivalry and economic jealousy with their merchant adversaries in Providence. But in the meantime, they began formulating their own plans for turnpiking the other major roads of northwestern Rhode Island.

In this respect, they were met by their own considerable local opposition. When first proposed in town meeting in 1799, the Glocester Turnpike was soundly defeated; only after a prolonged struggle was it finally accepted in 1804. But the native northwestern turnpikers eventually prevailed, largely because of weaknesses that are inherent to any kind of localist opposition. The turnpike proponents were an intelligent, powerful, and cohesive group. They had served together in the legislature and on county courts and had worked together politically at least since the days of the old Country party. Their opponents, on the other hand, were a scattered and politically inexperienced lot. In the case of the Glocester Turnpike Society, they lived in a variety of scattered locations, spread around the town's periphery. Area supporters of the turnpike, on the other hand, were concentrated in the town's southeastern corner, and thus could more easily develop a united strategy. The turnpike proponents also possessed superior skills in the area of persuasion and communication. This was particularly true of Theodore Foster and the Rhode Island and Connecticut Turnpike Company, whose ingenious construction plan showed a level of creative written expression that no doubt exceeded the abilities of the area's poorly educated farmers. As a result of these advantages, local turnpike proponents eventually gained a virtual ascendancy in their communities. Opposition to turnpiking persisted on the level of local harassment, but the concept of turnpiking itself gradually gained a measure of rural acceptance. By the 1820s, turnpikes had become an integral and vital part of the northwest's transportation network.

The Tragicomedy of the Farmers Exchange Bank

Somewhat less successful was the early development of banking in northwestern Rhode Island. The northwest's first and until 1818, only experience with chartered banking was the infamous case of the Farmers Exchange Bank. This "farmers" bank was the ninth such institution to be chartered in Rhode Island. As happened elsewhere in the nation, members of the Federalist party controlled the state's first several banks, including the Providence Bank, founded in 1791, and those of other maritime communities. The Federalist monopoly on banking was broken in 1803, when the Providence Republican clique incorporated the Roger Williams Bank. Shortly thereafter, the Republican party's rural wing began agitating for a bank of its own. Their petition for a bank charter explicitly called for "a Bank in the Country," which they claimed "would not only prove profitable to the proprietors, but also would facilitate and ultimately advance the trade and manufacturers in that part of the Country where Established." In February 1804 the Farmers Exchange Bank was incorporated with a capital stock limit of $100,000.[43]

The directors of the new bank included virtually the entire commercializing elite of northwestern Rhode Island. As usual, most of them came from the Scituate and Glocester area. Nine of the original thirteen directors had been supporters of either the Glocester or the Rhode Island and Connecticut turnpike companies. Also serving as directors were Daniel and Simeon Smith, original incorporators of the new town of Burrillville's first chartered cultural institution, the Burrillville Library Company. Rounding out the list were James Aldrich and Elisha Mathewson, who had served for several years as Scituate's deputies to the state assembly.[44] The bank's office was located in half of a town house in the village of Chepachet, town of Glocester. As such, the Farmers Exchange Bank became only the second bank in the country to be founded in an area unreached by commercial navigation, thus testifying to the ambitious and enterprising spirit of the northwest's modernizing elite.[45]

Unfortunately, the directors' speculative ambitions were not complemented in the area of financial expertise. From the bank's inception, its officers exhibited a remarkable ignorance concerning the principles of commercial banking. This incompetence, together with a gross kind of cupidity, soon reduced the bank to a state of near bankruptcy. Almost immediately, they began issuing notes in excess of the bank's total assets. After the first year of operation, in which the bank issued $72,211 in bills, it had only $53,275 remaining in capital. It must be remembered that some of these same directors had been the architects of the Country party's land bank of the 1780s. Both banks were founded on the premise that society's landed wealth should be convertible into liquid assets. But while the state could retire the land bank's currency by taxing it out of existence, the privately held Farmers Exchange Bank was continually called upon to redeem its bills in precious specie. Still more troubling was the directors' habit of treating the bank as if it were their own personal financial club. They suspended payment on the last three installments on their stock, without bothering to so inform the rest of the owners. They paid 8 percent dividends to all stockholders but then proceeded to divide the remaining profit, amounting in some years to $130 each, among themselves. Finally, in June 1805 they voted to give each other $200, a sum they never repaid.[46]

Predictably, the directors' policies soon led to a precipitous fall in the bank's capital, at which point they turned to more desperate strategems. At one point, they gave up on making money through banking and fell back on an area in which they had greater expertise: the grain trade. On April 29, 1805, Daniel Tourtellot was authorized by the other directors to use $2,875 in bank funds for purchasing rye and corn in Hartford, to be sold "for the profit of the Directors of said Bank in common." In fact, he just about broke even on the deal. By early 1808, the bank's notes-to-assets ratio had risen to around 60 to 1, leaving it on the brink of insolvency.[47]

The bank was now ready for plucking by a much more skillful swindler: Andrew Dexter, Jr. A Boston financier, Dexter achieved control over the bank by using the bank's own funds to buy out the other directors. Leaving Judge John Harris as its titular president, Dexter removed the bank's dies and printing blocks to his office in Boston and proceeded to print new bills by the hundreds of thousands. The fresh bills he sent to Glocester for signing by the bank's unfortunate cashier, William Colwell, who so labored, for the sake of secrecy, through many a sleepless night. Colwell then returned the signed bills to Dexter, under the guise of a "loan" at 2 percent interest. Dexter strove to keep this mountain of paper in circulation through a variety of ruses: instructing Colwell to "plague and delay" those who presented bills for redemption in specie, and shipping bills to faraway places, chiefly to another of his pet institutions, the Berkshire Bank of Massachusetts. In the meantime, he continually cajoled his cashier to sign the bills faster and faster.[48]

Dexter was surely a crook, but it is more difficult to evaluate the motives of his agents in Glocester. Certainly, they were willing assistants to Dexter's shenanigans. Yet they often seemed more confused than crafty, and as much victims as coconspirators. On December 5, 1808, when the bank's bubble was about to burst, President Harris wrote to Dexter, pleading for help and advice: "The present state of our affairs is to me truly alarming. We are threatened with prosecutions and almost every thing else bad. . . . [I] depend on your superiour knowledge and understanding in these things for my rule and guide." He also asked Dexter to send $8,000–$10,000 in specie and an equal amount in "Berkshire bills." Harris even expressed a sense of responsibility for the effect of the bank's troubles on the local population; for in the same letter he declared that "we shall not loan any more money at present, but endeavour to call in that which is out as fast as may be, and not distress the people too much."

Dexter replied, no doubt to Harris's disappointment, by sending only $300 in "Boston bills" and another $3,500 in relatively worthless securities. And instead of consenting to Harris's cautious loan policy, he urged him to sign more bills "without a moment's delay." Dexter then promised to send more specie, but he never followed through, offering instead a variety of lame excuses: "The banks are closed . . . it being after bank hours . . . I am unwell."[49] When the bank finally crashed in February 1809, Colwell was jailed for contempt, having been induced by Dexter into attempting to flee to Boston. President Harris was forced to leave the state altogether, with his estate under attachment by angry creditors. The swindler, Dexter, on the other hand, appears to have gotten off scot-free.[50]

As the upshot of this sorry affair, although the Republican-controlled legislature indefinitely stayed all court process against the offending directors, their local reputations were permanently disgraced. In October 1809, the Glocester town government was forced to declare that "Gloucester Farmers exchange Bank Bills to the amount of two hundred and odd Dollars now in the Possession of the Town Treasurer . . . should be a loss to the Town." In addition, many farmers were no doubt severely affected, having mortgaged their lands for worthless currency. On September 1, 1810, the town meeting instructed its representatives, in a vain attempt, "to get the [legislature's] Vote appealed staying the proceedings against the Directors" of the bank. The bank's opponents did succeed in ending the political career of Judge Harris. He was never again elected to office and, indeed, seems to have permanently vanished from the state. More generally, the northwesterners were badly burned by their experience with a set of bank directors whose speculative enthusiasm was far exceeded by their own financial imcompetence. Almost a decade would pass before another bank was incorporated in northwestern Rhode Island.[51]

The Impact of Social and Economic Problems

Fortunately, at least for those who favored continued economic development in the rural northwest, the economic fate of the region did not rest solely on the aspirations of a few energetic although occasionally misguided local entrepreneurs. The impetus toward commercializing the northwest resulted not only from the ambitions of a entrepreneurial minority, but also from the worries that all northwesterners must have shared because of population pressures and economic dislocation. The problem of overpopulation was relatively late in arriving to the northwest. Compared with the rest of southern New

England, northwestern Rhode Island was settled fairly late in the colonial period. As a result, while the revolutionary era was a time of land scarcity for
older communities like Concord, Massachusetts, the northwestern yeomen
continued to experience a relatively easy kind of subsistence agriculture. At
this time the average adult male in Glocester farmed seventy-eight acres of
land, as compared to only forty-three acres in Suffolk County, Massachusetts.[52] Rapid population growth, however, quickly eroded this advantage in
the next twenty to thirty years. In Glocester, farm holdings dropped to only
fifty-one acres by 1800. After 1820, the region's population leveled off and
even declined in some areas, suggesting that by then the land had reached a
saturation point.[53]

The economic vicissitudes of the 1800s and 1810s added to the woes of the
average farmer. The embargo of 1808 helped to cripple the farmers' already
meager ability to export foodstuffs, as did the numerous wars of the period.
The embargo did give Rhode Island's nascent cotton industry a tremendous
boost. Insulated from British competition, cotton-mill owners more than quin-
tupled their productive capacity between 1809 and 1815. Farmers benefited
briefly from this expansion, selling provisions to factory owners and workers,
and sending their own family members off to work in the mills. Unfortunately,
the return of peace and normal trading relations brought on the collapse of
the cotton industry, followed by a more generalized commercial panic and
contraction in 1818–1819.

Thus, just as the northwest began to suffer from overpopulation, it was also
hit by the nation's first serious economic recession. Pauperism became a major
problem for the first time in the area's history. In the towns of Glocester and
Burrillville, the proportion of adult men who owned no land rose from 26
percent in 1778 to 40 percent in 1822.[54] This increase came at a time when
employment off the farm was limited or unstable at best. Not surprisingly,
pauper rolls and expenditures soared in the first twenty years of the nineteenth
century. In Glocester, the poor-relief budget tripled from $103.53 in 1800 to
$317.00 in 1810 and more than doubled again to $756.50 by 1820. A similar
increase was registered in Foster, where relief costs rose from $132.50 in 1808
to $600.00 in 1820.[55]

Even those who still owned land could easily find themselves in a precarious
position. In the 1790s and early 1800s, many farmers entered into market for
the first time, drawn by the lure of increased foreign commerce, as well as by
the need to raise money for purchasing land for their sons. But the embargo
and continual oscillations between war and peace made trade volatile and uncertain, before it finally collapsed in the panic of 1819. As a result, indebtedness increased rapidly. In nearby Dudley and Oxford, Massachusetts, debt as
a proportion of total property rose from one-quarter in 1800 to one-third in
1820; of the farmers who died between 1810 and 1830, almost half had all
their lands auctioned off in order to pay their debts.[56] Of course, population
growth and commercialization also presented great opportunities for the area's

wealthier and more enterprising residents; but in the meantime, the towns of northwestern Rhode Island were faced with a new and perplexing set of social problems.

Fishway Rights Revisited

Perhaps the first to feel the effects of overpopulation were those unfortunate alewives, or herring, whose annual migration upstream had already caused so much controversy. As the northwest's population grew, more and more farmers came to rely on the springtime run of fish to supplement their diminishing supplies of food. Population growth also led to the erection of more grist- and sawmills, whose dams inevitably began to impede the herring's migration upstream. True, the needs of these traditional or petty forms of manufacturing did not generally conflict with fish migration; in springtime the water supply was usually sufficient to allow for the opening of "fishways" in dams, without detrimentally affecting the mills' operation. But by the early nineteenth century, the sheer number of these mills must have made upstream migration most difficult indeed. In 1778 the town of Glocester had about eighteen assorted mills and forges; but by 1799, the town of Foster, with only half of Glocester's size and population, boasted at least twenty of these enterprises.[57] The opponents of fishway rights had long contended, as the Greenes of Coventry had done in 1799, that for many years "no Alewives have come up to" their valuable dams.[58] Increasingly, this kind of contention was actually becoming true. As a result, the traditional harmony of interests that once existed between farmer–fishermen and mill owners became strained by the dynamics of population growth. This harmony had already been disrupted in 1799, when the Greene iron-forge owners had sided with Moses Brown and company in their dispute with the farmers of the south branch valley of the Pawtuxet River. In the next few years, a new and more locally divisive controversy would break out in the town of Scituate, through which flowed the north branch of the same river.

The controversy was set off when the Brown family closed down the Hope Furnace in 1800, thereby shifting the balance of power among farmers and mill owners on the north branch of the Pawtuxet. Prior to that year, fishway regulations had been alternately strengthened and loosened, largely in conjunction with the needs of the furnace's operation. The Browns and their co-owners had originally obtained a legislative exemption from the usual fishway requirements in 1768, soon after the furnace had commenced operation. When iron production slowed considerably in the 1780s due to the cessation of wartime demand for cannon, the furnace's fishway exemption was temporarily lifted as the legislature yielded to the farmers' demand for herring preservation. Ten years later, when demand for cannons briefly surged during the country's undeclared war with France, the legislature did an about-face, reenacting the Hope Furnace's exemption so "that the owners . . . shall not be obliged to open any fish-way through their dam, nor shall any fish-way be required to be opened above said dam." But with the return of peace in 1800, the Browns disbanded the furnace permanently, thus freeing the legislature from the need to disrupt the local fish population to accord with the requirements of one of the state's more influential families.[59]

Given the opportunity to reestablish traditional fishing rights, local farmers reacted quickly to take advantage of the Browns' withdrawal from Hope Furnace. In February 1801, 110 residents of Scituate, Cranston, and Warwick petitioned the legislature for an "Act directing that a Convenient fish way shall be made for the passing of Fish through or round . . . every . . . dam across" the north branch of the Pawtuxet River. To a large extent, the petition closely followed the pattern followed by earlier requests for fishway rights. It complained that "for several years past the Proprietors of the Dams across said North Branch of said River above the [Hope Furnace] . . . have been permitted to keep their Dams shut, and thereby have entirely prevented the passing of fish up said River."

But the petition also expressed a new sense of urgency as the farmers came to realize that continued mill construction and population growth threatened the long-term survival of the fish population; for at least in its earliest version, the petition advocated several extraordinary measures aimed at the preservation of fishing as an integral part of the rural economy: "We would further pray your Honors that the times and places for taking fish with nets in said river may be appointed by Law; and that the several Towns through which said river passes may be directed to dispose of the privilege of taking the fish called Alewives in the said Towns respectively, at public auction. . . . At the same [time] impowering said Towns . . . to fix the prices at which the fish shall be sold in their respective Towns."[60] The farmers were clearly worried about the local supply of fish. Only by restricting and regulating the right to fish could the alewife population be preserved. They feared that shortages would develop, hence the need for price regulations. The result, had these provisions been enacted, would have been an unprecedented effort to preserve the moral economy of the rural marketplace. Underlying the farmers' proposals was the assumption that the local economy was static, that production could not be increased and thus must be regulated to ensure an equitable division among an ever-growing population. Such an assumption conflicted directly with the aspirations of Moses Brown and his partners, for whom the Pawtuxet River was not a finite source of wealth, but rather a relatively untapped resource that should be made freely available to whoever could use its power most productively.

The result in the state legislature was a compromise. The farmers' more radical proposals for economic regulations probably never came to a vote; they were literally crossed off the original petition. At a time when market regulations elsewhere were being gradually dismantled, it would have been extraordinary for the assembly to embrace a whole new set of restrictions. But the farmers' more conventional requests were received with greater favor. After some delay, an act was passed in June 1802 requiring that "there shall be kept open a suitable and convenient fish-ways, through or round each and every dam across" the entire length of the north branch of the Pawtuxet.[61]

But the struggle was not yet over. Two years later a new drive against fishway rights was launched in the legislature, this time by ordinary mill owners of the north branch valley itself. Fifty-five inhabitants, mostly of the town of Scituate, petitioned for a repeal of fishway requirements for dams located in their own town. Since most of Scituate lies upstream of the old Hope Furnace, these millers would have benefited from the old Brown family exemption, an exemption that was terminated by the act of 1802. Emboldened, perhaps, by the success of Moses Brown and the Greenes in upholding a preexisting exemption on fishway requirements in the south branch, they now wanted the old conditions restored.[62] As a result, these new petitioners were threatening to burst asunder the old harmony of interests that had once united farmers and ordinary millers within rural communities. In Coventry just a few years before, small mill owners had united with farmers in opposition to the cotton and iron manufacturers' attack on fishway requirements. Now it seemed that the farmers would have to defend these rights on their own.

Although the fishway opponents were a relatively prosperous lot, including some of Scituate's wealthiest mill-owning families—the Angells, the Kimballs, and the Harrises—it would be a mistake to imply that the issue of fishway rights pitted rich millwrights against a few poor, unfortunate farmers. The advocates of traditional fishing privileges were hardly all poverty-stricken. Although not quite as uniformly prosperous as their antagonists, their numbers included several wealthy farmers, including Caleb Fiske and Eleazer Relph, the two wealthiest men in the town of Scituate.[63] The opponents and proponents of traditional fishing rights were not separated by their wealth so much as by their occupations (farmers versus mill owners), and more important, by their economic outlook. Collectively, the opponents of fishway rights appear to have developed what might be called an incipient entrepreneurial vision. At least ten of the fifty-five petitioners are known to have supported various modernizing improvements. Thomas Waterman and James Burlingame had already helped petition for the Glocester Turnpike charter, while Ezekiel Angell and Richard Rhodes helped create the Rhode Island and Connecticut and Foster and Scituate turnpikes, respectively. Angell and six other petitioners had earlier helped establish the Scituate Library Company, the region's first chartered institution. One of these six was none other than John Harris, that irrepressible local booster who had his fingers in nearly every scheme for improving the northwestern economy. By contrast, only two of the 110 men who sought to preserve traditional fishing rights could claim a prior connection with a turnpike, bank, or other local "improvement." Certainly, the opponents of the moral economy of fishing were wealthy mill owners; they were also early practitioners of the spirit of American boosterism.[64]

The advocates of water-power rights were defeated in this case, but only for the short run. They were outnumbered two to one in the quantity of signatures they could gather on their petitions, and probably by an even greater margin in northwestern society as a whole.[65] Their petition for a repeal of the 1802 fishing act was dismissed by the legislature in June 1806. Nevertheless, the victory for traditional fishway rights was only a hollow one. The act of 1802 was never explicitly repealed, but it was mysteriously deleted from the law books when the legislature issued its statutory compilation of 1822. In all probability, it had long since become obsolete. The growth of population and industry along the north branch of the Pawtuxet simply prohibited the survival of those unfortunate alewives. Besides, with so many mill owners actively opposed to upholding restrictions on their dams, the law must have quickly become unenforceable. Thus, after a brief but bitter controversy, the debate over the herring fishery gradually faded from the scene in northwestern Rhode Island.[66] In the late 1820s the issue was once again revived in the state, but then the conflict between dam owners and farmer–fishermen was confined to the Pawcatuck River valley, in Rhode Island's southwestern corner, a late-developing region that was now experiencing the economic growth—and consequent conflicts—that had disturbed the northwest a quarter of a century before.[67]

The Rationalization and Centralization of Town Government

Population growth led not only to squabbling over diminishing resources, like fish, but also to positive efforts to deal with local problems. After years of relative quiet and inactivity, the town meetings of the northwest's five municipalities suddenly began producing a plethora of new rules and regulations, most of which were aimed at dealing with the problems of poverty and economic dislocation. Poor-relief rules were changed to cut the soaring cost of relief and then revised again to help ensure that the poor were still decently treated. Public education, once rejected by the northwestern yeomanry as a useless and even threatening extravagance, was viewed increasingly as a possible solution to the problems of rural poverty and landlessness. Finally, just as some northwesterners were promoting private turnpikes as a spur to regional commerce, the town governments began strengthening public highway programs as another means to the same goal. These changes in local government did not come easily, nor without occasional disputes and disagreements; but by 1820, all of the towns showed a willingness to deal positively with social problems in ways that would have been unthinkable thirty years before.

The most immediately pressing problem confronting the towns was the rising cost of poor relief. The town meetings adopted a variety of measures aimed at improving the efficiency of the relief system. Under the relatively easy demographic circumstances of the eighteenth century, the care of paupers was assigned on an ad hoc basis. Various amounts of money were given to a variety of individuals who took care of poor persons—often relatives—in their own homes. Efforts to reduce costs centered on the enforcement of settlement laws by "warning out" wandering indigents.[68]

Beginning around the turn of the century, the assignments of relief money was systematized and more carefully regulated. Most of the towns passed ordinances that directed overseers of the poor to auction off their charges to the cheapest bidders. Glocester established such a low-bid system in 1791, Scituate followed suit in 1796, as did Foster in 1809. To further increase efficiency, the town meetings also began instructing the overseers to bid off all the indigent to a single bidder, who for an agreed-upon price would take care of anyone who was dependent at that time or would become so during the next year. This expedient was adopted by Coventry in 1821.[69]

Under these circumstances, the treatment of paupers must have become harsh. A contemporary petition from several Glocester citizens charged that under the auctioning system, the poor are sold "to the lowest bidder or him who would agree to starve them for the least sum." When the poor were "sold" in a single block, the winners were usually farmers of moderate means, who could scarcely afford to be indulgent in the care of their charges. At the very least, the auctioned poor were separated from their families and reduced to a state of utter dependency. When the town of Foster voted that "those Persons that bid off the Poor of this Town shall be entitled to all the Labor of such pauper," it effectively turned them into slaves for the ensuing year.[70]

Nevertheless, town policy was not unremittingly harsh in its execution of poor-relief policy. Indeed, the harshness resulting from governments' economizing expedients appears to have set off a humanitarian reaction among some sectors of the population. Town meetings passed several poor-law amendments that appeared to mitigate the effects of the low-bid system. In 1803 the town of Glocester agreed to procure directly "the Summer and Winter Cloathing for the poor," rather than rely on the discretion of the often unscrupulous low-bidders. A few years later, Foster passed a regulation requiring that upon the death of a pauper, the person charged with his or her care was to provide "a Decent Christian like Burial for which Trouble and Expence they shall be Remunerated out of the Town Treasury." The town meetings often seemed torn between conflicting desires for both economy and fairness in caring for the poor. The result could be a policy of vacillation. On April 18, 1821, the town of Coventry passed a harsh ordinance, calling for auctioning the poor in a single block to the lowest bidder; but on June 4, at the very next town meeting, this law was repealed. After a similar case of waffling occurred in Foster, the town meeting finally agreed in 1820 upon a compromise of sorts. The lengthy "Act for the Relief and siport [*sic*] of the Poor" provided for bidding off the poor all together or in parts, depending on the decision each year of the town meeting. The act provided for awarding the poor to low-bidders but also required that the bidders "must be able and willing to do justice by said Pauper or paupers by providing for their food and raiment."[71]

In practice, however, considerations of economy tended to outweigh humanitarian concerns. Although by law the Foster town meeting could choose to bid off the poor in parts, it almost always sold them off for one lump sum. Such was the case for every year, beginning in 1820 when the new law was passed, for at least the next decade. Moreover, by a law passed in 1819, indigents eligible for relief had to "be Personally Delivered by order of the overseers" to the town caretaker; exceptions to this rule were granted only if a Physician certified that the person was too sick to remove.[72] The result was the near elimination of outdoor relief, and the transformation of the caretaker's own farm and household into a quasi almshouse. Taking this process one step further, the town of Glocester, which always seemed to be the most advanced in creating modern institutions, already had an almshouse in operation by 1828. Elsewhere the almshouse movement was stalled by the usual reluctance of farmers to commit themselves to such a heavy capital expenditure.[73]

Still, it would be an oversimplification to suggest that poor-relief measures were guided only by the principle of parsimony. Elsewhere in the country, poor-law reform was motivated not only by a desire to save money, but also from the belief that in the more mobile and volatile society of the early nineteenth century, the poor had to be segregated from the community to save them from further corruption, perhaps even to "cure" them from the sins of idleness and debauchery. Accompanying this belief was the realization that in a highly mobile society poverty was a regional problem and could not be controlled by enforcing localistic settlement laws.[74] In the absence of more detailed records, it is difficult to evaluate whether these kinds of considerations were prevalent as well in the rural northwest. But certainly when the town of Foster effectively eliminated settlement requirements, as it did in 1825,[75] it signaled a realization that the relatively static economy of the eighteenth century had come to an end, that it was no longer possible or even desirable to impede the free flow of labor through the enforcement of old settlement regulations. Population growth and economic dislocation created a new set of problems—as well as opportunities—for northwestern farmers in the first quarter of the nineteenth century. The towns responded by shedding their earlier parochial, ad hoc approach toward poor relief, and adopting a more regularized and centralized policy that increased the role of local government as an agent in meliorating the problems (and taking advantage of the opportunities) of a new kind of society.

A still more dramatic change in town policy occurred in the area of public schooling. At the turn of the century the towns of the northwest had decisively rejected a statewide plan for creating free schools. Twenty years later, the same town meetings endorsed without any known opposition a similar plan for state funding of schools. Although the absence of literary documents makes it difficult to determine the reasons for this change in local opinion, the timing of the town meeting endorsements suggest that economic and demographic changes once again played an important role. The same concerns about economic dislocation that led to poor-relief reform also contributed to eventual rural acceptance of public education as a partial solution for local ills.

To begin with, even though northwesterners rejected tax-supported education in 1800, many of them began establishing their own private schools and academies. The area's first incorporated school society, the Union School House Company, was founded in Scituate in 1808. Three other schools received legislative charters in the next fifteen years: the Coventry School Society (1814), the Scituate and Foster Academy (1817), and the Central Society of Scituate (1818).[76] Less formally organized institutions must have predated these schools, although their exact number remains a mystery, until 1819, when Pease and Nile's *Gazetteer* was published, with its rough statewide census of educational institutions. By the *Gazetteer*'s count, there were forty-eight schools in the northwest, or about one school for every eighty-four children between ages five and sixteen.[77] Assuming an average class size of thirty in these one-room schoolhouses, about one-third of all school-age youth were probably receiving some kind of formal instruction. Although the five back-country towns ranked generally behind their neighbors to the east in terms of the ratio of schools to children, they still managed a respectable showing by contemporary Rhode Island standards. Outside of the more commercial towns of Providence, Pawtucket, Smithfield, Cranston, and East Greenwich, Scituate boasted the only academy in the fourteen towns that then made up Kent and Providence counties.

Nevertheless, one should not wax eloquent about either the quantity or quality of early-nineteenth-century education in northwestern Rhode Island. Most local schools operated only two to three months a year, in the dead of winter, when farmers could spare the labor of their children. Because private schools were funded only by local subscription, participation in schooling was probably limited to the area's wealthier families. Of the men who incorporated the area's four chartered schools, 65 percent ranked in the top fifth of tax assessments, with another 17 percent in the second fifth. Participants in less formal education were probably somewhat less affluent. Education in northwestern Rhode Island was still a fairly peripheral affair, supported by a small although relatively important section of the area's population.[78]

Still, by around 1820, this strong minority was sufficient to lead almost all of the town meetings to publicly support the establishment of state-funded schools. The industrial depression that followed the War of 1812, culminating in the panic of 1819, seems to have been a watershed in the history of public education in Rhode Island, and especially in the northwest. In October 1818, Governor Nehemiah Knight reintroduced the issue into the legislature when he proposed the establishment of schools for factory children. Spurred partly by Knight's initiative and partly by their own concerns, the backwoods towns soon began advocating public school proposals of their own. On September 23, 1819, Foster's town meeting voted to instruct its representatives "to get an act Passed for the purpose of Establishing free schools." At the same meeting, the town passed a sweeping reorganization of its poor-relief regulations, thus suggesting that the freemen viewed education as a possible remedy for the area's growing poverty and landlessness. On April 19 and August 29, 1820, the towns of Burrillville and Glocester also resolved to support broad proposals for "free schools," proposals that appear to have gone well beyond Knight's limited plan for factory education. Five years later, Glocester voted to send its poor children to school at the town's expense, thus further illustrating the connection, as perceived by rural leaders, between education and the melioration of poverty.[79]

After several years of legislative wrangling, a bill appropriating $10,000 in support of public schools finally passed in 1828. All but one of the northwest's representatives supported the measure.[80] The practical effect of the school act in the northwest was to encourage and further a preexisting movement toward educational improvement. It would be too much to say that the act revolutionized schooling in northwestern Rhode Island. Although the act's $10,000 grant was greater than the earlier Free School Act's grant of $6,000, it still amounted to a paltry forty cents for every school-age child in the state. More important, unlike its ill-fated predecessor in 1800, this later school act did not require towns to supplement the state's appropriation with their own funds: indeed, local matching funds were limited by the act to twice the amount of each town's state grant. In practice, every town in the northwest, except for Foster, established their own school taxes in 1828. The amounts raised locally ranged from $300 to $550 per town, a sum roughly equal to the funds received from the state.[81]

In spite of these successes by public school supporters, agrarian opposition to educational improvements continued. Between 1828 and 1846, the town of Burrillville continually voted down increases in its school fund, even though its population increased by 25 percent in the interim. Opposition to public schools was also expressed by sporadic acts of violence. For example, in Burrillville, a schoolhouse was seriously vandalized soon after it was constructed with funds made available by the new tax.[82]

But gradually significant opposition to public schools shifted away from the northwest to the southern portion of the state, an area that was either economically stagnant or underdeveloped. In this area, only three out of fourteen towns appropriated funds for education in response to the school act of 1828; and in the 1830s, bitter local disputes broke out between opponents and proponents of public schools.[83] In the northwest, more and more schoolhouses were built, continuing a trend set in place before 1828. As a result, the average number of children eligible to attend each school fell from 84 in 1819 to 60 in 1828 and again to 47 in 1831.[84] In a region where a generation ago public education was rejected as a threatening and needless innovation, it was now fast becoming an integral part of the cultural landscape.

Finally, in the same period during which towns were revamping poor-relief rules and creating a system of public education, they also moved to overhaul local highway-repair regulations. For decades, northwestern farmers had been content to make do with the existing inefficient and highly localistic set of rules. But suddenly, around the turn of the century, motions began to be heard in town meetings for improving the enforcement of highway regulations. Although generally successful, these reforms were not enacted without a certain amount of opposition. The intrusion of private turnpike companies into rural Rhode Island had already inflamed local discussion on the subject of highway repair. More generally, as the local economy changed in response to trade fluctuations and the introduction of textile factories, demands for new or improved highways arose, which further rankled those who were wedded to simply preserving the existing order. The movement for highway reform occurred in a highly charged atmosphere in which localistic traditions ran counter to the needs of a modern commercial economy.

As a first step, aided by the state legislature, the towns tried to improve enforcement of repair rules by monetarizing the entire process. In the colonial and revolutionary era, highway repair was accomplished by simply requiring one day's labor per year from every able-bodied adult male. But in 1794 the legislature gave towns the option of assessing a tax on every laborer or householder, who could then "pay" for the tax by working himself, or by sending an oxen team or another laborer in his place. Foster and Glocester both accepted this monetary option in the same year, and when the state made highway-repair taxation mandatory in 1808, Scituate quickly followed suit.[85] At first, the principal effect of this provision was that the area's rising gentlemanly minority could avoid physical labor by hiring others in their stead. But in 1816 the state turned the monetarization of highway labor into an enforcement provision: a new law gave individual surveyors the right to "levy and collect" delinquent taxes "by attachment, distress, sale of real estate, or otherwise, in the same manner as [town tax] Collectors" have in collecting other taxes "and shall have the same fees therefor." Prior to this, surveyors could only fine delinquent laborers at their own expense, an onerous and unrewarding duty.[86] A combination of new state laws and town regulations thus created a more powerful and flexible system for repairing local highways.

As a more central aim, highway law reformers sought to improve town control over the surveyors themselves, the officials who served as the linchpin of the entire repair process. Since most surveyors were farmers of above-average wealth, they could generally be counted on to keep local roads in passable shape, at least so that their own relatively considerable agricultural output could make it to market.[87] Still, supervising repair teams in the hard task of rebuilding roads must have been a disagreeable job, especially since they worked without recompense. It would only be natural for all but the most diligent to fall lax in their duties. Highway surveyors, after all, were the very officials whom the turnpike companies sought to bypass with their own work teams. One surveyor in particular, Barzillai Knight, had been an especially severe thorn in the side of Providence and Norwich Turnpike Society. Finally, the sheer number of surveyors—averaging thirty or so per town by 1800— made it difficult for central town authorities to supervise their activities and ensure the enforcement of their duties.

As one of the principal tactics adopted in cracking down on wayward surveyors, the towns tried to place them under the supervision of a more centralized, and presumably more responsible authority. In 1801 Foster created an unspecified number of new positions, called "highway inspectors," to whom each surveyor was to report annually. These presumably more reliable inspectors were then given the job of collecting fines from delinquent laborers.[88] In 1823, enforcement duties were further centralized when the town transferred the power to collect unpaid highway taxes from the surveyor to the town clerk. The town of Coventry had already adopted an identical procedure in 1819.[89]

Prior to that, in 1813, Coventry had created its own set of highway inspectors, in response to a clear case of resistance to a town meeting's directions by local highway workers. The conflict had its roots in yet another example of hostility between farmers and textile-mill owners. The Washington Factory opened in 1812, and its proprietors almost immediately began asking that a nearby bridge be repaired. In response, a small number of men called a "special" town meeting on January 14, 1812. Moderated by John Wood, a farmer of only middling wealth, who never served as moderator again, the meeting "voted that the Town make no Repairs on said Bridge at the Expense of the Town." Eleven months later, a more orderly town meeting reversed this decision, and, in a highly unusual measure, ordered in writing that the "Surveyor of the Eastern District, Richard Anthony . . . repair or Rebuild the Bridge at Washington Factory." Anthony was further "authorized to use Timber from the Town Land for . . . said Repairs in case he cannot procure timber in his district from them who owes Taxes," thus implying that local landowners might have refused to sacrifice their trees in order to repair the controversial bridge. But apparently even this admonition was not enough to effect the proper repairs. On June 7, 1813, the town meeting replaced Richard Anthony as the district surveyor with one Preserved Fish. Apparently, Anthony was either unwilling or unable to persuade a hostile local population to serve the needs of the Washington factory's owners.[90]

At the same meeting, the town rewrote its general highway regulations in order to prevent any further cases of local disobedience. As its chief innovation, the new highway act divided "the several Highway Districts into four grand Districts," each of which would be supervised by a "grand surveyor." The grand surveyors were given the authority to supersede a regular surveyor, should one of them "neglect or Refuse to Call out their Districts to work on the Highways." The act further required that each surveyor report on delinquent taxpayers in his district to his grand surveyor, who would in turn request that appropriate town officials issue warrants to seize their property. As a response to efforts by local surveyors to resist unpopular work orders, the act essentially created a new and more centralized layer of enforcement bureaucracy.[91]

Aggravated by the constant efforts of town leaders to discipline and control their activities, surveyors began making end runs around the local officialdom by appealing to the town meeting itself. Twice in the year 1804, and once in 1809, surveyors in the town of Glocester called town meetings "specially . . . for the purpose of suspending the Town Act for mending highways." Gathering their friends and neighbors to pack the meeting, they succeeded in obtaining a vote to postpone the normal deadline for working "out their . . . back taxes." To put a stop to this tactic, the town's leaders quickly devised a familiar counterstratagem. At a more "regular" meeting held on June 7, 1813, the town voted "that all surveyor or Surveyors that shall call a Town Meeting for the purpose of having their highway Taxes postponed by neglect of working them out, shall pay the expence [*sic*] of calling sd. Meeting." One might recall that a similar tactic was adopted by public school advocates a few years earlier: in a vain attempt to silence backwoods opposition to the Free School Act of 1800, they had tried to discourage opponents from calling for "special" town meetings.[92]

In still other towns, efforts proceeded apace to limit the surveyors' access to the town meeting. On September 20, 1813, the town of Foster amended its highway act to require surveyors to report to the town council, instead of the meeting itself. Coventry further extended the power of its council, voting in 1817 to give it the authority to replace wayward surveyors, a responsibility formerly held only by the town meeting itself. In all of these examples advocates of improved highways sought to restrict the license of town meeting–style democracy in favor of the authority of the six-member town councils, whose wealthy members could presumably be counted on to enforce highway regulations more severely, for the sake of improving regional commerce.[93]

Thus, as in the case of poor-relief and educational programs, highway regulations were changed in the direction of rationalizing, centralizing, and streamlining the structure and function of local government. Poor-relief reformers had sought to curb the waste and confusion caused by localistic tendencies, such as those bound up in settlement regulations and the granting of outdoor relief. In a similar way, many of the new highway repair rules were aimed at curtailing insubordination among local highway surveyors. By leashing local officials to a more responsible central authority, and by rationalizing the system through monetarization, highway reformers sought to turn town government into a more positive force in the promotion of community improvement. This same goal was effected in an even more direct way by public school advocates, who saw in free schools a possible means for meliorating local ills.

Of course, the reform of highway administration, unlike that of poor relief and education, did not arise so obviously from growing concerns over the problems of overpopulation and economic dislocation. Still, it was hardly a coincidence that all three reform movements arose at the same time. Until the 1790s, the town meetings had been stunningly quiet on all three issues. Then, in a period of growing scarcity and economic instability, almost all of the towns suddenly erupted with nearly simultaneous discussions on efforts to improve highways, reduce poor-relief expenditures, and create free schools.

The only town that failed to initiate improvements was Burrillville, the exception that proves the rule. An isolated and especially rocky town, Burrillville's population grew slowly in the period, and it never approached in density that of the rest of northwestern Rhode Island. Moreover, until the wool industry developed in the 1840s, the town remained largely unaffected by the fits and starts of Rhode Island's industrial revolution. In the first third of the nineteenth century, the specter of overpopulation and economic dislocation that troubled the other towns never appeared. Consequently, the town meetings were remarkably unaffected by the discussions over government "improvement" that so stirred Burrillville's neighbors to the south. There, in the more densely populated and economically mature sections of the northwest, efforts to improve poor-relief, highway, and educational systems arose as a general reform movement, a movement that sought to rationalize economic and social life as a means of meliorating local problems and welcoming the opportunities of a commercializing society.

Summary

The ambitions of an enterprising few therefore mixed with growing demographic and social problems in pulling the northwest into the commercializing and modernizing spirit of early nineteenth-century New England. In the 1780s and 1790s, backcountry Rhode Island seemed largely at odds with the commercial towns of Narragansett Bay. The farmers struggled in vain to block the new federal Constitution; and with somewhat more success, they sought to thwart attempts by East Coast merchants to modernize the rural hinterland. Whole communities were aroused to defend traditional fishing rights and the freedom of the highways, and to ward off expensive and threatening innovations like public schools.

But by the turn of the century, a native leadership had begun to develop from within some of the same institutions that the Providence merchants had sought to impose on the northwest from without. Residing generally in the populous and prosperous area of northern Scituate and eastern Glocester, a semicohesive group of wealthy farmers and millwrights worked together in building turnpikes and mills, incorporating schools and libraries, and establishing the area's first bank. Their efforts were warmly resisted at first, mainly by men of middling wealth who lived toward the geographical margins of northwestern society. But where the Federalist merchants from the east had generally failed, this native commercial leadership eventually succeeded in overcoming localist opposition to economic and cultural improvements. Localist oppositions, after all, have certain inherent weaknesses, especially when they are confronted by the rise of a modernizing elite within their own borders.

Besides, the native boosters of economic growth did not simply mimic the merchants of Providence when they planned their own improvements. As leaders of the state's Republican party, they offered alternative models to the modernizing institutions first proposed by the Federalists from Providence. The creators of the Rhode Island and Connecticut Turnpike, in particular, developed a blueprint for rural development that sought to combine the Federalist emphasis on outside, corporate coercion, with the native tradition of local participation and control. To a lesser, and disastrously unsuccessful extent, the directors of the Farmers Exchange Bank sought to bend the form of a commercial bank to the needs of a backwoods rural economy. This resulted most obviously in inflated currency and eventual bankruptcy, and less directly in a strengthened traditional opposition to the evils of banking.

In the meantime, localist attachment to traditional ways and mores was being undercut by the emergence of unsettling economic and social problems. Local control of highway-repair and poor-relief systems might have proved satisfactory in an economy of easy subsistence; but when the supply of land finally gave out, these traditions resulted in a kind of anarchistic confusion that was inimical to the orderly dispersion of scarce resources. In an economy based on a plentiful supply of land, public education might have seemed to be a threatening and useless innovation; but in a less abundant natural order, northwesterners came to embrace free schooling as a means of improving their options for success in an alternative commerical economy. Overpopulation also undercut the common-rights tradition, as symbolized by laws safeguarding the communal fish population. Mill dams and migratory herring might have happily coexisted in a time of rural plenty; but by the turn of the century the farmer–fishermen and their neighboring millwrights bitterly opposed each other over the need for fishways through dams. The traditionalists scored a victory with the passage of the 1802 law requiring fishways; but their victory was a symbolic one, as angry mill owners increasingly flouted and protested the law, which soon became a dead letter, leaving the area open to unbridled entrepreneurial expansion.

The ambitions of a native elite, and the influence of social problems that were felt by all, have been analyzed here separately for the purpose of clarity in exposition. In practice, of course, these forces worked together. Population growth rendered fishway requirements obsolete, but it also made viable the construction of regional turnpikes. Opponents of fishway requirements, whose cause was strengthened as the local population swelled, turned out to be some of the northwest's principal boosters of modernizing institutions. As for those who favored public schools and highway law reform, their names remain more obscure, thanks to the veil of anonymity that shrouds town meeting minutes. But they must have overlapped in identity with those who incorporated the northwest's earliest chartered schools and turnpikes; for together they all sought to both improve educational opportunities and straighten out a tangled old highway system.

More generally, the town officers who reformed local regulations and the assembly representative who helped charter new commercializing institutions belonged to the same Country wing of the state's Republican party. This party formed a natural home for those who sought to combine economic growth with the preservation of rural simplicity. The rural leadership were of necessity a practical lot, not given to philosophical musings. But as exemplified by the Rhode Island and Connecticut Turnpike Society's highway construction plans, they seem to have groped toward a view of political economy that melded localist traditions to the needs of an emerging commercial order.

In the 1780s, backcountry Rhode Island appeared to be almost a political and cultural entity unto itself, scorned by the rest of the nation as it clung stubbornly to its localist traditions. But within forty years' time, the northwest had developed a commercializing leadership that possessed links to a national Republican party. More broadly, most farmers had come to accept a variety of modernizing institutions—turnpikes, schools, and so forth—that they had previously denounced as the tyrannical trappings of an "enslaved" population in Puritan New England. In the next generation, these same institutions would help to link the northwest ever more firmly to an emerging regional economy and a national cultural ethos.

CHAPTER FOUR

Economic and Social Transformation

▼ ▼

THE ENTREPRENEURIAL victories of the 1800s and 1810s helped set the stage for a transformation in the living standards and material resources of a large portion of the northwestern population. Living standards rose dramatically, as is revealed by a quick analysis of the probate inventories of residents who died in the 1830s. Northwesterners dying in the 1780s and 1790s left behind personal estates of the barest proportions. Most households were stocked with only the basic essentials of rustic living: cooking utensils, metal or wooden plates, and a few pieces of furniture, chiefly beds. Luxury items, such as silver-plate utensils, were a rarity, even in the wealthiest of homes: about 6 percent of all households owned silverware. Fifty years later, material conditions were considerably more comfortable and refined. The total value of a northwesterner's personal estate now averaged $352, as opposed to only $272 in the 1780s and 1790s. More dramatic improvements occurred in the area of luxury goods. Fully one-quarter of all estates owned silverware. An equal proportion owned clocks or watches, rare items in the eighteenth century. A small proportion of local farmers were beginning to report ownership of bulky, imported goods. Personal riding chairs, or chaises, and mahogany furniture, both unheard of fifty years before, showed up in the inventories of about 7 percent of northwestern households.[1] By the 1830s, the region that Timothy Dwight once derided as "destitute of beauty" was beginning to display the adornments of a genuinely comfortable civilization. More to the point, farmers must also have increased their income from sales, in order to finance these new luxury purchases. Most northwestern farmers had once been inured to a semisubsistence type of economy, but they now were selling goods on the market at a heretofore unheralded rate.

99

The Causes of Market Growth

Although it may seem easy to posit the existence of a market economy, explaining its creation, especially in the northwest, is an altogether more difficult proposition. The region's soil and terrain, after all, were rocky, hard, and hilly. Foster, Rhode Island, along with its neighboring towns, was never destined to be a land of agricultural riches. Nevertheless, the demand of the powerful Providence market, together with the considerable exertions of a local group of boosters, combined to pull the northwest into a growing regional market.[2] In the 1820s and 1830s, Providence continued to boom as a major industrial and commercial center. Already the second-largest city in New England, its population grew by 43 percent in the 1820s, and by another 38 percent in the 1830s, to a total of over 23,000. Growth rates in the neighboring industrial towns of northeastern Rhode Island were just as dramatic: their combined population rose 81 percent in twenty years, reaching at least 31,000 in 1840.[3]

If northwestern farmers were able to take advantage of this burgeoning market, credit should be given as well to the infrastructural spadework begun by local boosters in the 1800s and 1810s. By their victories over a localist opposition, area modernizers made possible a greatly improved highway system. Local bankers, whose contribution up to 1820 was of a most dubious quality, made a comeback of sorts; and combined with the more powerful financial institutions of Providence, they made possible the beginnings of a cash-oriented economy. Finally, the mill owners' triumph over those stubborn alewives eliminated an important legal constraint on the expansion of textile mills. More subtly, but perhaps just as important, the extinction of the herring population removed an important prop from the livelihood of those who sought continued existence in a semisubsistence economy. In short, through the efforts of local boosters and entrepreneurs, it was becoming at once easier and more necessary for northwestern farmers to take part in the booming market economy of the Providence area.

Although spotty and occasionally contradictory, available evidence suggests that land transportation in the northwest improved considerably in the early decades of the nineteenth century. Northwestern Rhode Island was happily situated astride most major land routes leading west and north from Providence to the hinterland of New England. This geographical coincidence, together with some spirited competition among local boosters, resulted in the eventual construction of six turnpikes lying wholly or partly within the bounds of the northwest's five towns. Built only after overcoming considerable local opposition, these roads stretched to over a total of sixty-three miles, covering a fair proportion of the area's 276 square miles.[4] By their very existence they must have considerably rationalized what had been a crazy-quilt of local roads.

Unfortunately, the turnpikes of the early nineteenth century have received some weighty criticism from both contemporary observers and later historians. Most turnpike promoters insisted on running their roads in as straight a line as possible, in order to minimize highway length. But this entailed cutting through miles of uncleared land, when their efforts might have been more profitably spent in simply improving existing routes. Even more ludicrous, the commitment to straight-as-an-arrow roads often required travelers to climb the steepest of hills, when they might have more sensibly been directed around them. Some wonder whether turnpikes had more than a negligible effect on the overall cost of land transportation.[5]

Contemporary observers gave a decidedly mixed review of the quality of the northwest's own turnpikes. Individual travelers continued to snipe about highway conditions, even after mass popular resistance to turnpiking had faded away. In 1812, after almost two decades of construction on the Providence and Norwich Turnpike, its tollkeeper reported that "I am frequently told by Gentlemen traveling this road that I ought to give them 20 cts. for traveling such a road rather [than] the contrary." He even confessed himself that "our road is a horrible road indeed." As for the Glocester Turnpike, one of its stockholders, James B. Mason, felt obliged to admit that "I have this day passed over of our Turnpike road. I found it in a very unprofitable state. . . . if not repaired it will wash & be ruined." On the other hand, turnpikes continued to have their own champions. One of the travelers who had complained so bitterly about the Providence and Norwich Turnpike also reported that "the other road [by which he probably meant the rival Rhode Island and Connecticut Turnpike] is so much better." Timothy Dwight contributed a less backhanded compliment: writing in praise of the much maligned Providence and Norwich Turnpike, he termed it "tolerably well made" and contrasted it with the local roads that were "stony and ill, or rather not at all, repaired." Where the turnpike ended near the state border, "the former disagreeableness of the road was here renewed," before "we came to Sterling, where we were again relieved by a turnpike road."[6] Dwight's praise was quietly seconded, moreover, by the many newspaper advertisements for farms that listed turnpike location as a point in their favor. Contemporaries must have thought well of the turnpikes, if advertisers saw them as a promotional advantage.[7]

More to the point, the turnpike movement was really only a glamorous sideshow in the midst of the larger, more prosaic movement toward improved land transportation. In the first quarter of the nineteenth century, the highways of the northwest were being improved not only by private turnpikers, but also by the public efforts of local officials. Through the monetarization and centralization of town highway repair systems, local roads must have improved at least somewhat in their overall condition.[8] The advent of local highway reforms may also explain the bitterness with which travelers continued to criticize the turnpikes. When even the public roads were being gradually improved, travelers must have come to expect still more from the toll-charging turnpikes.

Finally, the debate over highway improvement can be settled less effectively by referring to the judgments of contemporaries or to the measurement of transport costs than by examining how it was that the farmers actually used their roads. Evidence from probate inventories suggests that by the 1830s rural roads in Rhode Island were considerably more passable than they had been a half century before. In the 1780s and 1790s, the transportation devices owned by northwestern farmers, when they owned any at all, consisted almost entirely of two-wheel carts. These small and crude devices were exceedingly slow and were also a menace to the animals that pulled them; nevertheless, they prevailed over the larger, four-wheel wagons because carts could operate much more easily over the miserable roads of the revolutionary era. By the 1830s, however, wagons had almost completely replaced carts in northwesterners' inventories. In the preceding fifty years, wagon ownership increased enormously from 3 to 53 percent of all households, while incidence of carts fell by nearly half, from 35 to 19 percent. Moreover, in the 1830s, 83 percent of cart owners also possessed a wagon; but only 62 percent of those who owned a wagon bothered to hold onto their carts. By shifting their preference so rapidly from carts to wagons, northwesterners indicated that road conditions must have improved considerably betweeen the 1780s and 1830s. They also showed that, with their larger wagons, they were now able to transport their produce faster and more efficiently than ever before.[9]

The contribution of the local banks to the northwest's economy was a bit more ambiguous. Nine years had passed, after the Farmers Exchange Bank debacle of 1809, before banks were again chartered in the northwest. Then, in quick succession, four banks were chartered in 1818; and with the opening of Foster's Mount Vernon Bank in 1823, each of the five northwestern towns had a bank within its borders. Nevertheless, almost all of these banks eventually ran into financial difficulties; and by themselves, they contributed relatively little to the area's economy.

For one thing, the rush to obtain bank charters in 1818 resulted not from real demand for banking facilities, but rather from an impending change in the state's banking laws. After 1818, all newly chartered banks were to be denied the privilege of "bank process," a power unique to Rhode Island under which banks were given the power of summary judgment and execution over defaulting debtors. In a massive case of logrolling, the legislature chartered sixteen banks, with most awarded one each to rural towns. Banks' incorporators were motivated not so much from a genuine desire to improve local credit, as from a speculative urge to obtain a set of valuable legal privileges, before they were legislated out of existence.[10]

It is not surprising, then, that the four banks chartered at that time, together with Foster's bank of 1823, compiled a financial record of dubious distinction.

The Burrillville Agricultural Bank effectively passed out of existence almost immediately when it came under the control of the powerful cotton manufacturer Samuel Slater. Slater opted to move the bank to his Slatersville manufacturing village, an obviously much more convenient location, and changed its name to the "Village Bank." Thus exited the second bank to be incorporated in the rural northwest.[11] The banks that remained did not exactly prosper. True, they managed to avoid the scandalous excesses of the Farmers Exchange Bank; but this success probably resulted less from the bankers' own wisdom and prudence than from the generally sound condition of the New England banking system. After 1819, the Suffolk Bank and its strong Rhode Island satellite, the Merchants Bank of Providence, agreed to redeem area bank notes at par, as long as the originating bank maintained a permanent deposit of $5,000 in specie. Although country banks like those in the northwest bitterly resented this constraint on their operations, they had no choice but to participate; and as a result, their note circulation remained fairly well controlled. Throughout the 1820s and 1830s, the ratio of specie to notes maintained by northwestern banks remained generally higher than the ratios of banks in the Middle Atlantic or Western states.[12]

Denied the ability to profit from inflationary circulation, rural banks might have turned to the business of collecting income from loans and paying dividends and interest on capital stock and deposits. During the 1820s, the banking industry boomed in Rhode Island because of the rise of the state's textile industry, whose demand for loans sucked in capital from all over New England. Total financial resources available to the state's banks almost doubled, rising from $4,305,456 in 1820 to almost $8.5 million in 1828. But the northwest's banks, operating on the periphery of the industrial revolution, were able to participate only partially in this financial bonanza. Between 1820 and 1830, the local bank assets rose from just under $160,000 to about $257,000, but their share of the state total fell from 3.7 to only 3 percent. Some local financial institutions, such as the Scituate Bank, eventually gave up on banking altogether. By 1834, Scituate Bank's bill circulation had dropped to a negligible $388, while its assets fell to $18,352. Unable to loan profitably to the countryside, and denied the ability to profit from circulation, the area's bankers could not translate the political perquisites of a bank charter into financial gains.[13]

With so many bank charters lying around, nearly useless for the local citizenry, the situation was ripe for manipulation by out-of-state swindlers. The first to fall was the Burrillville Bank, which had replaced the Burrillville Agricultural Bank in 1818, soon after the latter's exit to Slatersville. The bank slumbered along quite nicely until the fall of 1831, when Francis Y. Carlile and John L. Clark entered from whereabouts unknown, purchased a portion of the bank's stock, and arranged for the rest to be purchased by a few pliant local residents. Clark and Carlile proceeded to direct the printing of large sums of bills, raising the bank's circulation from a paltry $2,178 to $56,545. Happily for the bank's creditors, the Suffolk Bank soon forced it to default on its own notes, and the bank's assets and ledgers were seized by a legislative committee in time to redeem and destroy all outstanding bills. The committee then declared the bank permanently closed.[14] Four years later, the nearly moribund Scituate Bank was subject to a similar scam. On this occasion the swindlers' plot was uncovered in time for the legislature to resurrect the institution, under the appropriately conservative name of the "Hamilton Bank." But this revival was also to be short-lived; the new bank folded for good in 1851.[15]

The main deviation from the general weakness of northwestern banks was the Mount Vernon Bank of Foster, the exception that proves the rule. Like most northwestern banks, the Mount Vernon Bank was founded with a capitalization of only $50,000. But while all the other banks were able to subscribe for only half of their original capitalization, the Mount Vernon Bank had succeeded by 1835 in raising its stock value to over $69,000. The Mount Vernon Bank thrived not because of, but rather in spite of the nature of the local economy. Following the greatest line of return, the bank's directors simply invested most of their capital in the booming city of Providence. This tactic sparked considerable local resentment, but it also gave the bank unusual financial stability. Total assets climbed from $31,240 in 1825 to almost $150,000 in 1835, more than twice the average of other northwestern banks. Directors' debts as a percentage of total assets fell from an already low 12 percent to only 3.6 percent in 1835, well below the statewide average. By refusing to depend solely on the community's resources, the Mount Vernon Bank managed to thrive in an era of relative financial instability.[16]

Otherwise, banks in northwestern Rhode Island remained unstable. Indeed, they compiled the unenviable record of accounting for three of the state's first four bank failures. The financial ambitions of the northwest's boosters simply outstripped the potential of the local economy. This is not to say that the northwest was the state's poorest region. Other areas of Rhode Island remained even more backward: the southwestern part of the state, aside from the port town of Westerly, was still too inaccessible and underpopulated to participate in the commercial and industrial revolutions of the Narragansett region. But here, residents avoided bank failures by simply eschewing banks altogether. The region's leaders lacked the enterprising imagination—or foolhardiness, if one prefers—of the northwest's entrepreneurial elite. It was in the northwest, a border area between industrial riches and rural backwardness, that early banks sparked so fitfully, caught between the excessive ambitions of their founders and the realities of a largely agrarian economy.[17]

Still, banks did not have a completely nebulous effect on the local economy. In 1833, two more banks were chartered in the northwest, for a total of six, taking into account the failure of the Burrillville Bank. By 1835, their combined assets had grown to $425,777, rebounding to 3.4 percent of the statewide total; directors' debts as a percentage of assets fell to 12 percent. If they profited most from investing funds elsewhere, their stock nevertheless would be useful assets for a wealthy minority of local residents. In the 1830s about 5 percent of all northwesterners held bank stock as part of their probate inventories. Especially striking is the case of Pardon Holden, whose $1,540 investment in Mount Vernon Bank stock constituted three-fourths of his entire estate. The fluidity of these holdings helped allow him to devise his possession in a remarkably simple, and for his widow, generous manner: his wife would receive all of the dividends from the stock, until her death or remarriage, when the stock would simply be divided equally among his seven children. More broadly, the banks of the northwest, together with the more powerful financial institutions in Providence, succeeded in introducing paper money into the back country as a stable form of currency. In the 1830s, cash entered into local transactions for the first time as a common medium of exchange. Ownership of bank stock, together with the more widespread incidence of cash, signaled that economic and social relations in northwestern Rhode Island were becoming flexible and dynamic on a heretofore unimaginable scale.[18]

While the contribution of turnpikes and banks to the rural economy is in some ways debatable, the same certainly cannot be said of the booming new textile industry. Northwestern Rhode Island overlapped with the edge of the state's industrial area. Prior to 1840, mills were few in number in three of the area's towns: Foster and Burrillville each had only one mill in 1832; Glocester had two. In eastern Coventry and southern and eastern Scituate, on the other hand, a succession of cotton mills sprang up along the banks of the Pawtuxet River. In that area, they came to employ a significant portion of the local work force. Still more important, in terms of their overall effect on the rural economy, the mills of the northwest, together with those of nearby northeastern Rhode Island, created an unprecedented market and system of exchange for local farmers.

Following Moses Brown's victory in 1800 over the farmer–fishermen of Coventry and Scituate, the textile industry spread throughout the upper valley of the Pawtuxet River. Before long, local entrepreneurs joined Brown in furthering Rhode Island's industrial revolution: Richard and William Anthony opened the Coventry Manufacturing Company in 1806, followed by Lowry Arnold's Central Factory in 1809.[19] Business boomed when the embargo of 1807 and subsequent war cut off British imports; by 1812 there were at least ten mills in the northwest. Although this nascent industry nearly collapsed with the end of the war, it revived in the 1820s and by 1832 totaled about twenty-five factories. Operating 41,000 spindles and over a thousand looms, these factories accounted for about one-sixth of the state's textile capacity. As was the case with local banks, the industry gradually became more dominated by more powerful outside interests. Local entrepreneurs continued to build new mills, but their factories were increasingly subject to purchase and take-over by larger firms from the northeastern part of the state.[20] Still, although this development would perhaps eventually prove troubling to the local economy, for the time being, the textile industry was to exert a profound influence on the labor force and market structure of the rural northwest.

In the relatively industrialized towns of Coventry and Scituate, factory operatives amounted to a sizeable portion of the local work force. By 1832, almost 1,500 workers were employed in the local textile industry, or about a quarter of all town residents over the age of nine. Textile work was especially common for women and children, since they made up a disproportionate share of factory workers. About 28 percent of all women and 31 percent of all teenagers were employed in local factories. It is more difficult to gauge the effect of this employment on the preexisting farm population. Certainly, some native residents must have worked in the mills or at least profited from their children's labor, thereby bringing some much needed income into the home. But the workers in local mills were just as likely to have immigrated from further afield. About 60 percent of all employees in a mill in nearby Dudley, Massachusetts, arrived from distances of at least thirty miles. For a couple of decades, textile mills employed large numbers of local women as weavers, under the system of putting out nonmechanized aspects of the industry: between 1811 and 1819, one firm alone, the Blackstone Manufacturing Company of nearby Mendon, Massachusetts, issued outwork to over 150 households in the northwest. However, around 1820 local factory owners introduced power looms into their mills, thereby eliminating most outwork as an option for local farmwives. By 1832, over 1,000 looms were operating in the factories of northwestern Rhode Island, while at the same time ownership of hand looms was already declining.[21] Textile employment may have served more as a magnet for the distant unemployed than as a financial boon to the wives and children of local farmers.

The preexisting rural population was probably more materially affected by the factories' general impact on the regional marketplace. Among other things, the new industrialists needed lumber for constructing their mills, barrels for packing their products, and food for feeding their operatives. Their demand for these and other products greatly increased local opportunities for farmers to sell their goods on the market.[22] Less obvious, perhaps, the presence of factories also facilitated farmers' participation on the purchasing side of the market. Most mill owners, after all, operated factory stores in order to control their operatives' access to food, clothing, and other essentials of life. Apparently, they did not limit their sales to factory workers alone. Between June 1816 and May 1817, Hiram Salisbury, a Burrillville farmer and carpenter, recorded five different trips to nearby factory stores and villages, where he purchased textiles and hardware supplies. Later, in the 1820s, the spread of industrialization drew his shopping expeditions westward to the Connecticut mill village of Quoddick, located just across the state line from Burrillville.[23]

On the far southern side of northwestern Rhode Island, a farmer named John Waterman frequented factory stores still more often. A resident of Centerville in Warwick, just across the town line from Coventry, Waterman lived within just a few miles of the mills of the Pawtuxet River valley. Most of Waterman's surviving papers record only his payments to agricultural laborers; but these alone reveal a steady stream of visits to nearby mills, where he purchased goods for the purpose of paying his workers in kind. In the 1815 laboring season alone, he bought at the "old Factory" (a curious appellation, this early in the industrial revolution) $23.91 "worth of goods" for Stephen Wilcocks.[24] Located on the perimeter of the northwest's five towns, the new mill stores greatly increased local householders' access to a wide variety of consumer goods. Where once farmers depended on distant Providence for the purchase of imported consumer goods, they now could rely on several retail outlets, all located just a short distance away.

The intentional acts of a modernizing elite thus mixed with larger, more impersonal social developments in creating conditions ripe for market growth. The emergence of Providence as a major industrial and commercial center, perhaps more than any other factor, helped to pull northwestern farmers into a market economy. Certainly, northwesterners could hardly claim credit for this favorable economic development. But in other respects, the actions of a handful of local boosters and modernizers did contribute fundamentally to the beginnings of a market economy in the rural northwest. True, their actions often worked in ways that they could not have anticipated. Local bank owners hoped to profit from circulating inflated bills abroad, while extracting interest from loans at home. They were prevented from the first by the rigors of the Suffolk Bank system, and from the second by the inherent weakness of an agrarian economy. Still, they eventually played a useful economic role by channeling funds from the local moneyed elite into the more lucrative Providence market, and by working within the Suffolk system to create a stable system of paper currency. In a somewhat similar way, promoters of improved highways concentrated their conscious efforts on creating sparkling new turnpikes, but they probably accomplished more from the less glamorous business of improving existing public highways. In the area of textile mills, local entrepreneurs may have hoped to mimic the big industrial firms of Slater and the Browns; instead, many were simply bought out by them. Nevertheless, while they no longer controlled the destiny of the region's mills, local entrepreneurs did succeed in bringing the fruits, as well as the market demand of the industrial revolution a bit closer to the farms of the northwest. As will soon be demonstrated, banks and their currency, highways and turnpikes, and mills and their stores all played a vital role in pulling neighboring farmers into the vortex of an emerging regional economy. The modernization of the rural economy resulted not only from an impersonal brew of distant social forces, but also from the conscious efforts of a small number of boosters and shakers, and the consequences—albeit often unanticipated—that they engendered thereby.

The Development of Marketable Surpluses

The farmers of the northwest took advantage of these improved demographic, infrastructural, and market conditions by selling a variety of products to nearby merchants, factories, and storekeepers. Their efforts were constrained, of course, by the productive limits of New England's rocky soils and hilly terrain. Northwestern Rhode Island could never become the breadbasket of the nation, or even, for that matter, of the Narragansett trading region. Still, the land was suitable for pastoral agriculture, and as a result, local farmers profited increasingly from the sale of dairy and poultry products: chiefly butter, beef, and eggs. Of course, some areas were too rugged for even pastoral farming and hence remained forested. But these, too, furnished an important sideline to the local economy; for the farmers were able to sell firewood and timber to urban areas that had long since been deforested. Farming commercialized most dramatically in towns like Scituate, which bordered on Rhode Island's industrial core. In remoter areas and among the smaller farms, the development of rural capitalism occurred more slowly and subtly. In general, the transition from semisubsistence agriculture to market gardening did not always proceed evenly.[25]

Dairying probably led the way in the commercialization of northwestern agriculture. Dairy cows had long been the area's most common form of livestock. Eighty-eight percent of all farmers owned cows in the 1780s, a figure that would rise to 93 percent by the 1830s. The area's total herd size actually rose only modestly, by about one-quarter between 1780 and 1840; but both hay and grain production increased by half, thus suggesting that farmers were increasingly feeding their cattle with an eye toward commercial marketing. Perhaps more important, the withdrawal of rural women from domestic textile production allowed them to devote their energies to such dairy-related chores as milking cows and churning butter.[26]

Although local farms did not become really specialized in this field until the 1850s, many were already producing large quantities of butter and other dairy products for the regional market. As early as the late 1830s, William W. Knight of Scituate supplied prodigious quantities of butter to the large textile firm of Amasa and William Sprague, located in nearby Cranston and Warwick. Like other mill owners of the era, the Spragues purchased and sold a variety of goods through their factory stores. Throughout the spring and summer of 1839, Knight supplied the Spragues with an average of fifty-seven pounds of butter per week, yielding a steady weekly income of over $14. At the same time, he also managed to sell lesser amounts, averaging two to four pounds per week, to John Woodmaney and Emanuel Rice, store owners in Warwick and Coventry, respectively.[27] In order to produce this minimum weekly yield of sixty-three pounds of butter, Knight must have owned at least twenty-one cows. By contrast, on the Glocester Tax Valuation of 1778, only one out of 464 households reported a greater number of cattle. With annual sales totaling about 1,500 pounds of butter, the Knights' farm, although still not classifiable as a full-scale commercial dairy, ranked with some of the largest operations in the northeastern United States.[28]

Although not unusual, William Knight's farm was admittedly somewhat atypical of this era. In 1842 William and his kinsman Daniel R. Knight jointly paid a town tax of $2.86, placing them in the eighty-fifth percentile among the town's population.[29] Clearly, most local farmers could not match the size of the Knights' operation. Judging from probate inventories, average holdings of cows may have actually declined slightly between the 1780s and 1830s, as population growth reduced the average size of local farmsteads, and households turned to industrial by-employments as alternative sources of income.[30] In all likelihood, dairying commercialized slowly and unevenly in northwestern Rhode Island. For years the success of farmers like the Knights would stand in contrast to their poorer neighbors, many of whom were too marginal to compete in a commercializing economy. The future lay with the Knights, whose substantial sales were made possible by the arrival of cotton factories and their stores.[31]

To a lesser extent, farmers also began to market quantities of poultry and beef. Chicken and beef cattle were never owned by large numbers of northwesterners; but when they were, it was usually for commercial purposes: eggs, poultry meat, and beef were considerably more marketable than commoner fare, such as pork. In addition to the aforementioned butter, William Knight often sold chickens and turkeys to store owner Emanuel Rice. Sales usually occurred in the fall and winter, just as milk production began to dwindle. From October 1839 through January 1840, Knight sold Rice eighteen turkeys and forty-nine chickens, weighing a total of approximately 230 pounds. Although not typical of northwestern farmers, Knight's poultry business was by no means unique. Probate inventories reveal a slight increase in poultry ownership, from 8 percent of all farmers in the 1780s to 12 percent in the 1830s. To take an especially remarkable example, when Stephen Walker of Coventry died in 1837, his estate included ten hens, fifty chickens, fourteen geese, and a small (and indeterminate) number of turkeys. Like Knight, Walker must have sold poultry on a commercial scale.[32]

Evidence for increased marketing of beef is a bit more sketchy. Certainly, beef production was always an important sideline of the dairy industry: young males and farrow cows were usually slaughtered for sale, since they obviously could not produce milk. An increase in dairying would therefore normally lead to an increase in beef available for the market. Northwestern farmers also seem to have turned to beef cattle as an end product of its own. More and more often, farmers allowed male cattle to mature into "steer," thus suggesting that they were finding a market for the sale of heavier, adult beef carcasses. The proportion of estates reporting steer at the time of probate increased markedly, from 25 percent in the 1780s to almost 40 percent by the 1830s. Local beef production would eventually succumb to competition from the West, later in the century; but in the meantime, it furnished an important source of income for a prosperous minority of northwestern farmers.[33]

As happened elsewhere in the hill towns of New England, farmers also profited from the sale of nonfood items, principally firewood and lumber. Most revealing is the number of sawmills in the area, which tripled between 1780 and 1840. The booming city of Providence encountered firewood shortages by the early 1800s. As prices skyrocketed, city residents even complained to the *Providence Gazette*, chastising farmers for charging exorbitant prices at the expense of "the poor." By at least the 1830s, firewood was considered valuable enough to be listed in northwestern probate inventories, a practice unheard of in the eighteenth century. And by 1840, total sales in the northwest reached over 16,000 cords.[34]

Still more important than firewood was the sale of lumber and lumber products. The burgeoning industries of greater Providence needed large quantities of all kinds of forest products: timber for constructing factories and other buildings, boards for making wagons, smaller pieces for barrels and implements. Many northwesterners were able to respond to this demand. Estate ownership of lumber more than doubled between the 1780s and 1830s, rising from 6 to 13 percent of all probate inventories. Moreover, the size of these holdings increased considerably. In the 1780s and 1790s, estate inventories of lumber were valued at an average of $12 each; in fifty years' time, inventory values rose 150 percent to over $30 each.[35]

William Knight sold large amounts of timber for the construction of local textile mills, supplementing his dairy and poultry earnings. In July 1844, he supplied the Hope Manufacturing Company with over 3,800 feet of beams for constructing the water-powered factory's "flume" and "wheel pit." Located in southeastern Scituate, near the site of the old Hope Furnace, the new mill continued to occupy Knight's energies throughout the fall and winter of 1844–1845. In November and December, he supplied over 1,400 feet of beam wood, and after a brief lull in orders, finished off the job in March with about 475 feet of beams and over 2,000 feet of planking. In succeeding years, he furnished somewhat smaller amounts of timber to the Quidneck mill in Coventry and the Natick mill in western Warwick. Knight's sales to the Hope factory alone probably amounted to over $150.[36]

Burrillville resident Hiram Salisbury also profited from lumber sales in the Providence industrial market, albeit on a somewhat more modest scale. A farmer and local officeholder of moderate importance, Salisbury also earned income from his trade as a carpenter. Early in his adulthood, in the 1810s and 1820s, he plied his skills in making tables, chests, and other custom-made items, usually for relatives and neighbors within his own community.[37] In the 1830s, however, he progressed to a more profitable trade in the Providence mass market. Manufacturers and merchants of all kinds needed barrels and casks for shipping their goods; and these could only be made from wooden "hoops." With Providence denuded of trees, demand for these mundane items stretched far out into the hinterland, where Salisbury was happy to oblige. He sold several loads of hoops in Providence between 1829 and 1837, yielding $16–$18 at a time in income. By 1841, near the end of his active career, he had graduated to more ambitious tasks: parlaying his political contacts into a contract for building a schoolhouse, and finally "hewing some factory beams for [the mill at] Blackstone."[38]

Dairy, poultry, and forest products thus formed the backbone of the farm family's economy; but this list was undoubtedly not an exclusive one. As noted above, local women were already weaving cloth for textile manufacturers. And although local records do not speak for northwestern Rhode Island in particular, elsewhere in the northern United States farmers participated in a boom in the sale of raw wool, while their wives were busy selling a variety of domestic manufactures, including palm-leaf hats, buttons, and stockings.[39] At any rate, to judge from the prevalence of transportation equipment, local farmers were marketing goods in general on a much greater scale in the 1830s than they had a half century before. As has already been shown, highway improvements allowed local haulers to shift from carts to larger wagons. More generally, ownership of all kinds of transportation equipment increased greatly in the early nineteenth century. In the 1780s, only 49 percent of all farmers owned carts and/or wagons, with carts making up over 90 percent of the total. But by the 1830s, almost three-fourths of them owned some form of transportation, and of those over 95 percent owned a wagon. Moreover, the inventory value of this equipment increased considerably, thus suggesting that vehicles were generally becoming more numerous, as well as larger and sturdier in quality. In the 1780s, the median value of transport holdings was only $8; by the 1830s, this had more than doubled to $17.[40] Attracted by the booming market in Rhode Island's industrial and commercial towns, northwestern farmers were hauling a vastly increased supply of goods—butter, beef, poultry, and lumber—to nearby factories, villages, and ports.

Storekeepers and the Development of Capitalist Relations

The income from these sales soon spurred farmers into purchasing an increasing variety of consumer goods. As has already been demonstrated, by the 1830s, many local residents owned a number of luxury goods—watches, jewelry, and imported furniture—that were scarcely heard of fifty years before. Just as noteworthy was the widespread diffusion of more mundane imported items, such as clothing and kitchenware. Even a marginal farmer, like James Dorrance of Foster, turned up with a probate inventory that included items of foreign, or nonlocal origin: eight or nine cotton sheets, silver cups and spoons, and a set of six "blue edged plates."[41] More significant, rural demand for these kinds of products introduced a new character to the rural economic scene: the independent store owner. Store owners had been attracted to the hinterland by the farmers' new wealth; and their entry was further eased by the arrival of cheap goods from industrializing Great Britain, especially after the War of 1812 ended, reopening Anglo-American trade. The storekeepers' impact in rural consumer spending was qualitative as well as quantitative; for in providing households with the comfort of manufactured consumables, the storekeepers eventually altered the very structure of the rural economy. They helped to introduce not only cheap dishware, but also growth in village life, specialization in production, and, most significant, a revolution in credit relationships.

In the eighteenth century, before the arrival of storekeepers, necessities that could not be produced within each household were furnished by means of a complicated system of local exchange. A shoemaker would sell his wares to a carpenter in exchange for furniture; the carpenter would exchange with a blacksmith for horseshoeing services; and all three might trade their products for pork or grain from the owner of a particular large and productive farm. Urban goods were seldom imported, usually by only a handful of commercially active farmers, who disseminated them sparsely to their poorer neighbors through a complex pattern of patron–client relations. Stores were located in only the largest villages, such as Chepachet.[42]

By contrast, artisanal and retail shops proliferated in the early decades of the nineteenth century. As has already been indicated, stores associated with nearby factories greatly increased the availability of consumer goods. But increasingly, northwesterners could also avail themselves of the wares of local, independent storekeepers. Hiram Salisbury's account book, for example, indicates that in addition to frequenting nearby factory stores, he often bought provisions at Job Armstrong's store in Chepachet.[43] In nearby Dudley and Oxford, Massachusetts, the number of "shops" counted by tax valuation increased from two in 1791 to eighteen in 1811. Local probate inventories, which revealed no store owners at all in the 1780s, turned up at least three probable owners who died in the early 1830s. By 1840, the towns of the northwest could claim about a dozen stores each.[44]

In addition to serving farmers' consumer desires, shopkeepers also organized rural household production; their access to credit allowed them to serve as intermediaries between city merchants and farm households in the domestic manufacture of cloth and hats. In the first two decades of the nineteenth century, textile companies in Rhode Island employed weaving outworkers directly, but after 1820, they increasingly operated through independent merchants and store owners. Freeman Jones of Foster, for example, put out weaving work among several local women in the mid-1820s. When power looms eventually replaced textile outwork altogether, store owners turned instead to organizing the domestic manufacture of hats, buttons, and bonnets.[45] In general, by the 1830s, commercial trading patterns had reached a new level of sophistication, as specialized storekeepers emerged to service the consumer desires and productive capacities of an increasingly commercialized farm population.

The proliferation of shops through commercial specialization also resulted in the rapid growth of hamlets and villages. Crossroads hamlets were certainly not unknown to the northwest before the 1830s; each town had one or two of them as early as the 1780s. But by the 1830s, the number of these settlements had doubled or tripled and was thus growing at a rate all out of proportion to the general population. In addition, locales like Chepachet that were once mere hamlets had sprouted to village size. True, the greatest concentration of new urban areas occurred in the industrial areas of Coventry and Scituate, where Washington, Arkwright, Anthony, Hope, Fiskeville, and North Scituate all sprang up around local textile mills. Yet even in agrarian Foster, new villages continually developed during the first third of the nineteenth century. In the 1780s, village life in Foster was confined to the tiny hamlets of Hopkins Mills and Foster Centre. Fifty years later, these two had grown into sizeable villages, to which were added Mount Vernon, Clayville, North Foster, and Moosup Valley.

Located generally along Foster's new turnpikes, the new villages serviced the needs of both local farmers and regional travelers. They usually concentrated around a general store or tavern but might also have included a post office, a church, and a variety of artisanal shops or mills. Foster Centre (also known as Hemlock Village) grew up at the intersection of several important roads. By 1830 it could boast of a large store, an apothecary shop, a hotel, physician's office, and several substantial artisanal shops.[46] Villages like Foster Centre emerged, essentially, because increased demand for artisanal, retail, and other services allowed for the establishment of specialized shops. Where once practitioners of these trades had to run their artisanry as a sideline to a family farm, they now could sell the farm, move to a crossroads, and set up a specialized and independent business. The commercialization of the northwest's rural economy resulted, in short, in the beginnings of urban life.

Eventually, the process of specialization became almost self-sustaining because farmers themselves were becoming increasingly specialized as pure producers of foodstuffs and lumber. The establishment of factories, independent tradespeople, and village shops allowed farmers to purchase from afar products they had once made themselves or purchased from neighbors. As an example, farmers bought thread and cloth, instead of producing it on their own. Probate inventories from the 1830s reveal a steep decline in domestic textile manufacturing. Many households still owned looms or spinning wheels, but incidence of ownership had fallen to 66 percent, from 85 percent in the 1780s. The spinning trade was particularly affected: ownership of the inex-

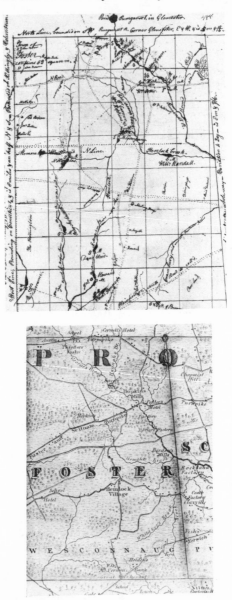

Figures 5 and 6. These maps reveal economic and demographic growth in the town of Foster. Above, the Plan of the town of Foster *(1799) shows the proliferation of sawmills (SM) and gristmills (GM); below, a detail from James Stevens'* Topographical Map of the State of Rhode Island and Providence Plantations *(1831) reveals the later emergence of the villages of Hopkins Mills, Hemlock Village (Foster Centre), Mt. Vernon, and, on the Scituate border, Clayville. Courtesy of Rhode Island Historical Society.*

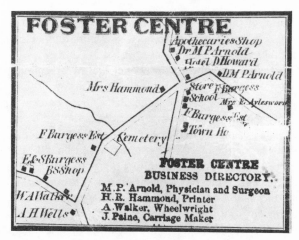

Figure 7. Map of Foster Centre *(1862) shows the growth of commercial, artisanal, and professional services. Detail from Henry F. Walling,* Map of the State of Rhode Island and Providence Plantations. *Courtesy of Rhode Island Historical Society.*

pensive wheels, which was almost universal at 80 percent of the population in the 1780s, fell to 57 percent by the 1830s. Looms, on the other hand, almost held their own because weaving had only recently been mechanized in local factories. Ownership of this complex and expensive tool remained at just under half of all inventories. Still, the value of domestic textile equipment, both wheels and looms, declined precipitously in this period. Probate inventories of textile implements had a median value of $5.00 in the 1780s; but by the 1830s, this had dropped to only $1.90, suggesting that the decedents' wheels and looms were either old and dilapidated or simply valued poorly in a new age of vastly more efficient factory production.[47]

In addition to abandoning domestic manufactures, farmers began to specialize in the area of husbandry. After an early-century boom in wool production, sheep ownership declined, as farmers shifted from wearing homespun wool to factory-produced cotton.[48] Pork production also began to diminish rapidly. Pigs were extremely common in the precommercial world of the 1780s; they were owned by 73 percent of all households, almost as high as a corresponding 76 percent figure for cows. Pig raising, after all, meshed well with the cultural norms and social realities of a semisubsistence economy. Unlike cattle, pigs can eat almost any kind of vegetation and could thus be raised to maturity simply by being allowed to run loose to graze on the wild and ample bushes and grasses of backcountry Rhode Island. Land was plentiful for all in the 1780s, even for those who owned little in freehold, thanks to the persistence of traditional notions about common grazing rights. True, pork was not an attractive commodity for the merchants of Providence, but the yeomen of the 1780s were probably more concerned with their own food needs, and those of their immediate neighbors. Besides, with labor in short supply, pigs must have been preferred over the more temperamental cows by many a household.[49]

On the other hand, once the northwest's economy had commercialized and its population increased, pigs began to fall into disfavor. From 73 percent in the 1780s, pig ownership by all households fell to 44 percent by the 1830s. Even among households identified as farmers, pigs showed up in only 61 percent of all probate inventories in the 1830s, a sharp decline from an 82 percent figure of a half-century before. Moreover, for those who did own swine, mean holdings dropped by over one-third, from 3.6 pigs to only 2.3.[50] In the 1780s, pork would have been a valued commodity, not only for the farm families' own consumption, but also for that of the neighbors with whom the farmers bartered and wrangled for a few basic needs. But by the 1830s, as farmers were enticed by the glittering luxuries of the urban market, and as nearby shopkeepers increasingly monopolized the local retail trade, the farmers were required by market demand to specialize in cows and cattle, the emerging mainstays of northwestern agriculture.

The demands of local shopkeepers and urban merchants helped to shape the nature of the farmers' agricultural output; just as fundamentally they also produced a revolution in credit relations. Indirect payment by book account, the traditional barterlike system of the s subsistence 1780s, was replaced by the direct exchange of notes of hand or cash. In the system of local exchange between relatively undifferentiated producers, which had prevailed in the 1780s, payment by book could satisfy the needs of most buyers and sellers. The shopkeepers of the 1830s, on the other hand, had little use for the book credits of local farmers. They could hardly offer such a credit in exchange for purchasing supplies from a Providence merchant. Instead, they began to require payment in cash, or in a secure note of hand, from their local customers. And for those farmers who had turned away from subsistence goods, like pork and textiles, to the more commercially favored butter and lumber, cash became more and more available in turn. Indeed, although the impetus for modernizing credit transactions came most directly from those who were especially vulnerable to a financial contraction—the storekeepers—cash and notes of hand eventually transfused many levels of northwestern society, from the mill owners of eastern Coventry to some of the poorest of the common field laborers.

In its broadest outlines, the credit revolution of the early Republic encompassed a sharp increase in the availability of cash, and in the formality and simplicity of debtor–creditor relations. The presence in probate inventories of "cash," "specie," or other forms of liquidity jumped markedly. About 46 percent of all households possessed at least some level of liquidity in the 1830s, nearly double the level of 26 percent in the 1780s. More striking was the increase in the size of cash holdings. Median liquidity levels for all households jumped almost sevenfold, from a paltry $3.67 to $21.50, while mean holdings increased still more dramatically from $12.60 to almost $150.00. Some died holding huge amounts of cash, upwards of $500 or even $1,000. Although manufacturers and merchants accounted for most of the largest holdings, seven "farmers," out of a total of seventy-two, owned over $100, and one died with $565 in cash. In contrast, the largest liquidity cache of the revolutionary era was only $58.67.[51] As a sidelight, reported inventories of "specie" actually declined by the 1830s, a development that suggests that "cash" had become so pervasive that it made ownership of "hard money" simply unnecessary.

While cash was becoming more prevalent, indebtedness was turning into an increasingly more formal financial relationship. In the semisubsistence world of the 1780s, "borrowing" usually occurred by means of simple book credit. When a blacksmith purchased grain from a farmer, he was in effect borrowing the value of the grain, because no cash exchanged hands. This suited the farmer because he could anticipate "repayment" in the form of horseshoes from the blacksmith, or in the form of some third party's goods and services. These debt patterns were at once extremely complex, because nearly everyone was both a creditor and a debtor, and also highly informal. Book accounts rarely charged interest, and, indeed, usually recorded only credits, as each person trusted their exchange partners to faithfully account for their debits. Even on the less common notes of hand, interest did not accrue for loans of under a year's duration.

By the 1830s, however, debt relations had changed considerably. Book accounts became more formal, as rural inhabitants adopted debit and credit—or double entry—systems of accounting. Both "book" and third-party debts also declined in frequency, to be replaced by interest-bearing notes of hand. Notes were present in 47 percent of all revolutionary-era inventories, a figure that increased to 59 percent by the 1830s. The total value of decedents' notes grew even more rapidly, from a median of $57.70 to over $160.00. Interest on notes, which had been charged in only a quarter of all probated estates in the 1780s, was now applied universally. The increasing availability of cash to some members of northwestern society probably made borrowing less and less necessary: but when debts were incurred, they tended to be simpler, more formal, and more costly in their execution.[52]

These changes in credit relations occurred slowly and unevenly, coming into place during the first three or four decades of the nineteenth century. In the early years of this period, a cash economy encompassed only a very few individuals in northwestern Rhode Island. When Theodore Foster settled in the area in the 1800s, he brought with him an easy access to cash and credit, which, although extraordinary to his new neighbors, was rather common for a member of Providence's mercantile class. Between 1801 and 1808, he listed in his account book over $1,650 in purchases. For these he paid $909 in cash and $712 in interest-bearing notes, well over 95 percent of the total. In addition to being extraordinarily liquid, Foster's credit arrangements were also rather short-lived. Unlike the book accounts of his neighbors in the northwest, which often remained open for seasons or even years at a time, Foster always settled his debts within the space of one or two months. Little wonder, then, that the northwestern yeomen greeted Foster and his modernizing dreams with a mixture of pleasure and uneasiness: although certainly beneficial, in a small way, to the local economy, Foster's spending and credit habits were decades ahead of his cash-poor rural neighbors.[53]

Although Foster's cash expenditures may have helped to loosen the credit relations of the backwoods economy, more important contributions came from the financial demands of the area's growing collection of shopkeepers. As a first step, storekeepers began to introduce the more formal practice of recording both credits and debits in their account books. When Freeman Jones of Foster opened his store in 1824, he immediately adopted a fairly consistent, albeit syntactically imprecise, double-entry accounting system.[54] Store owners also sought to reduce the number of third-party credits that they accepted in payment for debts. Farmers increasingly paid off their debts directly, instead of through an intermediary debtor, thereby sparing storekeepers from the burden of keeping track of complex credit relations. A storekeeper in Fitzwilliam County, New Hampshire, for example, reduced third-party payments from nearly one-half to 27 percent of all credits between 1830 and 1850. In northwestern Rhode Island, this development probably occurred still earlier, due to its proximity to the commercially dynamic Providence area.[55]

Finally, storekeepers succeeded in demanding cash, or at the very least, interest-bearing notes, instead of book credit and eventual payment in kind. Already initiated by the mid-1830s, at least in parts of rural Rhode Island, this development was accelerated nationwide in the aftermath of the depression of 1839. As always the most vulnerable to financial contractions, storekeepers went bankrupt in this period almost as often as they survived. Caught between the credit demands of their urban suppliers and the traditionalist expectations of their customers, they realized that the latter had to change. They started to require payment in cash, or by note payable in three months, instead of the customary year without interest. The same New Hampshire trader who in the 1830s and 1840s nearly halved his third-party receipts also increased the value of his cash receipts from 7 to 26 percent, while his notes income held steady at about 11 percent. In northwestern Rhode Island, this transformation may have occurred even earlier: Freeman Jones's store income in the mid-1820s was already 16 percent cash; by the late 1840s, a Chepachet trader, Jesse Potter, was dealing almost exclusively in currency.[56]

Eventually, farmers themselves adopted these more formal and cash-oriented business procedures. When Asa Steere, a Glocester farmer, recorded his accounts in the 1820s, he stuck fast to the traditional rural practice of noting credits only. But soon after his kinsman Samuel Steere took over the same book in the 1830s, the latter began to fill in the debits side of his trans-actions as well. Double-entry recording, which still occurred in only one-sixth of his accounts in the 1830s, increased to two-thirds by the 1840s and became universal after 1850.[57]

In the meantime, commercially oriented farmers were receiving and spend-ing cash and notes in increasingly larger and more regular amounts. When Hiram Salisbury first began to sell hoops in Providence, in the winter of 1828–1829, he appears to have received only book credit toward the purchase of store goods; as he noted in his daybook, on December 24, "I give away my hoops and get bbl. [barrel] of flour $6.00 . . . [and] 4 gals N.E. rum" for a total of $11.89. Within eight years, however, the financial terms of his trade seem to have been substantially altered. The simplicity of his notation on No-vember 28, 1837, "I . . . sell my hoops for $18.00," suggests that he received only cash in exchange. His return trip in February 1838 produced $16.00 under identical monetary arrangements.[58]

The trend toward cash and note accounting occurred most noticeably for large farms located relatively close to urban or mill-town markets. Dwarfing Salisbury's cash income were the transactions between the dairy farmer Wil-liam Knight and the Sprague brothers' textile firm. Recorded in proper credit and form, Knight's records show that in 1839 he sold the Spragues $270.60 in butter, for which he received $33.24 in kind, $55.00 in cash, and the re-mainder by note. Knight, in turn, was able to begin paying his laborers mostly in cash: in the following year, he paid Philip A. Colvin $76.00 in cash out of a total wage bill of $81.63. On the other hand, farmers with weaker market connections, or relatively modest operations, did not enjoy the benefits of a cash economy until much later. In the early 1840s, Samuel Steere of Gloces-ter, a farmer of below-average wealth, still paid or received cash for only a fraction of his accounts. The decades of the 1830s and 1840s seem to have been a transition period, in which the appearance of modern financial trans-actions occurred unevenly throughout the northwest.[59]

The coming of capitalist agriculture to rural Rhode Island is most dramat-ically and thoroughly revealed in the account book of the family of John Wa-terman, the west Warwick–area farmer who traded frequently with the factory stores of the Pawtuxet River valley. Spanning almost fifty years between 1790 and 1836, Waterman's records illustrate the process by which the complex, interlocking book-credit system of the eighteenth century was replaced by a series of single accounts between specialized producers and cash- or credit-paying customers.[60]

Beginning as the records of John's father, William, who preceded him as the owner of the family's farm, the accounts in the 1790s reveal all of the classic patterns of semisubsistence farming, recording credits only for a wide variety of goods, labor services, and third-party payments. William's accounts often remained unsettled for many months or even years at a time; and even though he was one of the area's wealthier farmers,[61] they rarely mentioned payment by cash. Important changes first begin to surface in 1812, when, after a gap of about ten years, the account book resumes under John's name.[62] By this time John was hiring laborers at the steady rate of about one per year, and he was able to pay them partly in simple cash, in addition to the in-kind or third-party payments. Still, traditional accounts with other farmers, worth $17.20 per year, continued to intermingle alongside his laborers' accounts. Consisting of the usual blend of food and carting and plowing services, these accounts reveal that the old world of complex, reciprocal relations had yet to disappear.

Steadily at first in the 1820s, and then dramatically in the 1830s, Waterman completed the commercialization of his farming practice and the modernization of his accounting procedures. Exchanges with neighboring farmers diminished considerably in the 1820s, to an average $10 per year, before disappearing altogether in the following decade, thus turning the record book into a specialized volume of laborers' accounts. The latter, in the meantime, continued to grow in importance, as a prospering Waterman was able to add two more employees to his work force.[63] Following the pattern of contemporary storekeepers, he reduced his third-party payments to his workers, paying them instead with his own goods, and, increasingly, with cash. For a brief period in the early 1830s, due perhaps to a local financial panic, Waterman's cash wages decreased markedly, while third-party payments rebounded. But soon thereafter, cash payments suddenly mushroomed, while the latter fell to nothing. He paid 41 percent of his wages in cash in 1833, a figure that rose to over 80 percent in 1834, to 90 percent in 1835, and finally to over 97 percent in 1836. Clearly, Waterman must have suddenly begun receiving sizeable sums of cash from local storekeepers and other purchasers of his agricultural produce.

Together with developments seen in other northwestern farms, the changes in Waterman's account book suggest that agriculture commercialized at an accelerating rate in the first third of the nineteenth century, thereby transforming the very structure of financial relationships in the rural northwest. For those farmers who were capable of specializing in dairy and other marketable products, sales expanded in this period, especially during the 1830s, when Rhode Island's nearby textile industry grew more rapidly than ever before.[64] As a sizeable trade developed, local storekeepers proliferated in number and importance, taking advantage of their access to urban credit; some of them, factory owners as well, were especially prominent. The storekeepers helped to further channel rural production into market-oriented directions. Some households, probably the lesser ones, turned for a time to the production of household textiles, in order to avail themselves of a storekeeper's goods. A more stable source of income came for those farmers, usually the larger ones, who were able to specialize in dairy, beef, poultry, and timber production.

More dependent now on stores for their supplies, rural households traded less and less often with their neighbors. In the meantime, responding to creditors' demands for greater liquidity, storekeepers and farmers alike untangled a pre-existing set of complex and interlocking credit relations: third-party payments diminished, while usury-free book credits were replaced by formal, interest-bearing notes, and eventually, by cash.

Although many of these changes occurred slowly and gradually, since they required a fundamental restructuring of rural production and trade, the final transition to a cash basis may have occurred rather suddenly, as Waterman's account book suggests. Between 1800 and about 1840, the northwest seems to have existed on the edge of a cash economy. Improved access to currency, from both store owners and urban interlopers like Theodore Foster, existed side by side with the maintenance of traditional credit and local trading rela-tionships. But eventually, in the face of periodic credit contractions of growing severity, this contradiction could no longer be maintained. At some point, creditors must have determined that only cash or notes would be accepted as a necessarily liquid form of exchange; and of course for those farmers who could produce meaningfully for the market, creditors would provide cash in return. For the area in which John Waterman lived, the panic of 1830 may have provided the impetus for a sudden conversion to a largely cash economy; in the more interior, less commercialized portions of the northwest, and else-where in New England, this transition may not have occurred until after the nationwide depression of the late 1830s. In either case, for those shopkeepers who survived the initial panic, the eventual return of prosperity allowed them to effect a revolution in rural credit relations. By the 1840s, farmers and shop-keepers together had created a cash economy in the rural northwest, an area that two generations before had been inured in the localized, barterlike trans-actions of general subsistence agriculture.

The Social Transformation of Traditional Household Society

The development of a more liquid and market-oriented economy consid-erably altered the social structure of the rural northwest, loosening and trans-forming the social bonds of traditional household society. In the eighteenth century rural society consisted of, and was viewed by contemporaries as a collection of "little commonwealths," or households, each headed by a male, independent proprietor. These households were fairly stable, geographically, and were relatively equal in status, if not in wealth. Men and women in society related to each other as members of one of these sturdy little structures. Men who were too young or too poor to form a household of their own belonged as sons or as laborers to a more viable "commonwealth." Of course, they would eventually move on, either to another farm set up by their father, or off in search of one of their own; but the original farm unit remained intact. As for women, whether they were wives or unmarried daughters, they contributed in essential ways to the family economy, chiefly through textile work and a few prescribed farm chores such as milking cows and feeding chickens. But their contribution always lay within a household, dominated by a husband, father, or master. Possibilities for making a living independent of this arrangement were almost nonexistent. In sum, households themselves were stable and relatively undifferentiated, and within them roles were well defined, allowing for little by way of independence or specialization.[65]

The leavening force of the northwest's emerging market economy left the old system of patriarchal households in disarray. Households lost their stable moorings as family heads, as well as sons and workers, moved about geographically with increasing velocity. In addition, households began to develop specialized roles. Whereas once almost all were farmers, even if practicing a trade on the side, by the 1830s, store owners, mill owners, and shopkeepers emerged as specialized household units. Finally, households lost their monopoly on the means by which men and women interacted with each other. A somewhat permanent class of farm laborers began to emerge, where once these workers were merely temporary members of independent households. Perhaps more important, women began to become separated from the family economy; they began to assume distinctive social roles, instead of serving largely as contributing adjuncts to each farming operation. As the market economy opened up new opportunities for individuals to succeed, as well as to fail, a profusion of new social and economic roles developed, freeing men and women from the stable strictures of a household society.[66]

Between 1780 and 1830, northwestern society became considerably more mobile geographically. In the eighteenth century, households were remarkably stable, once they settled on a farm in a particular area. This was especially true of the wealthier households. Of those households that were listed in the top two fifths of Foster's 1782 tax list, over three-quarters were still town residents ten years later. If one takes into account departures due to death, then only about one-tenth of these families moved voluntarily in each decade. Only the poorest and largely landless moved about frequently. In the semisubsistence economy of the 1780s, they would have few resources with which to care for their families. Established landowners, on the other hand, seem to have had little reason to move.[67]

By the 1820s this pattern had altered significantly. The rural population in general became much more mobile. Decadal persistence rates for Foster fell from 62 to 38 percent; in Coventry where greater opportunities existed, persistence was somewhat higher, at 48 percent. Even in the tumultuous world of contemporary Boston, families were no more unstable. By this time, moreover, geographic mobility had come to cut across all levels of wealth. Poorer families were still more likely than prosperous ones to move out of town; but differences between economic groupings narrowed significantly. In the 1780s, the wealthiest fifth of all households were nearly twice as stable as the poorest fifth. By the 1820s, they were 65 percent more stable in Foster, and only 48 percent more stable in Coventry.[68] The growth of a market economy, it seems, generated enough opportunities to attract even the most prosperous families into moving in and out of the towns of northwestern Rhode Island. In the 1780s, households moved about primarily because they had to, lacking the requisite land for forging a living in an agrarian economy. By the 1820s, north-westerners, and probably Americans everywhere, were moving more often, in the hope of better opportunities elsewhere.

Household heads not only began to move about more frequently; they also developed more distinctive roles. We have already described the emergence of specialized, village occupations, such as store owners and artisanal tradespeople. Still further distinctions were produced by the changing structure of credit. Creditors began to emerge as a more identifiable grouping in northwestern society. In the eighteenth century, debt patterns were extremely complex, as many people at any one time both borrowed from and loaned money to a large number of nearby residents. Of course, wealthier households tended to be greater net creditors, but they still owed money to others within the community. By the 1830s, on the other hand, storekeepers and banks began to provide a distinctively larger share of local credit. As revealed in the accounts of probate records, a few individuals or firms continually turned up as creditors to decedents' estates. In a sample of fourteen estates from the town of Glocester, the Franklin Bank and shopkeeper Ira P. Evans appeared as creditors five times each, while Chepachet store owner Job Armstrong was listed in four different estates. In the meantime, the average farmer was falling deeper in debt, especially in the 1810s and 1820s, when population pressures crested.[69]

Eventually, these changes in debt patterns may have effected the very proceedings by which probate courts conducted their business. Overwhelmed by the problem of settling nearly bankrupted estates, while operating in an era of stricter and more formal controls on credit, family members increasingly refused to administer decedents' estates, forcing probate courts to appoint non-kin in their stead. In the 1780s, over 90 percent of all intestate estates were administered by a family member. By the 1830s, this proportion had fallen to just 50 percent. The trend was especially pronounced for poorer estates, those that might be particularly hard-pressed to pay off debts.[70]

In about a third of cases for which information is available, the administrator appointed was a creditor of the estate, as was traditionally required by state law when family members refused the responsibility. But even creditors appear to have refused administration duty. In another one-third of all cases, a man was chosen who seemed to specialize in administering estates. Between 1830 and 1834, fifteen different intestates were administered by just six different people, none of whom was related to the deceased. Since these individuals were almost never creditors themselves, they were probably selected for their relative social standing, and increasingly, perhaps, for their knowledge of the law.[71] Thus, the growing formality of indebtedness together with the emergence of distinctive classes of debtors and creditors combined to encourage a further erosion in the old household structure of society. Probate administration, which had formerly been conducted almost exclusively by family relations, was increasingly being taken over by yet another, somewhat specialized figure: the court-appointed expert. In the not-too-distant future, perhaps, even lawyers would become attracted in substantial numbers to the once bucolic land of northwestern Rhode Island.

In the meantime, farm laborers increased in number and became separated from the household structure of society. The increase in farm laborers occurred within the context of growing social and economic inequality. Farm population growth subsided after 1820, but it had already squeezed many local residents out of an inherited estate. Many landless or nearly landless and impoverished households appeared in the probate inventories of the 1830s. While the median value of probate inventories increased by over 30 percent from the 1780s, and the mean skyrocketed from about $360 to over $1,200, a large number continued to leave behind only the smallest of personal estates. The lowest 10 percent of all estates were actually somewhat poorer in the 1830s than in the 1780s.[72] Alongside the success of John Waterman must be placed the case of Ezekiel Bishop, a marginal farmer in Scituate, who died in his fifties, leaving to his wife and four children an estate worth only $53, including, as its sole productive materials, one "hog," a woolen spinning wheel, and an "old loom."[73] True, as measured by tax valuations, property distribution remained relatively unchanged. In the 1830s, as in the 1780s, the poorest fifth owned about 3 percent of its wealth, while the richest fifth owned a little over half. But tax lists do not include the many landless, whose numbers increased by 140 percent while the population as a whole climbed by 84 percent. About three-tenths of all adult males owned no property in the 1780s, a proportion that rose to almost one-half by the 1830s. Although much of this increase occurred in the industrial towns of Coventry and Scituate, even in the still overwhelmingly rural towns of Foster and Burrillville landlessness rose to 40 percent.[74]

The growth of the class of landless men, women, and children had both a quantitative and a qualitative effect on the structure of farm labor. First of all, and most obvious, the supply of labor grew, benefiting those who operated sizeable farms. Wage rates on the Waterman family farm fell from $9 in 1814 and $11 in 1818 to $5 in 1829, outpacing a contemporary price decline by 72 percent.[75] Partly as a result of this trend, the Watermans' labor force increased from no regular workers in the 1790s, to one a year in the early 1810s, and finally to three by the late 1830s, thereby increasing their potential agricultural production.[76] Perhaps more important, the coming of a cash economy must have changed the quality of Waterman's relationship with his laborers. As long as he paid wages in kind or by purchases from a factory store, Waterman could help supervise the lifestyle of his employees. This sort of paternalistic responsibility would have ended, however, as soon as laborers began to experience the sense of independence engendered by the possession of cash. Evidence from elsewhere in New England suggests that other forms of paternalistic behavior were eroding as well. Farmers began to economize by hiring workers for only a short season instead of a full year. And where once laborers were treated almost as members of the farm family, increasingly they were not even allowed "to sit at [the dinner] table with the family."[77]

In a somewhat similar fashion, paupers were also becoming separated from household structures. In eighteenth-century rural society, poor relief usually entailed placing paupers singly or in small groups in the households of neighboring families. But in the early nineteenth century, northwestern towns began instead to auction off their paupers en masse to a single bidder. Initiated originally as an economizing reform, this policy presaged the creation of poorhouses, and thus the complete removal of poor relief from the context of a household economy.[78] The coming of a cash-oriented, commercialized economy may have increased wage-earning opportunities for the northwest's landless men, women, and children; but at the same time it served to further separate their interests and lifestyles from those of their employers and caretakers.

Finally, women in the rural northwest began to assume an identity of their own, apart from the structure of the household economy. Two different sorts of identities developed, depending on whether one was a married or unmarried woman. Unmarried women, for the first time, became household heads in significantly large numbers. Female-headed households surfaced most obviously on tax rolls, whereas in the 1780s they were almost nonexistent. By the early 1820s, 4 percent of all taxpayers were women, chiefly widows; and by the 1840s, this figure had nearly doubled to 7 percent.[79] To a large extent, this development was the result of an increasing gender imbalance in the local population. As often happened in a maturing rural society, the ratio of women to men increased in the early nineteenth century, especially for the older age groups. In the 1780s, women over forty-five were less numerous than men of the same age. But by 1800, the sex ratio had shifted to 1.05 in favor of women, and by 1820 to 1.11. In short, where widows were once in demand for a speedy remarriage, they now might spend the rest of their lives as single women, without direct support from a husband.[80]

Nevertheless, this does not mean that a widow's economic status was necessarily bleak or even unfortunate. As measured by tax rolls between 1780 and 1820, their livelihood fell only slightly in comparison to the male population. The proportion of female taxpayers ranking in the bottom fifth of all tax rolls rose from 36 percent in the 1780s to 38 percent in 1822, and to 42 percent twenty years thereafter. In the meantime, the value of female probate inventories as a percentage of male inventories fell from 67 percent to 53 percent.[81] What is remarkable, however, is that widows' status did not fall more steeply, given the significant decline that was also occurring in the availability of marriageable men.

In fact, their opportunities for living independently were actually growing, thanks to the contemporary development of a more liquid and market-oriented economy. To be sure, these opportunities did not lie in occupations that were, or were becoming, traditionally masculine. Although most owned land, very few of the widows attempted to operate a farm. Only 21 percent of them had more than one son in their household to assist them with farming, and a third had no male householders at all. Moreover, less than half of the widows' households had a member "employed," as defined by the federal census of 1820.[82] If anything, female participation in agriculture was declining substantially. Female-headed households had always owned fewer livestock than their more numerous male counterparts, but in the early nineteenth century this discrepancy widened considerably. In the 1780s, widows' probate inventories of livestock were about half the value of male inventories; by the 1830s, this fraction had fallen to only three-tenths. In the earlier period, women owned at least one cow almost as often as men (62.5% vs. 70%); in the next fifty years, cow ownership among female estates fell by one-half, to 32 percent, while the figure for men held steady.[83]

Female income in the early 1800s depended more on a variety of other sources that had emerged along with the northwest's commercializing economy. The industrial revolution, of course, created many jobs for women in factories, although these were mostly for girls who still lived at home or were under some form of patriarchal supervision. Manufacturing opportunities for older, independent women came more in the area of textile outwork. In the 1830s, occupation as a seamstress furnished Lydia Allen, of North Scituate, with a fairly independent livelihood, before marriage eventuated in her removal to Providence.[84]

More important, especially for the northwest's growing population of widows, was the creation through commercialization of a more formal and liquid credit system. Women had always been net creditors in the rural north, because they continually sold or rented land that they had inherited but could not farm themselves. Once interest became more readily chargeable on loans, they were able to exploit their creditor position much more thoroughly. Between the 1780s and 1830s, female holdings of notes of hand rose twelvefold, much faster than the rate for men. Possession of cash also skyrocketed, from an average of next to nothing to $20 per estate, rivaling the size of male holdings, even though the total value of men's estates remained much greater. In fact, by the 1830s, credits of all kinds constituted, on average, 28 percent of each widow's personal property, a figure much higher than the median male figure of 10 percent.[85] Thus, widows who owned land but did not farm could make a living by either renting it or selling it in return for mortgage interest. This may have been less lucrative than farming for the market, but then widows' needs were probably small: their average household size was only three, meaning few mouths to feed and bodies to warm or clothe.[86] The creation of a more modern credit system thus allowed for the beginnings of a separate and independent class of women: the rural widowed proprietor.

In the meantime, rural married women were beginning to become divorced from their own household's economy. In urban areas this pattern had already developed dramatically, at least for the middle class: when the advent of mercantile manufacturing led men to expand their shops, they eventually located their growing businesses outside of the confines of their homes, thus leaving their wives behind. In rural areas, trends in women's economic roles were less pronounced. The advent of factory-produced clothing relieved farm wives, as well as city women, from the tedium of spinning and weaving. To some extent, this was replaced by women's work as butter churners in the northwest's growing dairy economy; and women continued to feed chickens and grow vegetables for minor sales on the side.[87] But the preponderance of available evidence suggests that female involvement in the business of farming was declining. If probate inventories showed that widows were dying with fewer and fewer cows, pigs, and sheep in their possession, this data certainly suggests that wives as well were spending less time managing these animals and other aspects of a farm's operation.

More indirectly, changes in the administration of male estates suggests that wives were in general becoming excluded from the management of their husbands' property. The appointment of kin as administrators had declined rapidly during the early years of the Republic as probate courts selected non-related creditors and specialists in their place. As it turns out, nearly all of this decline came at the expense of widows; whereas formerly they adminstered 54 percent of all estates, by the 1830s this proportion had declined to only 14 percent. Husbands also named wives less often in their wills as executors. Widows executed about 37 percent of all wills in the 1780s, either on their own or jointly with a male kin or friend. In the 1830s, wives were selected to be executors just 20 percent of the time. Significantly, this occurred in only the poorest of households, where little property was at risk. Although certainly not yet purely housewives, as their urban counterparts were fast becoming, farm women were withdrawing increasingly from the rural men's world of cattle, crops, and lumber.[88]

The development of independence among widows and dependence among rural wives was both reflected in and furthered by changes in their husbands' testamentary behavior. In the 1780s, treatment of wives in inheritance usually followed certain specifically defined patterns. If a man died intestate, the law in Rhode Island and throughout English territories called for his widow to receive, as a life estate, the profits of or control over one-third of his real property. Many men wrote wills in order to alter the rules for intestacy, but they did so largely as a means of finagling with their sons' portions. They left their widows' customary portions unchanged, and many even invoked the usual language about giving the "power of thirds." Only about 38 percent appear to have willed more or less than a third.[89]

In the next fifty years, this pattern altered in two significant ways. While fewer men wrote wills,[90] those who did sought more frequently to increase or diminish their widows' inheritance from the usual rule of thirds. About 30 percent of all testament writers allocated less than a third: in a period in which population pressures continued to jeopardize farmers' hold on their land, it was always tempting for them to favor their sons at the expense of their widows' portions. But somewhat more often, in about 40 percent of all cases, husbands chose to bequeath a larger share of their estate to their surviving wives. In a few cases, men chose an extraordinarily modern manner in which to devise their estate, in terms of both the sophistication of their financial instruments and the preference with which they treated their wives over their children. When Pardon Holden devised his will in 1832, he bequeathed to his wife all the interest from the $1,540 of Mount Vernon Bank stock that made up most of his estate. His sons and daughters would not inherit until his wife died, or, more important, remarried.[91]

This brings us to a second departure from normal testamentary behavior: increasingly, men willed that their wives would lose their inheritance if they should remarry. In the 1780s only 29 percent of all wills required that widows forfeit their property upon remarriage; by the 1830s, this proportion had risen to 40 percent. The trend toward restrictions on remarriage was particularly pronounced among the northwest's wealthier husbands: the median inventory total for customarily devised estates was $262; for those who tried to control their wife's remarriage, it was four times as high, at $1,150. Stated another way, in the case of men dying with above-average estate values, 70 percent wrote remarriage restrictions into their wills. Certainly, men who had a larger fortune at risk had a greater incentive to keep it within the family.[92]

But more was at stake here than a simple matter of crude financial interest. First of all, by being more generous in their bequests, and yet also more restrictive, men encouraged women to remain widowed, thus helping to further an already existing demographic trend. Second, and more fundamental, the trend toward generous-but-restrictive widows' portions is suggestive of an important change in one's conception of marriage, a change that was occurring in middle-class homes throughout the United States and western Europe. If a husband wished that his wife remain his widow, so much that he expresses that desire in his last will and testament, it implies that he views marriage less as an economic arrangement and more as a life partnership of important emotional significance. Preserving widowhood forever may have also enhanced the widow's emotional ties with her children; for she would become a more important steward of their inheritance, while they would receive a stronger share of her parental affection, unencumbered now by a new attachment to a later husband.[93] The increasing importance of affective ties further explains why wealthier husbands would prefer this mode of inheritance: in their more prosperous households, wives were most likely to have become relatively divorced from economic affairs, while also becoming more richly involved in the world of domesticity.

Although these trends in the status of widows and wives were still rather sketchy and halting, altogether they indicate that a "woman's sphere" had begun to emerge from the traditional homogeneity of patriarchal society. Wives seem to have withdrawn somewhat from the business of running the household economy. At the same time, they were being encouraged to develop more fully their role as the family's chief source of affection and emotional ties. Widows, on the other hand, were actually becoming more independent of men, in that they at least could maintain their own households. But their independence was of a particular sort, based largely on income from rent and interest, as well as occasional work in domestic industry. Whether they were newly independent widows or emerging proto-housewives, rural women were carving, and there was being carved for them, a separate and uniquely "feminine" set of familial and societal roles.

By around 1840, the economic and social structure of farm life in northwestern Rhode Island had reached a sort of halfway point in the evolution of the modern family farm. Claims about the extent of farm commercialization need to be juxtaposed alongside qualifying reminders about the endurance of an older rural order. Farmers were clearly producing for the market on an unprecedented scale, but they still clung somewhat to subsistence production in the areas of pig and sheep raising. Cash had thoroughly entered the local economy, where once it had been scarce; but it must be remembered that one-half of all farmers still died with none in their possession. Farmers in 1840 bought from stores many items that they had once produced themselves, yet they still owned spinning wheels and looms in sizeable numbers. They became more and more indebted to store owners and shopkeepers, but some still traded products and debts with each other. Rural households lost their monopoly on economic and social reproduction: laborers and the poor began to live apart from farmers, while specialized occupations, such as store owners, substantial artisans, and lawyers, proliferated. But these trends had only been partially effected. Finally, the withdrawal of women from the economy, a process that had recently occurred among urban, middle-class families, had just begun on the farm, reaching only the wealthier household units.

Still, for all these caveats about the extent of these social and economic transformations, what is truly remarkable is that much change occurred at all. Northwestern Rhode Island could never be a land of agricultural riches. Probate inventories reveal, after all, that the actual size of livestock inventories grew very little, if at all, between the 1780s and 1830s. Yet many farmers were able to use these bare resources in order to effect important qualitative changes in their economic livelihood and social relations: they employed more laborers, owned much more cash, and possessed many more consumer goods, some previously unheard of. By contrast, the rural world of the 1780s had been in many ways an almost peasant society: economically self-sufficient, geographically stable, socially unspecialized—and religiously localistic in the form of Six-Principle Baptism. As their spiritual task in the early nineteenth century, farmers would need to find a new religious ethos, one that would be more in tune with the requirements of a commercializing rural order.

CHAPTER FIVE

Religious and Cultural Transformation

▼ ▼

THE FIRST decades of the nineteenth century saw new religious movements and denominations emerge to challenge the preeminence of the traditional Baptist order in northwestern Rhode Island. Throughout the United States, this era was one of tremendous religious activity, and the rural northwest was hardly immune to the revivals it engendered. Missionaries from Providence and other nearby cities toured the countryside, seeking to convert its inhabitants from the twin evils of religious idiosyncrasy and spiritual indifference. Meanwhile, relatively new denominations developed from within, as a more or less spontaneous response to changing social and economic conditions. In short, the northwest's traditional Baptist sects suddenly had to compete with a number of other religious orders for the allegiance of local souls. But the most immediate cause of the traditional Baptists' relative decline lay, ironically, in the very reasons that had once contributed to their success.

A collection of localist Baptist churches, the most common of which were of the General-Redemption, Six-Principle variety, the traditional Baptist order had emerged in the eighteenth century as the dominant religious expression of the rural northwest. Its communal practices and antihierarchical beliefs closely reflected the needs of a society of interdependent, self-sufficient farmers. The Baptists of the northwest met in small familial groups, oftentimes in each other's homes; and they kept a close and watchful eye on each other's behavior. Relatively isolated from the workings of the colonial economy, they hewed closely to an unorthodox set of religious practices. Most notable, of course, was the laying on of hands—the "sixth principle" required for church membership. They also eschewed religious modernisms of all kinds, such as formalized hymn singing and a paid and educated clergy, preferring instead the rustic simplicity of the uncorrupted Word of God.

In their adherence to these intimate rituals and antimodern beliefs, the rural Baptists came into sharp conflict with the emerging religious ethos of eastern, commercial Rhode Island. In doing so, they came to structure their religion not only in terms of their own local needs, but also in defense against the cultural encroachment of a more powerful social class: the urban merchants. Oriented to the much wider world of oceanic commerce, the prospering merchants of Providence and other port towns could only have been embarrassed by the intimate rituals and crude illiteracy of the Six-Principle Baptists. Preferring a more urbane religious experience, they successfully purged unorthodox practices from the Baptist churches in their midst and by the 1770s had even taken control of the Six-Principle Baptist Association.

In reaction to these defeats, the rural Baptists withdrew defensively into the hinterland. In 1774 they formed a new General Six-Principle association, called the Baptist Yearly Meeting, through which they could protect the purity of their sectarian practices from the encroachment of urbane respectability. By the turn of the century, when the Six-Principle Baptists reached the height of their influence and preeminence, the association boasted a membership of twelve churches in Rhode Island and nearby Massachusetts. In spite of the inroads made by more urban forms of Baptist religion, they were then by far the largest denomination in Rhode Island.[1]

Ironically, just as they seemed close to monopolizing religion in up-country Rhode Island, the Six-Principle Baptists suffered a temporary decline. The intimate practices and rural simplicity that appealed to the localist milieu of the eighteenth century may have appeared increasingly bizarre for the emerging new society of shopkeepers, turnpike builders, and educational improvers. At any rate, some of the sect's churches weakened and eventually disappeared. The Foster Six-Principle Church joined the yearly meeting in 1791, but it failed to prosper. The church had eighty members in 1790, one hundred in 1801, then dropped dramatically to only forty by 1815. Similar declines were registered in the Six-Principle churches of Glocester and Burrillville.[2] As described earlier, the area's variant Six-Principle Calvinist churches had already become defunct at the turn of the century. Traveling missionaries' reports from the area were full of tales about "ruined churches" and of congregations that had once been "considerable" but were now "much broken and scattered."[3] The traditional Baptist churches had thus become exceedingly vulnerable to the arrival of a host of new sects and religious forms, known as the Second Great Awakening.

A collective term used to describe a vast outpouring of religious activity in the early nineteenth century, the Second Great Awakening encompassed explosive camp meetings in the American frontier West, gentlemanly crusades in New England towns, and the great revivals of upstate New York. In north-

western Rhode Island the challenge to the existing Baptist order came principally from two sources. One group, consisting chiefly of urban missionaries,
preached to the farmers from without. Based among the established churches
of Providence and Boston, they sought to save rural Rhode Islanders from the
errors of both localist deviation and general religious indifference. In the
meantime, new religious movements developed within the northwest. Trig-
gered by the chance arrival of an itinerant preacher, they developed sponta-
neously in response to a need by rural Rhode Islanders to find spiritual meaning in the midst of a rapidly changing social order. The success and failure of
these two religious movements tell much about the nature of the old Baptist
order, which they sought to replace, as well as the broader development of
society and culture in the rural northwest.

Urban Missionaries in the Wilds of Western Rhode Island

The development of urban missions to the Rhode Island hinterland occurred as part of a larger, national, or rather northern, movement for religious
propagation and moral reform. Domestic missionary societies originated in
Connecticut and Massachusetts in the 1790s as an effort by the Congregational and Presbyterian orders to combat the evils of sin and heathenism on
the frontier, as well as the dangers of Unitarianism and Republicanism at
home. Before long, missionary societies developed in the Middle Atlantic
states, and among other denominational orders, including Baptists, Methodists, and Episcopalians. Eventually, many local and state denominational societies merged to form a series of interlocking, national benevolent organizations, including the American Bible Society and the American Tract Society,
founded in 1816 and 1825, respectively. Fueled by a series of quiet, gentlemanly revivals in New England in the 1800s and 1810s, the earliest societies'
efforts were fairly mild: distributing tracts and bibles, and sporadically sending
missionaries to preach to the unconverted. But the missionary impulse was
eventually reenergized by the Finneyite revivals of the late 1820s and early
1830s, leading proselytizers to work directly with their charges in building
churches, organizing temperance and bible societies, and educating the un-
catechized. Driven by revivalistic zeal and philanthropic dollars, the great "benevolent empire" of the early nineteenth century sought nothing less than a
complete moral regeneration of American society.[4]

In Rhode Island, the missionary societies developed along similar lines,
while also being influenced by the state's special history as a bastion of localism and religious liberty. As happened elsewhere, the earliest societies were
organized largely by Congregationalists and pursued only a limited and vague
set of missionary objectives. The first known organization, the Rhode Island
Missionary Society, was founded in 1803 for the purpose of promoting "the
gospel in any part of this State, where there may be opportunity for it; and to
assist Africans in coming to the knowledge of the truth."[5] Over time, the ac-

tivities of the organization became more sharply focused. Spurred by a series of revivals between 1815 and 1819,[6] the society was reformed and renamed the Rhode Island Domestic Missionary Society (RIDMS) in 1821, signifying a narrowing and hoped for strengthening of purpose. Finally, after a period of quiescence in the 1820s, Congregational missions were greatly energized by the revivals of the 1830s. By 1834, the state's denominational association had embraced the logic of immediatism on the subjects of total abstinence from liquor and the emancipation of slaves; and throughout the decade, it was able to staff four to five fairly permanent missions, placed in a variety of locations throughout the state.[7]

Rhode Island's Congregationalists were keenly motivated in proselytizing by their understanding of the state's peculiar religious history. Unlike the parent American Home Missionary Society, to which it was an auxiliary, the RIDMS eschewed the needs of religion on the frontier in order to concentrate on more pressing problems at home, in their own state of Rhode Island. To the old Puritan churches, Rhode Island, especially in its rural areas, had long been a "cesspool" of irreligion and heresy. They now hoped to return this blighted area to the New England Congregational fold. Missionary organizations in orthodox Massachusetts and Connecticut pitched in to help their beleaguered brethren in wayward Rhode Island. A Boston tract society sent a missionary of its own to the rural northwest in 1812; and in the 1830s, the Massachusetts and Connecticut missionary societies contributed about $1,000 per annum to RIDMS, or about 40 percent of its annual budget. In the meantime, the Congregationalists' local base of support grew steadily, at least in the state's booming commercial and industrial towns. Three new churches were established in Providence alone between 1800 and 1840, and a large one began flourishing in nearby Pawtucket.[8] After the society's earliest missions revealed a shocking degree of irreligion and spiritual decay in rural Rhode Island, the newly galvanized denomination viewed the area as a great opportunity for advancing the cause of religion, and in particular, of their own Congregational way.

In the meantime, the state's urban Baptists were developing their own missionary organization, although they began rather later than the Congregationalists, in 1825, with the formation of the Rhode Island Baptist State Convention. Prior to that time, Baptist proselytizing in Rhode Island was limited to the sporadic efforts of the Massachusetts Baptist Missionary Society. The Baptist State Convention consisted of all of the Rhode Island members of the Warren Association, a Calvinistic, Five-Principle network of churches. In practice, most of the convention's active membership, and almost all of its financial support, came from the commercial towns of Providence, Warren, Pawtucket, and Newport. As with the Congregationalist organizations, the original aims of the state convention were rather diffuse, comprising both foreign and domestic missions, as well as the education of men for the ministry. But the revival of 1830 soon had a wonderfully focusing effect on the convention's proselytizing activities. Energized by an unprecedented wave of religious fervor, the Baptists put aside plans for converting the distant heathen in Asia in order to concentrate instead on creating the millennium here, in Rhode Island. During the 1830s, they spent most of their funds in either establishing missions where there were no churches, or offering financial support to those that were weak in resources.[9]

The Baptists' proselytizing activities thus developed parallel to those of the Congregationalists; but their motivations in some ways differed. Essentially, the urban Baptists of the 1830s were driven by the same search for respectability that had preoccupied their forebears in the 1770s. The state convention was led, after all, by the First Baptist Church of Providence, the same church that in 1760 had replaced its Six-Principle elder, Samuel Winsor, with the orthodox, college-educated pastor, James Manning. And one of the convention's chief financial supporters was Nicholas Brown II, the son of one of Winsor's principal antagonists. The earlier generation of urban Baptists had been content with purifying their own churches of the embarrassing rites of rural obscurantism; but in an era of heightened missionary zeal, the goals and expectations of their descendants were necessarily much greater.

The Baptist leaders of the 1830s were acutely aware of the opprobrium that had been cast upon all Baptists by virtue of Rhode Island's reputation as the state where Baptism and anarchy cohabited in sinful fecundity. They knew that, in the view of church leaders elsewhere in the nation, the state's policy of religious liberty had led inevitably to the growth of irreligion, apostasy, and generalized wickedness. As the state convention spokesmen summarized their feelings: "We cannot forget that [this] is the land of Roger Williams, nor are we insensible to reproach which has been cast upon us, on account of the many disagreeable things which are said to result from the prevalence of our principles." They hoped that "this reproach will be wiped away, by the successful labor" of the convention's own missionaries. Thus, while the Congregational societies could look upon the rural hinterland as a wide-open field, in which they had nothing to lose and everything to gain, the Baptists had to be more careful in their proselytizing activities: they needed to gently prod their wayward rural neighbors toward a more civilized religion, without offending them in the process.[10]

Still, although they differed somewhat in their motives, the Congregational and Baptist missionaries shared the same basically upright and evangelical notions about religion. Like the Congregationalists, the Baptists generally embraced the ideals of Sabbatarianism, total abstinence, and immediate emancipation. Equally important, they agreed that the rural preference for unpaid and uneducated ministers was simply no longer respectable. "One of the great evils in our churches," the convention leaders admitted, "has been the inadequacy of support for the ministry." This evil "has been partially removed among the churches connected with us; but among our Baptist brethren not connected with us," the urban Baptists continued, referring to the rural back-woodsmen, "there is still greater deficiency." Finally, the Baptists and the Congregationalists held the same severely moralizing attitude toward their objects of proselytization. Most typical was the view of the Providence Female Tract Society, an interdenominational organization founded in 1815, on the subject of teaching rural youth: the society instructed its missionaries "to impress upon young and tender minds a deep sense of their entire dependence upon God . . . the duty . . . of obedience and submission to parents and guardians . . . and of forming such habits of industry, temperance, and of prudence, as will qualify them to be useful and respectable members of Society." The urban missionaries sought to transform the countryside morally in the image of respectable bourgeois civilization; they were the cultural equivalents of the turnpike and cotton-mill builders who had tried to transform the countryside economically a generation before.[11]

When they first entered the rural northwest, the missionaries reacted as if they had encountered a strange and almost savage civilization. The earliest proselytizers were shocked by the region's economic and cultural backwardness. The world of turn-of-the-century rural Rhode Island differed dramatically from the bustling urban ports in which the missionaries had been born and raised. Ephraim Abbott, a representative of a Boston-based tract society, evangelized in the area of Chepachet between 1812 and 1813. He was particularly surprised by the prevalence of illiteracy among the local population. On October 6, 1812, he noted, "I have today as on some other days conversed with several who could not read." A trip to a nearby schoolhouse revealed that "the children . . . are large [but] so ignorant as to read with difficulty." A few years later, in 1817, Miss Sarah Walker reported to the Providence Female Tract Society that the people of Scituate "were generally very poor." She even found one family "in the woods . . . who were almost wholly destitute of clothes." The children were illiterate and "knew no more than wild creatures." By the 1830s, the area's cultural conditions may have changed considerably, for missionaries ceased to express such consternation over the north-westerners' impoverished and ignorant behavior.[12]

In any case, while the missionaries "often felt" for their charges' cultural and material deprivation, as Miss Walker phrased it, they were concerned "most for [the condition of] their immortal souls." In this regard, the religious behavior of the rural inhabitants, or rather lack thereof, proved to be still more appalling. Freedom of religion in Rhode Island had always allowed for the persistence of irreligion and old-fashioned peasant anticlericalism. In the 1810s and 1820s, when the northwest's traditional Baptist sects reached a deep state of decay, these traits may have become especially pronounced. The missionaries were shocked by the inhabitants' general ignorance of and disregard for what they considered to be the basic elements of Christian religion. Many if not most rural Rhode Islanders were simply not accustomed to observing the Sabbath. As one missionary reported in 1817, on Sundays "the parents in general *worked*, the young people *visited*, and the children *strolled* at pleasure." When residents did attend services, they turned them into social occasions. This was especially true of the troublesome "young people," who went to church "only to assemble their company." As one missionary detailed, they then "are in the habit of going *in and out* [of the meetinghouse] in time of public worship, so that solemnity and even decorum are destroyed." In addition, many inhabitants lacked basic knowledge of the fundamentals of Christian theology. A schoolteacher from the Providence Female Tract Society reported that "a great proportion [of her students] were ignorant of the Lord's prayer, and did not know there was a commandment."[13]

Even worse than ignorance and Sabbath-breaking was the general hostility to authority and religion that the missionaries often encountered. The area's schoolchildren were a generally unruly lot. As Ephraim Abbott noted, "they appear to be impatient of restraint and unaccustomed to subordination." It was a similar lack of deference, after all, that had enabled an earlier generation of northwesterners to resist the turnpiking ambitions of the Providence mercantile elite. Other examples of hostility took the form of traditional anticlericalism. When Ephraim Abbott tried to spread the good news to Obadiah Windsor, a resident of Glocester, the man rebuffed him, exclaiming that "ministers were a pack of good for nothing fellows going about to get their living out of other people." Less hostile but just as sinister for the missionaries was the reaction of those who simply were not religious. By the early 1800s, a sort of commonsense deism had developed in rural Rhode Island. Typical was the case of a Mrs. Appleby of Smithfield, who "thinks as many others do, that a person be as good without making a profession [of belief] as with it." According to Abbott, local residents had grown indifferent to Christian theology in reaction to the bizarre practices of the existing Six-Principle Baptist churches. Dr. Anthony of Foster, for example, had been turned off by the "irregular conduct" of Elder Williams, the local Six-Principle pastor. As a result, he "appears to be indifferent respecting religion, and converses more like a Deist than a Christian." Over and over again, the missionaries described the rural northwest as a land "destitute of moral and religious life."[14]

By the 1830s, the spiritual condition of rural areas appears to have improved somewhat. The missionaries, of course, were fond of taking credit for these changes. The Congregational pastor in Scituate, the Rev. Allen, reported that when he first came there, "darkness and moral death reigned. Immorality and vice of every kind were practiced to an alarming degree." But by the time of his report in 1838 conditions had much improved, especially in the area of liquor consumption.[15] Progress was more uneven in other areas: in the Washington factory village in Coventry, as another Congregational missionary observed, the Sabbath was still "more generally desecrated here than . . . in any other place." Baptist missionaries were generally less critical of rural morality.

Sensitive to the charge that it was Baptism that caused these errors in the first place, they preferred to simply express sorrow for a people who lived "destitute" of proper pastoral care.[16] At any rate, by the late 1820s they were also able to report their own improvements, citing in 1827 that "opposition [to missionary activities] has become less prominent [and] jealousies are subsiding."

Judging from church membership rolls,[17] the northwest had indeed become considerably more "Christian" by the fourth decade of the nineteenth century; but contrary to the missionaries' claims, they deserved little credit for this remarkable development. As happened elsewhere in backcountry America, these avatars of urbane respectability and complex theology simply provoked an outpouring of antielitist opposition from the northwest's rural inhabitants.[18] For all their money and effort, the Congregationalists and Baptists succeeded in forming only three churches in northwestern Rhode Island prior to the middle of the century. In general, the local population treated them with the same suspicion and hostility that it had reserved in the 1790s for the Providence and Norwich Turnpike Society.

The Congregationalists fared especially poorly because of their unpopular connection with the system of ministerial "slavery" that reigned in establishmentarian Massachusetts and Connecticut. Their missionaries continually complained about the population's "most blind and deep-rooted prejudices against, what we believe to be, the truth and order of the gospel."[19] Antipathy toward New England orthodoxy was so great that the citizens of pious Connecticut came to be ridiculed by the rural inhabitants. Villagers in Washington were greatly amused when "people from Connecticut" technically violated Sabbatarian restrictions by traveling through Rhode Island on Sundays in order to trade "early" in the Providence market on Mondays. "Such practices," the local missionary lamented, "embolden the people in this part of Rhode Island to ridicule the steady habits of Connecticut and to go on with an higher hand in their violations of the sabbath."[20] Finally, the local populace had an understandable, if somewhat misguided fear that all Congregationalist missionaries were out for their money. Congregational religion had become synonymous in the minds of rural Rhode Islanders with the payment of church taxes for ministers, or "hirelings" as they deprecatingly called them. Little wonder, then, that as one missionary reported, "many of the people were extremely suspicious and expected me of some sinister designs or were in fear lest I should ask them to pay me for preaching to them." And in a sense, the people were correct in their suspicions; for while the missionaries might come free of charge, the RIDMS hoped that eventually self-sustaining churches would be established, with a salaried pastor paid for by local contributions.[21]

But for all the tribulations of the Congregationalist missionaries, their Baptist brethren fared only slightly better. The urban Baptists had simply become too "Congregational" for the rural people's sensibilities: they, too, favored salaried and educated ministers, and the creation of stately, visible churches. Although northwesterners may have begun to tire of the Six-Principlists' rusticity, they still opposed any high-church ornamentation that interfered with the workings of the religious spirit. In their view, "those who made any preparation for the ministry were destitute of piety and could not preach by inspiration." For many residents, missionary activity itself was suspect because of its planned, "systematic . . . nature."[22] And even those who accepted the need for proselytizing endeavors might naturally look askance at those who, like the members of the Baptist State Convention, originated in Providence, the city of Federalist turnpikers.

Finally, both Baptists and Congregationalists alike must have offended northwesterners with their arrogant criticisms of rural life, and their snobbish insistence that theirs was the only valid religious experience. When "Brother Weaver" of the Baptist State Convention toured through Foster in 1830, he reported that the region was "destitute" of churches. He was wrong—the area had at least two or three churches; but Weaver ignored them, probably because they belonged to denominations that did not believe in "support for the ministry," Calvinistic theology, and other elements of a proper Christian religion. One missionary seemed aware of how thoroughly his brethren could alienate their charges. He complained: "I have had to labor under much embarrassment from prejudices growing out of my predecessors."[23] More fundamentally, the missionaries betrayed a condescending attitude toward their wayward charges that could only have alienated them further. At one point in his travels, Ephraim Abbott attempted to soften one resident's intense anticlericalism by explaining that "it was from pitty [*sic*] to this region that I had come to preach the Gospel here." The infidel's response: "He damned me over and over again."[24]

The three churches that the missionaries did succeed in establishing were located in areas with strong economic ties to the missionaries' hometowns on Narragansett Bay. Two were located in Scituate, a town where by 1830 most textile factories were owned by outside entrepreneurs. One of these, the Arkwright and Fiskeville Baptist Church, was even located on the property of mill-owner Charles Jackson, a resident of Providence who later moved to Scituate. The third missionary church was located in Chepachet, where most of the mills were owned by Elisha Dyer, a major Providence industrialist.[25]

In Coventry, Foster, and Burrillville, on the other hand, where industrial establishments were sparse, or remained locally owned, the missionaries failed completely. For at least ten years the RIDMS employed full-time pastors in the village of Washington; but they eventually left with little to show for their efforts. As the Rev. J. N. Whipple, the latest in a long line of exhausted and discouraged missionaries, was forced to admit in May 1840, "it would be a matter of great satisfaction to me, could I report that the little church of which I have acted as stated supply for three years last past, had been greatly strengthened; but such is not the fact." Service in Washington, he complained, "has been a term of much labor and fatigue."[26] The Christianization of northwestern Rhode Island would be accomplished not by these self-appointed guardians of backcountry souls, but rather by the northwesterners themselves, using new forms of religious experience for a new kind of society.

The Christians and Freewill Baptists

Two completely new denominations, both indigenous to the United States and only a generation or two old, were primarily responsible for evangelizing the countryside of northwestern Rhode Island: they were the Freewill Baptists and the Christians. Although separated by a few significant differences, these two new denominations shared an important set of religious traits: qualities that enabled them to offer rural northwesterners a meaningful compromise between the backwoods sectarianism of the Six-Principle Baptists and the urbane condescension of the Providence missionaries. Both denominations developed out of rural societies that were only a generation or two removed from frontier conditions; and they both emerged as religions of protest, in an age of extraordinary democratic ferment, expressing a kind of backwoods resentment against the hierarchical structures and abstruse theologies of existing, urban-based denominations. The Freewill Baptists and Christians advocated a religion of rural simplicity and a theology of commonsense morality.

Ironically, they also laid the groundwork for an eventual rapprochement with the very mainline churches against which they had once rebelled; for under the influence of Finney's commonsense revivalism, the Presbyterian and Congregational churches would also gradually abandon Calvinist piety in favor of the pragmatism of freewill morality. In a further irony, the two new religions, and in particular the Freewill Baptists, became more "established" themselves, for they eventually shed their original frontier emotionalism and rural antiformalism for the more urbane trappings of ecclesiastical learning and denominational order. The Christians and Freewill Baptists had roots in the explosive, sectarian past of frontier religion; yet they also looked forward to the stabler virtues of evangelical denominationalism. In the first half of the nineteenth century they would function as key cultural vehicles, allowing northwesterners to express continued opposition to the Providence elite, while at the same time transcending the communal, peasantlike mentality of the Six-Principle Baptist sect.

The Freewill Baptists originated during the 1770s and 1780s in the rapidly growing backcountry towns of central New Hampshire and western Maine. Prior to the revolutionary war, the Congregational establishment predominated in this area; but its hold on local residents was tenuous at best, partly because they received little support from parent institutions in Massachusetts, and partly because of the general frailty of social institutions on the northern frontier. When New Light revivals swept through the area during the revolutionary war, the remaining Congregational edifice was largely torn asunder. Of the many sects that flourished in its place, the Freewill Baptists were the most numerous and the most enduring. From a total of 21 churches in 1781, their fledgling sect grew to 51 churches in 1800, 100 by 1810, and 185 a decade later.

The Freewill Baptist movement was born out of local dissatisfaction with the Congregational order. Politically, the Congregationalists represented a Federalist establishment of local gentlemen and absentee landlords that was detested by the hill-country farmers. Religiously, their Calvinist doctrines became suspect once the experience of a great revival rendered doubtful the validity of predestinarian theories. As untutored backwoodsmen, the New Hampshire farmers had little patience for the niceties of Edwardsean theology. The revival had proved to them that people could be brought to confession by their own human exertions; hence they deliberately rejected Calvinism, choosing instead the "Freewill" appellation.[27]

Over the first few decades of their existence, the Freewill Baptists evolved from a schismatic and volatile sect to the beginnings of a stable denomination. In their early years they were given to extreme emotionalism and the practice of bizarre rituals. Freewill revivals were marked by "screaming, loud laughing, and . . . exhibitions of animal excitement"; and almost all of the early churches insisted on such Biblicist practices as washing the saints' feet.[28] But eventually a reaction against these excesses set in, as church leaders realized that emotionalism only produced continuing schisms in their new religious polity. Besides, by the 1800s, the first stirrings of commercialization in the region may have prompted Freewill members, who were generally more prosperous than their neighbors, to press for a more respectable and stable form of religious experience. As a first step, a rough institutional hierarchy was established in the 1790s and 1800s. It consisted of monthly meetings of individual congregations for devotional exercises; quarterly meetings of representatives from several churches, for clerical and disciplinary concerns; and yearly meetings of the entire denomination for discussing general issues of theology and policy. They also began to consider educating their pastors and paying them a steady salary, staid practices that would have been fiercely opposed in the denomination's early, more primitivist era. Thus, ironically, by the 1820s the Freewill Baptists had actually begun to assume many of the institutional characteristics of the mainline denominations that they had once rebelled against.[29]

The second new sect, the Christians, emerged about a generation after the Freewill Baptists, with whom they shared several denominational tendencies, while also differing in a few important respects. Arising simultaneously in the early 1800s in three separate areas—the Ohio Valley, the upper South, and New England—the Christians originated as Republican-inspired protest movements against the existing ecclesiastical order. In the West, they emerged out of opposition to the Presbyterians' hierarchical church structure and Calvinist theology. In the South, Christians formed in reaction to authoritarian excesses by the Methodist episcopacy. And in New England, the reviled establishments were the haughty and gentlemanly Congregational order, and the increasingly respectable Calvinist Baptist denomination. Not surprisingly, the New England group, which undoubtedly supplied the inspiration for Christians in Rhode Island, originated as an offshoot of, and were sometimes close cooperators with, the Freewill Baptists. In all areas, the new sect sought to replace established denominations with a faith based on the New Testament alone, as democratically interpreted by the common people themselves. They insisted on abandoning all other existing theological and ecclesiastical systems, believing that these systems produced only tyranny, contention, and error.

But unlike the Freewill Baptists, the Christian sects never solidified into an enduring denomination. Except for the western branch, which eventually merged with the Campbellites to form the Disciples of Christ, the Christians remained loose and unformed. Their theology was deliberately vague and ill defined, although like the Freewill Baptists they were generally Arminian on the subject of human exertions. In their early history, the two sects considered merging, but the Christians' increasing tendency toward Socianism eventually drove them apart. Moreover, unlike the Freewill Baptists, the free-thinking Christians never developed a secure denominational structure. Their church polity remained extremely localistic: regional conferences were weak or even nonexistent; and proselytizing activities occurred only through the efforts of a loose collection of itinerant evangelists.[30]

In 1812, one of these itinerants just happened to stumble upon northwestern Rhode Island; and by an unusual coincidence, in precisely the same year a Freewill Baptist missionary began proselytizing in the rural northwest. Their timing could not have been more propitious. By 1812, many of the region's original Six- and Five-Principle Baptist churches had almost completely decayed, leaving a spiritual void in much of the countryside. Moreover, the Christian and Freewill itinerants had distinct advantages when it came to proselytizing the northwest, for they espoused a set of beliefs and practices that naturally resonated with the local residents' own predilections. Their freewill theology approximated the old Baptists' belief in general redemption;[31] and their loose organizational style meshed well with rural Rhode Islanders' fierce localistic proclivities. Finally, and perhaps most important, both the Christians and the Freewill Baptists originated in opposition to the Federalist politics and Calvinist beliefs of an existing religious establishment. This formative experience must have bound them psychologically to many a rural northwesterner, who would still have remembered bitterly both the arrogance of Federalist turnpikers and the influential urbanity of the merchant Baptists of Providence. Partly as a result of these advantages, the Christians and the Freewill Baptists would soon succeed in transforming the religious culture of northwestern Rhode Island.

The flowering of the "Christians" in northwestern Rhode Island was a classic example of the effect of rapid commercialization on the workings of the human spirit. The Christian revival first blossomed in the western Coventry hamlet of "Rice City," a village whose very name says much about the boostering mentality of commercializing, rural Rhode Island. The village owed its existence to its fortuitous location on the Providence and Norwich Turnpike: it was situated about a day's ride between the terminal points of Providence and Norwich, and it was also the site of one of the company's tollgates. In spite of the company's many problems in building the turnpike, traffic eventually boomed along the highway, because of Providence's emergence as the area's largest port. By the turn of century, three taverns had sprouted in the village to service the needs of weary and thirsty travelers. Delusions of metropolitan riches must have been envisioned by one of the tavern owners, Samuel Rice; it was he who named the village, in a booster's characteristically bombastic fashion, "Rice City."[32]

Crowded with transients and self-important entrepreneurs, Rice City quickly became a leading center of tavern-based sin. Local religious establishments, which might have reigned in the growth of immorality, had reached an all-time low; for Rice City was at the center of what missionaries achingly called a "destitute" region: its "ruined churches" included Five-Principle Baptist churches in Coventry and Foster and a Six-Principle church in Hopkins Mills. As a result, "gambling, drinking, horse-racing . . . and other kinds of wickedness" proliferated to an alarming degree. The village's three watering holes were the center of this dissolution; and the most notorious of all was the one owned by, naturally enough, Samuel Rice. "Esquire Rice" was "a very noted gambler" who succeeded in attracting men of similar moral standing to his establishment. Before long, the village developed a reputation as a place where "pride, rioting and licentiousness were the general characteristics of its inhabitants."[33]

When the British navy blockaded coastal traffic during the War of 1812, inland transportation boomed, bringing commercial prosperity and moral dissolution to a temporary peak. Great must have been the consternation of the few remaining righteous citizens. But the possibility of deliverance finally arrived when one Elder Douglas Farnum, a wandering evangelist, appeared in the vicinity. Hoping to prey on the guilty consciences of the morally corrupt, they invited him to preach in town in November 1812, just at the height of the village's war-induced speculative boom.[34]

The result was probably the most emotionally explosive revival in the history of Rhode Island. In the space of a year, 250 local residents were converted to the preacher's calling. As they agonized for their souls, men and women fell "on the floor, rolling and creeping about." The most powerfully affected were the adolescents: children upwards of ten years old, "made happy in their souls," began "clapping their hands and singing hosannas to the Son of God." Some likened the young people's cries "to the barking of dogs" and "the hooting of owls." Those who were older and well established also embraced the fervor of the revival. As one participant later related, "the principal men in the town were taken by the word, and brought on their knees to cry for mercy." Even Samuel Rice, formerly the prince of sin, was driven to conversion. The new converts took over the meetinghouse of the defunct Coventry Separate Baptist Church; and from there the revival spread east to the new factory villages of the Pawtuxet River valley, north through Foster, and west to the Connecticut towns of Plainfield and Sterling. By the summer of 1816, five "Christian" churches had been founded in Connecticut alone.[35]

For a time, however, the heat of the revival produced schisms among the new disciples of Christ. As often happened in American revivals, the converts soon disagreed about the merits of emotional theatrics. Those who were "old professors" from nearby defunct churches took special offense at the "wildfire and confusion" of the Rice City revival. They left the new church, accusing the Christians of having "run into the Methodist delusion." Even among those who remained, a distinctly conservative faction soon came into conflict with Elder Farnum, whose preaching consisted, as a supporter described it, not of the "enticing words of man's wisdom," but "in demonstration of the Spirit and with Power." When the new connection's conservative elders censured his conduct in 1818, Farnum departed for more fertile religious fields in Ohio, as did many of his supporters, including Samuel Rice. An even more extreme group "came out" altogether by joining the Shakers. Shattered by religious schisms and dispirited by the panic of 1819, the church in Rice City soon fell to a temporary low. When the church was finally stabilized in 1824, it could count only forty men and women on its membership rolls.[36]

Nevertheless, from this brief nadir, the church managed to grow steadily, even dramatically at times, over the next two decades. Having averaged about seventeen new converts per year in the 1820s, membership suddenly spurted in the revival years of 1832–1834. Over two hundred men and women were converted in those years, resulting in the formation of three more churches: one in the hamlet of Foster Center, a second in the mill village of Rockland in western Scituate, and a third in Phenix, a factory village on the Coventry and Warwick border. A fifth church, in the village of Clayville in Scituate, was established at mid-century. By 1840, the Christians had grown to at least 750 members; they were then overwhelmingly the largest denomination in a one-hundred-square-mile area that consisted of southern Foster, western Coventry, and the southwestern quarter of Scituate.[37]

The attraction of the Christians lay principally in the utter simplicity of their theological beliefs. They called themselves Christians not because they claimed to be the only exemplar of such a title, but because they wished to practice a simple, primitive Christian faith, stripped of all the theological and ecclesiastical baggage that "Christianity" had accumulated over the centuries. The Christians claimed to rely on "the New Testament . . . as our Only Rule of Faith and Practice." Tired of decades of what seemed to be petty theological disputes, they rejected "as Antichristian . . . all man-made Scripture, Crude Disciplines, Confessions of faith, in short, everything not named in the Scriptures." In practical terms, the Christians tended toward freewill beliefs instead of predestinarianism and required complete immersion for baptism; but they made a point of accepting anyone who held evangelical beliefs.[38] Of greater importance to Christians was the personal behavior of prospective converts. The main requirement for membership in the Clayville (Scituate) church, for example, was the exhibition of "Christian character" and "a life of vital Christian piety."[39] What mattered most to the Christian was not a person's system of beliefs, but rather the quality of his or her character.

The members of this new denomination, it seems, were practical individuals of the world. In an age of unprecedented economic growth, they ranked among the more prosperous and upwardly mobile residents of their communities: 59 percent of their members were taxed in the upper two-fifths of their town's population. By 1850, the Christians were clearly the wealthiest denomination in the northwest, consisting chiefly of commercial farmers and substantial shopkeepers, such as wheelwrights, house carpenters, and stonemasons. They embraced and participated in rural commercialization, but they also felt disturbed by its less savory effects, such as the drinking and gambling that had plagued prerevival Rice City. Troubled by the appearance of sin amidst God-given prosperity, they reacted at first with the emotional intensity of the Rice City revival. But eventually, once the noisier ones had departed for points west, they turned to a simple and commonsensical religion as a suitable spiritual framework for a confusing, new world.[40]

As practical men, they had little use for the unorthodox rites and contentious dogmas of the Six-Principle Baptists. They preferred instead a straightforward faith in the New Testament, and the practice of "good works" through the development of Christian character. These differences reveal themselves in their church meeting minutes: gone are the Six-Principlists' otherworldly references to being "in love and unity" with each other. The Christians concentrated instead on the practical business of cultivating good behavior. Like other contemporary evangelical denominations, the Christians employed church committees "to labor with" wayward communicants and, if necessary, suspend or excommunicate the recalcitrant.[41]

The Christians also differed from the old-order Baptists in the manner of their relations with other Protestant believers. Little attached to a particular set of beliefs or practices, the Christians lacked the Six-Principlists' zealous commitment to preserving sectarian purity. Instead of condemning all intercourse with rival beliefs, the Christians actively cooperated "with all who sincerely trust in Jesus as their Saviour, making no distinction for opinion's sake."

This spirit of toleration was reflected in their membership policy. Unlike the Six-Principle Baptists, who would accept into the covenant only communicants from "sister" churches, the Christians opened their doors to adherents from many different congregations. In 1835, the Foster church, for example, admitted Letitia Seamans from Elder Richard Knight's church "without their giving [her] a letter." "Knight's church," being of the Six-Principle persuasion, had probably refused Seamans a letter of dismission because she committed the unpardonable transgression of joining a rival denomination. The Christians even invited to communion those who retained membership with a different evangelical denomination. This practice, known as "open communion," was rigorously opposed by the Six-Principle Baptists.[42]

More generally, the Christians condemned the very sort of sectarian contentiousness that the Six-Principlists seemed to relish. Of course, like any new denomination, especially in the tumultuous antebellum period, the Christians suffered at first from their share of internal schisms. By the 1830s, these had largely faded away. Instead of promoting sectarian divisiveness, the Christians rejected "all Party Names, Party Spirit [and] Bigotry,"[43] because petty doctrinal issues made little sense in an era of great practical concerns and accomplishments. Perhaps more important, denominational rivalry was simply evil for the Christians, because it hindered the more important goal of encouraging proper "character": petty bickering over insignificant doctrines would only alienate those most in need of Christian fellowship and character development. By the 1830s, the Christians had developed a uniquely ecumenical form of evangelical religion. They hoped to combine spiritual enthusiasm with practical character development, in order to forge a new moral order for a changing rural society.

Still, although Christians dominated—at least for several decades—a large section of northwestern society, their influence was ultimately neither extensive nor permanent. As happened elsewhere in the country, the Christians never developed a requisite level of denominational identity and institutional strength. Ecumenicalism may have opened Christian churches to believers of all kinds, but it also effectively closed them to those who desired a more identifiable theological dogma. In particular, the Christians' openness to the Socinian, or Unitarian heresy must have alienated the majority of rural Protestants, who continued to hold to trinitarian beliefs. Perhaps more important, the Christians adhered to a strong tradition of congregational independence, thereby forsaking the strengthening advantages of hierarchical organization. They created a General Conference of New England Christian churches, but this never amounted to more than a loose and informal institutional structure. Lacking the requisite strength for building an extensive and long-lasting new denomination, the Christians in Rhode Island never expanded much beyond their initial stronghold in the area of Coventry, Foster, and Scituate. They gradually weakened after 1850 and were eventually absorbed by other Protestant churches.[44] The development of a more enduring, new religious order in rural Rhode Island would be the work of yet another denomination: the Freewill Baptists.

The Freewill Baptists may have arrived in northwestern Rhode Island without the emotional explosiveness of the Rice City revival of 1812, but their overall influence on rural life was more extensive and permanent. While the Christians generally lived only in parts of Foster, Coventry, and Scituate, Freewill Baptist churches proliferated over the entire remaining area of northwestern Rhode Island. By the 1830s, they were by far the strongest denomination throughout Burrillville, Glocester, and the northern halves of Foster and Scituate. Perhaps more important, unlike the Christians, the Freewill Baptists spread beyond the rural northwest and into the burgeoning manufacturing towns and commercial centers of eastern Rhode Island. Having a broader base of support helped to ensure their longevity, since their churches had access to the superior personnel and financial resources of the state's urban areas.

In comparison to the Christians, Freewill Baptists were able to strike a more harmonious balance between competing demands for practical behavior and rural simplicity on the one hand and theological orthodoxy and ecclesiastical structure on the other. The Freewill Baptists were the first church to satisfy the rural folks' need for a religion of practical and simple beliefs, without succumbing to the inherent vulnerability of localistic polity and excessive rusticity. As a result, they were able to remain influential in northwestern Rhode Island through the early decades of the twentieth century.[45]

Freewill Baptism first arrived in Rhode Island in the person of John Colby, an itinerant missionary sent to the town of Burrillville from the denomination's stronghold in central New Hampshire. Like the Congregational and orthodox Baptist missionaries who were his contemporaries, Colby initially encountered hostility and opposition from the area's unchurched and anticlerical population. One "old man" reacted so angrily when Colby began singing a hymn in his home that he "violently caught hold of his gun . . . ran out of the house where I was singing, and discharged the piece." Fortunately, the man missed his target, probably on purpose, because, as Colby later surmised, he had only meant to "scare" him. The rest of the irreligious population may have been more good humored in its opposition. Once when Colby planned to preach a service in eastern Burrillville, the local heathens organized a competing "Thanksgiving Ball within about a mile of [his] meeting, and . . . [gave] out word that they intended to see who would draw the greatest party."[46]

Nevertheless, however violent and well organized the opposition, it seems to have paled in comparison to the widespread antagonism that the urban Calvinists had aroused; for Colby was able to establish a church in Burrillville the year he arrived. The new sect grew slowly at first, but a revival ensued in

1819–1820, leading to the founding of two more churches in the northwest, in Glocester (1822) and northern Foster (1824). In the meantime, the denomination expanded rapidly throughout Rhode Island and southeastern Massachusetts, leading to the establishment of a quarterly meeting for the region in 1821. Revivals continued to spread in the 1820s and 1830s, resulting in the formation of about one church per year during the entire period. From three churches and 375 members in 1821, the quarterly meeting grew to include twelve churches and 1,074 members in 1830, and twenty congregations with 2,640 communicants in 1840. In the northwest, two more churches were established in the 1830s, located in western Glocester and the small mill village of North Scituate. By 1840, rapid growth had resulted in the creation of a separate quarterly meeting for the northwest alone, to which was added the Morning Star Church (in Glocester) in 1846, and a Coventry church in 1847.[47] With congregations located in rural areas, mill towns, and cities, the Freewill Baptists became the second most widely based denomination in the state of Rhode Island, and the fourth largest in total membership.[48]

Moreover, the new denomination grew not only in numbers, but also in terms of its institutional strength and organizational apparatus. Unlike the highly congregational Christians, the Freewill Baptists eventually established a whole series of hierarchical, professional, and educational organizations. When it first began proselytizing in Rhode Island, the denomination as a whole had reached about the halfway point in its evolution from a primitivist sect to a stable and structured religious order. And in Rhode Island, this process continued to unfold.

By the late 1830s, an elaborate network of denominational institutions had been established in the Rhode Island area. In addition to the usual quarterly meetings that had been established in 1821 and 1840, an elders conference was created on a regional level in 1822. The conference gave the denomination's elders a forum for expressing their views together, allowing them to increase their authority over the more scattered laity. To improve local visibility, the quarterly meeting published magazines at various times during the antebellum period: these included the *Free-Will Baptist Magazine*, 1828–1830, the *Rose and Lily* in the 1840s, and the *Freewill Baptist Quarterly*, 1853–1869.[49] Although unstable and short-lived, these publications heralded the development of a written, religious culture in an area formerly limited by the oral folk traditions of the Six-Principle Baptists.

In a further development in 1835, the Rhode Island Quarterly Meeting established domestic and foreign missionary societies, following the lead of the national denomination, which had created similar organizations two years before. The quarterly meeting also instructed individual churches to have "a meeting of prayer for Missions on the first Monday . . . in every month." These prayers would presumably be accompanied by the opening of parishioners' pockets and purses to provide the missions with much needed financial support. Local congregations in the northwest seem to have responded favorably to this appeal for assistance. The Glocester and North Scituate churches established fund-raising committees in 1840, and the Second Foster Church followed with its own "Home and Foreign Missionary Society" in 1841.[50] In embracing this kind of well-financed missionary activity, the Rhode Island Freewill Baptists showed that they had come to accept not only the need for institutional structure, but also the desirability of deliberate efforts to spread the gospel. The denomination thus succeeded in overcoming traditional rural preferences for locally spontaneous, as opposed to regional "systematic," efforts at increasing church membership. Unlike the Christians, the Freewill Baptists did not remain a loose body of congregations that relied upon chance revivals for their continued growth and vitality. Instead, they created a number of institutional structures aimed at deliberately increasing the strength and visibility of their new religious order.

More important still, in this regard, were the efforts by local Freewill Baptists at improving the standing and respectability of their ministers. As a first step, the elders conference began to regulate the credentials of all local pastors. Unordained preachers, who had traditionally preached freely throughout the rural northwest, were required after 1828 "to preach before the members of the [elders] conference" in order to be "lysanced." In 1835, this procedure was further strengthened when the conference voted that preachers' licenses must be renewed annually.[51]

More ticklish were questions concerning education and salaries for Freewill Baptist ministers. Rural Baptists had long opposed these stately innovations, since they believed that educating pastors would only inhibit their ability to communicate God's spirit; and paying them salaries would set them apart from society and grievously tax the meager earnings of their parishioners. The quarterly meeting, consisting of the denomination's regional leadership, usually took the lead in proposing these controversial measures. The leadership continually fretted over the fact that many of their congregations lacked steady pastorates, a fault they attributed to the absence of sufficient salaried support. It chided the local churches for failing to appreciate "the value and necessity of a constant enlightened and godly ministry." Seeking to alleviate this shortage of elders, the quarterly meeting reminded its members of "their duty to make systematic and unremiting [*sic*] exertions" to give their pastors "a suitable support." In the meantime, regional leaders sought to reassure local parishioners that regular salaries would not make ministers "proud and idle." While attempting to steer their denomination in the direction of steadier pastorships, the leadership had to continually assuage traditionalists' fears about the evil effects of money on a minister's spiritual power and purity.[52]

Eventually, albeit somewhat grudgingly, the churches of the northwest appear to have responded to their leaders' directives about ministerial support. As early as 1833, the Foster church recorded that its members regularly "bring their tithes and offerings into the store House of God." At least part of these contributions may have been given to the congregation's minister. A few years later, in 1836 and 1840 respectively, the North Scituate and Second Foster churches initiated more formal subscription systems for ministerial support, which in the case of the Scituate congregation soon provided its elder with a guaranteed salary of $400 per annum. Not surprisingly, this strikingly formalistic innovation provoked occasional opposition from local traditionalists. In 1841, Deacon Parker of the Scituate church resigned to express his disapproval for "Support of the Ministry . . . and other Benevolent objects of the day." And at the smaller, more rural Foster church, subscription support of the ministry remained weak—ranging "from 50 to 150 dollars"—throughout the 1840s. Although large by contemporary rural standards, this amount was undoubtedly too low to ensure a steady pastorate, as a succession of ministers came and went every two or three years during the next decade. Still, when the elders conference surveyed its churches in 1851, it discovered that the proportion with "settled pastors" had increased to 46 percent, up significantly from 25 to 30 percent in 1836. Thus, the Freewill Baptists appeared to have already eliminated, to some degree, the stigma that rural churches once applied to the employment of salaried, "hireling" ministers.[53]

Even more remarkable were the gains achieved by the Freewill Baptists in educating their ministers. Concerned about the quality of its early pastors, most of whom had at best a common-school education, the Rhode Island Quarterly Meeting voted to establish a seminary of its own in 1838. A subscription had raised $10,000 by January 1839, and the school, located in the Scituate village of Smithville, opened its doors the following autumn. The seminary was housed in a large, three-story building, which, with its massive Greek-revival frontispiece, was by far the most imposing structure then built in the still rustic confines of northwestern Rhode Island. The Reverend Hosea Quinby, a graduate of Waterville (now Colby) College in Maine, served as its first president. In the 1840s, the seminary enrolled 350 students annually, attracting them from all over New England.[54]

In time, however, the school experienced a number of difficulties. The rural churches may have continued to believe that higher education was inimical to the cultivation of Christian spirituality. In 1842, for example, the Western Rhode Island Quarterly Meeting expressed concern that the "precious youth" of the seminary, while possessing "promising talents," remained "unconverted to God." The denomination's leaders also insisted, seeking to assuage the concerns of their more traditional followers, that "a learned ministry" must always be "connected with piety and zeal."[55] More serious were the school's financial problems, which in 1850 forced the Freewill Baptists to temporarily relinquish control; the seminary reopened in 1863 under the denomination's auspices but never achieved its earlier level of success. In 1877 it was closed for good. At this time, the school probably had succumbed not to popular

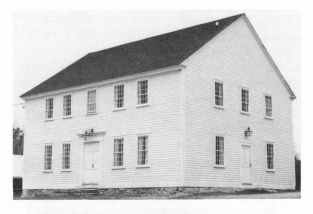

Figures 8, 9, and 10. These photos demonstrate the evolution of ecclesiastical architecture in northwestern Rhode Island. From top to bottom: Elder Hammond's Meetinghouse (1796–1797) is totally devoid of religious ornamentation; the Rice City Christian Church (ca. 1830) displays a modest steeple; and the Smithville Seminary (1840) boasts a massive Greek Revival–style portico. Courtesy of Rhode Island Historical Preservation Commission.

opposition to ministerial education, but rather to competition from nearby Brown University, which itself was a leading institute for the education of Baptist ministers.[56]

The more remarkable fact is that, in an area that once bitterly opposed the founding of Rhode Island College, the Freewill Baptists were able to establish a seminary dedicated to the education of pastors for a largely rural denomination. By the 1840s, the Freewill Baptist congregations of the northwest were supporting denominational missions, paying their ministers' salaries, and participating in the creation of an education clergy. They had thus begun to rival even the Congregationalists and urban Baptists in respect to their commitment to institutional structure, systematic proselytizing activities, and the creation of a trained, salaried, and stable group of ministers.

At the same time, the Freewill Baptists were able to retain a kind of folksy simplicity in their doctrinal views. Like the Christians, they emphasized the importance of practical character over the need for theological sophistication. Church and quarterly meeting minutes were remarkably devoid of doctrinal statements or disagreements. The sole theological statement of the Second Church of Foster was simply to announce in its covenant that "we take the bible for our rule of faith and practice." The Freewill Baptists were much more interested in the development of proper, Christian behavior. The elders conference, when it agreed to renew preachers' annual licenses, required only that the licentiates show "satisfactory evidence of their moral and christian character." This practice contrasts sharply with the pastoral oversight of the Six-Principle Baptists, in which they regularly excommunicated elders for preaching improper doctrine.[57] As for the individual churches, they concentrated on encouraging proper behavior among their parishioners. In most churches, a standing committee was formed for the purpose of visiting negligent and wayward members. Members were often disciplined for absenteeism, argumentativeness, or profaning the Sabbath, but never for holding improper beliefs.[58]

As was the case with the Christians, the Freewill Baptists' relative indifference to doctrinal issues manifested itself in extremely open membership and communion policies. They seem to have cared relatively little for the doctrinal views of prospective church members. Even the elders conference accepted ministers who, contrary to Freewill tradition, believed in predestination, and who had been "sprinkled only" in Baptism instead of "immersed."[59] It was equally as easy to leave the Freewill Baptist denomination as it was to join it. Members who wished to affiliate with another denomination were given letters of dismission by their churches, instead of being excommunicated, as was the practice of the Six-Principle Baptists. As the Foster church stated in 1849: "any member in good standing . . . who desire [*sic*] to have a letter of dismissal upon giving his or her reason (the request lying on the table for six months) be granted by a vote of two-thirds of the members present." The passage of such a tolerant policy by a Six-Principle church would have been inconceivable. Freewill Baptists were concerned not with doctrinal purity or denominational loyalty, but rather with the "good standing" or proper character of their members.[60]

As a corollary to their liberal membership rules, the Freewill Baptists also adopted an extremely open communion policy. The Second Foster Church, for example, opened communion to members of any "evangelical Church" who "maintain . . . Christian Character." Even more liberal was the elders conference, which in 1842 opened its own organization to participation by ministers of other faiths, voting that the "conference . . . shall have discretionary power to admit such other ministers and deacons as it may deem proper." As with the Christians, the Freewill Baptists' concern for advancing godly character took precedence over theological issues. In their view, the most efficient way to accomplish this goal was to include as many persons as possible who shared their interest in creating a godly and moral community.[61]

Still, the Freewill Baptists were not entirely indifferent to doctrinal issues and the need for traditional evangelical zeal. Unlike the Christians, they never elevated theological indifference to the status of a covenantal agreement. Although the elders conference was generally lax about doctrinal qualifications, it did bar "fellowship" with any minister who denied the divinity of Christ. This restriction may even have been aimed specifically at the Christians, some of whom dabbled in the Unitarian heresy. Many Freewill Baptists, moreover, seem to have clung to the primitivist beliefs of their earliest years. The practice of washing the saints' feet, although no longer a requirement, was still accepted by the elders conference as late as 1825. The elders agreed, then, that members who "felt free" to follow this rite should "have a privaledge [*sic*] to practice it at the next conference."[62]

The Freewill Baptists also seem to have conducted themselves with greater spirituality than the practical-minded Christians. Church meeting minutes frequently included references to the members being "all in Harmony and Friendship," a phrase that, although less otherworldly sounding than the Six-Principlists' "love and unity," still suggests a note of ardent spirituality. Less commonly used phrases were still more powerfully religious: for example, "the children of the Lord were relating to each other the exercise of their mind, talking of the goodness and telling of his power." And in times of revival, church meetings sang with evangelical zeal. The meeting of the First Foster congregation, on August 8, 1829, "was a unanimous, harmonious, glorious, reviving and feasting time to the Children of God, while singing, praying, and speaking of the goodness of God to their souls."[63] The Christians, on the other hand, although born in the highly emotional revival of 1812, seem to have settled down in their maturer years to a distinctly less exuberant pattern of religious experience.

By preserving spiritual zeal in their religious devotions, and by building a strong institutional framework for their newfound faith, the Freewill Baptists created a more enduring denomination than their "Christian" neighbors in northwestern Rhode Island. After an explosive and tumultuous beginning, the Christians appear to have mellowed into a perhaps overly pragmatic and undogmatic denomination. Because they drew their membership increasingly from the northwest's more prosperous families, their original democratic rejection of all creeds appears to have evolved into more of a rationalistic denial of Christ's divinity. In this respect they uncoincidentally approached the theological position of their still wealthier, but institutionally stronger, religious cousins, the Unitarians. The utter simplicity of the Christians' limited dogma must have originally come as a relief to hundreds of troubled farmers for whom the contemporary mélange of competing beliefs and sects seemed an unnecessary cause of mental confusion and community discord. But in time, their theology of pragmatic moralism began to sound uninspired, perhaps even jejune.

By preserving a decidedly more spiritual tone in their religious services, the Freewill Baptists maintained a steadier hold on the hearts of the local population. Throughout the antebellum period, they drew adherents from a more representative slice of northwestern society, finding support from all but the wealthiest and poorest families. By creating a stronger institutional framework than the Christians', they also became more successful at riding out those periods of religious indifference that inevitably occur. The genius of the Freewill Baptists lay in their ability to mix a strong and simple faith of piety and good works with an institutional network of growing sophistication. They were able to introduce formalistic concepts, such as missionary fund-raising and the need for an educated and professional ministry, which a generation earlier would have been summarily rejected by antielitist backwoodsmen. In the first half of the nineteenth century, the Freewill Baptists served as a crucial bridge in the cultural development of northwestern Rhode Island, linking its intensely localistic and semiliterate past to a mid-century world of commercial prosperity and respectable middle-class life.

The Emergence of Moral Reform

Two of the principal good works supported by both Christians and Freewill Baptists are deserving of special consideration: the temperance and antislavery crusades. Interest by rural evangelicals in these causes stemmed partly from their strong concern for the practical improvement of human society. As one of the more energetic congregations, the Freewill Baptist Church in the northeastern town of Smithfield stated in its covenantal agreement: "We agree to promote the benevolent enterprises of the day, such as Temperance, the Abolition of Slavery . . . and Moral Reform, together with every other that may have the present and eternal well-being of mankind for its object."[64] The churches of the northwest were not so all-inclusive in their moral reformist zeal. While support for abolitionism was occasionally lukewarm, interest in the temperance crusade among the evangelicals was nearly universal. In fact, so strong was the antiliquor movement in the northwest that it attracted support from secular as well as religious circles. The temperance crusade was fueled by the mighty energy of the evangelical revival, but its strength testifies as well to a larger transformation in the culture of the rural northwest.

In supporting antiliquor and abolitionist ideals, Rhode Island's rural evangelicals were participating in a larger, national religious crusade; for temperance and antislavery agitation had been both broadened and transformed throughout the North by the great revivals of the 1830s. Prior to then, both movements consisted of politely run societies devoted to the use of only "moderate" tactics: moderate abstinence and moral suasion in the case of the antialcohol crusade, and colonization of freedmen to Africa for avowed opponents of slavery. For the converts of the 1830s, however, neither of these tactics would suffice. They called for total abstinence from liquor, and the "immediate" abolition of slavery (at least in Theodore Weld's formula of immediate abolition "gradually accomplished"). Anything less was simply an ineffective compromise with sin. By the late 1830s, perhaps a majority of all evangelical churches in Providence, and indeed throughout the northeastern United States, had pledged to support both of these absolutist ideals.[65]

The Freewill Baptists, and to a lesser extent the Christians, came to approve of temperance and abolitionist goals, although in some cases they lagged behind their evangelical brethren in the cities. As was true in their support for ministerial education and salaries, the denomination's leadership generally outpaced local churches in favoring absolutist moral pledges. This was particularly true in the case of abolitionism. On a national level, the Freewill Baptists' periodical, the *Morning Star,* supported immediate abolition of slavery as early as 1834. Soon thereafter, the doctrine secured the unanimous approval of the denomination's clergy, although lay opposition delayed approval by the general conference until 1840.[66] In Rhode Island, the quarterly meeting first supported immediatism in August 1837, voting "that we highly approve the course that the conductors of the [Morning] 'Star' have hitherto taken on the subject of American Slavery." In the next year, the meeting declared further that "all the moral means in the power of the free states ought to be exercised to create throughout our land a Sound publick opinion averse to Slavery which may secure its extermination." Quarterly meeting members expressed concern, however, over local disinterest in the antislavery cause, stating in 1837 that "we deeply lament the indifference of many members of the church of Christ on this subject." Seeking to prod local parishioners from their moral apathy, the elders conference later urged that each minister should "preach a sermon once or more a year on the subject of slavery."[67]

Regional leaders were justified in their concerns, for the record of individual congregations—both Freewill Baptist and Christian—was decidedly mixed. In 1842, the North Scituate Freewill Baptist Church resolved that

"American slavery . . . should be speedily and peaceably abolished."[68] But churches in more western and rural areas were ambivalent in their support for the antislavery cause. The issue was debated for several years in the First Foster congregation without ever coming to complete resolution. A four-part statement on slavery, of unknown text, was introduced at a church meeting at the relatively late date of May 4, 1844. While the first two resolutions passed the following August, the third and fourth were tabled, and at a subsequent meeting, "voted out." Another unstated resolution on slavery was introduced in 1848, only to be indefinitely tabled. The minutes of two other congregations—the Second Foster and Glocester churches—were completely silent on the slavery issue, although an anonymous history of the Second Foster Church, written by a member in the 1840s, reported vaguely that its adherents were "Anti-Slavery in sentiment." The Christian churches, on the other hand, seem to have ignored antislavery altogether, perhaps because regional leadership in their denomination was almost nonexistent. The murkiness of local records leaves much in doubt; but in general, the rural churches seem to have been lukewarm on the subject of immediate abolition.[69]

Still, it would be an oversight to negate the antislavery activity of northwestern evangelicals. Individual church members played prominent roles in the region's antislavery activity. In 1836 Rhode Island's first antislavery convention attracted delegates from all over the state. Of the five representing Foster and Glocester, the only towns for which evangelical church membership lists have been completely analyzed, two attended Christian or Freewill churches. These two delegates were also members of the state antislavery society's board of directors, and one of them, Job Armstrong, served as its first vice-president. Armstrong, a Chepachet store owner with whom many farmers often traded, was secretary of the Western Rhode Island Quarterly Meeting of Freewill Baptists. It is no coincidence that he first appeared publicly in the northwest in 1804, when he supported the local mill owners' drive to abolish fishway rights on the Pawtuxet River. By the 1830s, his belief in freedom of the waterways appears to have transmuted first into a spiritual belief in Freewill theology, and from thence to a moral insistence on freedom from human bondage. Antislavery activity, although weak in much of the northwest, received strong support from many of the area's entrepreneurial and evangelical leaders.[70]

On the question of temperance, the Christians and Freewill Baptists acted much more decisively. Although they initially lagged several years behind the urban evangelicals in joining the total abstinence movement, they eventually adopted a series of temperance resolutions that in some ways exceeded those of the more conventional churches in ultraist ardor. Regional religious leaders, once again, led in supporting the cause. The Freewill Baptists' elders conference adopted total abstinence as a goal in 1833 when it voted that "it is right for Churches to reject candidates for admission on the ground that they are in the habit of using ardent spirits though not to intoxication." Two years later, the conference made this injunction against liquor more obligatory, resolving that ministers must "use all their influence, moral, political or religious . . . to put a stop to the retail traffic in ardent spirits." As for the leadership of the Christian denomination, Elder James Burlingame, the pastor for several local congregations, worked tirelessly in behalf of the temperance cause. Named the first state temperance agent by the Rhode Island Temperance Society, he lectured throughout the countryside in favor of total abstinence from liquor.[71]

The individual churches acted more slowly, but in time they also embraced the total abstinence pledge. In much of the country, Freewill Baptist and Christian congregations reacted with suspicion, at first, to the total abstinence crusade. Still, betraying their origins as backwoods schismatics, they tended to view the movement as a "federal plot" by Congregationalist proselytizers. But by the late 1830s, local churches began to accept the advice of their regional leaders. Once again the North Scituate church took the lead, declaring in 1838 "that we will admit no person to membership who does not wholly abstain from the use of ardent spirits . . . or that furnishes the same."[72]

Then, in 1842 and 1843, the total abstinence campaign completed its sweep of the northwest in a great rush, knocking aside all remaining opposition. On May 14, 1842, the [North] Foster Freewill Baptist Church passed the area's first such pledge, resolving that "all Christians (Church members especially) [should] speedially embrace the principles and adopt the practice of total abstinence" and that "we as a Church will not receive any one as a member . . . that use[s] it as a Beverage." In the meantime, rumors of a coming total abstinence crusade began to sweep through the Christian Church in Foster Center. One self-confessed drinker, Solomon Wilcox, felt obliged to resign his church membership, having "heard from some one that there was to be a sifting of the tares from the wheat and more especially all the inebriates from the list, and Temperance inforced." Wilcox's anxious prediction eventually proved true; after several more recalcitrant drinkers resigned, the church voted in 1844 that "we in future will abstain from all intoxicating drink." By this time, the Second Foster Freewill Baptist Church had also passed a temperance pledge, making total abstinence the nearly unanimous policy of the region's new evangelical churches.[73] Moreover, some churches even banned wine from their communion tables, thereby adopting an ultraist position that many of the more orthodox, urban churches refused to accept.[74] By the 1840s, thanks to the Christians and Freewill Baptists, the temperance crusade had become a powerful force in northwestern Rhode Island.

This is not to suggest, however, that temperance agitation was exclusively the province of the evangelical crusaders; adherence to the movement went beyond just the evangelicals to include a vast number of men and women who were disturbed by the rise of alcoholism and general chaos in the midst of a changing social order. The temperance crusade grew out of a larger concern for the integral role that liquor had traditionally played in rural society. Before the 1820s, the use of alcoholic beverages was widely condoned at all levels of northwestern society. Even respectable church members defended liquor as "a great benefactor in keeping off disease, and assisting in times of arduous labor." Farm work was dull and strenuous, after all, and was seldom viewed as a commercial, profit-making enterprise requiring the direction of sober and hardworking men. It was not surprising, then, that a yeoman would take "his glass of West Indian at the end of each swath" of his scythe and share it in turn with his laborers. Liquor was perhaps even more prevalent at social and political occasions. As a later temperance advocate once related, "at all elections voters were at the expense of the candidates . . . At weddings, the bride and groom were pledged in a full bumper . . . He who went to the house of a friend thought himself insulted if he was not asked to drink." In short, in work, business, politics, and friendship, drinking was fully condoned by all levels of society.[75]

By the late 1820s, however, many in the northwest had begun to reconsider this easy acceptance of alcoholic drinking. Both tippling and alcoholism, at this time, seem to have reached record proportions. In boomtowns like Rice City, rootless men and women turned to gambling and rum, their thirsts fired by the sudden possession of new commercial wealth. In the meantime, traditional religious establishments, which might have reigned in the proliferation of drinking, were steadily declining. The appearance of urban life also increased the visibility of drunken behavior: where once drinking was mostly restricted to the isolation of a farmer's cabin, it now occurred publicly in village taverns and crossroad inns. In the rural northwest, and throughout the nation as a whole, liquor consumption probably reached a historic peak in the 1820s and early 1830s. Public drunkenness must have proliferated to an alarming extent.[76]

In the meantime, changes were occurring in the organization of society that had once made drinking acceptable. The introduction of occasional textile mills created a small but influential class—the factory owners and managers—who were most obviously interested in reducing alcoholic consumption; they needed sober and reliable workers in order to operate efficiently their expensive machinery. In Burrillville, especially, the "manufacturing interest" was a leading advocate of restrictive temperance legislation. Even so, opposition to drinking was hardly limited to the new men of industry. Farmers and shopkeepers who now produced actively for the market could ill-afford to have their time and wits wasted on the alcoholic drink. And where once they paid their laborers partly in rum, as a sign of easy sociability among near equals, they now lived apart from their field hands, paid them in cash, and generally maintained separate lifestyles and economic interests. In short, in a society made up increasingly of practical, commercial-minded men, drinking simply no longer made sense. Even worse, given the perils of a market economy, drunkenness—and indeed wasteful behavior of all kinds—could lead to bankruptcy and ruin.[77]

Aghast at the contemporary proliferation of drinking, and troubled by the social changes produced by commercialization, hundreds of northwesterners joined the temperance crusade in the late 1820s and 1830s. They signed temperance pledges, joined societies for moral support, and eventually sought restrictive ordinances and legislation to curb social drinking. Temperance activity was strongest in the region's more heavily populated and industrial areas; but local abstinence societies were also formed in Glocester and the almost completely agrarian town of Foster. One hundred and fourteen men and women joined the Foster Total Abstinence Society between its founding in the 1830s and 1851.[78] Throughout the northwest, manufacturers and shopkeepers refused to allow drinking on their premises, and farmers kept rum out of their fields. Some store owners even sacrificed their profits by declining to sell drink. Among these was Jeremiah McGregor, owner of one of the original, infamous Rice City taverns, who turned his establishment into one of the state's first "temperance" inns.[79]

The result was a remarkable drop in local consumption of alcohol. According to a contemporary's estimate, in the year 1829 alone liquor consumption halved in the Coventry village of Washington. Over a longer time period, between 1824 and 1834, a still more remarkable advance in temperance was observed in the northwestern town of Scituate. As described by the local Congregational missionary, the Reverend Allen, in 1834: "Ten years since, this town was inundated with *rum:* there was a grog shop in almost every corner. But now I do not know of a farmer of respectability in this town, who furnishes rum for his workmen; nor do I know of a mechanic," as Mr. Allen continued, confirming the class basis of temperance, "except the lowest, that keeps it in his workshop." Only less respectable and "low" farmers and mechanics, probably too poor to engage in the northwest's growing commercial economy, continued to mix business with booze. The influence of the more "respectable" portion of society also helped to control and even eliminate drinking at the town's social events. At funerals, for example, "gallons" of liquor had once been "considered indispensable"; but by 1834, as Reverend Allen related, "these solemn occasions" occurred "without the aid of rum."[80]

Thus, although the temperance movement was often led by the churches, and it attracted their members in disproportionate numbers, the new evangelicals hardly monopolized the northwest's antidrinking agitation. One of the more prominent supporters of temperance was none other than the venerable Solomon Drowne, Theodore Foster's friend and fellow gentleman farmer: he was a churchgoer perhaps, but hardly an evangelical convert. Still alive in the early 1830s, Drowne was too old to participate actively in the antiliquor crusade, but he worked through his son William, who often delivered temperance addresses in the vicinity of Foster. On a more general scale, of the first thirty persons who joined the Foster Total Abstinence Society, fourteen belonged to a local Christian or Freewill Baptist church or were related to a church member; but most of the rest presumably preferred to stay home on Sundays.[81]

So great was this support for temperance by nonevangelicals that it elicited a considerable and confused commentary from the area's urban itinerants. The missionaries from Providence falsely assumed that opposition to alcohol could only be produced by evangelical fervor. They therefore expressed surprise, oftentimes, at the growth of temperance societies in the absence of avowed Christian zeal. As one missionary noted in 1836, writing from an area in which "infidelity Sabbath breaking and vice prevail" to a large extent: "it is a matter of astonishment in that as many attend [temperance] meetings as do, considering the abounding error, opposition and sin." He reported that while only fourteen belonged to his bible class, about 400 had sworn membership to the local temperance society. Showing somewhat less surprise, the Congregationalists' missionary to Coventry reported in 1829 that intemperance was "the only . . . vice that has suffered any dimminution [*sic*]." In fact, the Coventry missionary's report suggests that temperance activity actually preceded the northwest's first powerful revivals in the early 1830s. In general, throughout the age of evangelical crusades, many of the northwesterners who flocked to temperance societies showed not the slightest interest, much to the missionaries' distress, in the fate of their souls.[82]

Temperance reform often coincided with the area's evangelical revivals, because both cultural movements believed strongly in the freedom of human will—either to save one's soul from damnation or to save one's body from drunkenness and poverty—and both relied on the power of personal and group influence in attracting new converts. But many who opposed drinking seem to have remained unmoved by revivalistic preachings, especially those that were authored by arrogant urban missionaries. This is not to minimize the crucial role played by Christians and Freewill Baptists in the temperance movement. Rural evangelicalism and support for moral reform were not one and the same; rather, they were parallel and overlapping responses to the disjunctive emergence of a new kind of society in the midst of a culture still steeped in traditional mores. The precipitous decline in local alcohol consumption, all by itself, testifies to the success of the moral reformers in challenging these traditions, thereby transforming the cultural life of northwestern Rhode Island.

The Decline of the Six-Principle Baptists

The traditional cultural order, however, was not bereft of its ardent defenders: these consisted primarily of the Six-Principle Baptists. The old Baptists had already declined considerably in the first two decades of the nineteenth century; and it would have been analytically convenient for them to have continued this descent, during the remainder of the antebellum period, into an early oblivion; but such was not exactly the case. The Six-Principle Baptists were too closely linked to the area's cultural identity to be abandoned so soon by the northwestern population. Local Six-Principle churches, after suffering some earlier declensions, experienced a series of powerful revivals between 1825 and 1845. Meanwhile, the denomination's leaders attempted with some success to strengthen their religious order by modernizing their churches' policies on ministerial support, congregational singing, and missionary activity.

Ultimately, however, the forces of tradition proved stronger, as Six-Principle adherents clung to old rustic ways. The Six-Principlists' newfound strength, although numerically impressive, was qualitatively fragile. Church schisms occurred repeatedly, especially in the more economically advanced areas where members were continually tempted to renounce outdated doctrines in favor of rival denominational beliefs. Church membership began declining again as early as 1845, and it collapsed completely after the Civil War. By the 1930s, only three churches remained statewide, out of what had once been the dominant religious order in all of Rhode Island.

Early declines in many Six-Principle churches led the association to reach a temporary nadir in the early 1820s. Some churches in the northwest disappeared altogether. After many years of declension, the churches of Glocester, Burrillville, and Foster disbanded in 1819, 1833, and 1837, respectively. Elsewhere in the Six-Principle Baptists' regional association, which comprised Rhode Island and southeastern Massachusetts, churches dwindled and became moribund. The Rehoboth North Church reported only intermittently after 1818, and the church in Swanzey suffered a catastrophic loss in membership in 1819, following a local doctrinal schism.[83]

In some cases, Six-Principle churches suffered directly from competition with the new, evangelical disciples of the Christians and Freewill Baptists. It was a Freewill Baptist who helped cause the schism at Swanzey, drawing away all but 50 of the church's 260 members. Elsewhere, the new evangelicals simply came to the fore where Six-Principle churches were already nearly extinct. In Burrillville, the old Baptists' congregation was so weak by the time of the Freewill Baptists' first revival, in 1812, that they were forced to allow the newcomers to share their meeting house in return for some much needed repair work. The arrival of the Freewill enthusiasm in Foster, shortly thereafter, occasioned a final collapse in local Six-Principle membership, from forty in 1819, to twenty-five in 1825, and only intermittent reporting thereafter. In the northeastern Rhode Island town of Cumberland, Six-Principle membership had fallen to only eleven in number, when the area fell under the sway of a "Christian" evangelist, who wooed away the remaining old Baptist adherents. As a result of these declensions, schisms, and rival encroachments, membership in the entire yearly meeting fell from about 1,100 in 1800 to 951 by 1826. Within the northwest, during the same time period, membership increased at first from about 550 to 730, because of revivals in the Coventry and Scituate churches, two of the denomination's largest. But in the meantime, churches located in the three other northwestern towns were fast disappearing; and the area's total membership eventually fell as well, declining to 665 by 1825.[84]

Following this troublesome decline, however, the Six-Principle churches underwent a remarkable recovery. The revivals of the Second Great Awakening, after all, were rarely limited to just a few denominations, and similarly in the case of northwestern Rhode Island the enthusiasm engendered by the Christians and Freewill Baptists eventually spilled over into the Six-Principle churches. Beginning in the late 1820s, a series of powerful revivals occurred in the Scituate and Coventry churches. Membership in Scituate increased from about 275 in 1827, to 370 in 1832, to over 440 ten years later. The size of the Coventry church jumped even more dramatically, from 330 adherents to just over 800 during the same time period. In some periods, over 100 new members were added in a single year. Two new churches were formed in the northwest as a result: the Coventry Central and Union Scituate, both established after a particularly powerful upsurge in 1841. In the entire regional association, membership more than doubled by the early 1840s to over 2,000, while the number of churches increased from ten to eighteen. Although the Six-Principle Baptists were overtaken in numbers by the combined membership of their Christian and Freewill rivals, they remained the largest single denomination in the rural northwest.[85]

The Six-Principle churches, or at least some of their adherents, worked to modernize and strengthen their denomination by building a more stately and dynamic religious order. As early as the late eighteenth century, several churches had come to accept congregational singing, one of the "modern" practices that had originally alienated Elder Winsor and his agrarian supporters when the merchants gained control over the Providence church. A split even developed in the general association between advocates and opponents of hymn singing. The two sides reached a compromise in 1789: they agreed that when the association's yearly meeting was held "in churches where they practice singing," a hymn would precede the concluding prayer; the reverse would occur when meetings were held in nonsinging churches, giving the traditionalists a chance to exit gracefully before the offensive hymns began to sound.[86]

The denomination's leaders also sought to steer their churches in the direction of copying other respectable innovations from their more urbane rivals, particularly in the areas of ministerial salaries and regularly funded missionary societies. In a denominational history written in 1827, author Richard Knight, the elder of the Scituate church, tried subtly to encourage parishioners to be more generous in their ministerial support. He quoted from one of the sect's original seventeenth-century divines in order to indirectly scold his contemporaries for having "been too short, in caring for their ministers"; as a result of this, as he continued to quote, "the ministers are rendered . . . the less capable to serve . . . being much diverted by worldly employments from . . . serious study and [the] exercise of reading." Meanwhile, yearly meeting leaders also exhorted their adherents to strengthen the denomination's proselytizing activities by establishing mite societies and regularly funded missions.[87] In fact, by the early 1830s, with congregational singing, ministerial support, and other urbane innovations possibly on the rise, the Six-Principle Baptists seemed on the verge of making the same transition that the Freewill Baptists had already achieved—changing from a primitivist sect to a stately and professionally organized denomination.

Unfortunately, the old Baptists' efforts in these areas ultimately met with only mixed success. Congregational singing may have found some measure of acceptance in Six-Principle churches; but instrumental music remained absolutely forbidden as an impure accompaniment to the sacred Word of God. One church was even banished from the yearly meeting because it introduced this heretical practice into its Sunday services.[88] Furthermore, the leadership's appeals for ministerial salaries and mission assistance received only lukewarm support. In 1816, the yearly meeting began to solicit funds from individual churches in order to send missionaries to New York and Pennsylvania, where a separate western conference of Six-Principle Baptists had just been established. Noting that "the temporal things of the world" are necessary "for the promulgation of the Gospel," the denomination's leaders urged that $200 be raised annually for sending "some public brethren" to the western churches. The ensuing fund-raising effort, however, fell far short of this goal. During 1817–1818, the only year for which there are complete records, the Rhode Island churches contributed only $31.02 toward the western missions. By 1839, the yearly meeting seems to have realistically lessened its financial expectations: it began to send only one messenger a year to the western conference, at a cost of a mere $35. But in the ensuing year even this modest solicitation yielded only $8.59, forcing the Six-Principle leaders to ask for an "additional . . . $25."[89]

Finally, Elder Knight's hints about the need for greater ministerial support seem to have fallen on deaf ears. Even his own church in Scituate paid little or no money to its resident elders. In fact, the church's yearly budget usually amounted to only $5 to $30 per year, most of which was spent on church maintenance and firewood. Since the Scituate church, with over 350 members, was the second or third largest in the conference, the budgets of most Six-Principle congregations must have been even smaller. By comparison, in 1840 the Second Freewill Baptist Church of Foster, with only a quarter of the Scituate church's membership, raised $80 for ministerial salaries alone. Next to this effort, Six-Principle Baptist fund-raising seems positively feeble.[90]

Like many of modest means elsewhere in rural America, the old Baptists viewed mission assistance and ministerial support as a plot conjured up by urbane, cold-spirited clergymen to tax and control the common people. In arguing against ministerial support, they declared that "as we freely received the gospel, we are freely dispensing it to others." Using almost Jacksonian rhetoric in favor of voluntary, as opposed to coercive, giving, they rejected subscriptions for salaries, the selling of pews, and other costly fund-raising schemes. Much more essential, in the Six-Principlists' view, was the ability to preach, like the "illiterate Apostles . . . with . . . power and demonstration"; for "without this power, it will be but a form of words, like the dry wind from the wilderness, that will neither fan nor cleanse."[91]

A similar kind of Jacksonian aversion to coercion colored Six-Principle Baptist proclivities in the area of moral reform. On the subjects of temperance, antislavery, and the promotion of general orderliness, they remained decidedly lukewarm, especially when compared to the Christians and Freewill Baptists. The yearly meeting's first general pronouncements on drinking and slavery did not occur until the late 1830s. Even then, they spoke against these ills only obliquely and halfheartedly. On the subject of slavery, the meeting could only muster a vote against southern laws that "deny to a portion of our fellow men, the right to learn, to read the bible, upon the penalty of fines and scourges." As for the sin of drinking, the Six-Principlists' general meeting merely urged members to pray and admonish "the grovelling victim of intemperance." Not until the late date of 1857 did the old Baptists speak more imperatively with respect to these two important moral reforms; at that time, they finally called for "total abstinence" from liquor and the "utter" abolition of slavery.[92]

As for the individual Six-Principle churches, they ignored the temperance and antislavery crusades almost completely. Their minute books are devoid of the many resolutions on these subjects that filled the pages of Christian and Freewill Baptist church records. The only example of moral reformism in a Six-Principle church occurred late in the antebellum period, in 1854, when a newly ordained elder of the Scituate church "gave his testimony in favor of the Temperance cause" and "spoke against Slavery as an abomination in the sight of God."[93] In general, advocacy of these kinds of coercive moral reforms arrived late, or not at all, to the Six-Principle churches.

This is not to say that Six-Principle Baptists never participated in temperance or antislavery activity. Three of the northwest's sixty-three representatives to the state's first antislavery convention belonged to Six-Principle churches, although this proportion, about 5 percent, was just over half of the Six-Principlists' share of the entire adult population.[94] In 1835, one Six-Principle member, John Tillinghast of the Johnston church, published a short-lived religious periodical, *Zion's Friend*, which ardently supported temperance and the abolitionists' cause.[95] Nevertheless, the magazine's views do not seem to have been representative of the denomination's membership: although Tillinghast strongly defended the Six-Principle faith throughout, the denomination never bothered to return his support. The yearly meeting failed to endorse

Zion's Friend and in fact never mentioned the publication in its minutes. As for individual churches, only one voted to "recommend" *Zion's Friend:* Tillinghast's own congregation in Johnston, a body that was expelled from the yearly meeting altogether just eight years later, in 1844.[96]

Finally, the magazine's subscribers, whose names and residences were published therein, hardly typified the denomination as a whole. About half of them lived either in factory villages or in coastal towns, where Six-Principle churches were continually splintered and seduced by Freewill Baptist beliefs. Where Six-Principle churches were strong, supporters of *Zion's Friend* were scarce: only 8 percent belonged to the Coventry and Scituate churches, even though those two churches contained over half of the denomination's membership. In November 1835, Tillinghast published a general appeal for support from the Six-Principle churches; but his call went unanswered, forcing him to abandon *Zion's Friend* after a short eleven-month run.[97] Individual members or Six-Principle leaders may have embraced temperance and abolitionist beliefs, but the denomination as a whole long rejected the kind of coercive behavior prescribed by antebellum moral reforms.

The Six-Principle Baptists were simply more interested in preserving the strength and purity of their own religious order than they were in spreading morality and orderliness to the rest of the population. This does not imply that the Six-Principlists were advocates of drunken revelry. Far from it: they continued to strictly regulate the morals of their own members throughout the antebellum period. The East Greenwich church, for example, "suspended" one member in 1812 for drinking "Strange Lickquer to Excess." And a few years later, it excommunicated another for bearing a child out of wedlock.[98] But the Six-Principle Baptists refrained from applying these same standards to the rest of the population, preferring instead to concentrate on the spiritual and disciplinary needs of their own individual members.

An important reason for this lack of interest in coercive moral crusades may have been the old Baptists' relatively humble social and economic status. Unlike their rivals among the Christians and Freewill Baptists, the Six-Principle Baptists were generally poorer than the average northwesterner. This was especially true after 1820 when the newer denominations appear to have successfully competed for the region's wealthier churchgoers. In the 1820s and 1830s, only 27 percent of all Six-Principle converts ranked in the top two-fifths of local tax lists, while 54 percent ranked in the bottom two-fifths. The corresponding figures for the evangelicals, on the other hand, were 48 and 26 percent, respectively. By 1850, this socioeconomic gap had widened still further: the median value of real estate held by Six-Principlists was only $400, less than one-half and one-quarter, respectively, of the amount held by a typical Freewill Baptist or Christian Connection member.[99]

The Six-Principle Baptists may thus have simply lacked the self-assurance of their more prosperous rivals, a quality that allowed the new evangelicals to preach confidently to all people of the possibility of gaining earthly riches and heavenly rewards through leading a sober and orderly life. After all, much of the impetus behind antebellum moral reform stemmed from a strong belief in the power of personal example: the total abstinence campaign, in particular, was partly motivated by the hope that the relatively affluent in society could reduce drinking among the more humble, simply by abstaining from alcohol themselves. For the Six-Principle Baptists, however, so often among the more humble in rural society—be they laborers, petty artisans, or small, uncommercialized farmers—the power of the moral reformers' logic would be simply annoying or even incomprehensible.[100] Bewildered and buffeted by a changing economic world, the Six-Principlists preferred to turn inward among each other in order to cultivate a sense of purpose and spiritual unity. In essence, they remained determinedly sectarian in an era of increasing denominationalism: in place of the Freewill Baptists' reliance on education, ecumenicalism, and societal moral reform, the old Baptists preferred tradition, doctrinal purity, and communal moral discipline.

The sectarian nature of the Six-Principlists' worldview is most starkly revealed in their handling of the often disorderly crowds that surrounded their annual September leadership meetings. A three-day, weekend affair of discussions and sermons, the conference was rotated among the denomination's larger churches. Although most business was conducted inside the hosting church building, the final Sunday service was always held outdoors for the benefit of those who could not be seated inside. Large numbers of rural inhabitants attended these services, especially once the revivals of the era began swelling Six-Principle membership; in 1829, between 400 and 500 "brethren and sisters partook" of this outdoor "communion."

The earliest services were marked, in the words of the yearly meeting, by "order and decorum"; but trouble eventually arose when the outdoor communicants, along with the warm September air, attracted an even larger crowd of victuallers and entertainers. Before long, this gathering of onlookers began committing, as a local missionary once observed, "the most terrible profanations of the sabbath. Many persons were selling to the people various kinds of food and drink. In a house, opposite the meeting house, there was dancing during the day, some were engaged in Jockeying horses, others in gambling. It was a scene of rioting and wickedness."[101] In short, right under the noses of the Six-Principle leaders, the crowd practiced all of the favorite traditional pastimes—drinking, gambling, and general merrymaking—that the moral reformers were trying so strenuously to eliminate.

To the astonishment and disgust of these same moral reformers, the Six-Principle annual meeting members appeared reluctant, and even impotent at times, in their attempts to eliminate these abuses. As heirs of a traditional rural culture, the Six-Principle Baptists did not seem to share the evangelicals' obsession with keeping the Sabbath holy. In 1829, at a time when the crowd was still fairly orderly, the yearly meeting had even thanked the crowd "for the good entertainment" that they "provided." For the evangelical moral reformers, "entertainment" was never something for which one should be thankful, especially during a time of religious observance.[102]

Only when the crowd's "noise and confusion" threatened to disturb the conference's services did the Six-Principlists attempt, and then only haltingly, to tame its bacchanalian excesses. In 1836, the meeting formed a committee to seek a legal prohibition on "sales" of food or drink "at our next yearly meeting." But the committee's solution, if any were found, must have been ineffectual; for by the late 1840s, conference leaders were complaining once again about the "noise and confusion" brought on by the "long continued practice" of victualling the meeting's participants. Ironically, they could have solved the problem quite easily by simply terminating the practice of offering outdoor services. This solution was proposed in 1849, when "a resolution was introduced to adjourn the conference" and cancel the Sunday service, "by reason of the great amount of outdoor confusion which surrounded the meeting." But after considerable discussion, the "resolution was finally refuted by a majority of 14 [out of a total of forty-five]," and the custom of outdoor worship continued unabated.

Unwilling to sacrifice tradition for the sake of social orderliness, and reluctant to impose their own moralizing standards on the unchurched population, the yearly meeting could only plaintively "request," as it recorded in 1852, "that no person will so disturb our worship under the excuse of furnishing us something to eat." Unlike the evangelical moral reformers, who would have scolded the Sabbath-spoilers, and tried to convert them to Christian morality, the Six-Principlists simply wished "to disconnect ourselves from the sin" of outdoor sales "and its consequences." They were thus reduced to begging the unwanted "rabble" to cease and desist. One doubts that this request was fulfilled, because the meeting repeated it once again in the following year.[103]

An even more self-destructive aspect of old Baptists' restrictive sectarianism was its tendency to embarrass and alienate its more energetic members. The newer, more evangelical members of the Six-Principle order felt continually discomforted by their church's uncooperative stance toward other denominations. The key stumbling block in most cases was the issue of "closed communion," the practice of barring members of other denominations from sharing at the Eucharist table. Orthodox Six-Principle Baptists believed that only those who had come under the "laying on of hands"—the sixth principle—could participate in their church's communion. From this requirement followed their belief in closed communion; only fellow church members could qualify under such a strict definition of "Christian."[104] In true sectarian fashion, the Six-Principle Baptists' communion policy emphasized doctrinal purity and spiritual oneness over the need for ecumenical cooperation.

The denomination's moral reformers, on the other hand, came to reject the sixth principle as a requirement for Christian conversion and hence began to accept the possibility of opening communion to other evangelical denominations. As Ray Potter, one of the first to leave the Six-Principle order over the issue of closed communion, once described his position: "I was convinced from the Bible, that the laying on of hands . . . could not be proved from the same to be required to be done in order to constitute a person a visible member of the church of Christ; and consequently, that I did not conceive that we had any right to withhold fellowship or communion from those who had not conformed to it." For Potter, the sixth-principle and closed-communion restrictions were not spiritually purifying regulations; rather, they constituted a "partition wall . . . between the people of God."[105] This "wall," instead of strengthening Christianity, would only hinder Christians of all denominations from uniting in an evangelical crusade against the evils of intemperance, disorderliness, and general immorality.

During the first half of the nineteenth century, a series of schisms and wholesale excommunications occurred within the Six-Principle denomination over the issue of closed communion, as the moral reformers struggled unsuccessfully to seek room for their latitudinarian ways in an otherwise orthodox, sectarian order. Significantly, demands for open communion—and consequent excommunications—occurred most frequently in relatively commercialized and industrialized regions, areas in which temperance, antislavery, and other moral crusades were at their strongest.

The first church to go was the one that Ray Potter belonged to, located in the relatively commercialized town of Cranston. The Cranston church had been formed in 1816 as a branch of the Six-Principle church of Johnston; and in the next few years, thanks to its elder's spirited preaching, it grew faster than any other congregation in the entire yearly meeting. Unfortunately, the church and its elder, Henry Tatem, soon fell prey to latitudinarian thinking. In 1819, Tatem decided to break the closed-communion barrier once and for all by attending services at Colby's Freewill church in Burrillville. The Six-Principle association then reacted against this doctrinal treachery by excommunicating Tatem and seizing control of his church on behalf of its small Anti-Tatemite minority. Having been tossed out of their own church, Potter, Tatem, and the open-communion majority then formed a new one of their own in the Freewill Baptist denomination.[106]

For the next several decades similar scenarios would be played out over and over again. In 1830, a Six-Principle church was organized in highly commercialized Providence. Predictably, it soon offended the denomination's leaders by embracing both open communion and the use of instrumental music. The entire church was expelled in 1835; two years later it found refuge in the Freewill Baptist order.[107] In 1844, the Six-Principle association also "withdrew fellowship" from the Johnston church, home of the editor of *Zion's Friend*, when it discovered that the church had been practicing open communion.

After a few years of independent existence, the congregation, following the path already prepared by other Six-Principle excommunicants, decided to join the Freewill Baptist denomination.[108]

Finally, in 1850, the open-communion heresy invaded the Six-Principle churches of the northwest; in that year the Coventry Central and Lippitt and Phenix churches dropped out of the old-Baptist yearly meeting. Typically, both churches were located in highly industrialized areas: the Coventry Central Church in the factory village of Anthony, and the Lippitt and Phenix church a few miles away in the village of Phenix. After their establishment in 1841 and 1845 respectively, they soon ran into trouble with the general association. The Lippitt and Phenix church never joined the yearly meeting, its petition having been rejected in 1845. Nor did the yearly meeting ever make clear the reasons for the rejection; however, the denomination was probably none too pleased at finding a total-abstinence pledge in the church's constitution. Having been spurned by the yearly meeting, the young Six-Principle church quickly adopted a variety of other heretical practices. Its members began paying their minister in 1848, introduced instrumental music into their church in 1850, and in the same year, adopted open communion. In the meantime, the Coventry Central Church had also withdrawn from the Six-Principle conference over the issue of open communion. Together with the Six-Principle church of Taunton, Massachusetts, another dropout from the yearly meeting, the Coventry Central and Lippitt and Phenix churches formed a new "General Baptist Association of Rhode Island and Massachusetts," devoted to the practice of open communion with all evangelicals, and to the principles of absolute temperance and the abolition of slavery.[109]

Thus, gains in Six-Principle membership were continually eroded by the departure of the denomination's newer, more evangelical adherents. In the six years that followed its founding in 1841, the Coventry Central Church added over 150 members to the Six-Principle denomination; but these gains were lost at a single stroke when the entire congregation withdrew from the Six-Principle yearly meeting. Similar wholesale departures cost the denomination 55 members when Elder Tatem's supporters withdrew, 41 members from the Providence church, and almost 250 adherents from Johnston. Untold others must have left their churches individually, motivated by a desire to build a universal Christian society, instead of a narrow sectarian order. By the mid-1840s, these departures began to outnumber new converts, as membership in the northwest's Six-Principle churches fell from a peak of 1,427 in 1844 to 1,073 by 1850. A similar decrease occurred in the entire yearly meeting, from 2,790 adherents to just under 2,000,[110] wiping out half of the denomination's gains of the previous two decades and leaving it in a serious and this time, permanent state of decline.

The Six-Principle Baptists were ultimately weakened by two interrelated trends in contemporary rural religion. As rural society became increasingly prosperous and commercialized, many men and women cherished a more urbane and culturally sophisticated religious experience: they built grander meetinghouses, introduced harmonized singing and instrumental music, and cultivated a learned and salaried clergy. At the same time, commercialization was altering the structure of rural society, creating a more mobile, and in some ways more disorderly social milieu. Troubled by the rise of drunkenness and general licentiousness, northwesterners began seeking a simpler and more commonsensical form of religion, one that would emphasize personal character over doctrinal beliefs, and interdenominational cooperation over sectarian exclusiveness. In rural Rhode Island, as elsewhere in the nation, these trends intersected in a mighty evangelical revival, which refashioned the beliefs of existing denominations and generated entirely new ones. Measured purely in terms of church adherence, the resulting transformation was truly remarkable: church membership, as a proportion of the population over age fifteen, rose from one-tenth in 1790 to over one-third in 1840. Northwesterners had once displayed a penchant for disorder and dissolution that shocked urban missionaries, but by the 1840s they appeared increasingly sober and respectable in their everyday behavior.[111]

In its earliest, most spontaneous stages, the Second Great Awakening resulted in heightened religious conflict as new sects challenged old standing orders in the democratic ferment of the postrevolutionary era. But as once radically antielitist groups such as the Freewill Baptists stabilized into respectably professional denominations, and as older hierarchical ones modified their once rigid Calvinist theology, conflict and hostility diminished. Perhaps more important, evangelicals of all persuasions came to realize the need to create a network of interlocking mission and reform organizations aimed at ushering in a new age of cooperative piety and Christian moral order.[112]

After an initial decline, the Six-Principle Baptists benefited, however briefly, from this powerful religious revival. The people of the northwest's commercializing farms and villages had grown up, after all, in a society that had long been accustomed to Six-Principle beliefs. When revivals swept through the area, they naturally joined the denomination their parents and kin may have once belonged to. But, in time, many of the new Six-Principle adherents sought to modify their old religion, liberalizing its doctrinal strictures against interdenominational cooperation in order to promote a united evangelical drive against irreligion and sin. The new moral evangelists were particularly prevalent in relatively commercialized or industrialized areas, where the rearrangement of social relations had created the greatest demands for temperance, sabbatarianism, and other moral reforms. Unfortunately for the moral reformers, however, control of the Six-Principle denomination remained in the hands of the traditionalists. When the yearly meeting refused to countenance gaps in the "partition wall" that separated (or in the traditionalists' view, protected) the Six-Principle religion from other denominations, the moral reformers simply withdrew from the conference and eventually found spiritual refuge in one of the newer religions, such as the Christians or Freewill Baptists.

Six-Principle Baptism thus remained a religion of the traditional, rural order. Its adherents, mainly marginal farmers, artisans, and humble laborers, sought spiritual meaning not in spreading moral reform to the rest of the population, but rather in turning inward to the familiar forms of a long-established sect. Yet the social order that once supported their vision was being rapidly eroded. What remained of the old economy of semisubsistence agriculture disappeared after the Civil War, and with it collapsed the Six-Principle denomination. Church membership in the northwest, which had already declined by 30 percent before 1860, fell by another 45 percent in the next three decades.[113]

The remaining Six-Principle members seemed aware of the terminal unpopularity of their "ancient" spiritual order; but they stubbornly refused to budge from primitivist sectarian ways. In 1866, the yearly meeting's circular letter admitted that because "[we] contend for the simplicity of primitive christianity, we have not become popular in the world, and consequently, our denomination has not spread." Nevertheless, the letter's author refused to advocate "popular" reforms but preferred instead: "to pray that God would revive the Six Principle Baptists denomination, that he would enable them to restore their Association to its former standing, [and] that our churches may be reanimated with a spiritual life."[114] This plaintive prayer may have been designed to rouse Six-Principle adherents to an era of former glory; but since the denomination only continued its decline, it served instead as a sort of swan song of despair for a dying cultural order. The future for religion in northwestern Rhode Island would lie not with plaintive callings of sectarian traditionalists, nor with the well-financed missionary efforts of urban religious organizations, but rather with the pragmatic strivings of the Christians and especially the Freewill Baptists, whose simple, moralistic, and increasingly urbane religious faiths best fit the needs of a commercializing rural society.

CONCLUSION

The Place of Northwestern Rhode Island in Rural History

⊽ ⊽

In 1853, the Hartford, Providence, and Fishkill railroad line was built through the south end of Jeremiah McGregor's farm lot in Rice City, bypassing his "temperance tavern" and the village that had played such a richly important role in the area's economic and cultural history. Rail freight quickly reduced wagon traffic on the old and once controversial Providence and Norwich Turnpike, forcing Rice City's shops and storekeepers out of business in favor of the rising rail-stop village of Greene.[1] But the coming of the railroad signaled something more fundamental than just the replacement of one market center for another: the decline of the rural farm and shopkeeper classes that had only recently experienced commercial prosperity. Between the 1780s and 1850s, what was originally a society of isolated, semisufficient yeoman households had been transformed, at least for those who survived the transition, into a land filled with prosperous crossroads shopkeepers and a somewhat modern looking collection of family-run farms. But from the 1850s on, the continuing centralization of the country's economy meant that the main lines of the new nation's rural development would run elsewhere than among the hills of northwestern Rhode Island.

The most seriously affected by the creation of a national market were the rural artisans. By the 1840s, domestic textile workers had already been displaced by the area's cotton and woolen mills. In succeeding decades, the work of rural shoemakers, tailors, and carpenters would all be replaced by factory-produced goods, thanks to the efficiencies of mass production and the ability of railroads to supply the northwest with these products from afar. In Chelsea,

Vermont, for example, an area geographically similar to northwestern Rhode Island, the number of resident artisans fell from seventy-nine in 1850 to only thirty by the end of the century.[2]

Meanwhile, opportunities for factory building in the northwest became spotty at best. During the 1860s, war-induced demand led to a brief spurt in textile-mill construction. Scituate, Glocester, and Burrillville all reported upwards of forty factories by 1865, and even agrarian Foster numbered fourteen. But most of these new enterprises were small and undercapitalized, and they generally collapsed with the end of the war. Thereafter, industrial development occurred unevenly in the northwest. Towns that were blessed with railroad lines—mainly Burrillville and Coventry—continued to expand their textile operations, while in others manufacturing declined considerably.[3]

As for the farmers, the development of a national economy forced them to continually readapt to changing market imperatives. The Hartford, Providence, and Fishkill railroad, together with a parallel line that passed through Burrillville on its way to Springfield, Massachusetts, connected Rhode Island not only to the rest of New England, but also to the great agricultural lands of the Middle Atlantic and midwestern states. Competition from New York's dairy land forced northwestern farmers to turn from cheese production to butter, and then to the more perishable milk. Meanwhile, the importation of midwestern beef effectively ended northwestern cattle raising. Local farmers turned instead to market gardening, growing vegetables such as cucumbers and lettuce, planting peach and apple orchards, and raising poultry for meat and eggs. The poor soils of the northwest left them continually vulnerable to competition from more fertile lands in the West, as well as in the nearby coastal areas of southwestern Rhode Island, where farmers were catching up with the northwest, after a late start in rural commercialization.[4]

Most farmers, however, did not suffer economically. Many inhabitants, especially in the agrarian towns, migrated from the northwest following the Civil War. After stabilizing for a time in the prosperous 1840s and 1850s, between 1860 and 1900 the population of Foster and Glocester declined by 40 percent to just over 1,100 and 1,400, respectively. But much of this decline stemmed from the loss of artisanal employment and the gradual mechanization of agriculture. Relatively few farms were actually abandoned. In the town of Foster, for example, total farm acreage declined by only 13 percent between 1850 and 1895, and the number of individual farms rose. Those farmers who left were not forced out by impoverished conditions so much as they were attracted elsewhere by more profitable employments, either in farmland further west, or in the booming cities of the Northeast. In fact, to judge from the experience of Chelsea, Vermont, rural standards actually improved in the late nineteenth century. In Chelsea the number of mercantile stores rose by 67 percent between 1850 and 1900, while the population nearly halved, thus suggesting that farmers were able to spend more and more money on imported goods.[5]

Yet if those who stayed behind were not deprived economically in the post-bellum period, they seem to have become impoverished culturally, perhaps even spiritually. The exodus of the northwest's shopkeepers and entrepreneurs emptied many of the crossroads hamlets and villages that had once served as the focal point for the area's cultural activity. Rice City boomed as a place where farmers, travelers, and local artisans all met to exchange goods and services; and it was there that the Christian revival first came to Rhode Island, altering dramatically the religious and cultural values of the rural northwest. Other villages provided locations for banks, grammar schools, and even the Smithville Seminary, an important regional institute that attracted students from all over New England. But the coming of railroads deprived many local entrepreneurs of their livelihoods, as a once dynamic area became drawn into the cultural and political orbit of the city of Providence.

Still, one should not minimize the extent to which the rural northwest was socially and economically transformed in the first several decades of the nineteenth century. It is true that the development of a national economy would eventually reduce the northwest agriculturally to an area of only minor importance. But U.S. capitalism was originally built around regional economies, and in this respect, the northwest played an important role in the development of a thriving trading area centered in Providence and the Narragansett Bay area. By mid-century, northwesterners were trading large quantities of increasingly specialized goods — butter, cheese, beef, lumber, and lumber products — to the ports and mill towns of industrial Rhode Island. A similar process occurred throughout the Northeast, as rural hinterlands were drawn into the vortexes of a series of regional economies.

Nor should one overestimate the ease with which northwesterners affected this transformation in their political economy. Like backcountry farmers throughout the United States, the northwestern yeomen of the 1780s looked across a deep political and cultural divide toward their economic superiors in towns and along the commercialized coast. Although they participated occasionally in urban markets, they oriented their production and credit relations more toward the preservation of household independence and a reciprocal network of community exchanges. Backwoods farmers usually supported commercial elites in the struggle for American independence. But the proliferation of revolutionary, republican ideals quickly led them to challenge the gentlemanly prescriptions for credit rules, taxes, governmental structures, and ecclesiastical formulations.

In the case of Rhode Island, the northwest's relatively late settlement and highly localistic cultural traditions seemed to reinforce the backward and self-sufficient nature of its agrarian economy. The absence of an effective provincial or state government meant that highway building would be dictated not by the needs of regional commerce, but rather by local whim and prejudice. The existence of strong, established churches, a rudimentary public-school system, and an educated elite, which in neighboring Connecticut and eastern Massachusetts had inculcated habits of orderliness and eventuated in widespread literacy, was unthinkable in backcountry Rhode Island. Indeed, contemporary travelers uniformly commented on the poverty and backwardness of northwestern Rhode Island, in comparison with neighboring sections of Connecticut. The culture and political economy of the northwest more closely resembled that of adjacent Worcester County, Massachusetts, with its strong tradition of "Popular" gentry leadership and steadily growing Baptist dissent.

In sharp contrast to the commercial backwardness of the rural northwest stood the bustling orderliness of Providence and its environs. Contemporary travelers unanimously praised Providence residents for their "spirit of industry, enterprise and perseverance" and their faithful observance of the Sabbath. They reported further that an orderly devotion to hard work prevailed as well "in the neighborhood" farms, which were not as "miserably cultivated" as those of the backcountry northwest.[6]

It was this sharp contrast between urban industriousness and rural entropy that fueled conflicts between Providence and the northwest in the 1780s and 1790s. The juxtaposition of one of New England's most economically dynamic areas with a relatively backward one led inevitably to heated confrontations. Merchant efforts to build turnpikes and cotton-mill dams in the northwest were resisted with considerable ferocity. Many yeomen had little interest in abandoning the easy, if slovenly, lifestyle of semisubsistence agriculture for the demands and possible rewards of commercial and industrial capitalism. Their sense of resentment found further expression in a political ideology of local rights, and in a religious culture of communal sectarianism. As contemporary travelers noted, even church architecture in the two areas differed in an especially striking way. The Baptist Church in Providence had an "uncommonly handsome steeple," and the Congregational Church was pronounced "one of the handsomest . . . in New England." In the northwestern countryside, on the other hand, where the Six-Principle Baptists cared little for refinement and ornamentation, churches were described by gentlemanly travelers as "small buildings resembling miserable barns."[7] For the northwestern yeomen, turnpikes emanating from Providence threatened to spread not only urban industriousness, but also a fundamentally alien way of life.

In Connecticut and eastern Massachusetts, on the other hand, where established churches and a long-settled gentry forged ties between city and countryside, conflicts over turnpikes and mill dams occurred less frequently. Harvard- and Yale-trained clergy imported into rural areas the elegance of church-steeple architecture and the values of orderliness, industry, and sobriety. In short, the Puritan established church may have played an important role in the transfusion of capitalist values among a rural people who otherwise might have chosen a different worldview.

In time, however, even in the culturally isolated rural northwest, capitalism proved too powerful a force to be resisted by a localist opposition. The yeomanry might have succeeded in harassing urban turnpike companies, but they could only slow the pace of commercial development. They were politically impotent in the state legislature, where merchants could receive charters for their turnpikes and legal exemptions for their mill dams with relative impunity.

Moreover, the northwesterners eventually became divided among themselves, as local entrepreneurs and boosters emerged to sponsor their own turnpikes, schools, and other improvements. In some ways they simply copied the commercializing schemes and plans of the Providence merchants, yet their creations also bore the imprint of their original localist proclivities. Freed from cultural and personal ties to an urban elite, their enterprises could be as brilliantly imaginative as the Rhode Island and Connecticut Turnpike or as comically unsuccessful as the Farmers Exchange Bank in Glocester. But in any event, social status and superior organizing skills allowed the northwest's entrepreneurs to defeat the remaining localist opposition.

In the meantime, the traditional subsistence lifestyle was becoming untenable, thanks to the pressures of population and industry on land, fish, and other natural resources. The remaining semisubsistence farmers were gradually forced to either seek employment in nearby towns and cities or else adapt to the new rhythms of commercial agriculture. As a third option, they could move west, seeking to preserve their social and economic independence amidst the plentiful spaces of the frontier. There, battles between localists and the agents of commercializing agriculture would occur again and again, culminating, perhaps, in the Populist rebellion of the 1890s, when midwestern and southern farmers joined in a futile attempt to free themselves from peonage and market dependence.

For those who stayed behind, however, the defeat of a localist political economy soon resulted in the linking of the northwest to an emerging regional economy and a national cultural ethos. The growth of industry in the Providence area, together with improvements in banking, transportation, and demographic conditions, allowed farmers to sell their products on a greatly increased scale. They could vend their dairy, cattle, and lumber products in a variety of ways, either by traveling to Providence or a nearby mill town, or perhaps more significantly, by trading through local storekeepers. Indeed, the rise of this latter group during the 1820s and 1830s meant that rural trading patterns changed in quality as well as in quantity. Storekeepers and shop owners introduced into the northwest not only imported "luxury" goods, such as clocks and English pottery but also greatly increased economic specialization (through the "putting out" system and their own artisanal skills) and the beginnings of a capital market and cash economy. Finally, the emergence of a more fluid and dynamic economy also helped produce specialization in family and social roles. The structure of the traditional patriarchal family fell into disarray: laborers who once lived and worked alongside their employers became separated from the farm family, and wives began to develop distinctive roles, relatively divorced from the workings of a commercializing agricultural economy. Rural commercialization brought cash and a higher standard of living to the more prosperous farmers, but it also divorced others from the material and social benefits of the commercial economy.

These changes, in turn, helped draw northwesterners into a developing national, or rather northern culture of evangelical zeal and moral reformism; for families throughout the northeastern United States were experiencing similar problems with social differentiation and upheaval. In cities like Providence, Rhode Island, and Rochester, New York, middle-class citizens turned by the thousands to religions that preached moral reformation, seeking a way to both counter and separate themselves from the social disorder and moral dissolution spawned by the breakdown of the traditional patriarchal household. For the most part, in these urban settings the established Protestant denominations—Congregationalists, Presbyterians, and Calvinist Baptists—were strong enough to maintain the allegiance of the righteous, needing only to modify their theologies in the direction of an Arminian emphasis on good works, and to redirect their energies through the myriad voluntary associations that made up the era's "benevolent empire."

In northwestern Rhode Island, many inhabitants joined with this "evangelical empire," or war against sin; but their social structures and cultural traditions dictated that they do so more indirectly, by adapting different ecclesiastical forms. When the mainline denominations tried to evangelize the countryside by sending out missionaries from Providence, they were doomed to failure by their own paternalistic condescension, which necessarily aggravated long-standing rural animosities toward the Providence economic and cultural elite. The sectarian and backwoods heritage of the Six-Principle Baptist order was simply too strong to be overcome by a few missionaries, however well financed, because they originated from an alien urban culture. Instead, the more prosperous northwesterners tended to turn toward two new Protestant denominations: the Christians and the Freewill Baptists. Born amidst the rough-hewn conditions of northern New England, the Christians and the Freewill Baptists espoused a simple, backwoods faith that resonated sympathetically with the cultural affinities of northwestern farmers. But they differed from the existing Six-Principle Baptists by emphasizing the need for social outreach and moral reformation, rather than the preservation of ecclesiastical insularity and theological purity. As the countryside commercialized in the Jacksonian era, the more prosperous farmers and shopkeepers rejected Six-Principle orthodoxy in favor of the practical, commonsense preaching of the Christians and Freewill Baptists. Troubled by the rise of sin and dissolution in the midst of their own commercial prosperity, they found solace and encouragement in the new denominations' forthright attention to the moral needs of society.

Eventually, this religious evolution brought many northwesterners to a kind of cultural rapprochement with the once hated city of Providence. Providence's own traditionally Calvinist denominations, after all, had also been slowly abandoning theological purity in favor of a practical regard for improving society. In both the urban setting of Providence and the rural northwest, church rhetoric shifted away from sectarian concerns about the laying on of hands, or the efficacy of adult baptism, to a broader interest in the moral reformation of society. The temperance and antislavery crusades, the two most important movements to grow out of this religious reorientation, further tied together the inhabitants of rural and urban Rhode Island. It is true that northwesterners were relatively late in joining the abolitionist and antidrinking crusades, and their efforts in this regard were strongest in the mill villages and other commercial centers where capitalist rearrangements of social relations had proceeded the furthest. But even in agrarian Foster in the 1830s and 1840s, 114 men and women, out of an adult population of about 1,000, joined the Foster Total Abstinence Society, an affiliate of a Providence-based statewide organization.[8]

Finally, as commercialization gradually provided the more prosperous northwesterners with the trappings of bourgeois comfort, they began to abandon their region's traditional hostility to urban respectability and religious refinement. Spurred by their denominational leaders, the Freewill Baptists adopted once unheard of ecclesiastical practices: they began paying their ministers, educating a new generation of religious leaders, and introducing liturgical ornamentations, such as organ music, into their services. Indeed, the success of the Freewill Baptists best testifies to the northwest's steady incorporation into the larger culture of northern evangelical Protestantism: for by the 1830s, they maintained large and growing congregations in largely agrarian towns such as Foster and Glocester and in the emerging industrial areas of Pawtucket, Olneyville, and even Providence.[9]

Ultimately, this religious and cultural rapprochement also translated into long-lasting political ties between northwestern farmers and the Providence industrial elite. Analysis of the byzantine workings of Rhode Island's Jacksonian politics lies well beyond the realm of this book, but the political history of the northwest deserves to be briefly sketched, nevertheless. When the Jeffersonian party split apart in the late 1820s, most area residents turned to the Democrats, largely because of the farmers' traditional antipathy to urban merchants and industrialists, who favored instead the National Republican and Whig parties that generally dominated Rhode Island politics. As was the case across the border in Worcester County, Massachusetts, support for the Jacksonians came more from cultural sentiments than economic interests. After all, by this time most farmers were enjoying the benefits of trade with regional merchants and manufacturers. Democratic presidential candidates usually received fewer votes than their gubernatorial counterparts, thus suggesting that some northwestern farmers split their votes, supporting Whig economic policies on the national level, while electing Democrats to local offices.[10]

The farmers' allegiance to the local Democratic party was shaken, however, by the ramifications of the Dorr War rebellion. Advocates of increased suffrage rights and legislative reapportionment, the Dorrites originated as moderate reformers with close ties to the Whig party. But as the reformers radicalized in the late 1830s in the face of conservative intransigence, they increasingly turned their allegiance to the Democratic party, particularly its workingman, Locofoco faction. Alarmed by the prospect of losing control of the party to legions of mill-town workers, farmers in parts of the northwest began to desert to the anti-Dorrite "Law and Order" party, and later to the Whigs.[11]

More fundamentally, as commercialization altered social relations in the countryside, the area's burgeoning temperance crusade lifted the Whig party to power. Hiram Salisbury, the Burrillville resident who mixed farming with carpentry and local office holding, chronicled in his diary the ultimate triumph of the Whig–temperance politics. Salisbury may have sold lumber and produce to the Whig capitalists of Providence; but he followed an older tradition, politically, by working for the Democratic party. "Huzza for Jackson," he exclaimed when his party beat the opposition by a "36 majority" at a town meeting in 1833. But when the Whigs latched on to the temperance movement, the continuing commercialization of the countryside led to their eventual triumph. A part-time peddler, such as Salisbury, might have continued to feel antipathy toward the Whigs of urban Providence; but for more prosperous farmers and storekeepers, the temperance crusade induced them to switch sides in favor of the proponents of moral order. The "Temperance Whigs," as Salisbury termed his opponents, gradually narrowed their losses to the Jacksonians, losing by nineteen votes in June 1838, before finally winning four years later. Salisbury recorded this event with a stunningly simple expression of rejection, noting on June 6, 1842, "I lost all my offices."[12]

Thereafter, Burrillville became a leading center for temperance agitation in Rhode Island, for the town meeting prohibited the sale of liquor locally for several years prior to the enactment of a state "Maine Law" in 1852. When the Whig party collapsed in the 1850s in the wake of antislavery divisions, northwesterners briefly reverted to their traditional Democratic moorings, before transferring their allegiance to the Know-Nothing and, soon thereafter, Republican parties.[13] By this time, the specter of Irish Catholic immigration provided an extra impetus toward sealing the farmers' political marriage to the once hated industrialists of Providence. At the time of the Civil War, the rural northwest, an agricultural region once infamous for its parochial isolation, had already become an integral part of the nation's capitalist civilization.

APPENDIX

The Churches of Northwestern Rhode Island, 1780–1850

Six-Principle Baptists

Burrillville Church, 1749?–1832: met in Chepachet, 1756–1786; in Burrillville, 1786–1832; meetinghouse taken over by Freewill Baptist Church of Burrillville, ca. 1820.

Coventry Central "Knotty Oak" Church, 1840– : majority of members left in 1852 over closed-communion issue; remaining Six-Principle church eventually recovered and reoccupied meetinghouse in 1859; joined Warren Association of Five-Principle churches in 1916.

Coventry "Maple Root" Church, 1762– : meetinghouse built in 1797, located in south-central part of town.

Foster Church, 1769–1837: met in various homes, 1769–1790; in meetinghouse near Hopkins Mills, 1791–1837.

Glocester Church, 1780–1827?: located in southwest Glocester.

Scituate Church, 1725–1922?: located on Providence and Norwich Turnpike, near center of town.

Scituate Union Church, 1841–1921?: formed by members of Coventry Church who lived in southern Scituate.

Freewill Baptists

Burrillville Church, 1812– : met in old Six-Principle church, 1812–1839, then moved to Pascoag village; merged with Methodists, 1928.

Coventry Church, 1847–1906?.

Foster Church, 1824– : also called the North Foster Freewill Baptist Church.

Glocester Church, 1822–   : met in meetinghouse in Chepachet financed by the "Proprietors of the Chepachet Meeting House," a society formed in response to the decline of a local Calvinist Baptist congregation and the consequent destruction of its church building.

Morning Star Church, 1846–1939: located in Foster near Glocester boundary.

North Scituate Church, 1835–   : formed when ministers were excluded from local Congregational Church.

Second Church of Foster, 1835–1913: name changed to the Freewill Baptist Church of Foster and Glocester, ????; actually located in northwestern Scituate.

Other Baptists

Arkwright and Fiskeville Church, 1829–1855: result of missionary work of Rhode Island Baptist State Convention; building located on property owned by the Jackson Mills in the southeastern corner of Scituate.

Coventry Church, 17??–1810?: New Light or Separate Baptist in origin; located at west end of town; probably taken over by Christians in Rice City around 1812.

Foster Church, 1750?–1805?: Six-Principle Calvinist in beliefs.

Foster Church (Elder Hammond's meetinghouse), 1780–1825: formed by Five-Principle Baptists after schism in the town's Six-Principle Baptist Church.

Glocester Baptist Church, 1742–1802: formed as Separate Baptist Church and eventually joined Warren Association; Six-Principle Calvinist in beliefs.

Second Separate Baptist Church of Coventry, 1795–1846?: formed in 1795 from above-named Coventry Church; located in eastern end of town.

"Christian" Churches

Clayville Church, 1850–   : formed from Foster Center Church; located near center of Foster–Scituate town border.

Foster Center Church, 1834–   : formed from Rice City Church.

Harris and Phenix Church, 1833–   : located on border of Coventry and Warwick.

Rice City Church, 1812–   : located in western end of town.

Rockland Church, 1825–   : located in west-central Scituate.

Other Denominations

Adventists—large camp meeting held in 1843; church formed in Glocester, possibly by 1848.

Laurel Hill Methodist Episcopal Church (Burrillville), 1847–

SOURCES: The Historical Records Survey, *Inventory of the Church Archives of Rhode Island: Baptist* (Providence, 1941); Margery I. Matthews et al., *Churches of Foster* (Foster, 1978); Richard M. Bayles, ed., *History of Providence County, Rhode Island* (New York, 1891), chaps. 12–15.

Notes

Abbreviations Used in Notes

RIHS   Rhode Island Historical Society
ABHS   American Baptist Historical Society
RISA   Rhode Island State Archives
NYHS   New York Historical Society
RIDMS   Rhode Island Domestic Missionary Society
OSVRL   Old Sturbridge Village Research Library

Preface

1. On the differences between backcountry and commercial economies, see James A. Henretta, "Families and Farms: *Mentalité* in America," *William and Mary Quarterly* 35 (January 1978): 3–32; Michael Merrill, "Cash Is Good to Eat: Self-Sufficiency and Exchange in the Rural Economy of the United States," *Radical History Review* 3 (Winter 1977): 42–71; Christopher Clark, "Household Economy, Market Exchange, and the Rise of Capitalism in the Connecticut Valley, 1800–1860," *Journal of Social History* 13 (Winter 1979): 169–89; Clark, *The Roots of Rural Capitalism: Western Massachusetts, 1780–1860* (Ithaca, N.Y.: Cornell University Press, 1990).

2. On backcountry religious awakenings, see Rhys Isaac, *The Transformation of Virginia, 1740–1790* (Chapel Hill: University of North Carolina Press, 1982), 161–80, 278–304; Richard L. Bushman, *From Puritan to Yankee: Character and the Social Order in Connecticut, 1690–1765* (Cambridge, Mass.: Harvard University Press, 1967), chaps. 10–14; Stephen A. Marini, *Radical Sects of Revolutionary New England* (Cambridge, Mass.: Harvard University Press, 1982).

3. For examples of backcountry rebellions, see Thomas P. Slaughter, *The Whiskey Rebellion: Frontier Epilogue to the American Revolution* (New York: Oxford University Press, 1986); David P. Szatmary, *Shays' Rebellion: The Making of an Agrarian Insurrection* (Amherst: University of Massachusetts Press, 1980); Andrew R. L. Cayton, *The Frontier Republic: Ideology and Politics in the Ohio Country* (Kent, Ohio: Kent State University Press, 1986); Alan Taylor, *Liberty Men and Great Proprietors: The Revolutionary Settlement on the Maine Frontier, 1760–1820* (Chapel Hill: University of North Carolina Press, 1990).

4. On the impact of radical republicanism on religion, see Nathan O.

Hatch, *The Democratization of American Christianity* (New Haven, Conn.: Yale University Press, 1989); Taylor, *Liberty Men and Great Proprietors,* 123–54.

5. Of the several studies that emphasize Rhode Island's uniqueness, see especially Irwin H. Polishook, *Rhode Island and the Union, 1774–1795* (Evanston, Ill.: Northwestern University Press, 1969); Sidney V. James, *Colonial Rhode Island: A History* (New York: Charles Scribner's Sons, 1975), 287–89.

Chapter One

1. Edwin T. Corwin, comp., *Ecclesiastical Records of the State of New York* (Albany, 1901), I: 399–400, quoted in Carl Bridenbaugh, *Fat Mutton and Liberty of Conscience: Society in Rhode Island, 1636–1690* (Providence: Brown University Press, 1974), 3.

2. New Shoreham Town Meeting Minutes, July 12, 1785, quoted in Polishook, *R.I. and the Union,* 36.

3. Francis Brinley to Francis Nicholson, Newport, R.I., Nov. 4, 1709, Massachusetts Historical Society Misc. Bound Documents, vol. 7, quoted in Polishook, *R.I. and the Union,* 25; for more on Rhode Island's colonial government, see Polishook, chap. 2.

4. Rhode Island's legislature did not pass a general highway act until 1715, decades after similar acts were passed in Connecticut (1645) and Massachusetts (1647). Philip E. Taylor, "The Turnpike Era in New England" (Ph.D. dissertation, Yale University, 1934), 34–35.

5. James, *Colonial R.I.,* 287–89.

6. James, *Colonial R.I.,* 170–85; Polishook, *R.I. and the Union,* 6–8.

7. John Montgomery to Edward Hand, July 26, 1784, quoted in Polishook, *R.I. and the Union,* 96.

8. Timothy Dwight, *Travels in New England and New York,* (New Haven, 1821–22) II: 29–30; III: 36–37.

9. James B. Hedges, *The Browns of Providence Plantations: Colonial Years* (Cambridge, Mass.: Harvard University Press, 1952), 219.

10. James, *Colonial R.I.,* 250–56; Julian Ursyn Niemcewicz, *Under Their Vine and Fig Tree, Travels through America in 1797–1799,* trans. and ed. Metchie J. E. Budka, New Jersey Historical Society Collections, vol. 14 (Elizabeth, N.J., 1965), 141–47; Francisco De Miranda, *New Democracy in America: Travels, 1783–84,* trans. Judson P. Wood, ed. John S. Ezell (Norman, Okla.: University of Oklahoma Press, 1963), 148–49.

11. Rose C. Tillinghast, *The Tillinghast Family, 1560–1971* (1972). In 1769, Newport had twenty-two distilleries. See Peter J. Coleman, *The Transformation of Rhode Island, 1790–1860* (Providence: Brown University Press, 1963), 10.

12. Polishook, *R.I. and the Union,* 69–75.

13. Both cows and heifers are mentioned throughout this discussion because Rhode Island tax records counted them both, contrary to the practice in Massachusetts.

14. See Table IA for figures on Glocester agriculture. In 1782 Glocester (which at the time included the future town of Burrillville) accounted for one-third of the northwest's population and 40 percent of its land area. Situated in the extreme

northwest corner of the state, the town may have been slightly less commercialized than Scituate or Coventry. See Edward Cook's "Commercial Index," in *Fathers of the Towns: Leadership and Community Structure in Eighteenth-Century New England* (Baltimore: Johns Hopkins University Press, 1976), 211.

15. See Table IB for estimated farm-household production and consumption.

16. Figures on agriculture elsewhere in southern New England were obtained from Robert A. Gross, "Culture and Cultivation: Agriculture and Society in Thoreau's Concord," *Journal of American History* 69 (June 1982), 42–61; and Bettye Hobbs Pruitt, "Self-Sufficiency and the Agricultural Economy of Eighteenth-Century Massachusetts," *William and Mary Quarterly* 41 (July 1984), 333–64.

17. Nehemiah Atwood Account Book, RIHS; Paul G. E. Clemens and Lucy Simler, "Rural Labor and the Farm Household in Chester County, Pennsylvania, 1750–1820," in *Work and Labor in Early America*, ed. Stephen Innes (Chapel Hill: University of North Carolina Press, 1988), 106–43. Clemens and Simler computed a ratio of .6 for landless to landed households in 1760. In Glocester in 1778 the ratio was only .23.

18. Nicholas and John Brown to Israel Arnold, Dec. 20, 1763; Thomas and Solomon Owen to N. Brown & Co., Nov. 22, 1771; Nicholas Brown to Solomon Owen, Jan. 4, 1776 (Brown Family Papers, John Carter Brown Library). In the 1778 tax assessment, Solomon Owen's estate ranked in the top 5 percent; Israel Arnold died before 1778, but of the Arnolds listed who survived him, five out of seven ranked in the first decile. See Table IA for farm production figures.

19. See Table IC for a breakdown of farm production by family life cycle. See Table 4A, part 1 for distribution of "luxuries" among the rural population.

20. Glocester Town Tax Valuation, 1778. For probate records, see Table 4A. Actually, only 2.7 percent of all decedents owned wagons in the 1780s, but I use "less than 5 percent" in the text because probate records tend to understate ownership of material possessions.

21. Nathaneal Greene, Jr., to N. Brown & Co., Mar. 29, 1771 (Brown Papers); see also Owen's correspondence with the Browns, cited in note 18.

22. Hedges, *Browns*, 127, 142–43, 149; Owen to N. Brown & Co., Nov. 22, 1771 (Brown Papers); Rhode Island Historical Preservation Commission, *Preliminary Survey Report: Town of Scituate* (Providence, 1980), 7.

23. Thomas and Solomon Owen to N. Brown & Co., Nov. 22, 1771; Nathaneal Greene, Jr., to N. Brown & Co., Mar. 29, 1771 (Brown Papers).

24. Charles C. Beaman, "Sketches of Scituate and Foster, R.I.," No. 3, clippings from the *Providence Journal*, in Rider Collection, Box 343, No. 9, John Hay Library.

25. The argument that follows is based partially on Henretta, "Families and Farms," 3–32; Michael Merrill, "Cash Is Good to Eat: Self-Sufficiency and Exchange in the Rural Economy of the United States," *Radical History Review* 15 (Winter 1977): 42–71; Clark, "Household Economy," 169–89; Clark, *Roots of Rural Capitalism*, 21–58; and Carole Shammas, "How Self-Sufficient Was Early America?" *Journal of Interdisciplinary History* 13 (1982–1983): 247–72. See also additional works as cited below.

26. See Table IA for Glocester Town Tax Valuation, 1778.

27. Glocester Town Tax Valuation, 1778. Forrest McDonald and Grady McWhiney have suggested that a similarly easy lifestyle, based on open-range grazing, was pursued by the piedmont farmers of the antebellum South; see McDonald and McWhiney, "The South from Self-Sufficiency to Peonage: An Interpretation," *American Historical Review* 85 (December 1980): 1085–1118.

28. Dwight, *Travels*, II: 38; Elias Boudinot, *Elias Boudinot's Journey to Boston in 1809*, ed. Milton Halsey Thomas (Princeton, N.J.: Princeton University Press, 1955), 27; Sir Augustus John Foster, *Jeffersonian America: Notes on the United States of America Collected in the Years 1805–6–7 and 11–12* (San Marino, Calif.: Huntingdon Library, 1954), 319; Niemcewicz, *Travels through America in 1797–1799*, 141. For a general discussion of rural "slovenliness" in the late eighteenth century, see Jack Larkin, *The Reshaping of Everyday Life* (New York: Harper and Row, 1988), 127–32. Since, as Larkin suspects, the Connecticut countryside was probably unusual in its orderliness, rural Rhode Island may simply have suffered by comparison: it may have been no more untidy in appearance than the more recently settled parts of Massachusetts. See Larkin, "From 'Country Mediocrity' to 'Rural Improvement': Transforming the Slovenly Countryside in Central Massachusetts, 1775–1840" (Paper presented at the Boston Area Seminar in Early American History, April 18, 1991), 19.

29. See Table 1C for statistics on farm production for different household sizes and stages in the family life cycle.

30. Over 80 percent of all households owned spinning wheels. This and other data cited on local services was gathered from a file of probate inventories from all four towns, spanning the years 1784–1791. On midwifery, see Laura Thatcher Ulrich, "Martha Ballard and Her Girls: Women's Work in Eighteenth-Century Maine," in Innes, ed., *Work and Labor in Early America*. Women's role in the rural economy will be discussed at greater length in Chapter Four.

31. See Figure 2 for a comparison of food prices in northwestern Rhode Island and Philadelphia. In "A Price Index for Rural Massachusetts, 1750–1855," *Journal of Economic History* 39 (December 1979): 975–1001, Winifred B. Rothenberg purports to show a close correlation of prices in rural Massachusetts with those in New York and Philadelphia. A year-by-year comparison of New York prices with her rural index actually reveals the following trends: (1) largely negative correlation between urban and rural prices in the colonial years; (2) weak correlation during the revolutionary war, when rural prices increased, but at a much slower rate than urban prices; (3) mixed correlation in the 1790s, when rural prices inexplicably "led New York and Philadelphia prices by a year or two"; and (4) establishment of a fairly steady correlation in the early 1820s.

32. Of the seven extant account books for northwestern Rhode Island and neighboring Connecticut and Massachusetts, none show payment of interest. Four of the seven record customers' credits sporadically, usually only in the case of laborers who would not have compiled account books of their own. The other three record no customer credits at all. See the Bibliography for a list of account books used. In "The Emergence of a Capital Market in Rural Massachusetts, 1730–1838," *Journal of Economic History* 45 (December 1985): 781–808, Winifred B. Rothenberg suggests that a capital market only began to emerge in the 1780s.

33. Erratic and incomplete accounting practices may also cause under-estimation of the frequency with which interest was charged on notes of hand.

34. For Mathewson's inventory, see Glocester Town Probate Records, vol. 2, 112.

35. Theodore Foster Account Book, 1802–1809, John Hay Library; Ledger of Samuel Butler, 1780–1800, in Butler Family Papers, RIHS. For a similar pattern of different credit rules, see Clark's discussion of "local" versus "long-distance" trade in *Roots of Rural Capitalism*, 28–38.

36. See Atwood and Smith account books, noted above.

37. While living in the United States in the late 1700s, Richard Parkinson was shocked to find that Americans of all ranks considered it a "custom . . . to take fruit wherever they saw it." The locals, in turn, were outraged to learn from Parkinson that fruit stealers faced severe punishment in England. As one merchant protested: "What! transport a man for getting a little fruit! . . . thank God, we have no such doings here. Give me liberty and equality, my boys! . . . Give me a republican country!"; see Parkinson, *A Tour in America, in 1798, 1799 and 1800* (London, 1805), 616–19.

38. Recent scholarship suggests that religion in Connecticut and Massachusetts was also rather heterogeneous, or at least not as uniform as historian Perry Miller's work once suggested. For example, Laura Becker has shown that opposition to new forms of congregational singing was more intense in rural churches than in urban ones. This suggests that urban/rural divergence in religious practice was not unique to Rhode Island. See Laura L. Becker, "Ministers vs. Laymen: The Singing Controversy in Puritan New England, 1720–1790," *New England Quarterly* 55 (November 1982), 79–95.

39. See Table IE for church membership in 1790. Even at the height of the Great Awakening, church membership in Concord, Massachusetts, did not exceed about 190 out of a population over age fifteen of 780, or about 24 percent. Membership before the Great Awakening was only 11 percent. (Population over age fifteen was assumed to be 52 percent of the total.) See Robert A. Gross, *The Minutemen and Their World* (New York: Hill and Wang, 1976), 3, 19. In 1810 church membership in Cortland County, New York, was 9.5 percent of persons over age nine, or about 12 percent of those over age fifteen. See Curtis D. Johnson, *Islands of Holiness: Rural Religion in Upstate New York, 1790–1860* (Ithaca, N.Y.: Cornell University Press, 1989), 182. Sydney E. Ahlstrom estimates that only 5–10 percent of all Americans were church members at the end of the eighteenth century; see Ahlstrom, *A Religious History of the American People* (New York: Image Books, 1975), 443.

40. For the best description of the rite of laying on of hands, see Ezra Stiles, *The Literary Diary of Ezra Stiles*, ed. Franklin Bowditch Dexter (New York, 1901), 122.

41. A. C. Underwood, *A History of the English Baptists* (London: Baptist Union Publishing Department, 1947), 49–158; Richard Knight, *History of the General Six-Principle Baptists, in Europe and America* (Providence, 1826), 95–115. The Particular Baptists, although sharing some of their rival's sectlike traits, were generally less radical and otherworldly. They considered laying on of hands and other rites to be merely optional; and early on they began developing an educated ministry. Philip F.

Gura, *A Glimpse of Sion's Glory: Puritan Radicalism in New England, 1620–1660* (Middletown, Conn.: Wesleyan University Press, 1984), 93–103; Edwin Scott Gaustad, "Baptists in Seventeenth-Century England" (Master's thesis, Brown University, 1948).

42. Morgan Edwards, "Materials for a History of the Baptists in Rhode Island," RIHS *Collections*, VI (1867), 313–15; William G. McLoughlin, *New England Dissent, 1630–1833: The Baptists and the Separation of Church and State* (Cambridge, Mass.: Harvard University Press, 1971), 10–11. Reuben Aldridge Guild gives a slightly different account, alleging that the original Particular Baptist church simply died out and was replaced by a General Baptist rival. But in any case, the town's Baptist community as a whole gradually shifted from Five-Principle, Particular to Six-Principle, General Baptism; see Guild, *Early History of Brown University, including the Life, Times and Correspondence of President Manning, 1756–1791* (Providence: Snow & Farnham, 1896), 199.

43. Isaac Backus, *The Diary of Isaac Backus*, ed. William G. McLoughlin (Providence: Brown University Press, 1979), 475n.

44. The two Six-Principle Calvinist churches in the northwest were located in western Scituate (Foster after 1782) and Glocester (see the Appendix). McLoughlin, *New England Dissent*, 421–22, 704–5; McLoughlin, ed., *Diary of Backus*, 538–40.

45. For rural singing practices, see McLoughlin, ed., *Diary of Backus*, 590.

46. Dexter, ed., *Diary of Stiles*, 123.

47. The Stony Lane, Maple Root, and Wood River churches were located, respectively, in North Kingston, Coventry, and Richmond, Rhode Island. (Richmond was a backcountry town in southwestern Rhode Island.)

48. Dexter, ed., *Diary of Stiles*, 49; James, *Colonial R.I.*, 47. For church meeting minute books, see the General Six-Principle Baptist Archives, RIHS.

49. Record Book of the General Six-Principle Baptist Church of Scituate, June 4, 1785; many other examples occur in the Johnston church records: Apr. 5, 1783; Aug. 5, 1786; 1790s, *passim* (RIHS).

50. For this and other examples of church-mediated disputes, see Six-Principle Baptist Church of Smithfield and Glocester, misc. MSS. records, Apr. 23, 1764; Oct. 24, 1764; and June 29, 1768–Jan. 16, 1769 (ABHS); Johnston Six-Principle Church Records, Mar. 2, 1793 (RIHS).

51. Records of the Church Meetings of Business, Scituate church, Aug. 17, 1833; Scituate church records, June 4, 1785, July 2, 1785, June 2, 1787; Records of the Six-Principle Baptist Church of East Greenwich, June 25, 1762; Records of the General Six-Principle Baptist Church of West Greenwich, Mar. 5, 1825 (RIHS).

52. David Jones, *The Doctrine of "Laying on of Hands" Examined and Vindicated* (Philadelphia, 1786), 3–4, 16, 27; Jones, *A True History of the Laying on of Hands . . .* (Burlington, N.J., 1805); Records of the General Six-Principle Baptist Church of West Greenwich, 8–9, *passim*; Isaac Backus, "Thots about Laying on of hands. Feb. 1764" (ABHS).

53. For the wealth and residence of Six-Principle Baptists, see Tables 1D and 1E. In "The Singing Controversy," Laura Becker discusses the ways in which

the Massachusetts clergy struggled to overcome the local particularisms of rural congregations.

54. For development of "high-church" religion among other colonial elites, see Bernard Bailyn, *The New England Merchants in the Seventeenth Century* (Cambridge, Mass.: Harvard University Press, 1955), 138–39; E. Digby Baltzell, *Puritan Boston and Quaker Philadelphia: Two Protestant Ethics and the Spirit of Class Authority and Leadership* (New York: Free Press, 1979).

55. James, *Colonial R.I.,* 188–207.

56. Hedges, *Browns,* 194; McLoughlin, *New England Dissent,* I: 491–500.

57. "Elder Young" was probably Nathan Young, who served (1754–1775) as pastor of a Six-Principle Calvinist church in western Scituate (later Foster). By "illiterate," Stiles probably meant that Young was simply ignorant of Greek and Latin. As reported earlier, Stiles found that the rural pastors could at least read the Bible. Dexter, ed., *Diary of Stiles,* 48–49; McLoughlin, *New England Dissent,* I: 491–500; McLoughlin, ed., *Diary of Backus,* 601n.

58. S. L. Caldwell, *History of the First Baptist Church in Providence, 1639–1837* (Providence, 1877), 12; Guild, *Brown University,* 210–12.

59. James Brown's sermon, n.d., Brown Papers, Folder L31–90M.

60. Coleman, *Transformation of R.I.,* 26, 71, *passim;* Henry C. Dorr, *The Planting and Growth of Providence* (Providence, 1882), 135–55, 230–40.

61. Hedges, *Browns,* 194–97.

62. Guild, *Brown University,* 210–11; Dexter, ed., *Diary of Stiles,* 49.

63. Records of the First Baptist Church, Providence, vol. 1, RIHS; Guild, *Brown University,* 214–17.

64. In "The Singing Controversy," Laura Becker found that an interest in "harmony and order" lay behind Bostonians' support of hymn singing.

65. Backus, "Thots about Laying on of hands. Feb. 1764" (ABHS).

66. Isaac Backus, "Remarks upon David Jones's vindication of Laying on of Hands. 1788" (ABHS).

67. Records of the First Baptist Church, Providence, vol. 1; Guild, *Brown University,* 217–18; Caldwell, *First Baptist Church in Providence,* 12; Warren Association, *Minutes,* 1782; McLoughlin, *New England Dissent,* I: 504. For a similar, albeit more violent example of religious conflict between yeomen and gentry, see Rhys Isaac, *The Transformation of Virginia, 1740–1790* (Chapel Hill: University of North Carolina Press, 1982), chap. 8.

68. Knight, *History of the Baptists,* 260.

69. Rhode Island Six-Principle Baptist Association Minutes, 1764–1775, John Hay Library. There were actually eleven churches in the Six-Principle association, but the congregations of East Greenwich and Coventry rarely bothered to send delegates to the association's annual meeting.

70. *Ibid.*

71. The Coventry Six-Principle church joined the yearly meeting in 1783, twenty-one years after its founding in 1762; the Burrillville and Foster churches joined in 1786 and 1791, having been founded in 1749 and 1769, respectively. See the Appendix.

72. See the Appendix. Isaac Backus was chiefly instrumental in persuad-

ing Six-Principle Calivinist pastors to abandon the "hands" requirement. See Mc-Loughlin, ed., *Diary of Backus*, 267.

73. The Separate Baptist Church of Coventry, organized in 1774, foundered over political conflicts engendered by Shays' Rebellion. An offshoot, "Second Separate Baptist Church," flourished briefly after its founding in 1795, before it, too, began to decline. Meanwhile, the Five-Principle Calvinist church of Foster declined, due to westward immigration, from a peak membership of thirty-eight in 1790 to eventual dissolution in 1825. Composed disproportionately of wealthy members, the Five-Principle Calvinists may have been particularly disposed to arouse controversy by opposing locally popular Shaysite sentiments. See the Appendix and discussion of Shays' Rebellion in the following section of this chapter.

74. *Ibid.*; Records of the Baptist Yearly Meetings, 1774–1800, RIHS.

75. See Table 1D. Edward Cook's figures for New England were 40 percent for the top decile and 73 percent for the top quarter. See Cook, *Fathers of the Towns*, 80.

76. David S. Lovejoy, *Rhode Island Politics and the American Revolution, 1760–1776* (Providence: Brown University Press, 1958), 16–17. The figure for suffrage eligibility was calculated from the number of Glocester polls who owned more than the minimum qualification of forty pounds in real estate on the 1778 tax valuation. This figure is somewhat lower than Lovejoy's because in estimating the total number of adult males, Lovejoy did not include men who paid a poll tax but who did not have any taxable wealth. The number of polls on the 1778 tax valuation (555) is very close to the number of adult men listed in the census of 1782 (567).

77. On Rhode Island politics, see James, *Colonial R.I.*, 156–86. On the Massachusetts scene, the best work is Robert Zemsky, *Merchants, Farmers and River Gods: An Essay on Eighteenth-Century American Politics* (Boston: Gambit, 1971).

78. James, *Colonial R.I.*, 156; Hedges, *Browns*, 137.

79. Israel Arnold to Nicholas and John Brown, Apr. 15, 1763, Brown Papers; Lovejoy, *R.I. Politics*, 24–25.

80. The correspondent who referred to Rhode Island as a "republick" was Israel Arnold, *ibid.*; Lovejoy, *R.I. Politics, passim*. Bruce C. Daniels, "The 'Particular Courts' of Local Government: Town Councils in Eighteenth-Century Rhode Island," *Rhode Island History* 41 (May 1982): 64.

81. Forrest McDonald and Ellen Shapiro McDonald have recently argued that high and discriminatory taxes, instead of debt, played the most important role in triggering Shays' Rebellion and other agrarian disturbances of the 1780s. See McDonald and McDonald, *Requiem: Variations on Eighteenth-Century Themes* (Lawrence: University Press of Kansas, 1988), 59–84. For another view, see John L. Brooke, "To the Quiet of the People: Revolutionary Settlements and Civil Unrest in Western Massachusetts, 1774–1789," *William and Mary Quarterly* 46 (July 1989): 425–62.

82. Petitions to the General Assembly, vol. 22, pt. 1, no. 84, RISA; Joseph Hadfield, *An Englishman in America, 1785, Being the Diary of Joseph Hadfield*, ed. Douglas S. Robertson (Toronto: Hunter-Rose, 1973), 26–27.

83. Horace A. Keach, *Burrillville, As It Was, and As It Is* (Providence: Knowles, Anthony, 1856), 24–26. Glocester residents also participated in tax riots

across the border in Douglas, Massachusetts; see John L. Brooke, *The Heart of the Commonwealth: Society and Political Culture in Worcester County, Massachusetts, 1713–1861* (New York: Cambridge University Press, 1989), 204. For economic conditions and protests, see David P. Szatmary, *Shays' Rebellion: The Making of an Agrarian Insurrection* (Amherst: University of Massachusetts Press, 1980); and Robert A. Becker, " 'Combustibles in Every State': A Frame of Reference for Shays' Rebellion" (Paper presented at the Annual Meeting of the Organization of American Historians, Philadelphia, Apr. 3, 1982).

84. Polishook, *R.I. and the Union*, 103–24. Polishook demonstrates that sixteen merchants alone owned 30 percent of the entire state debt in 1784.

85. *Ibid.*, 124–54, 163–65; Merrill Jensen, *The New Nation: A History of the United States during the Confederation, 1781–1789* (New York: Alfred A. Knopf, 1950), 313–26. The paper-money laws enacted by the Country party in the 1780s also stand in contrast to the currency schemes of Rhode Island's colonial period. Colonial "land banks" were actually enacted at the behest of Rhode Island's merchants, who needed a sizeable currency in order to expand their trade. Legal tender laws were not enacted because the currency was designed for paying off debts owed to Boston merchants, instead of debts owed to fellow Rhode Islanders, as was the case in the 1780s. Farmers, on the other hand, often opposed paper money in the colonial period: they had little desire to trade with Boston, and they preferred specie as a more secure intermediary for purchasing occasional necessities from their own local merchants. See James, *Colonial R.I.*, 168–78.

86. David Daggett, *An Oration . . . July 4, 1787* (New Haven, 1787), quoted in Jackson Turner Main, *Political Parties before the Constitution* (Chapel Hill: University of North Carolina Press, 1973), 305.

87. No modern history has yet been written of the agricultural areas along Narragansett Bay. The reasons for planter support of paper money are therefore offered here mostly as conjecture. See James, *Colonial R.I.*, 250–55; Coleman, *Transformation of R.I.*, 19–21; Polishook, *R.I. and the Union*, 108–9.

88. The most famous example of a scornful view of Rhode Island by outsiders was the Connecticut Wits' satirical poem, *Anarchiad*.

89. Charles C. Beamen, "History of Foster," RIHS MSS. For more on popular opposition to federalism, see Saul Cornell, "An Aristocracy Assailed: The Ideology of Backcountry Anti-Federalism," *Journal of American History* 76 (March 1990): 1148–72.

90. Foster, *Jeffersonian America*, 321–22; Henry Bradshaw Fearon, *Sketches of America*, 2d ed. (London, 1818), 99–100.

91. Polishook, *R.I. and the Union*, 115–18. For the insight into the "social audacity" of the farmers, I should credit Carl E. Prince, "From War to Peace: New Jersey in Transition, 1780–1790" (Lecture delivered at The Treaty of Paris and American Independence: A Bicentennial Symposium, Princeton University, Oct. 29, 1983).

92. Beaman, "History of Foster," 39–42, Richard Bayles, *History of Providence County* (New York, 1891), II: 515.

93. Polishook, *R.I. and the Union*, 163–230; *Providence Gazette*, June 5, 1790; Bayles, *History of Providence County*, II: 518–19. Other Country party leaders also admitted privately of their support for ratification. See John P. Kaminski, "Political

Sacrifice and Demise—John Collins and Jonathan J. Hazard, 1786–1790," *Rhode Island History* 35 (August 1976): 91–98.

94. Polishook, *R.I. and the Union*, 223–24, 234–35; Foster Town Meeting Minutes. For state politics in the Federalist era, see Joseph Michael Norton, "The Rhode Island Federalist Party: 1785–1815" (Ph.D. dissertation, St. John's University, 1975). I am also indebted here to Edward Cook and his extensive knowledge of Rhode Island politics.

Chapter Two

1. Coleman, *Transformation of R.I.*, 9–11, 38–70; Dwight, *Travels*, II: 35–36.

2. Coleman, *Transformation of R.I.*, 77–95. As an example of the shift from commercial to manufacturing investment, in 1831 the Brown and Ives Co. for the most part discontinued maritime operations in order to concentrate on its booming textile business.

3. *Ibid.*, 182–88, 208–20; *Petitions to the General Assembly*, RISA, vol. 32, no. 88; *Public Laws of the State of Rhode Island and Providence Plantations, 1798–1813* (Newport, 1813), 31–35.

4. *Petitions to the General Assembly*, RISA MSS., vol. 33, pt. 2, no. 5; for the case in North Providence, see Gary Kulik, "The Beginnings of the Industrial Revolution in America: Pawtucket, R.I., 1672–1829" (Ph.D. dissertation, Brown University, 1980), 50–65, 154–59; and Kulik, "Dams, Fish, and Farmers: Defense of Public Rights in Eighteenth-Century Rhode Island," in *The Countryside in the Age of Capitalist Transformation: Essays in the Social History of Rural America*, ed. Stephen Hahn and Jonathan Prude (Chapel Hill: University of North Carolina Press, 1985), 25–50. Much of the following discussion on fishing rights in colonial America is based on Kulik's work.

5. Howard S. Russell, *A Long Deep Furrow: Three Centuries of Farming in New England* (Hanover, N.H.: University Press of New England, 1976), 6, 13, 43, 319; Bayles, *History of Providence County*, I: 235.

6. Joseph K. Angell, *A Treatise on the Common Law in Relation to Water-Courses* (Boston, 1824), 74–75.

7. Rhode Island Colony Records, vol. 4, 221; *Public Laws of Rhode Island, 1744*, 185–87.

8. *Petitions*, vol. 13, pt. 2, no. 20; *Acts and Resolutions of the Rhode Island General Assembly, February 1767*, 72–73; Kulik, "Pawtucket, R.I.," 60.

9. *Petitions*, vol. 22, no. 90. The fishway-rights petition was also endorsed by the upper-valley town of Scituate. See Scituate Town Meeting Records, Feb. 24, 1787.

10. *Ibid. Acts and Resolutions*, March 1786, 11; March 1788, 20–21. See Table 2A for residence and tax information on opponents and proponents of restricting dams and fishing nets. The results are somewhat difficult to interpret, partly because the town of Cranston, although generally an upriver region, also borders on the mouth of the Pawtuxet River. Tax figures show that neither group was wealthier than the other.

There were, however, a few noteworthy exceptions to the unanimity with which upper-valley residents supported the free passage of migratory fish. As the table shows, about 27 percent of those who signed the second petition (in support of less restrictive fishing regulations) were residents of the upper valley. This group consisted chiefly of the Medberry, Harris, and Kimball families of Scituate and the Thorntons and Williamses of Johnston, whose above-average tax payments suggest ownership of large milling establishments. These families sided with residents of the lower valley in seeking fewer restrictions on dams and seines. Twenty years later, when conflict over fishing rights would break out again, they would find more support for dam-owner privileges from their own neighbors. (See Chapter Three.)

11. The only other example of conflict among rural Rhode Islanders occurred in 1766, when Warwick farmers opposed Samuel Greene's plans to build a corn mill, largely because Greene was believed to be a rather obnoxious character. See *Petitions*, vol. 13, pt. 2, nos. 15, 17.

12. Arthur Cecil Bining, *Pennsylvania Iron Manufacture in the Eighteenth Century* (Harrisburg: Pennsylvania Historical and Museum Commission, n.d.), 64–73.

13. *Petitions*, vol. 11, no. 206; vol. 13, no. 77.

14. *Petitions*, vol. 4, no. 70; vol. 13, no. 13.

15. Hedges, *Browns*, 312–14; Mathias P. Harpin, *Prophets in the Wilderness, A History of Coventry, R.I.* (Oneco, Conn.: Harpin's Connecticut Almanac, 1973), 11; Nathaneal Greene, *The Papers of Nathaneal Greene*, ed. Richard K. Showman (Chapel Hill: University of North Carolina Press, 1976), I: 35–39; II: 381n.

16. Deed of William Potter, Job Greene and James Greene, and John Allen to Almy & Brown, Aug. 31, 1799; James Greene to Almy & Brown, Dec. 25, 1799. For the mill owners' efforts to buy more machinery, see correspondence between Levi Arnold, Richard Crosbie, and David Dickson and Almy & Brown, Jan.–Mar. 1800. Almy & Brown Co. Papers, 1789–1846, RIHS. See Figure 1 for location of Moses Brown's mill.

17. *Petitions*, vol. 33, pt. 2, no. 5. For notions in rural England about a "moral economy," see E. P. Thompson, "The Moral Economy of the English Crowd in the Eighteenth Century," *Past and Present* 50 (February 1971): 76–136.

18. *Acts and Resolutions*, October 1799, 6; see Table 2B. In 1800, the number of adult males in Coventry, Scituate, and West Greenwich was approximately 540, 376, and 380, respectively.

19. *Petitions*, vol. 33, pt. 2, no. 6.

20. See Table 2B. Petition signers William Richmond and Amasa Mason (textile manufacturers) and Charles and Benjamin Dyer (pharmaceutical sellers and manufacturers) are prime examples of middling artisans who became wealthy industrialists. For their relative wealth and occupations, see Providence city directories and tax ratables, RIHS.

21. Providence Association of Mechanics and Manufacturers, *The Charter, Articles of Agreement, Bye-Laws, Rules and Regulations of the Providence Association of Mechanics and Manufacturers* (Providence, 1798), 37–40. See also John S. Gilkeson, Jr., *Middle-Class Providence, 1820–1940* (Princeton, N.J.: Princeton University Press, 1986), 14–18, 55.

22. *Petitions*, vol. 33, pt. 2, no. 6.

23. Showman, ed., *Papers of Nathaneal Greene*, I: 4n.

24. *Ibid.* See Table 2B. Tax information came from the Coventry Town Tax List, 1798 (RISA).

25. *Petitions*, vol. 33, pt. 2, no. 6. Nathaneal Greene, one of six brothers who inherited the family ironworks in 1770, achieved national fame as a general in the revolutionary war. Greene died in 1786 and so was not one of the petition signers.

26. Coleman, *Transformation of R.I.*, 21, 225.

27. *The Public Laws of the State of Rhode Island . . . 1798* (Providence, 1798), 384–90. For highway laws of other colonies or states, see Philip E. Taylor, "The Turnpike Era in New England" (Ph.D. dissertation, Yale University, 1934), 34–39; Bernard Bush, comp., *Laws of the Royal Colony of New Jersey, 1760–1769*, New Jersey Archives, 3d ser., IV: 36–49.

28. Taylor, "Turnpike Era," 71–75.

29. For the actual success of the turnpikes in improving land transportation, see Chapter Four. In financial terms, the turnpikes were mostly failures: very few of them earned the maximum 12 percent return on investment.

30. Taylor, "Turnpike Era," 135–50, 208.

31. Probate inventories from the 1780s reveal that 12 percent of sampled farmers owned sleds: a remarkable figure, when one considers that only 38 percent owned vehicles of any kind whatsoever.

32. Records of the Scituate Turnpike Company reveal that in 1798, small wagons and carts outnumbered large vehicles by a ratio of 6 to 1. See Taylor, "Turnpike Era," 115–18.

33. England's first turnpike act was passed in 1663, although most dated from the 1690s or later. On the continent, the persistence of aristocratic and royal privileges meant that many roads remained subject to tolls for centuries. See William Albert, *The Turnpike Road System in England, 1663–1840* (Cambridge: Cambridge University Press, 1972), 17–23.

34. Taylor mentions a few examples of antiturnpike protests in "Turnpike Era," 115–18.

35. *Acts and Resolutions*, October 1794, 8. Of the six charter members, three lived in Glocester and three lived in Connecticut. (See census of 1800.)

36. Glocester Town Meeting Records, Aug. 28, 1798.

37. *Petitions*, vol. 32, no. 80; Glocester Town Meeting Records, June 3, 1799; *Acts and Resolutions*, October 1798, 3; February 1880, 11.

38. *Petitions*, vol. 33, pt. 2, no. 17. For Manton's wealth, see Johnston tax data in Jay Mack Holbrook, *Rhode Island 1782 Census* (Oxford, Mass.: Holbrook Research Institute, 1979); Glocester Town Meeting Minutes, Apr. 16, 1799.

39. *Petitions*, vol. 28, no. 128; *Acts and Resolutions*, October 1794, 13; January 1795, 3, 10; Foster Town Meeting Minutes, June 12, 1797. For the relative wealth of John Waterman and William Battey, see Holbrook, *R.I. 1782 Census*, and the Scituate tax list of 1783, Scituate Town Papers (RIHS).

40. Foster Town Meeting Minutes, June 12, 1797; Coventry Town Council Minutes, July 1, 1799.

41. Charles Angell to Jabez Bowen, July 28, 1801; Turnpike Society to John Harris, Apr. 15, 1802; in Providence and Norwich Turnpike Society MSS, John Hay Library.

42. Accounts of Almy & Brown Co. with James Gordon for repairing road, 1795–1797, Brown Papers, Box P-T9PN.

43. *Acts and Resolutions,* January 1795, 10; *Petitions,* vol. 32, pt. 2, no. 58; *Charters Granted by the General Assembly,* vol. 2, no. 31 (RISA).

44. *Petitions,* vol. 32, no. 45; vol. 33, no. 49; *Acts and Resolutions,* February 1800, 11. According to company records, in April 1799 representatives of the town of Scituate approached the society's directors, offering to pay a portion of the town's highway taxes or labor, in return for free turnpike passage by all its citizens. No record exists of any further history of this initiative. See Providence and Norwich Turnpike Society MSS, Apr. 1, 1799.

45. *Acts and Resolutions,* February 1800, 11.

46. Record Book of the General Six-Principle Baptist Church of Johnston, Apr. 5, 1783 (RIHS); Providence County Court of Common Pleas, Index to Defendants, 1785–1810, Providence College Archives.

47. *Petitions,* vol. 33, pt. 2, no. 42. In 1787, Barzillai Knight paid a Cranston town tax of £1.3, placing him in the middle of the tax list. See Cranston Town Tax List, 1787 (RIHS).

48. *Petitions,* vol. 33, no. 49.

49. *Ibid.* Remington's tax payment of £1.1 in 1782 was slightly less than the town median of £1.5.

50. *Acts and Resolutions,* February 1801, 20.

51. *Petitions,* vol. 33, pt. 2, no. 42; Agreement between the town of Cranston and Jabez Bowen, Mar. 2, 1802, Providence and Norwich Turnpike Society MSS.

52. Providence County Court of Common Pleas, Index to Defendants, 1785–1810; *Petitions,* vol. 39, pt. 2, no. 59.

53. Taylor, "Turnpike Era," 115–21. Much more work needs to be done on the nature of early turnpike development.

54. Fearon, *Sketches of America,* 96; Dwight, *Travels,* II: 37–38.

55. Welcome Arnold Greene, *Providence Plantations for 250 Years* (Providence, 1886), I: 57.

56. *Petitions,* vol. 32, no. 88. The need of a self-governing people for enlightened knowledge was almost universally recognized by gentlemen leaders of the new Republic. See Lawrence Cremin, *American Education: The National Experience, 1783–1876* (New York: Harper and Row, 1980), 103–5.

57. Foster Town Meeting Minutes, June 17, 1786; *Newport Mercury,* Mar. 29, 1803.

58. The literacy estimate of 75 percent is based on examining all wills probated in the northwest between 1783 and 1792. For evidence of rural opposition to public schooling, see Michael B. Katz, *The Irony of Early School Reform* (Boston: Beacon Press, 1970), 19–22; Alice Felt Tyler, *Freedom's Ferment: Phases of American Social History from the Colonial Period to the Outbreak of the Civil War,* reprint (New York: Harper and Row, 1962), 243.

59. *Petitions,* vol. 32, no. 88.

60. Foster Town Meeting Minutes, Aug. 27, 1799; Glocester Town Meeting Minutes, June 7 and Aug. 27, 1799. Minutes for the Coventry and Scituate town meetings do not exist for this time period.

61. *Public Laws of the State of Rhode Island and Providence Plantations, Passed since . . . 1798* (Providence, 1810), 31–35. New York's state school law of 1795 expired in 1800 when the legislature refused to renew it. Of the thirteen original states, only Connecticut provided a system of statewide financial support for schools. See Edwin Grant Dexter, *A History of Education in the United States* (London: Macmillan, 1906), 76–89; Lawrence A. Cremin, *The American Common School: An Historic Conception* (New York: Columbia University Teachers College, Bureau of Publications, 1951), 90–101.

62. The names of town deputies are recorded in *Acts and Resolutions,* 1800–1820, *passim.*

63. Glocester Town Meeting Minutes, 1800–1801, *passim; Acts and Resolutions,* June 1801, 8; October 1802, 25.

64. Glocester Town Meeting Minutes, Dec. 23, 1800; Nov. 1, 1802.

65. Charles Caroll, *Public Education in Rhode Island* (Providence: E. L. Freeman Company, 1918), 69, 81.

66. Letters by A. Z. and Delta, *Providence Gazette,* Apr. 9 and 16, 1803.

Chapter Three

1. Coleman, *Transformation of R.I.,* 21, 35–48, 220.

2. For the population of Rhode Island, see Coleman, *Transformation of R.I.,* 21, 220.

3. Why most of the northwest's leading modernizers came from this particular area remains unclear: northern Scituate and eastern Glocester are certainly closer to the Providence marketplace. This area had long been traversed by a major transportation link—the Providence to Killingly highway—and the commercial opportunities engendered thereby may have contributed to the inhabitants' entrepreneurial enthusiasm. Still, southern Scituate and eastern Coventry were just as close to Providence, and even closer to minor ports like Pawtuxet and Wickford. This more southern area was blessed with its own major highway—the Providence to Norwich road that the merchants of Providence had tried to improve in the 1790s, only to be mostly outdone by a heated local opposition. But unlike their more northern neighbors, the leaders of this subregion were slow to introduce turnpikes, banks, and other innovations of their own. The Pawtuxet River valley in eastern Coventry became a leading cotton manufacturing area by 1815, but most of its early mills were built and owned by outside entrepreneurs (see Table 4C, part 2). During the generation after the revolutionary war, the once powerful Greene family iron makers either died out or moved south to Georgia. It is puzzling that no native families rose to the occasion to continue the Greene manufacturing tradition.

4. Inventory of Mowry Smith, Glocester Probate Records, vol. 4, 182–84.

5. The specific locations in which the residents of Scituate lived were obtained from Bayles, ed., *History of Providence County,* II: 587–89. For the location of the Kimball family mill and Angell's tavern, see "Map of Scituate," in RIHS MS. 1414. For Angell and the turnpike company, see Chapter Two.

6. *Acts and Resolutions,* February 1796, 77. The Aldrich, Angell, Harris,

Kimball, and Mathewson families accounted for thirteen of the Scituate Library Company's original twenty-eight incorporators.

7. Arthur Fenner to Theodore Foster, July 17, 1790, Theodore Foster Papers (RIHS); Bayles, ed., *History of Providence County*, II: 5.

8. Beaman, "History of Foster," 19–32; William Drowne, "Sketch of the Life of Solomon Drowne, M.D.," RIHS MSS, 177, *passim*.

9. Foster to Judge Robert Hopkins, Feb. 24, 1806, quoted in Beaman, "History of Foster," 35.

10. Drowne, "Solomon Drowne," 126–27; *Acts and Resolutions*, June 1815, 17–23.

11. Foster Town Meeting Minutes, June 17, 1786. Theodore Foster was eventually elected Moderator on Mar. 25, 1811.

12. Beaman, "History of Foster," 23; Drowne, "Solomon Drowne," 138–48; Solomon Drowne to Dr. James Thayer, Nov. 9, 1820, Solomon Drowne Collection, John Hay Library. For Foster's law practice, see advertisement in the *Providence Phoenix*, Oct. 22, 1803.

13. Theodore Foster to Solomon Drowne, Dec. 25, 1801, Theodore Foster Papers (RIHS).

14. *Acts and Resolutions*, May 1802, 13; February 1803, 10. Theodore Foster's name did not appear on the original petition for a turnpike charter, probably because he was still living in Washington.

15. *Ibid*. For the location of contemporary roads in relation to Mount Hygeia, see the map entitled, "Plan of the Town of Foster, by Conjecture from the Best Information," 1799, Isaac Davenport, corrected by Theodore Foster, RIHS MSS, vol. 8, 9.

16. *Ibid*. The Providence and Norwich Turnpike was about twenty-two miles long. These mileages were estimated from the lengths of the twentieth-century highways that have descended from the Rhode Island and Connecticut and Providence and Norwich turnpikes: routes 101 and 14. The former's toll rates were set slightly lower than the average for turnpike companies.

17. *Charters*, vol. 2, no. 21. For the location of the petitioners' residences, see "Plan of the Town of Foster." This map does not locate all of the petitioners; but of those who are located, all lived in the northern half of the town.

18. For the residence and relative wealth of the petitioners, see Table 3A. For the location of the preexisting road relative to the Rhode Island and Connecticut Turnpike, see "Plan of the Town of Foster" and James Stevens, *Topographical Map of Rhode Island and Providence Plantations* (Newport, 1831). This road appears to have later been incorporated into the Foster and Scituate Turnpike.

19. *Petitions*, vol. 35, pt. 2, no. 42.

20. *Acts and Resolutions*, October 1804, 18–21. *Reports to the General Assembly*, vol. 6, nos. 66, 72, RISA. Only five individuals actually petitioned the legislature to complain about compensation for property used by the turnpike; but another fourteen men were awarded remuneration by the committee. For the beginning of construction on the turnpike, see the notice in the *Providence Gazette*, Mar. 16, 1805.

21. *Providence Gazette*, July 9 and 16, 1803; also *Providence Phoenix*, July 16 and 23, 1803.

22. *Ibid.*

23. See, for example, the advertisement in the *Providence Gazette*, July 23, 1804, for sale of subscriptions on the following Aug. 22.

24. *Providence Gazette*, Mar. 4, 1809; Connecticut and Rhode Island Turnpike Co. MSS, NYHS; Stevens, *Topographical Map of Rhode Island.*

25. For a general discussion of Republican political economy, see Drew McCoy, *The Elusive Republic: Political Economy in Jeffersonian America* (Chapel Hill: University of North Carolina Press, 1980), *passim.* For examples of Republican-sponsored compromises between localist and Federalist antagonists, see Cayton, *The Frontier Republic;* and Taylor, *Liberty Men and Great Proprietors.*

26. Foster Probate Records, vol. 5, 479ff. Probate inventories dated 1830–1834 include two other residents who owned Rhode Island and Connecticut Turnpike Company stock. All three ranked in the top one-third of the area's property owners.

27. Unfortunately, little information exists on how well the turnpike company's plan actually worked, aside from the observation offered above that ownership was probably less democratized in practice than had been hoped for in theory. Newspaper advertisements suggest that the road was in operation by 1809; and by 1832, its route was prominently displayed on local maps. See *Providence Gazette*, Mar. 4, 1809; and Stevens, *Topographical Map of Rhode Island.*

28. *Charters*, vol. 2, nos. 40, 42. The relative wealth of the Providence merchants who signed the petition was gauged from city tax lists located in the Rhode Island Historical Society. Henry Smith was a leader of a particular faction in the Republican party that was most influential in the commercial towns of Providence, Newport, Warren, Warwick, and Bristol. This faction would later break with the Fennerite–Country wing of the Republican party, nominating a separate slate of candidates in 1806 and 1807. See Joseph Michael Norton, "The Rhode Island Federalist Party: 1785–1815," chap. 5.

29. *Ibid.*

30. See Table 3B. Since many farmers paid no taxes at all, the "lower-middle" section of the tax list was actually closer to the average of all local residents—taxpayers and nontaxpayers included.

31. See Chapter Two for an analysis of the Greene family iron business.

32. See Table 3B.

33. See Figure 4.

34. The evidence suggests that the opponents of the Glocester turnpike did not reject the new road simply out of preference for another turnpike project. In the first thirteen years of the nineteenth century, three turnpikes were initiated through northern Foster, all of which would have improved access to Providence for the residents of Pine Hill village. But none of the opponents to the Glocester turnpike ever supported any of these turnpikes.

35. Glocester Town Meeting Minutes, June 4, 1804. Petition of Elijah Armstrong to the General Assembly, June 9, 1804, in *Charters*, vol. 2, no. 40.

36. *Acts and Resolutions*, June 1804, 22. None of the turnpike's opponents ever served in the state legislature, according to the *Acts and Resolutions*, 1784–1820, *passim.*

37. Henry F. Cauchon, Jr., "The New London Turnpike and the Rhode Island Turnpike Era" (M.A.T. thesis, Brown University, 1960), 17–20. For the wealth of Foster and Scituate Central Turnpike advocates, see Table 3C. Data on the original sponsors of the Foster and Scituate Turnpike Company is not available.

38. *Charters*, vol. 3, no. 18. Three of the ten petitioners whose tax valuation could be identified ranked in their towns' top fifth, with another five ranking in the second fifth.

39. *Charters*, vol. 5, no. 13. For the residence and relative wealth of opponents and proponents of the Foster and Scituate Turnpike extension, see Table 3D.

40. *Charters*, vol. 2, no. 47. Brown Papers, Box P-T9PN. The political success in 1805 of the Providence and Norwich Turnpike Society may have resulted from a developing rapprochement between the Federalists who controlled the turnpike and the Fennerite–Country wing of the Republican party. In the elections of 1806 and 1807, the Fennerites united with the Federalists to run a victorious coalition slate of candidates. See note 28 above for more information on these political alignments.

41. See, for example, *Charters*, vol. 3, no. 35; "Petitions Voted Out," Box 110, May 1816, and Box 112, May–June 1818; and *Petitions*, vol. 41, no. 28.

42. The Turnpike Society to John Harris, Apr. 15, 1807, Providence and Norwich Turnpike Society, Correspondence, John Hay Library. For fines on turnpike vandals and toll-evaders, see *Acts and Resolutions*, February 1810, 19; February 1813, 8–9, 17.

43. *Charters*, vol. 2, no. 37. For a chronological table of banks founded in Rhode Island, see J. Van Fenstermaker, *The Development of American Commercial Banking, 1782–1837*, (Kent, Ohio: Kent State University Press, 1963), 174–77.

44. Information on the directors of the Farmers Exchange Bank was obtained from petitions for turnpike companies and *Acts and Resolutions*, January 1822, 5; for the town of Scituate's assembly representatives, see *Acts and Resolutions, 1780–1810, passim*.

45. The first bank found on nonnavigable waters was the Bedford Bank in Massachusetts. See Fenstermaker, *Commercial Banking*, Appendix A.

46. *Report of the Committee Appointed by the General Assembly . . . 1809, to inquire into the situation of the Farmers Exchange Bank in Glocester* (Providence, 1809), 1–4.

47. *Ibid.*, 5–6, 26–27, 31.

48. Bray Hammond, *Banks and Politics in America: From the Revolution to the Civil War* (Princeton, N.J.: Princeton University Press, 1957), 172–78.

49. *Report of the Committee*, 15, 43–51.

50. *Rhode Island American*, Mar. 7, 1809.

51. *Ibid.*, Glocester Town Meeting Minutes, Oct. 7, 1809; Sept. 1, 1810.

52. The average farm size was calculated by dividing the total number of acres listed in the Glocester tax assessment of 1778 by the number of adult males over age twenty-one. Kenneth Lockridge used a similar formula for determining farm size in Suffolk County, Massachusetts, in "Land, Population and the Evolution of New England Society, 1630–1790," *Past and Present* 39 (April 1968): 62–80. In Concord, Massachusetts, the population reached a natural limit of around 1,500 by 1725 and remained at that level through the time of revolution, creating a prolonged period of relative scarcity for farmers. See Gross, *Minutemen and Their World*, 3, 15, 68–108.

53. For the population of Rhode Island, see Coleman, *Transformation of R.I.*, 21, 220.

54. Landless rates were calculated by dividing the number of property owners on tax rolls by the total number of men over age twenty-one, as presented by the censuses of 1782 and 1820, respectively. In the case of the 1820 census, the number of men age twenty-two to twenty-six was conservatively estimated at one-third of the number between sixteen and twenty-six years old (the closest age bracket to twenty-one).

55. For poor-relief expenditures, see Table 3E.

56. Figures on Dudley and Oxford, Massachusetts, came from Jonathan Prude, *The Coming of the Industrial Order: Town Life in Rural Massachusetts, 1810–1860* (Cambridge: Cambridge University Press, 1983), 52–54. For the commercialization of agriculture in the early Republic, see Chapter Four.

57. Glocester Tax Valuation, 1778. For the location of mills in Foster, see "Plan of the Town of Foster," a map revised by Theodore Foster that probably underestimated the actual number of mills.

58. *Petitions*, vol. 33, pt. 2, no. 6.

59. *Acts and Resolutions*, March 1788, 20–21; *The Public Laws of the State of Rhode Island . . . as revised by a Committee . . . in January 1798* (Providence, 1798), 501–3. For the history of the Hope Furnace's final years, see Hedges, *Browns*, I: 312–14. See Chapter Two for the Hope Furnace's original exemption from fishway requirements.

60. *Petitions*, vol. 34, no. 38.

61. *Petitions*, vol. 33, pt. 2, no. 39; *Public Laws of the State of Rhode Island and Providence Plantations, Passed Since . . . 1798* (Providence: Jones & Wheeler, 1810), 83–84.

62. *Petitions*, vol. 35, pt. 2, no. 54.

63. For the wealth distribution of opponents and proponents of fishway rights, see Table 3F.

64. To match up fishing-rights petitioners with turnpike and bank promoters, the names of all were combined and sorted in a single data base. Petitioners for the following chartered corporations were included in the data base: the Rhode Island and Connecticut Turnpike, the Glocester Turnpike, the Foster and Scituate Turnpike, the Foster and Scituate Central Turnpike, the Farmers Exchange Bank, and the Scituate Library Company. A few of the proponents of fishway requirements helped establish chartered institutions at a later date, in particular, the United Library Company in 1808.

65. Two additional petitions by fishway proponents arrived in the legislature in November 1800 and October 1801. The first was signed by only three mill owners from the lower valley of the north branch. The second petition has since been lost. See *Petitions*, vol. 33, pt. 2, no. 39; *Acts and Resolutions*, October 1801, 12.

66. *Petitions*, vol. 35, pt. 2, no. 54; *The Public Laws of the State of Rhode Island and Providence Plantations, as revised by a committee . . . in 1822*, (Providence, 1822), 510–18.

67. For fishing rights in the Pawcatuck River valley, see B. Michael Zuckerman, "The Political Economy of Industrial Rhode Island, 1790–1860" (Ph.D. dissertation, Brown University, 1981), 35–45.

68. Bruce C. Daniels, "Poor Relief, Local Finance, and Town Government in Eighteenth-Century Rhode Island," *Rhode Island History* 40 (August 1981): 82.

69. Glocester Town Meeting Minutes, Apr. 20, 1791; Foster Town Meeting Minutes, May 29, 1809; Coventry Town Meeting Minutes, Apr. 18, 1821. Margaret Creech, *Three Centuries of Poor Law Administration: A Study of Legislation in Rhode Island* (Chicago: University of Chicago Press, 1936), 166–67. A similar drive toward economy in poor relief occurred in New York City and its rural environs in the wake of economic dislocations brought on by the War of 1812. See Raymond Mohl, *Poverty in New York, 1783–1825* (New York: Oxford University Press, 1971), chap. 5; and Robert E. Cray, Jr., *Paupers and Poor Relief in New York City and Rural Environs, 1700–1830* (Philadelphia: Temple University Press, 1988).

70. *Petitions*, Box 110, May 1816, unnumbered; Foster Town Meeting Minutes, Sept. 27, 1814. Of the six farmers selected to care for the poor in Foster in the 1820s, four ranked in the middle quintile of taxpayers, and two ranked in the second highest quintile.

71. Glocester Town Meeting Minutes, June 18, 1803; Foster Town Meeting Minutes, Sept. 27, 1814; Sept. 23, 1820; Coventry Town Meeting Minutes, Apr. 18, 1821, June 4, 1821.

72. Foster Town Meeting Minutes, Sept. 18, 1819, 1820s, *passim*.

73. Glocester Town Meeting Minutes, Aug. 26, 1828. Glocester Town Meeting Records do not indicate exactly when a poorhouse was established, although the subject was debated as early as Aug. 31, 1790. Scituate established a "poor farm" in 1844; see Creech, *Poor Law*, 171. In this respect, Rhode Island's rural towns appear to have lagged behind those that neighbored on New York City, most of which formed almshouses by the 1820s. See Cray, *Paupers and Poor Relief*.

74. Mohl, *Poverty in New York*; M. J. Heale, "Humanitarianism in the Early Republic: The Moral Reformers of New York, 1776–1826," *Journal of American Studies* 2 (October 1968): 161–76; David J. Rothman, *The Discovery of the Asylum: Social Order and Disorder in the New Republic* (Boston: Little, Brown, 1971), 155–205.

75. Foster Town Meeting Minutes, Sept. 24, 1825.

76. *Acts and Resolutions*, February 1803, 8; February 1814, 16; June 1817, 40; February 1818, 13.

77. John C. Pease and John H. Niles, *A Gazetteer of the States of Connecticut and Rhode Island* (Hartford, 1819), 335–48, 367–76. See Table 3G for educational statistics.

78. Caroll, *Public Education in Rhode Island*, 104–5. Statistics on the wealth of school incorporators are derived from the seventeen (out of a total of thirty-five) who appeared on town tax lists.

79. Foster Town Meeting Minutes, Sept. 23, 1819; Burrillville Town Meeting Minutes, Apr. 19, 1820; Glocester Town Meeting Minutes, Aug. 29, 1820; Nov. 25, 1825. The Coventry Town Meeting Minutes do not mention schools in this period. Scituate's minutes have been lost.

80. Nathan K. Stone of Scituate voted "absent" on the public education bill, a vote that should be considered negative under the procedural circumstances in which it was made. In the assembly as a whole, eight other representatives also voted

"absent," two voted no, and one voted yes who had previously opposed the bill. All of these opponents came from economically and demographically stagnant areas along the Narragansett Bay—areas that had once been commercially strong but were now declining relative to the rest of the state. William Smith of Scituate was "excused" from voting, making his position on the bill unclear. Caroll, *Public Education*, 91.

81. Caroll, *Public Education*, 91–93, 104. The figure of $.40 per child is based on an estimated 38,000 children, age five to fifteen, as tabulated in the census of 1830.

82. Keach, *Burrillville*, 71–72; Rev. William Fitz, *An Historical Sketch of the Public Schools of Burrillville* (Providence, 1876), 4–6.

83. Caroll, *Public Education*, 104–7; *Petitions*, vol. 59, no. 2; vol. 63, no. 10.

84. See Table 3H.

85. *Acts and Resolutions*, March 1794, 11; Foster Town Meeting Minutes, June 19, 1794; Glocester Town Meeting Minutes, Aug. 26, 1794; *An Act for Repairing the Several Highways and Bridges within the Town of Scituate; Passed in Town-Meeting, May 27, 1812* (Providence, 1812). Since Scituate's town meeting minutes have been lost, it is possible that the town adopted highway taxes earlier.

86. *Public Laws*, 1810–1822, 229.

87. The wealth distribution of highway surveyors was determined by looking up the tax quintile of the sixty surveyors who served for Glocester in the year 1804. Of the forty-three who appeared on tax lists, over 60 percent ranked in the top two quintiles.

88. The highway law amendment was never clearly spelled out, although its provisions are implied in the Foster Town Meeting Minutes of May 30, 1801; Apr. 17 and May 17, 1805; and October (third Monday) 1807.

89. Foster Town Meeting Minutes, May 26, 1823; Coventry Town Meeting Minutes, Dec. 6, 1819.

90. J. R. Cole, *History of Washington and Kent Counties* (New York, 1889), 1197–98. Coventry Town Meeting Minutes, Jan. 14 and Dec. 7, 1812; June 7, 1813. Coventry Town Tax List of 1798.

91. Coventry Town Meeting Minutes, June 7, 1813.

92. Glocester Town Meeting Minutes, Feb. 25 and Mar. 2, 1804; June 19, 1809; June 7, 1813. For a review of attempts to control town meeting opposition to public schools, see Chapter Two.

93. Foster Town Meeting Minutes, Sept. 20, 1813. Coventry Town Meeting Minutes, Aug. 26, 1817.

Chapter Four

1. See Table 4A. On changes in rural living standards generally, see Larkin, *The Reshaping of Everyday Life*, chap. 3.

2. For more on the importance of regional economies in the era of the early Republic, see Diane Lindstrom, *Economic Development in the Philadelphia Region, 1810–1850* (New York: Columbia University Press, 1978), 1–18. Lindstrom demonstrates that, prior to the creation of a nationwide railway system, a national market did

not really exist in the United States. Instead, trade was located regionally around major cities or groups of cities.

3. For population figures for Rhode Island, see Coleman, *Transformation of R.I.*, 220.

4. The six turnpikes extended for the following mileages in the northwest: the Providence and Douglas Turnpike, only a small portion of which passed through the northwest, four miles; the West Glocester and Glocester turnpike, thirteen miles; the Rhode Island and Connecticut Turnpike, twelve miles; the Foster and Scituate Turnpike, eleven miles; the Foster and Scituate Central Turnpike, nine miles; and the Providence and Norwich Turnpike, fourteen miles.

5. For criticism of turnpike construction and economics, see Taylor, "The Turnpike Era," 282–86. Winifred Rothenberg estimates that the cost of land transport changed little between 1750 and 1865 in "The Market and Massachusetts Farmers, 1750–1855," *Journal of Economic History* 41 (June 1981): 298.

6. Job Angell to Jabez Bowen, Aug. 19, 1812, Providence and Norwich Turnpike, Correspondence, John Hay Library; James B. Mason to Elisha Mathewson, July 22, 1811, Papers of Elisha Mathewson, RIHS; Dwight, *Travels*, II: 21.

7. For examples of farm advertisements mentioning turnpike location, see the *Providence Gazette*, Mar. 14, 1795, and Jan. 19, 1805; and the *Providence Phoenix*, Apr. 20, 1805.

8. See Chapter Three.

9. See Table 4A, parts 1 and 2. On the relative advantages of carts and wagons, see John T. Schlebecker, "Agricultural Markets and Marketing in the North, 1774–1779," *Agricultural History* 50 (June 1976): 21–36.

10. Edward Field, *State of Rhode Island and Providence Plantations: A History* (Boston: Mason, 1902), II: 290–92. In keeping with the U.S. Supreme Court's Dartmouth College case, bank process was not denied by local courts to banks that had already been granted the privilege. For a general survey of statistics regarding Rhode Island banks, see Fenstermaker, *Commercial Banking*, 174–77, 226–27.

11. Reverend T. E. Ryan, *Burrillville, R.I. and the Catholic Church* (Harrisville, R.I., 1925), 38; Fenstermaker, *Commercial Banking*, 174–77.

12. Fenstermaker, *Commercial Banking*, 78–80; Field, *Rhode Island*, II: 284–86. For a comparison of specie/note ratios, see Table 4B.

13. See Table 4B; for figures on the Scituate Bank, see "Abstract of the Returns of the Several Banks . . . October 1834," *Acts and Resolutions*, October 1834, 52.

14. For the results of the Burrillville Bank investigation, see *Acts and Resolutions*, May 1832, 5–8; June 1832, 60–65; October 1834, 60–61; May 1840, 42–46; see also Ryan, *Burrillville, R.I.*, 38.

15. *Acts and Resolutions*, October 1836, 49–50; October 1838, 50; January 1841, 82; Field, *Rhode Island*, II: 304.

16. "Abstract of the Returns of the Several Banks in this State," *Acts and Resolutions*, May 1825, 44; October 1835, 76; Field, *Rhode Island*, II: 300. The figure on loans to the bank's directors is undoubtedly underestimated because the only available figures come from somewhat unreliable reports filed by the directors themselves. Actually, contemporary banks typically loaned much of their capital to their own direc-

tors' extended kinship networks. See Naomi R. Lamoureaux, "Banks, Kinship and Economic Development: The New England Case," *Journal of Economic History* 46 (September 1986), 647–67.

17. For a list of Rhode Island banks and their failures, see Fenstermaker, *Commercial Banking*, 174–77. The only other bank to fail was the Mount Hope Bank of Bristol.

18. For Pardon Holden's will and inventory, see Foster Town Probate Records, vol. 6, 114. For more discussion on cash and inheritance patterns, see the section on the social transformation of traditional household society in Chapter Four.

19. J. R. Cole, *History of Washington and Kent Counties* (New York: W. W. Preston & Co., 1889), 1193–94, 1203.

20. See Table 4C, parts 1 and 2; see also Coleman, *Transformation of R.I.*, 71–107.

21. See Table 4C, part 3. For the textile industry in Dudley, see Jonathan Prude, *The Coming of the Industrial Order: Town and Factory Life in Rural Massachusetts, 1810–1860* (Cambridge: Cambridge University Press, 1983), 88–89. Although two-thirds of the Blackstone Manufacturing Company's weaving customers were identified as men, most of the actual work was probably done by their wives and teenage daughters; the remaining one-third were entirely single women or widows. See Gail Barbara Fowler, "Rhode Island Handloom Weavers and the Effects of Technological Change, 1780–1840" (Ph.D. dissertation, University of Pennsylvania, 1984), 190–229, 341–43. For ownership of home textile equipment, see Table 4A and the section on storekeepers and the development of capitalist relations in Chapter Four.

22. Farmers' sales to factories are detailed in the section on the development of marketable surpluses in Chapter Four.

23. Daybook of Hiram Salisbury, 1815–1844, from typescript version in possession of Edna Kent, Chepachet, R.I.; original manuscript owned by Harrison Salisbury.

24. Account Book of William and John Waterman, 1790–1836, RIHS. The location of the Waterman farm was determined by examining the Warwick Tax Valuation of 1822 and Henry F. Walling, *Map of the State of Rhode Island and Providence Plantations* (1855). The exact identity or location of the "Old," "Greene," and "Stone" factories could not be determined. For a more thorough analysis of the Watermans' Account Book, see the section on storekeepers and the development of capitalist relations in Chapter Four.

25. On the commercialization of agriculture in the rural north, see the sources cited below and Rothenberg, "The Market and Massachusetts Farmers, 1750–1855," 283–314; Robert A. Gross, "Culture and Cultivation: Agriculture and Society in Thoreau's Concord," *Journal of American History* 69 (June 1982): 42–61.

26. For agricultural production, see Table 4D; on women's roles in dairy farming, see Joan M. Jensen, *Loosening the Bonds: Mid-Atlantic Farm Women, 1750–1850* (New Haven: Yale University Press, 1986), 79–91.

27. On commercial dairying, see Charles Danhof, *Change in Agriculture: The Northern United States, 1820–1870* (Cambridge, Mass.: Harvard University Press, 1969), 171–75; Account Book of William W. Knight, 1838–1846, John Hay Library, 25–27, 31. The Spragues' industrial holdings were one of the state's largest complexes

of cotton mills; see Coleman, *Transformation of R.I.*, 131. Woodmaney's and Rice's residences were inferred from the census of 1830.

28. Butter requirements were calculated from James T. Lemon, *The Best Poor Men's Country: A Geographical Study of Early Southeastern Pennsylvania* (New York: W.W. Norton, 1972), 163. Comparisons with the 1778 tax valuation are difficult because the tax assessors counted all cattle over two months old, which would include non–milk producing heifers and calves. Only James Fenner's herd of forty such cattle may have outnumbered Knight's inventory.

29. Scituate Town Tax List of 1842, Town Clerk's Office.

30. See Table 4A, part 2. Average probate inventories of cows fell from 2.3 to 2.0 for the entire northwest.

31. In *Loosening the Bonds*, 86, Jensen calculates that even in the highly commercialized Philadelphia "butter belt," only 5–10 percent of all farms sold over 1,500 pounds per year. I have adopted her definition of "commercial dairies" as those very few that produced over 8,000 pounds of butter per year.

32. Account Book of William W. Knight, 39–40. Unfortunately, Knight did not list his dollar earnings from poultry sales. For Walker's estate see Coventry Town Probate Records, vol. 5, 11, June 14, 1833. Poultry production probably expanded more rapidly after the 1840s; see Danhof, *Change in Agriculture*, 179.

33. See Table 4A, part 1. For an overview of the antebellum cattle industry, see Danhof, *Change in Agriculture*, 166–75; and Lemon, *Best Poor Men's Country*, 160–64.

34. See Table 4D; *Providence Gazette*, Feb. 2, 1805; for examples of firewood listings in probate inventories, see Coventry Town Probate Records, vol. 4, 285, 373; vol. 5, 11; *Sixth Census . . . 1840*, 58–59. Christopher Clark also discovered a boom in forest products by farms on the edges of the Connecticut River valley, although it occurred a bit later, in the 1840s and 1850s. See Clark, *The Roots of Rural Capitalism*, 291–92.

35. See Table 4A, parts 1 and 2.

36. Account Book of William W. Knight, 131–36. The value of Knight's lumber was estimated by assuming a price of $16 per thousand board feet for planking, and twice that for beams. See Arthur Harrison Cole, *Wholesale Commodity Prices in the United States, 1700–1861* (Cambridge, Mass.: Harvard University Press, 1938). The price for Philadelphia was used.

37. Daybook of Hiram Salisbury. See entries for June and July 1816; Jan. 20 and Apr. 9, 1826.

38. *Ibid.*, Dec. 23, 1829; Jan. 3, 9, 21, 28, Mar. 1, 1830; Mar. 18, July 7, 8, 15, Nov. 28, 1837; Feb. 12, 1838; Apr.–June 1841. In another case of rural woodworking for the textile industry, Shadrach Steere, a Burrillville farmer, produced bobbins and quill wheels between 1810 and 1813. See Carolyn Cooper and Patrick Malone, "The Mechanical Woodworker in Early 19th-Century New England as a Spinoff from Textile Industrialization" (Paper presented at the Old Sturbridge Village Colloquium on Early New England Society and Culture, March 1990).

39. For sheep production, see Danhof, *Change in Agriculture*, 164–66. On female domestic manufactures, see Rolla Milton Tryon, *Household Manufactures in the United States, 1640–1860: A Study in Industrial History* (Chicago: University of Chicago

Press, 1917), 281–90; Prude, *Industrial Order*, 71–78; Thomas Dublin, "Women and Outwork in a Nineteenth-Century New Hampshire Town: Fitzwilliam, New Hampshire, 1830–1850," in *The Countryside in the Age of Capitalist Transformation: Essays in the Social History of Rural America*, by Steven Hahn and Jonathan Prude (Chapel Hill: University of North Carolina Press, 1985), 51–70.

40. See Table 4A, parts 1 and 2.

41. Foster Town Probate Records, vol. 6: 354–55.

42. For more on reciprocal exchange in the revolutionary era, see Chapter One. The only known store in eighteenth-century northwestern Rhode Island was the Chepachet partnership of Owen and Gadcomb. The Rhode Island Historical Society once catalogued their account book for the years 1795–1802, but it has since been lost.

43. Daybook of Hiram Salisbury. See, for example, Sept. 9, 1827 and Feb. 8, 1828. For more information on Job Armstrong's store, see Bayles, ed., *History of Providence County*, II: 527.

44. Prude, *Industrial Order*, 7; Coventry Town Probate Records, vol. 4, 366; Foster Town Probate Records, vol. 6:60, 103; *Sixth Census . . . 1840*, 58–59.

45. Account Book of Freeman Jones, OSVRL. On the history of textile outwork, see Fowler, "R.I. Handloom Weavers," 245–321; and Tryon, *Household Manufactures*, 314, 370. On the domestic manufacture of hats, etc., see Clark, "Roots of Rural Capitalism," 176–91; and Dublin, "Women and Outwork."

46. *Foster, Rhode Island: Statewide Historical Preservation Report P-F-1* (Providence: Rhode Island Historical Preservation Commission, 1982), 23–25.

47. See Table 4A, parts 1 and 2. For a more detailed study of domestic textile equipment in probate inventories, see Gail Fowler Mohanty, "Rhode Island Handloom Weavers: A Probate Perspective," in *Early American Probate Inventories* (The Dublin Seminar for New England Folklife, Annual Proceedings, 1987), 86–96.

48. For sheep herd size, see Tables 4A and 4D. In *Landlords and Farmers in the Hudson–Mohawk Region, 1790–1850* (Ithaca, N.Y.: Cornell University Press, 1946), 194–99, David Meldwyn Ellis suggests that wool production served as a transition industry, following the decline of general subsistence agriculture, but preceding specialization in dairy products.

49. McDonald and McWhiney, "The South from Self-Sufficiency to Peonage," 1085–1118. Most of McDonald's and McWhiney's comments on the antebellum South apply as well to eighteenth-century New England.

50. Table 4A, parts 1 and 2. Although Table 4D shows that the total number of pigs in Burrillville and Glocester rose slightly between 1778 and 1840, the number per farm must have declined considerably, because the number of men over age twenty-one—in these towns that remained largely agricultural—nearly doubled in this period.

51. *Ibid.* To check against the possibility that "cash" levels were unusually low in the 1780s, a time of financial contraction, probate inventories were examined from the early 1770s. The results were rather similar: the percentage of those owning cash was somewhat higher, 39 percent (vs. 26 percent in the 1780s), but average holdings were significantly lower, at $9.20, as opposed to $12.63.

52. See Table 4A, parts 1 and 2. For a discussion of debt structure in

the 1780s, see Chapter One. Winifred Rothenberg found that the proportion of administrators' accounts that charged interest doubled between 1790 and 1830, as did the number of debtors in each estate; see Rothenberg, "The Emergence of a Capital Market in Rural Massachusetts, 1730–1838," *Journal of Economic History* 45 (December 1985), 789, 793.

53. Account Book of Theodore Foster, John Hay Library, 162–69. The area's textile manufacturers used similarly formal, cash-laden accounting and business practices. See, for example, the Account Book of Perez Peck (a Coventry industrialist), 1820–1839, in Perez Peck Papers, OSVRL.

54. Account Book of Freeman Jones, OSVRL. Jones betrayed his roots in the traditional world of credits-only accounting by improperly using the preposition "to" in his debits column, instead of the correct word, "by."

55. Thomas Dublin, "Women and Outwork," 55–57. Unfortunately, Freeman Jones's account book—the only extant store records for northwestern Rhode Island in the early 1800s—does not record enough detail to allow for an analysis of his third-party debits and credits.

56. *Ibid.*; Account Book of Jesse Potter, Glocester Heritage Society. (Unfortunately, Freeman Jones's account book does not extend beyond 1825.) In the Connecticut River valley of Massachusetts, cash income by stores grew from about 30 percent in the 1830s to almost 100 percent in the mid–1850s. See Clark, *Roots of Rural Capitalism*, 170–72, 221–27.

57. Account Book of Asa and Samuel Steere, 1819–1850, RIHS.

58. Daybook of Hiram Salisbury, Dec. 24, 1828; Nov. 28, 1837; Feb. 12, 1838.

59. Account Book of William W. Knight, John Hay Library, 27–28, 51; Knight's receipt of payment by note was not explicitly recorded in his account book but rather inferred by comparing his overall credits with those of the Sprague textile firm. Account Book of Asa and Samuel Steere, *passim.* Samuel Steere ranked in the second quintile of the Glocester Town Tax Valuation of 1822.

60. The following discussion is based on the Account Book of William and John Waterman, RIHS, as analyzed in Table 4E.

61. William Waterman's 1822 property valuation of $5,960 placed him in the top tenth of Warwick's annual tax assessment; RIHS.

62. Although William and John Waterman's households were listed separately in the censuses of 1800, 1810, and 1820, they probably operated the same farm, or at least owned adjacent properties. Their names were always placed next to each other on census and tax returns, thus suggesting that their households were similarly adjacent. According to the 1822 valuation, William still owned the lion's share of his family's holdings, but the farm had probably long been actually operated by John. William was already at least sixty years old by 1810, and his household was devoid of younger men who could have helped him in its operation.

63. Waterman's total labor costs actually fell at first in the 1820s, largely because his employees' monthly wages fell from $11 in 1818, to $6 in 1823, to $5 in 1829.

64. Coleman, *Transformation of R.I.*, 120–21, reports that, between 1832 and 1840, textile capitalization increased by 40 percent, while the number of spindles doubled.

65. For background on colonial household society, see John Demos, *A Little Commonwealth: Family Life in Plymouth Colony* (New York: Oxford University Press, 1970), *passim*; on patriarchy, see Toby L. Ditz, *Property and Kinship: Inheritance in Early Connecticut, 1750–1820* (Princeton, N.J.: Princeton University Press, 1986), 119–22.

66. For an excellent discussion of the decline of patriarchy in commercializing rural Connecticut, see Ditz, *Property and Kinship*, 134–37.

67. See Table 4F for geographic mobility. Estimates of death rates were based on figures from Lincoln and Bedford, Massachusetts, as analyzed in Richard Holmes, *Communities in Transition: Bedford and Lincoln, Massachusetts, 1729–1850* (Ann Arbor, Michigan: U.M.I. Research Press, 1980), 98–99, 186–87.

68. *Ibid.* For mobility in Boston, see Peter R. Knights, "Population Turnover, Persistence, and Residential Mobility in Boston, 1830–1860," in *Nineteenth-Century Cities: Essays in the New Urban History,* ed. Stephen Thernstrom and Richard Sennett (New Haven, Conn.: Yale University Press, 1969), 258–74.

69. Tabulated from Glocester Town Probate Records, 1830–34. For farm indebtedness, see Chapter Three. For a more dramatic example of the effects of commercialization on the debt structure of a rural area, see Steven Hahn, *The Roots of Southern Populism: Yeoman Farmers and the Transformation of the Georgia Upcountry, 1850–1880* (New York: Oxford University Press, 1983), 190–91.

70. See Table 4G, part 1. Under Rhode Island law, which remained essentially unaltered between 1780 and 1830, the widow or next-of-kin was granted the right to administer intestate estates. If they refused or neglected to accept this responsibility, the probate court was required by law to appoint one of the "principal Creditors" of the estate. See *Acts and Laws of the English Colony of Rhode Island and Providence Plantations, in America* (Newport, 1767), 214–19. *Acts and Laws . . . Made and Passed since the Revision of June 1767* (Newport, 1772), 25–28; *The Public Laws of the State of Rhode Island . . .* (Providence, 1798), 281–95.

71. See Table 4G, part 2. The trend toward nonkin, noncreditor administrators may have been spurred (or more probably, simply echoed) by a minor change in the law: the revision of 1798 (p. 295) allowed probate courts to grant administration to "such others as the Court shall think fit," in case both kin and creditors refused the same.

72. See Table 4A. The median value of the poorest tenth of all 1780s estates was $49.33, slightly more than $47.85 for the 1830s.

73. For Bishop's estate, see Scituate Town Probate Records, vol. 5: 521. Bishop's age and family composition were obtained from the census of 1830.

74. For landlessness and property distribution, see Table 4H. The increase in numbers of propertyless males was calculated by using, as the 1780s base, data from Glocester and Burrillville, the only towns for which full tax records exist from the revolutionary era.

75. While contemporary prices declined by 32 percent between 1818 and 1829, Waterman's wage rates fell by 55 percent. Wages may have begun to rise again after 1830; see Danhof, *Change in Agriculture*, 73–79. For contemporary prices, see Herman M. Stoker, *Wholesale Prices for 213 Years, 1720–1932* (Ithaca, N.Y.: Cornell University Press, 1932), 8–9.

76. See the section on storekeepers and the development of capitalist relations in Chapter Four.

77. Patrick Shirreff, *A Tour through North America* (Edinburgh, 1835), 25.

78. See Chapter Three. For background on colonial household care for the poor, see David J. Rothman, *The Discovery of the Asylum: Social Order and Disorder in the New Republic* (Boston: Little, Brown, 1971), 30–38.

79. See Table 4I, part 1.

80. Calculations were based on U.S. census data.

81. See Table 4I, parts 2 and 4.

82. See Table 4I, part 3.

83. See Table 4I, part 4. For a fascinating exception to this trend, see Jensen's discussion of the life and business of Esther Lewis, a Chester County, Pennsylvania, widow, in *Loosening the Bonds*, 129–41. Jensen also suggests that women's experience with butter making increased their economic independence and control over family farm operations.

84. Lydia Angell Papers, RIHS.

85. See Table 4I, part 4.

86. See Table 4I, part 2.

87. For changes in women's roles in urban areas, see Paul E. Johnson, *A Shopkeeper's Millennium: Society and Revivals in Rochester, New York, 1815–1847* (New York: Hill and Wang, 1978), 43–58.

88. See Table 4G, part 1. For a different view, see Lisa Wilson Waciega, "A 'Man of Business': The Widow of Means in Southeastern Pennsylvania, 1750–1850," *William and Mary Quarterly*, 3d ser., 44 (January 1987), 40–64.

89. See Table 4G, part 3. On Rhode Island inheritance law, see note 70. On widows' inheritance generally, see Richard B. Morris, *Studies in the History of American Law*, 2d ed. (New York: Octagon Books, 1964), 155–64.

90. For reasons that remain unclear, huge numbers of men, about 62 percent of all cases, wrote wills in the 1780s and 1790s, twice the usual eighteenth-century average. This may be attributed to the fact that statutory provisions for the eldest son's portion were currently in flux. Their traditional double portion, which had been restated in statutes as recently as the revision of 1772, was replaced by equal partibility in the Public Laws of 1798. By the 1830s, the proportion of estates probated by wills had fallen to only one-quarter, a much more typical figure for that period.

91. See Table 4G, part 3; Foster Town Probate Records, vol. 6, 114. In *Property and Kinship*, 128–32, Ditz details more thoroughly the trend toward more generous widows' portions in commercializing areas of New England.

92. See Table 4G, part 3. Lisa Waciega ("A 'Man of Business,' " 54) found the opposite to be true: men's restrictions on their widows' remarrying decreased somewhat between 1750 and 1850.

93. On the considerable literature on the development of affectionate family relations, see especially: Lawrence Stone, *The Family, Sex and Marriage in England, 1500–1800* (New York: Harper and Row, 1977), which traces this development in upper-class England to the mid–eighteenth century; Edward Shorter's *The Making of the Modern Family* (New York: Basic Books, 1975) places it for Europe generally a bit later, in the early nineteenth century. In American society, Nancy F. Cott and Dan-

iel Scott Smith find the origin of affectionate marriages in the late eighteenth century. See their respective articles: "Divorce and the Changing Status of Women in Eighteenth-Century Massachusetts," *William and Mary Quarterly* 33 (October 1976): 586–614; and "Parental Power and Marriage Patterns," *Journal of Marriage and the Family* 35 (August 1973): 419–28.

Chapter Five

1. The last three paragraphs are a summary of material from the section on religion in backcountry Rhode Island in Chapter One.

2. Membership figures were obtained from John Aplund, *Annual Register of the Baptist Denomination in North America to the First of November, 1790* (1791); Records of the Foster Six-Principle Baptist Church, microfilm copy at RIHS; Records of the Baptist Yearly Meeting, RIHS, 1814.

3. See the section on religion in backcountry Rhode Island in Chapter One; Journal of Ephraim Abbott, RIHS, Oct. 30 and Nov. 6, 1812; *Minutes of the Rhode Island Baptist State Convention . . . June 21, 1827* (Providence, 1827).

4. From the voluminous literature on the development of moral reform in the antebellum years, see especially Clifford S. Griffin, *Their Brothers' Keepers: Moral Stewardship in the United States, 1800–1865* (New Brunswick, N.J.: Rutgers University Press, 1960), 1–98. Sydney E. Ahlstrom, *A Religious History of the American People* (New Haven, Conn.: Yale University Press, 1972), chap. 26; Ronald G. Walters, *American Reformers, 1815–1860* (New York: Hill and Wang, 1978), 21–37. For the effect of Finney's revivals, see especially Johnson, *A Shopkeeper's Millennium*, 116–21.

5. For the early history of the Rhode Island Missionary Society, see Rhode Island Domestic Missionary Society, *Proceedings of the Evangelical Consociation and Missionary Society of Congregational Churches in Rhode Island, June 1834* (Providence, 1834), 16–18.

6. For revivals in Providence, see Henry Jackson, *A Discourse in Commemoration of the 46th Anniversary of the Mite Society, and the 250th Anniversary of the 1st Baptist Church of America* (Providence, 1854), 9–19.

7. *Proceedings*, June 1837, 11; June 1834, 5–6.

8. *Proceedings*, June 1834, June 1836, June 1837, June 1838, June 1840, *passim*. The tract society missionary was Ephraim Abbott, referred to in this chapter. See also "Thirty-third Annual Report of the Rhode Island Domestic Missionary Society," Rider Collection, John Hay Library. (The RIDMS's reports are often available in manuscript form, which is generally more complete than the printed reports cited in the *Proceedings*.)

9. Works Projects Administration, *Inventory of the Church Archives of Rhode Island: Baptist* (Providence, 1941), 47–49; *Minutes of the RIBSC*, 1827, 1829, 1830.

10. *Minutes of the RIBSC*, 1830, 7. For the earlier history of the First Baptist Church of Rhode Island, see Chapter One.

11. C. Allyn Russell, "Rhode Island Baptists, 1825–1831," *Rhode Island History* 28 (1969): 35–48; *Minutes of the RIBSC*, 1835, 13–14; the Providence Female Tract Society, *First Annual Report* (Providence, 1816), 8. This is not to say that urban missionaries and industrialists always shared the same goals and interests. Missionaries

sometimes criticized mill owners for working their child laborers so hard as to deprive them of the possibility of education and proper Christian catechism. For a more detailed discussion, see Mark S. Schantz, "Missionaries and Mills: Religion in the Rhode Island Countryside" (Paper presented at the Annual Meeting of the Society for Historians of the Early American Republic, 1987).

12. Journal of Ephraim Abbott, Oct. 6, 1812; Dec. 22, 1812, RIHS. Providence Female Tract Society, *Third Annual Report* (Providence, 1818), 8–9.

13. Providence Female Tract Society *Third Annual Report*, 7–8; *Fifth Annual Report* (1820), 10–11.

14. Journal of Ephraim Abbott, Nov. 6 and 17; Dec. 19, 22, and 24, 1812, RIHS; Providence Female Tract Society, *Second Annual Report* (1817).

15. *Proceedings*, June 1838, 10. The subject of liquor and temperance will be discussed at greater length later in this chapter.

16. *Proceedings*, June 1837, 14–15; *Minutes of the RIBSC*, June 21, 1827, *passim*; April 14, 1830, 4.

17. See Table 5B.

18. Nathan O. Hatch, *The Democratization of American Christianity* (New Haven, Conn.: Yale University Press, 1989), 17–66.

19. *Proceedings*, June 1834, 13; *Proceedings*, June 1838, 7; Journal of Ephraim Abbott, Oct. 21, 1812, RIHS.

20. Documents of the RIDMS, John Hay Library MSS, 18.

21. Journal of Ephraim Abbott, Dec. 18, 1812, RIHS; Documents of the RIDMS, 22.

22. Documents of the RIDMS, 25–26; *Minutes of the RIBSC*, April 8, 1929, 10.

23. *Minutes of the RIBSC*, April 14, 1830, 5; April 8, 1835, 13–14. The churches that Weaver overlooked were the Christian Church of Rice City in western Coventry, which had many members in Foster; the North Foster Freewill Baptist Church; and the ailing but still functional Six-Principle Baptist Church of Foster. *Proceedings*, June 1840, 13.

24. Journal of Ephraim Abbott, Dec. 24, 1812, RIHS.

25. The third missionary-sponsored church was the Scituate Congregational Church; see also the Appendix. For information on textile-mill ownership, see the section on the causes of market growth in Chapter Four and Table 4C and the sources cited thereunder. On Charles Jackson and the Arkwright Baptist Church, see *Inventory of Church Archives: Baptist*, 82.

26. *Proceedings*, June 1840, 13.

27. For background on the Freewill Baptists, see Norman Allen Baxter, *History of the Freewill Baptists: A Study in New England Separatism* (Rochester, N.Y.: American Baptist Historical Society, 1957); Stephen A. Marini, *Radical Sects of Revolutionary New England* (Cambridge, Mass.: Harvard University Press, 1982), 25–101. On Freewill Baptist resistance to Federalist proprietors in Maine, see Taylor, *Liberty Men and Great Proprietors*, 123–53.

28. John L. Lincoln, "Report on the Origin and Present Operations of the Free Will Baptists" (Paper read before the Missionary Society of Newton Theological Institute, Feb. 14, 1839), in John Hay Library, MSS, Baptist Collection, Box 27, no. 11.

29. Marini, *Radical Sects*, 97, 116–22; Baxter, *History of the Freewill Baptists*, 68–82, 87–92; Lincoln, "Free Will Baptists."

30. Winfred Ernest Garrison, *An American Religious Movement: A Brief History of the Disciples of Christ* (St. Louis: Christian Board of Publication, 1948), 41–47, 58–59; Ahlstrom, *A Religious History*, 540–48; Hatch, *The Democratization of American Christianity*, 68–81; Hatch, "The Christian Movement and the Demand for a Theology of the People," *Journal of American History* 67 (December 1980): 545–67.

31. Reverend I. D. Stewart, *The History of the Freewill Baptists* (Dover, N.H.: Freewill Baptist Printing Establishment, 1862), I: 314.

32. Rhode Island Historic Preservation Commission, *Preliminary Survey Report: Town of Coventry* (Providence, 1978), 4–7; Margery I. Matthews, Virginia I. Benson, and Arthur E. Wilson, *Churches of Foster: A History of Religious Life in Rural Rhode Island* (Foster, R.I.: North Foster Baptist Church, 1978), 28–34.

33. *Ibid.*; *Herald of Gospel Liberty*, June 11, 1813; Samuel R. Hopkins, *A Short History of the Reformation and Establishment of the Church of Christ, or Christian Church, in Coventry, R.I., since 1812* (Providence, 1821), 5. See Table 5A for the decline of local churches around 1810.

34. Matthews et al., *Churches of Foster*, 29; *Pawtuxet Valley Gleaner*, Jan. 13, 1893.

35. *Herald of Gospel Liberty*, June 11, 1813; Hopkins, *A Short History*, 5–8; "Elder James Burlingame," newspaper-clipping scrapbook in possession of Mrs. Lester Underwood, Greene, Coventry.

36. Matthews et al., *Churches of Foster*, 28–34; Hopkins, *A Short History*, 9–30.

37. For general membership statistics, see Table 5B. For members added in individual churches, see Records of the Church of Christ in Coventry, in the possession of Audrey Hall, church secretary; Records of Foster Center Church, in the possession of Margery I. Matthews.

38. "Covenant," Records of the Church of Christ in Warwick and Coventry at the Phenix and Harris villages, in possession of Audrey Hall; Anna M. Whipple, *Historical Facts and Stray Thoughts from the Old Elder Ballou Meeting House* (Woonsocket, R.I.: Charles E. Cook, 1897).

39. *Members' Manual of the First Christian Church of Scituate, Rhode Island* (Phenix, R.I.: John H. Campbell, 1878), 3–4, 7.

40. See Table 5A.

41. For examples of church discipline, see the records of the Church of Christ in Warwick and Coventry, Nov. 2, 1835, June 28, 1840; Rice City and Foster Center Church Records, *passim*.

42. *Members' Manual*, 3–4; Foster Christian Church Records, Nov. 25, 1835, Jan. 8, 1837. For a discussion of the Six-Principle Baptists' membership rules, see the section on religion in backcountry Rhode Island in Chapter One and the section on the decline of the Six-Principle Baptists in Chapter Five. For a similar example of openness by a Christian church in the Midwest, see Don Harrison Doyle, *The Social Order of a Frontier Community: Jacksonville, Illinois, 1825–1870* (Urbana, Ill.: University of Illinois Press, 1978), 165–66.

43. Records of the Church of Christ in Warwick and Coventry, "Cove-

nant." Schisms could occur for more overtly political reasons. For example, the Foster Center Christian Church split for a time over the Dorr's War disturbances of 1842. For a different view, see Hatch, *The Democratization of American Christianity*, 81. I believe, however, that Hatch's view, based on the Christians' earliest history, tends to exaggerate their later divisiveness, at least in the case of Rhode Island. Unfortunately, no modern, nationwide history has been written of the Christians for the period after 1830.

44. *Ibid.*, 46, 99. The Foster Center Christian Church joined the Rhode Island Baptist State Convention in 1927; the others were absorbed by the Congregationalists in 1930. On the weakness of the Christian Connection nationally, see Hatch, *The Democratization of American Christianity*, 80.

45. Rhode Island's Freewill Baptist churches were absorbed into the State Baptist Convention in 1912, but they retained a separate identity through membership in the exclusively Freewill-Baptist "Roger Williams Association." In 1941, this association still had over twenty-three churches, four of which were located in the northwest. See *Inventory of Church Archives: Baptist*, 156.

46. Stewart, *Freewill Baptists*, 313; John Colby, *The Life, Experience, and Travels of John Colby* (Dover, N.H.: Free-will Baptist Printing Establishment, 1854), 151–52, 158.

47. See Table 5B and the Appendix for membership figures and lists of churches. See also *Inventory of Church Archives: Baptist*, 154–82; Minutes of the Rhode Island Quarterly Meeting of Free-will Baptists (RIQM), RIHS.

48. Henry Jackson, *An Account of the Churches in Rhode Island presented at . . . the Rhode Island Baptist State Convention*, Providence, Nov. 8, 1852, 102. A denomination is considered to have been "widely based" if it had congregations in a large number of Rhode Island's towns. In 1853, the Rhode Island Baptist State Convention was the most widely based in the state, with fifty-one churches containing 7,146 members in twenty-two towns; the Freewill Baptists had twenty-seven churches containing 2,644 members in eighteen towns. In total membership the Freewill Baptists ranked just behind the Congregationalists and Methodists, who were concentrated in highly populated eastern Rhode Island.

49. Records of the elders conference of the Rhode Island Quarterly Meeting of Free-will Baptists, RIHS. *Free-Baptist Magazine* (Providence, R.I.), vols. 1–3 (1826–1830). The publication dates for the *Freewill Baptist Quarterly* were obtained from the *Union List of Serials in Libraries of the United States and Canada*, 3d ed. (New York, 1965). The existence of the *Rose and Lily* is more uncertain, as it was not listed in any of the relevant guides to periodicals; but it was mentioned by the quarterly meeting on Aug. 21, 1844, as a "Freewill Baptist Periodical" published in Pawtucket.

50. RIQM, Jan. 23 and May 21, 1835; January 1836. Minutes of the Glocester Freewill Baptist Church, in the possession of Mrs. Clifford W. Brown, Providence, Feb. 29, 1840; Minutes of the North Scituate Baptist Church, July 25 and Sept. 26, 1840; Minutes of the Second Foster Freewill Baptist Church, RIHS, May 1, 1841.

51. Elders conference, Aug. 12, 1828; Jan. 21, 1835.

52. RIQM, May 20, 1836; M[artin] Cheney, *Circular . . . written by M. Cheney, Pastor of the Free-will Baptist Church in Olneyville* (Providence: W. Marshall, n.d.), 3–7.

53. Minutes of the Foster F-W. B. Ch., located at the church, Oct. 12, 1833; N. Scituate F-W. B. Ch., Apr. 23, 1836; Oct. 24, 1841; Apr. 23, 1846; Second Foster F-W. B. Ch., January–April 1840; Apr. 20, 1844; and the manuscript history written in the minute book. *Minutes of the Ministers' Conference and also of the Quarterly Meeting Conference of the Rhode Island Quarterly Meeting of Freewill Baptists, held at Greeneville, R.I.* (Pawtucket, R.I., 1851), 9. Fragmentary opposition to clerical professionalism may have also expressed itself in a brief upsurge in Millerite fervor, which led to the dismissal from their churches of several Freewill Baptist members. Some historians believe that Millerism emerged partly as a reaction to growing respectability among Baptist clergy. See David L. Rowe, *Thunder and Trumpets: Millerites and Dissenting Religion in Upstate New York, 1800–1850* (Chico, Calif. Scholars Press, 1985).

54. *Inventory of Church Archives: Baptists*, 157–58; RIQM, Jan. 24, 1838; Jan. 25, 1839; Rhode Island Historical Preservation Commission, *Historic and Architectural Resources of Scituate, Rhode Island: A Preliminary Report* (Providence, 1980), 16, 32–33.

55. Western Rhode Island Quarterly Meeting of Free-Will Baptists, RIHS, Mar. 2, 1842; Cheney, *Circular*, 3.

56. *Inventory of Church Archives: Baptists*, 157–58.

57. Minutes of the Second Foster F-W. B. Ch., "Covenant"; elders conference, Jan. 21, 1835. Examples of Six-Principle Baptist elders disqualified for doctrinal heresy include Elder Pendleton of the Richmond church, 1784; Elder Place, 1812; and Henry Tatem of the Cranston church, 1820. See Baptist Yearly Meeting Minutes, RIHS.

58. Minutes of the Second Foster F-W. B. Ch., May 6, 1837; Minutes of the Foster F-W. B. Ch., *passim.*

59. Elders conference, Aug. 22, 1834; Oct. 24, 1834; Aug. 18, 1835.

60. Foster F-W. B. Ch., Aug. 23, 1845; May 1, 1847; July 5, 1848; Dec. 5, 1849.

61. Elders conference, May 22, 1834; Oct. 18, 1842; Second Foster F-W. B. Ch., "Covenant."

62. Elders conference, Jan. 11, 1833. The Christians' tendency toward Unitarianism has been discussed above. Elders conference, Oct. 22, 1824; May 6, 1825.

63. Foster F-W. B. Ch., Aug. 8, 1829, *passim.*

64. *Covenant of the Second Freewill Baptist Church in Smithfield, R.I., adopted February 28, 1841* (Providence, 1841), 3.

65. For a general background on the evangelical origins of temperance and antislavery, see John L. Thomas, "Romantic Reform in America," *American Quarterly* 17 (Winter 1965): 656–81; Ian Tyrrell, *Sobering Up: From Temperance to Prohibition in Antebellum America* (Westport, Conn.: Greenwood Press, 1979); Robert L. Hampel, *Temperance and Prohibition in Massachusetts* (Ann Arbor, Mich.: UMI Research Press, 1982); Gilbert Hobbs Barnes, *The Anti-Slavery Impulse, 1830–1844* (New York: Harcourt, Brace and World, 1964). The views of urban Rhode Island churches on antislavery and temperance can be found in *Proceedings*, June 1834, 5–7; *Minutes of the RIBSC, 1833*, 10ff; Russell, "R.I. Baptists, 1825–1831," 38–42; and John S. Gilkeson, Jr., *Middle-Class Providence, 1820–1940* (Princeton, N.J.: Princeton University Press,

1986), 23–25. Advocacy of immediate emancipation was somewhat less widespread than devotion to total abstinence.

66. Baxter, *Freewill Baptists*, 94–97.

67. RIQM, August 1837; May 24, 1838; some disagreement over abolitionist resolutions seems to have occurred in 1839, but they were passed by a "large majority" in 1840: see May and August 1839; Jan. 22, 1840. Elders conference, May 23, 1838; May 18, 1841.

68. N. Scituate F-W. B. Ch., Jan. 22, 1842. In the previous year, a freewill church in Georgiaville, a manufacturing village located just two miles from the Scituate border, made abolitionism part of its church covenant. See *Covenant of the Second Freewill Baptist Church in Smithfield*, 3; *Inventory of Church Archives: Baptist*, 166.

69. Foster F-W. B. Ch. Minutes, May 4, Aug. 2, and Oct. 5, 1844; Mar. 11, 1848; Second Foster F-W. B. Ch., anonymous history written in back of minute book.

70. *Proceedings of the Rhode Island Anti-Slavery Convention* (Providence: H.H. Brown, 1836); delegate lists were checked against extant church membership lists.

71. Elders conference, May 8, 1832; Oct. 23, 1838; "Elder James Burlingame," news clippings, 6.

72. Foster F-W. B. Ch. Minutes, May 4, Aug. 2, and Oct. 5, 1844; Mar. 11, 1848; Second Foster F-W. B. Ch., anonymous history written in back of minute book.

73. Foster F-W. B. Ch. Minutes, Apr. 30, May 14, 1842; Feb. 3, 17, Aug. 2, 1844; Foster Center Christian Church Minutes, Mar. 25, 1843; April 1843; July 13, 1844; Second Foster F-W. B. Ch., Feb. 18, Aug. 5, 1843. Of area churches whose minutes were examined, only the Christian churches of Rice City and Warwick/Coventry failed to mention temperance pledges. A total abstinence resolution was discussed at the Glocester Freewill Baptist Church in 1843, but discussion was broken off by intra-church schisms over the Dorr's War and the Adventist crusade.

74. Second Foster F-W. B. Ch., Mar. 20, 1839; N. Scituate F-W. B. Ch., Nov. 23, 1839. Nationally, the Freewill Baptist General Conference adopted a resolution against communion wine in 1841. For more on "ultraist" temperance positions, see Whitney Cross, *The Burned-Over District: The Social and Intellectual History of Enthusiastic Religion in Western New York, 1800–1850* (New York: Harper and Row, 1965), 211–16; Tyrrell, *Sobering Up*, 125–51.

75. "Elder James Burlingame," news clippings, 2–3; Keach, *Burrillville*, 79–80; Daniel Dow, *A Discourse in Chepachet, R.I., December 5, 1830, before the Glocester Temperance Association* (Providence: H. H. Brown, 1831), 10.

76. See W. J. Rorabaugh, *The Alcoholic Republic: An American Tradition* (New York: Oxford University Press, 1979), 8.

77. Keach, *Burrillville*, 87. "Constitution of the Foster Total Abstinence Society," in possession of Margery I. Matthews. For social developments on northwestern farms, see Chapter Four. The best account of the social basis for the temperance movement is Tyrrell, *Sobering Up*, especially chaps. 4–6.

78. Ian Tyrrell found agrarian support for temperance in the Worcester area, especially among commercial farmers who espoused innovative agricultural techniques. See *Sobering Up*, 102–4.

79. "History of the John H. Place Family Homestead and Adjoining Farms," misc. MSS, RIHS, 15. Hiram Wood ran a liquor-free store in southern Foster, 1843–1853; see the *Pawtucket Valley Gleaner*, Jan. 13, 1893. For other sources on local temperance societies, see the previous three citations. The tactics of antebellum temperance crusades are too familiar to bear repetition here. For more details, see Johnson, *A Shopkeeper's Millennium*, 111–35; and Hampel, *Temperance and Prohibition, passim*.

80. Documents of the Rhode Island Domestic Missionary Society, Rider Collection, John Hay Library, 19; *Proceedings*, June 1834, 14.

81. William Drowne, "Short Sketch of the Life of Solomon Drowne, M.D.," MSS, RIHS, 172–76; Foster Total Abstinence Society Records, in possession of Margery I. Matthews.

82. *Proceedings*, June 1836, 13; Documents of the Rhode Island Domestic Missionary Society, 19.

83. For Six-Principle Baptists' membership statistics, see the yearly tabulations compiled by the Baptist Yearly Meeting, 1814–1854, RIHS.

84. *Ibid.*; Richard Knight, *History of the General Six-Principle Baptists in Europe and America* (Providence: Smith & Parmenter, 1827), 280, 297–300; Whipple, *Historical Foster and Stray Thoughts*; see also Table 5B.

85. Baptist Yearly Meeting Records.

86. *Ibid.*, 1789.

87. Knight, *History*, 104. For citations on Six-Principle missions, see the next several paragraphs.

88. For more details on the use of instrumental music, see the discussion below on the Providence and Phenix Six-Principle churches.

89. *Minutes of the Baptist Yearly Meeting in the Ancient Order of the Six Principles of the Doctrine of Christ*, 1816 (Providence: H.H. Brown, 1816), 8; *Minutes . . .*, 1817, 6–7; Records of the Baptist Yearly Meeting, 1815, 1817, 1839, 1840.

90. Financial records of the Scituate Six-Principle Baptist Church, 1858–1886, *passim*. For the Second Foster Freewill Baptist Church's finances, see the section on the Christians and the Freewill Baptists in this chapter; this freewill church's membership was seventy-eight in 1839, according to the RIQM. As late as 1881, Six-Principle Baptists continued to lack "an academy or college, or periodical organ or distinctive literature, or missionary society for home or foreign work." William Cathcart, ed., *The Baptist Encyclopaedia: A Dictionary of the Doctrines, Ordinances . . . of the Baptist Denomination in All Lands* (Philadelphia, 1881), 1060.

91. *Minutes . . .*, 1847, 6–7; On antimission sentiment generally, see Hatch, *Democratization of American Christianity*, 174–79.

92. *Minutes . . .*, 1837, 8; *Minutes . . .*, 1839, 7; *Annual Report of the Rhode Island and Massachusetts General Baptist Yearly Conference . . . 1857* (Providence, 1856).

93. Minutes of the Scituate Six-Principle Church, Aug. 31, 1854.

94. The delegate list from *Proceedings of the R.I. Anti-Slavery Convention* was matched against membership lists from the Six-Principle Baptist churches of Foster, Coventry, and Scituate. Total male membership was estimated by dividing total membership of 992 (both male and female) by three. The northwest's adult male

population in 1835 was about 3,820, an extrapolation between U.S. census figures for 1830 and 1840.

95. *Zion's Friend*, published Feb. 7, 1835–Jan. 1, 1836, was paginated consecutively throughout. For examples of its temperance and antislavery sentiments, see pages 12, 25, 31, 32, and 35.

96. *Zion's Friend*, Nov. 6, 1835. The expulsion of the Johnston church is related below in further detail.

97. *Zion's Friend*, Nov. 6, 1835; *passim*. Membership figures were obtained from the Baptist Yearly Meeting Minutes.

98. Minutes of the East Greenwich Six-Principle Baptist Church, RIHS, Aug. 24, 1812; Dec. 24, 1814.

99. See Table 5A.

100. For another example of indifference to temperance by poorer, downwardly mobile members of rural society, see Randolph A. Roth, *The Democratic Dilemma: Religion, Reform and the Social Order in the Connecticut River Valley of Vermont, 1791–1850* (Cambridge: Cambridge University Press, 1987), 230–46.

101. Rhode Island Domestic Missionary Society, 11; Baptist Yearly Meeting, 1829; Mathias P. Harpin, *Prophets in the Wilderness: A History of Coventry, R.I.* (Oneco, Conn.: Harpin's Connecticut Almanac, 1973), 15–25.

102. Baptist Yearly Meeting Minutes, 1829.

103. Baptist Yearly Meeting Minutes, 1836, 1849, 1852, 1853.

104. Ironically, in this respect, the Six-Principlists' policy approximated the practice of their ancient adversaries, the Calvinist Baptists, who continued to close communion to all but those who had experienced adult baptism. Perhaps because they both originated as schismatic outcasts from an oppressive established church, the Six-Principle and Calvinist Baptists shared an insistence on preserving their own denominational purity and identity. See McLoughlin, *New England Dissent*, 1132–34.

105. Ray Potter, *Statement of Facts Relative to the Six-Principle Church in Cranston, R.I.* (Providence, 1820), 5, 13–14.

106. *Ibid.*, 5–10; Minutes of the Johnston Six-Principle Church, RIHS, Dec. 2, 1815; June 1, 1816; Baptist Yearly Meeting Minutes, 1816–1820. RIQM, Oct. 11, 1828.

107. Baptist Yearly Meeting Minutes, 1830–1835; RIQM, August 1837; Historical Records Survey, *Baptist*, 165.

108. Baptist Yearly Meeting Minutes, 1844; *Inventory of Church Archives: Baptist*, 176–77.

109. Minutes of the Lippitt and Phenix Six-Principle Baptist Church, RIHS, 1845–1851, *passim*. Baptist Yearly Meeting Minutes, 1851; Coventry Central Baptist Church, *Articles of Faith and Covenant of the Central Baptist Church in Coventry, R.I.* (Providence: M.B. Young, 1853); Harpin, *Prophets in the Wilderness*, 18–19.

110. Baptist Yearly Meeting Minutes.

111. See Table 5B and the section on religion in backcountry Rhode Island in Chapter One.

112. On increasing denominational cooperation in promoting moral reform, see Johnson, *Shopkeeper's Millennium*, 109–35.

113. *Ibid.* Other denominations also declined after the Civil War, because

of the general diminution of the rural northwest population; but the Six-Principlists' fall in membership was much more pronounced. Their membership declined by 75 percent between 1840 and 1900, whereas the Freewill Baptists' fell by only 47 percent.

114. [Samuel Arnold], "Circular Letter," *Annual Report of the Rhode Island and Massachusetts General Baptists Yearly Conference* . . . (Providence: Crawford Greene & Brother, 1866), 20, 21–22.

Conclusion

1. "History of the Place Family Homestead," 6–7, 14–15; Rhode Island Historic Preservation Commission, *Preliminary Survey Report of the Town of Coventry* (Providence, 1978), 10.

2. Hal S. Barron, *Those Who Stayed Behind: Rural Society in Nineteenth-Century New England* (Cambridge: Cambridge University Press, 1984), 70–73.

3. John Modell, "Mobility and Industrialization: Countryside and City in Nineteenth-Century Rhode Island," *Essays from the Lowell Conference on Industrial History*, 1980 and 1981, ed. Robert Weible, Oliver Ford, and Paul Marion (Lowell, Mass.: Lowell Conference on Industrial History, 1981), 90–91, 103. After a late start, the woolen industry boomed in Burrillville between 1840 and 1900. See Coleman, *Transformation of R.I.*, 136–41.

4. Rhode Island Historical Preservation Commission, *Foster, Rhode Island: Statewide Historical Preservation Report P-F–1* (Providence, 1982), 29–35; Rhode Island Historical Preservation Commission, *Preliminary Survey Report: Town of Burrillville* (Providence, 1982), 12–13; Modell, "Mobility and Industrialization," 89–92, 102.

5. Coleman, *Transformation of R.I.*, 220; *Twelfth Census of the United States . . . Population, part 1* (Washington: United States Census Office, 1901), 350. *Foster, Rhode Island: Statewide Historical Preservation Report*, 31. Barron, *Those Who Stayed Behind*, 65–75.

6. Dwight, *Travels*, II: 35–36; Boudinot, *Journey to Boston*, 27–30.

7. Dwight, *Travels*, II: 28–29, 38.

8. Records of the Foster Total Abstinence Society, in the possession of Margery I. Matthews.

9. For Freewill Baptist membership figures, see the minutes of their Rhode Island Quarterly Meeting, RIHS.

10. See Table 6 for voting statistics. On Jacksonian politics generally in Rhode Island, see Edward Francis Sweet, "The Origins of the Democratic Party in Rhode Island, 1824–1836" (Ph.D. dissertation, Fordham University, 1971). For Worcester County political alignments, see Brooke, *Heart of the Commonwealth*, 313–19, 327. The Antimasonic party was relatively weak in Rhode Island, garnering no more than 15 percent of the vote statewide. It was strongest in neither the agrarian west nor the Whig heartlands of Newport, Bristol, and Providence, but rather in a middle belt of towns dominated by mill villages and highly commercialized farmers. See Goodman, *Antimasonry*, 195–210; Susan Porter Benson, " 'A Union of Men and Not of Principles': The Rhode Island Antimasonic Party," (Master's thesis, Brown University, 1971).

11. It is difficult to generalize about the Dorrites. Although farmers generally opposed Dorrite reforms, because they feared being overwhelmed by legions of

newly enfranchised, propertyless workers, the largely rural towns of Glocester and Burrillville supported Dorr strongly. For more on Dorr's Rebellion, see Marvin Gettleman, *The Dorr Rebellion* (New York: Random House, 1973); and Patrick T. Conley, *Democracy in Decline: Rhode Island's Constitutional Development, 1776–1841* (Providence: Rhode Island Historical Society, 1977).

        12. Diary of Hiram Salisbury, Aug. 27, 1832; June 4, 1838; June 6, 1842. On temperance and the Whig party, see Hampel, *Temperance and Prohibition in Massachusetts, 1813–1852*, chaps. 5 and 6.

        13. See Table 6; Keach, *Burrillville*, 80–88.

Tables

TABLE IA. Glocester Town Tax Valuation, 1778

	Mean	Median	% Owning
Livestock			
Horses	0.8	0.7	59
Oxen	1.0	0.4	43
Cows and heifers	6.1	4.8	92
Cows only	3.9	3.1	
Heifers only	2.2	1.7	
Sheep and goats	8.0	6.3	69
Pigs	3.1	2.4	87
Acreage			
Pasture	12.5	7.0	72
Tillage	4.2	3.5	77
Meadow	11.9	9.2	71
Orchard	1.0	0.3	40
Waste	54.5	35.2	79
Total	84.1	62.0	82
Products			
Grain (bu)	51.6	39.7	77
Hay (tons)	6.8	4.6	71
Cider (gal)	3.0	0.3	39
Other assets			
Money and trading stock (£)	2.5	0.0	19
Plate (£)	0.8	0.0	6

SOURCE: Random sample of one-fifth of the households listed in the Glocester Tax Valuation of 1778, located in the Glocester Town Clerk's Office. Tax valuation figures counted all horned livestock over two months of age as "cattle" and thus included both heifers and fully mature cows in its totals. Separate figures for the two were derived by multiplying the cattle total by .64 for cows and .36 for heifers, the proportions present in contemporary probate inventories.

TABLE IB. Agricultural Production and Consumption for a Typical
(Median) Household in Northwestern Rhode Island, ca. 1780

Food Type	Production (Annual)	Consumption (Annual/Daily)	Nutritional Yield (Calories, Daily)	Surplus (Annual)
Grain	40 bu	36 bu/4 lbs flour	6,480	4 bu[a]
Milk	300 gal	136 gal/10 cups	1,600	164 gal
Beef	380 lbs	360 lbs/1 lb	1,000	20 lbs
Pork	180 lbs	180 lbs/0.5 lb	500	none
Cider	3 gal	3 gal/34 oz	510	none
Produce	9 bu	9 bu/7.5 lbs	3,000	none
Total			13,090	

a. The surplus grain would undoubtedly have been used for livestock feed in the winter. All other
surpluses were potentially marketable.

SOURCES: Production determined from Glocester tax figures in Table 1A; and James T. Lemon,
The Best Poor Man's Country: A Geographical Study of Early Southeastern Pennsylvania (New York:
W. W. Norton, 1972). Figures were extrapolated downward to reflect the fact that Glocester's
farms were less productive than Pennsylvania's. Produce production was estimated by multiplying
average probate holdings by 5, the factor by which they appear to underestimate annual production.

Consumption figures were derived from Catherine F. Adams, *Nutritive Value of American Foods
in Common Units* (U.S. Department of Agriculture, Agriculture Handbook No. 456, 1975); and
Bettye Hobbs Pruitt, "Self-Sufficiency and the Agricultural Economy of Eighteenth-Century
Massachusetts," *William and Mary Quarterly* 41 (1984), 344. I estimate that colonial farm families
needed somewhat less than the 15,000 total caloric intake suggested by Pruitt. I believe that Pruitt
incorrectly assumes that all family members would be involved in year-round "strenuous exercise"; in fact, the rhythms of farm life meant some seasons—winter, in particular—brought idleness as well as hard work.

TABLE IC. Agricultural Holdings and Production (Median Figures)

Based on Household Size

No. in Household	Cattle[a]		Pigs	Grain Production	N
	Heifers	Cows			
1–2	0	2	2	24	23
3–4	1	3	2	36	57
5	1	3	3	46	50
6	2	3	3	45	49
7	2	4	3	48	41
8–9	3	5	3	49	54
10–13	3	6	4	75	33

Based on Place in Family Life Cycle

Household Stage[b]					
Young couple	1	2	2	24	55
Young family	1	3	3	50	87
Medium family	2	4	3	49	84
Mature family	3	4	4	60	45
Elderly family	2	3	3	50	33

a. Separate figures for heifers and cows were derived by multiplying the cattle total by .64 for cows and .36 for heifers, the proportions present in contemporary probate inventories.

b. Stages were determined by linking households on the Glocester Tax Valuation of 1778 with the Rhode Island Census of 1782, using the following definitions:

Young couple: both parents under age 45 with fewer than 3 children, all under age 16

Young family: both parents under age 45 with 3 or more children, all under age 16

Medium family: at least one parent under age 45 with children both under and over age 16

Mature family: both parents over age 45 with children both under and over age 16; *or* at least one parent over age 45, provided they have more children over age 15 than under

Elderly family: both parents over age 45 with children only over age 15.

SOURCES: Glocester Tax Valuation, 1778 and Rhode Island Census, 1782.

TABLE ID. Agricultural Holdings and Production Based on Family Life Cycle Stage and Household Size

Household Stage/ No. of Members	Cattle	Pigs	Grain Production	N
Young Couple				
2	2	2	22	10
3	1	1	22	16
4	4	2	20	24
Young Family				
4–5	3	2	49	24
6	4	3	40	25
7	5	4	60	17
8+	8	3	60	21
Medium Family				
4–5	3	3	37	8
6	5	2	32	10
7	4	2	35	10
8	9	4	70	11
9	8	2	60	19
10	9	3	75	16
11–12	10	5	68	10
Mature Family				
1–4	9	4	82	12
5	5	4	58	10
6	8	4	64	10
7–14	7	5	48	13
Elderly Family				
1–2	4	2	45	11
3–4	6	4	60	13
4+	8	4	60	9

SOURCE: See sources for Table IC.

TABLE IE. Church Membership in Northwestern Rhode Island, ca. 1790

	Cov.	*Foster*	*Gloc.*	*Scit.*	*Total*	*% of All Members*	*% of Pop. >15*
Baptists							
6-Prin. Gen.	107	80	85	60	332	61	6.1
6-Prin. Calv.	0	0	85	0	85	15	1.5
5-Prin. Calv.	0	38	0	0	38	7	0.7
Separatist	20	0	0	0	20	4	0.4
All Baptists					475	87	8.7
Quakers (est.)	20	10	20	20	70	13	1.3
All church members					545	100	10.0

SOURCES: John Asplund, *The Universal Register of the Baptist Denomination in North America* (Boston, 1794; reprint, New York: Arno Press, 1980); Isaac Backus, *A Church History of New-England. Extending from 1690, to 1784.* . . . vol. 2 (Providence, R.I., 1784), 424–25.

TABLE 2A. Controversy between Upper-Valley and Lower-Valley Residents of Pawtuxet River Area over Fishing Rights, 1780s

	Petition for Fishways					
	Residence		*Tax Data*			
	No.	*%(N=69)*	*Mean*	*Median*	*No.*	*Town Median*
Upper Valley						
Coventry	11		$0.85	$0.88	8	$0.74
Scituate	16		£2.40	£1.11	3	£1.7
Glocester	0		—	—		
Johnston	2		£0.65	£0.65	2	£1.5
Total	29	42				
Lower Valley						
Providence	0		—	—		
Warwick	6		Not Available			
Total	6	9				
Cranston[a]	34	49	£2.95	£2.53	2	£1.1
	Petition against Fishways					
Upper Valley						
Coventry	0		—	—		
Glocester	4		$605	$605	2	$250
Johnston	3		£5.0	£5.7	3	£1.5
Scituate	9		£3.1	£3.4	9	£1.7
Total	16	27				
Lower Valley						
Providence	2		Not Available			
Warwick	23		Not Available			
Total	25	42				
Cranston[a]	18	31	£2.1	£1.3	13	£1.7

a. Cranston is treated separately because it was situated in both the upper and lower valleys of the Pawtuxet River.

SOURCES: Rhode Island Census, 1800; Scituate Town Tax List, 1783; Coventry Town Tax List, 1798 (RISA); Glocester Town Tax Valuation, 1778; Johnston Town Tax List, 1782.

TABLE 2B. Controversy over Moses Brown's Cotton-Mill Dam

Petitioners for Fishways

Residence	No.		Tax Quintiles				
		Lowest	Lower-Mid.	Middle	Upper-Mid.	Highest	N
Coventry	120	11%	25%	26%	20%	18%	(108)
Scituate	34		Not Available				
West Greenwich	33		Not Available				
Other	8						
Unlisted	40						
Total	235						

Petitioners against Fishways (First Supporting Petition)

	No.	%(N=302)	Mechanics Assoc. Members
Providence			
West ward	151	51	14
North[east] ward	54	18	6
South[east] ward	30	10	46
Prov.—unknown	24	8	15
Prov.—total	259	87	81
Narragansett Bay	15	5	0
Northeast R.I.	24	8	0
Unlisted	108		

Petitioners against Fishways (Second Supporting Petition)

	No.	Tax Quintiles				
		Lowest	Lower-Mid.	Middle	Upper-Mid.	Highest
Coventry	9	33%	0%	22%	11%	33%
Warwick	35		Not Available			
Unlisted	19					

SOURCES: U.S. Census, 1800; Coventry Town Tax List, 1798 (RISA); Providence Association of Mechanics and Manufacturers, *Annual Report* (1798).

TABLE 3A. Petition against Rhode Island and Connecticut Turnpike

Residence	Lowest	Lower–Mid.	Middle	Upper–Mid.	Highest	Totals
			Tax Quintiles			
Foster (1798 tax)	11	11	13	15	18	68
Foster (1822 tax)	1	0	2	1	1	5
Scituate (1783 tax)	1	0	2	1	1	5
Scituate (1822 tax)	1	0	5	5	5	16
Total (No.)	14	11	22	22	25	94
Total (%)	15	12	23	23	27	100
Tax rate unlisted						65

SOURCES: *Charters*, vol. 2, no. 21, RISA; various town tax lists.

TABLE 3B. Petitions for and against Glocester Turnpike

	Petition for Turnpike (Residence)				
	NW R.I.	*NE R.I.*	*Prov.*	*Non–R.I.*	*Totals*
Number	72	9	25	23	129
Percentage	56	7	19	18	100

	Petition for Turnpike (Tax Quintiles)					
Residence	*Lower*	*Lower-Mid.*	*Middle*	*Upper-Mid.*	*Highest*	*Totals*
Glocester (1778 tax)	3	0	1	4	7	15
Glocester (1822 tax)	6	1	4	9	12	32
Burrillville (1822 tax)	1	0	0	1	1	3
Scituate & Foster (1822 tax)	0	0	1	0	2	3
Johnston and North Providence (1782 tax)	0	0	0	0	2	2
Total (No.)	10	1	6	14	24	55
Total (%)	18	2	11	25	44	100
Tax rate unlisted						18

	Petition against Turnpike (Tax Quintiles)					
Glocester (1778 tax)	6	4	2	5	6	23
Glocester (1822 tax)	3	1	3	3	4	14
Burrillville (1822 tax)	0	0	5	1	2	8
Johnston and North Providence (1782 tax)	0	0	9	0	1	10
Total (No.)	9	5	19	9	13	55
Total (%)	16	9	35	16	24	100
Tax rate unlisted						62

SOURCES: *Charters*, vol. 2, nos. 40, 42, RISA; various town tax lists.

TABLE 3C. Petition for Foster and Scituate Central Turnpike

Residence	Lowest	Lower-Mid.	Middle	Upper-Mid.	Highest	Totals
			Tax Quintiles			
Foster (1798 tax)	2	0	0	1	0	3
Foster (1822 tax)	1	1	2	5	14	23
Scituate (1822 tax)	0	2	1	0	2	5
Cranston (1822 tax)	0	0	0	1	0	1
Total (No.)	3	3	3	7	16	32
Total (%)	9	9	9	22	50	99
Tax rate unlisted						31

SOURCES: *Charters*, vol. 5, no. 1, RISA; various town tax lists.

TABLE 3D. Petitions for and against Foster and Scituate Turnpike Extension

Petition against Extension

Residence	Lowest	Lower-Mid.	Middle	Upper-Mid.	Highest	Totals
			Tax Quintiles			
Foster (1822 tax)	1	0	0	0	0	1
Scituate (1822 tax)	2	6	5	12	8	33
Johnston (1782 tax)	0	0	1	1	2	4
Johnston (1822 tax)	0	0	1	0	2	3
Total (No.)	3	6	7	13	12	41
Total (%)	7	15	17	32	29	100
Tax rate unlisted						9

Petition for Extension

Residence	Lowest	Lower-Mid.	Middle	Upper-Mid.	Highest	Totals
Foster (1798 tax)	0	1	0	0	0	1
Foster (1822 tax)	1	7	2	4	2	16
Scituate (1822 tax)	1	2	2	3	3	11
Total (No.)	2	10	4	7	5	28
Total (%)	7	36	14	25	18	100
Tax rate unlisted						14

SOURCES: *Charters*, vol. 5, no. 13, RISA; various town tax lists.

TABLE 3E. Poor-Relief Expenditures in Burrillville, Foster, and Glocester, 1800–1820

	Burrillville	Foster	Glocester
1800	$ —	$ —	$104
1801	—	—	—
1802	—	—	—
1803	—	—	—
1804	—	—	315
1805	—	—	275
1806	—	—	—
1807	200	—	300
1808	185	133	289
1809	224	169	369
1810	195	229	317
1811	191	238	308
1812	279	330	250
1813	270	356	275
1814	249	391	332
1815	338	—	605
1816	275	524	695
1817	279	310	645
1818	264	373	757
1819	319	479	462
1820	250	600	374

SOURCE: Town Meeting minutes for Burrillville, Foster, and Glocester.

TABLE 3F. Petitions for and against Fishway Requirements on the North
Branch of the Pawtuxet River, 1801 and 1805

Petition for Fishways, 1801

| | Tax Quintiles | | | | | |
Residence	Lowest	Lower-Mid.	Middle	Upper-Mid.	Highest	Totals
Scituate (1783 tax)	2	1	2	2	6	13
Scituate (1822 tax)	0	8	5	3	7	23
Coventry (1798 tax)	2	1	3	2	2	10
Cranston (1787 tax)	2	1	4	1	3	11
Total (No.)	6	11	14	8	18	57
Total (%)	11	19	25	14	32	101
Tax rate unlisted						53

Petition against Fishways, 1805

Residence	Lowest	Lower-Mid.	Middle	Upper-Mid.	Highest	Totals
Scituate (1783 tax)	0	0	1	0	0	1
Scituate (1822 tax)	0	3	3	4	7	17
Coventry (1798 tax)	0	0	0	1	0	1
Cranston (1787 tax)	0	0	0	1	0	1
Johnston (1782 tax)	0	0	0	0	1	1
Glocester (1822 tax)	1	0	1	0	0	2
Total (No.)	1	3	5	6	8	23
Total (%)	4	13	22	26	35	100
Tax rate unlisted						32

SOURCES: Petitions to the General Assembly, vol. 34: 38; vol. 35, pt. 2: 54 (RISA); U.S. Census, 1800; various town tax lists.

TABLE 3G. Educational Statistics for Northwestern and Northeastern
Rhode Island, 1819

	No. of Schools	School-Age Population	Ratio: Children per School
Northwest			
Burrillville	10	644	64
Coventry	8	930	116
Foster	10	904	90
Glocester	12	753	63
Scituate	8[a]	814	102
Total/Average	48	4,045	84
Northeast			
Cranston	9	578	64
Cumberland	9	720	80
East Greenwich	6	398	66
Johnston	7[a]	397	57
North Providence	10	639	64
Smithfield	20	1,317	66
Warwick	10	920	92
Total/Average	71	4,969	70

a. Figures include one or two academies as well as common schools.

SOURCES: John C. Pease and John H. Niles, *A Gazetteer of the States of Connecticut and Rhode Island* (Hartford, 1819), 325–48, 367–76; U.S. Census, 1820, from which school-age population (ages 6 through 16) was calculated by multiplying the population age 0 through 16 by .65.

TABLE 3H. Educational Statistics for Northwestern Rhode Island, 1819, 1828, 1831

	Number of Schools		
	1819	*1828*	*1831*
Burrillville	10	12	16
Coventry	8	21	18
Foster	10	15	19
Glocester	12	13	17
Scituate	8	10	20
Total	48	71	90
	Ratio: School-Age Population/No. of Schools		
Burrillville	64	53	40
Coventry	116	51	60
Foster	90	53	42
Glocester	63	57	43
Scituate	102	105	52
Average	84	61	48

SOURCES: See Table 3G; also, Charles Caroll, *Public Education in Rhode Island* (Providence: E.L. Freeman, 1918), 104; U.S. Census, 1830 (population ratios for 1828 and 1831). For those years the school-age population (ages 6 through 16) was calculated by adding the 6–10 and 11–15 age brackets to one-fifth of the 16–20 age bracket.

TABLE 4A. Probate Inventories of Personal Property (Men Only), 1780s and 1830s

Part 1. Percentage Owning Key Possessions for Total Sample (Farmers Only)

	1780s		1830s	
Livestock				
Horses	48	(58)	34	(44)
Cows	76	(88)	65	(93)
Steer	21	(25)	22	(35)
Oxen	37	(47)	30	(43)
Pigs	73	(82)	44	(61)
Sheep	56	(69)	36	(53)
Poultry	12	(8)	10	(12)
Tools				
Spinning wheels	80	(87)	54	(74)
Looms	48	(60)	43	(53)
Wheels and looms	85	(90)	66	(83)
Iron plows	0	(0)	23	(28)
Wagons	3	(3)	55	(68)
Carts	35	(48)	19	(26)
Wagon, cart, or sled	39	(52)	59	(74)
Lumber	6	(7)	13	(20)
Credits				
Notes	47	(47)	59	(60)
Capital stock	0	(0)	9	(6)
Cash and specie	26	(31)	46	(50)
Luxuries				
Clock or watch	7	(7)	25	(25)
Plate	3	(4)	24	(29)
Chaise	0	(0)	7	(1)
Mahogany furniture	0	(0)	7	(1)
Books	18	(19)	27	(26)

Part 2. Median and Mean Holdings of Key Possessions for All Samples (Farmers Only)
(Figures Exclude Holdings with Zero Values)

	Median		Mean	
	1780s	1830s	1780s	1830s
Livestock				
Cows	1.9 (1.9)	1.5 (1.7)	2.5 (2.6)	2.1 (2.2)
Steer	2.0 (2.0)	2.0 (2.0)	2.2 (2.4)	2.3 (2.3)
Pigs	3.0 (3.0)	2.0 (2.0)	3.6 (3.7)	2.3 (2.3)
Sheep	9.0 (10.0)	8.0 (7.0)	11.2 (11.6)	10.0 (10.0)
Poultry	6.0 (7.5)	6.5 (7.0)	7.7 (9.0)	12.5 (14.5)
Total value ($)	75.0 (83.0)	78.0 (100.0)	88.0 (100.0)	102.0 (117.0)
Tools (Total Value)				
Transport equip. ($)	8.3 (8.0)	18.0 (17.0)	11.0 (10.7)	27.4 (27.3)
Textile equip. ($)	5.0 (5.7)	2.5 (2.8)	6.3 (7.0)	3.4 (3.7)
Farm equip. ($)	10.0 (10.0)	10.8 (11.6)	12.7 (12.8)	12.9 (13.4)
Credits				
Notes ($)	57.7 (57.0)	162.1 (143.3)	126.5 (130.3)	897.0 (414.5)
Cash and Specie ($)	3.7 (6.3)	21.5 (13.5)	12.6 (14.9)	146.0 (63.8)
Total value of inventory ($)	272 (340)	358 (407)	362 (413)	1,238 (770)

SOURCE: Probate inventories for all northwestern towns, 1780s and 1830s. A 100% sample of inventories for 1783–1792 and 1830–1834 yielded 112 male estates in the earlier period and 122 male inventories in the 1830s.

"Farmers" were identified as those households that contained livestock and farm equipment holdings greater than zero, and that did not own more than $33.3 worth of carpentry, blacksmith, or textile tools. Since inventories in the 1780s and early 1790s were quoted in pounds sterling, they were converted to dollars at the official state rate of six shillings to the dollar. Although prices fluctuated considerably in between the two periods, scholarly indices suggest that by the 1830s they had again reached the level of the 1780s and early 1790s. There was therefore no need to adjust for inflation or deflation.

Since probate inventories are recorded at the time of a person's death, they probably underestimate the size of a typical household's possessions, especially in the areas of livestock and other occupational materials. Nevertheless, they should still be valid for the purpose of comparing one period with another.

TABLE 4B. Banking Statistics for Rhode Island, New York, and
Pennsylvania, 1820, 1828, 1835

	1820	1828	1835
Northwestern Banks			
No.	4	5	6
Total assets ($)	159,321	256,942	425,777
Directors' debts ($)	20,952	59,597	49,001
Specie ($)	35,911	22,653	40,903
Notes in circ. ($)	83,453	81,100	156,079
Specie as a % of notes	43	28	26
All Rhode Island Banks			
No.	33	45	61
Total assets ($)	4,367,857	8,475,461	12,661,377
Directors' debts ($)	622,622	741,961	985,407
Specie ($)	323,955	344,412	566,416
Notes in circ. ($)	601,050	913,438	1,644,289
Specie as a % of notes	54	38	34
New York Banks			
Specie as a % of notes	9	15	29
Pennsylvania Banks			
Specie as a % of notes	49	29	36

Note: Total assets consist of debts due the bank, specie, notes of and deposits in other banks,
investments, and real estate.

SOURCES: Rhode Island General Assembly, *Acts and Resolutions*, May 1820, 49; May 1828, 38;
October 1835, 76; J. Van Fenstermaker, *The Development of American Commercial Banking, 1782–
1837* (Kent, Ohio: Kent State University Press, 1963), 226–27.

TABLE 4C. Textile Industry in Northwestern Rhode Island, ca. 1810 and 1832

Part 1. Cotton and Woolen Mills, 1832

	No. of Mills	Employees				Machinery		
		Men	Women	Children	Totals	Spindles	Looms	Cards
Foster	3	10	13	5	28	500	13	0
Burrillville	1	6	11	11	28	408	0	1
Glocester	2	19	38	55	112	2,474	65	2
Scituate	8	148	294	248	690	18,884	487	0
Coventry[a]	9	189	257	343	789	18,750	514	0
Total	23	372	613	662	1,647	41,016	1,079	3
Percent of state total					17	18		

Part 2. Factory Ownership (Locals vs. Nonresidents), ca. 1810 and 1832

	ca. 1810			1832		
	Locals	Outsiders	Both	Locals	Outsiders	Both
Scituate	4	2	2	0	8	0
Coventry	2	3	0	6	3	1
Total	6	5	2	6	11	1

Part 3. Factory Employment as Percentage of Work-Age Population, 1832

	Women	Men	Children[b]	Totals
Scituate	16	29	25	24
Coventry	22	26	37	28
Average	19	28	31	26

a. Totals for Coventry are estimates; source gave combined totals for several mills located in both Coventry and neighboring West Greenwich.

b. Children were estimated to be all those between ages 10 and 19.

SOURCES: *Part 1.* Henry Lane, *Documents Relative to the Manufacturers in the United States . . . 1832* (New York: Burt Franklin, 1832), I: 958–74. *Part 2.* Richard M. Bayles, ed., *History of Providence County, Rhode Island* (New York: W.W. Preston, 1891), II: 600–613; J. R. Cole, *History of Washington and Kent Counties* (New York, 1889), 1193–1215. *Part 3.* Lane, *Documents;* U.S. Census, 1830.

TABLE 4D. Total Agricultural Production for Burrillville and Glocester,
1778, 1840, 1850

	1778	*1840*	*1850*
Livestock			
Cattle (3 years or older)	1,714	n.d.	2,369
Oxen	420	n.d.	647
All horned livestock	2,134	2,689	3,016
Horses	363	502	471
Sheep	3,558	2,664	1,193
Pigs	1,395	1,524	1,319
Products			
Grain (bu)	23,220	36,230	42,676
Hay (tons)	3,060	4,506	6,589
Acres			
Improved land	13,739	n.d.	24,687
Unimproved land	25,299	n.d.	26,683
Mills			
Grist mills	8	9	n.d.
Saw mills	8	25	n.d.

Note: Burrillville was part of Glocester in 1778.

SOURCES: Glocester Town Tax Valuation, 1778; U.S. Census, 1840 and 1850.

TABLE 4E. John Waterman's Account Book, 1812–1836

| | Accounts with Laborers | | | | | | | All Payments | | Other Accounts |
| | In-Kind | | Third-Party | | Cash | | | | | |
	Amount	% of Total	Amount	% of Total	Amount	% of Total		Amount	% of Total	Amount
1812–1819	$201.99	51	$104.45	26	$ 89.61	23		$396.05	100	$137.66
1820–1829	128.87	70	4.21	2	50.84	28		183.92	100	98.29
1830–1832	94.98	65	36.30	25	15.72	11		147.00	101	3.75
1833	23.62	44	8.04	15	22.31	41		53.97	100	0.00
1834–1836	24.21	10	0.00	0	229.79	90		254.00	100	11.37

SOURCE: Rhode Island Historical Society.

TABLE 4F. Geographic Mobility in Foster and Coventry, 1780s, 1800s, 1820s (Minimum Persistent Rates)

| | Foster | | | Coventry | | |
Tax Quintile	1780s	1800s	1820s	1780s	1800s	1820s
Highest	79%	69%	48%	n.d.	65%	59%
Upper-middle	74	58	47	n.d.	68	53
Middle	55	54	38	n.d.	60	55
Lower-middle	59	47	26	n.d.	49	35
Lowest	43	43	29	n.d.	38	40
All	62	53	38	n.d.	56	48

SOURCES: Foster and Coventry Town Tax Lists for 1782, 1798, and 1822, matched with the censuses of 1790, 1810, and 1830, respectively. Results extrapolated logarithmically to even ten-year periods. Persistence rates are "minimum" because they do not include those who died during each decadal period. The lack of comprehensive vital records makes it impossible to adjust for deaths.

TABLE 4G. Inheritance Patterns, 1780s and 1830s

Part 1. Administration of Male-Owned Estates

	1780s			1830s		
	No.	%	Median Estate Value	No.	%	Median Estate Value
Administrators						
Widows	22	54	£ 46.3	12	14	$ 551
Male kin	10	24	40.8	24	27	414
Other male	3	7	33.3	43	49	244
Widow and male	4	10	153.7	9	10	2,864
Misc.	2	5	—	0	0	—
Total	41	100		88	100	
Executors						
Widows	6	9	27.8	3	10	267
Male kin	35	55	105.9	17	59	856
Other male	2	3	92.3	6	21	240
Widow and male	18	28	179.3	3	10	998
Misc.	3	5	—	0	0	—
Total	64	100		29	100	

Part 2. Non-kin Administrators in the 1830s

	Type of Administrator[a]		
	Unique	Specialized	Total
Relation to deceased			
Creditor	8	1	9
Not creditor	10	8	18
Unknown	18	6	24
Totals	36	15	51

Part 3. Widows' Portions

	1780s (N = 48)		1830s (N = 20)	
Amount of Portion				
> ⅓	21%		40%	
= ⅓	40		15	
< ⅓	17		30	
Indeterminate	21		15	
	%	Median Estate Value (£)	%	Median Estate Value ($)
Portion granted until				
Death	67	113	55	262
Remarriage	29	131	45	1,150
Unclear	4		0	

a. "Unique" administrators are those who administered only one estate in the period surveyed. "Specialized" administrators managed more than one.

SOURCES: See Table 4A.

TABLE 4H. Landlessness and Property Distribution, 1778–1842
(Percentage of Adult Males Owning Real Estate)

Part 1. Landlessness

	1782	1822
Coventry	n.d.	57
Foster	n.d.	62
Glocester	68	57
Burrillville	n.d.	56
Scituate	n.d.	51
Total	68	56

Part 2. Property Distribution

	Tax Quintiles				
	Lowest	Lower-Mid.	Middle	Upper-Mid.	Highest (2d 10th/1st 10th)
	1778–1798				
Coventry (1798)	8%	12%	16%	22%	15%/27%
Foster (1782)	3	6	13	23	19 /35
Glocester (1778)	2	7	14	23	18 /38
Scituate (1783)	6	8	13	23	18 /33
	1822				
Coventry	3	7	13	22	17 /37
Foster	3	8	14	23	18 /35
Glocester	2	7	13	23	17 /38
Burrillville	2	7	14	24	19 /33
Scituate	4	8	13	22	17 /36
	1842				
Scituate	4	8	14	23	19 /33

SOURCES: Town tax lists; Rhode Island Census, 1782; U.S. Census, 1820. Figures from the latter were extrapolated to take into account population change between 1820 and 1822. Of the tax lists available for 1782, only Glocester's was detailed enough to gauge the number of real estate owners. Calculations for Coventry, Foster, and Scituate in the earlier period include those who paid only a poll tax. In practice, this may have resulted in underestimating the inequality of property distribution.

TABLE 41. Female-Headed Households

Part 1. Number in Each Town (No. Women/All)

	Taxpayers				Probated Estates	
	1782	*1798*	*1822*	*1842*	*1780s*	*1830s*
Coventry	n.d.	15/429	23/396	n.d.	0/19	5/32
Foster	3/250	1/331	19/371	n.d.	3/28	5/35
Glocester	5/464	n.d.	16/324	n.d.	2/34	4/25
Burrillville	—	n.d.	9/263	n.d.	—	5/19
Scituate	6/418	n.d.	1/346	31/418	3/38	2/30
Total (No.)	14/1,132	16/760	68/1,700	31/418	8/119	22/141
Total (%)	1	2	4	7	7	16

Part 2. Wealth Distribution (No. Households)

Tax Quintiles	*1782*	*1798*	*1822*	*1842*
Highest	1	1	1	1
Upper-middle	2	1	6	5
Middle	3	1	12	2
Lower-middle	3	0	23	10
Lowest	5	13	26	13
Total	14	16	68	31

Part 3. Demographic Characteristics of the Female Taxpayers of 1822

	Household Size					No. Employed			No. Men			
	1	*2*	*3*	*4*	*5+*	*0*	*1*	*2+*	*0*	*1*	*2*	*3+*
No. households	3	8	7	7	5	17	10	3	10	13	3	4

Part 4. Probate Inventories

	1780s	*1830s*
Cows (% owning)	63	32
Sheep (% owning)	50	23
Median value of		
Livestock	$ 37.3	$ 23.5
Notes of hand	10.0	128.0
Cash	0.0	19.5
Total inventory	183.7	189.6

SOURCES: *Parts 1 and 2.* Town tax lists; for source of data on probabted estates, see Table 4A. *Part 3.* U.S. Census, 1820. *Part 4.* See Table 4A.

TABLE 5A. Relative Wealth and Occupations of Northwestern Church Members

Part 1. Relative Wealth of Members Joining between 1780 and 1850

	Tax Quintiles					
Denomination	Lowest	Lower-Mid.	Middle	Upper-Mid.	Highest	No.
Evangelical						
Christians[a]	9%	14%	18%	32%	27%	44
Freewill Baptists[b]	11	18	31	27	13	62
All Evangelicals	10	16	25	29	19	106
Six-Principle Baptist[c]						
Joined by 1800	23	21	13	26	17	53
Joined 1801–1820	11	17	25	27	21	72
Joined after 1820	18	35	21	9	18	34

Part 2. Occupations and Relative Wealth of Members Joining between 1830 and 1850

	Denomination		
	Christians	F-W. Bapt.	6-P. Bapt.
Merchants/Manufacturers/Professionals	7%	5%	4%
Farmers	61	54	49
(median property value)	($2,000)	($1,500)	($750)
Artisans	24	23	16
(median property value)	($1,350)	($550)	($750)
Skilled workers/factory overseers	0	1	10
Factory operatives	2	6	6
Laborers	5	8	14
Students	0	2	0
None stated	0	1	1
Median property value (all occup.)	$1,850	$1,050	$400
Number	41	119	81

a. Rice City Church; Foster Center church.

b. Foster Church; Glocester church; Second Foster church; North Scituate church.

c. Coventry Church; Foster church; Scituate church.

SOURCES: Church membership lists, matched with town tax lists; U.S. Census, 1850.

TABLE 5B. Church Membership by Denomination in Northwestern Rhode
Island

	1815	1820	1825	1830	1835	1840	1900
Evangelicals							
Freewill Baptists							
Membership	n.d.	143	263	266	486	742	396
No. of churches	1	1	3	3	5	5	8
Christians							
Membership	n.d.	40	n.d.	450[a]	n.d.	750[a]	n.d.
No. of churches	1	1	2	2	4	4	5
All Evangelicals							
Membership	n.d.	183	350[a]	716[a]	1,100[a]	1,492[a]	n.d.
No. of churches	1	2	5	5	9	9	13
Six-Principle Baptists							
Membership	497	729	665	775	992	1,033	380
No. of churches	5	4	4	3	3	2	4

a. Estimated figure.

SOURCES: Minutes of the Rhode Island Quarterly Meeting of Freewill Baptists, RIHS; Records of the Baptists' Yearly Meetings, RIHS. No official membership records are available for the Christians. Estimates were gleaned instead from "Thirty-third Annual Report of the Rhode Island Domestic Missionary Society," John Hay Library; Margery I. Matthews, Virginia I. Benson, and Arthur E. Wilson, *Churches of Foster: A History of Religious Life in Rural Rhode Island* (Foster, R.I.: North Foster Baptist Church, 1978), chaps. 4–7; and Richard M. Bayles, ed., *History of Providence County, Rhode Island* (New York: W.W. Preston, 1891), II: 611.

TABLE 6. Voting Statistics in Northwestern Rhode Island for Key Statewide
Races, 1832–1860

1832 Gov.	50% Dem.	38% Nat. Rep.	12% Antimasonic
1832 Pres.	49% Dem.	38% Nat. Rep.	13% Antimasonic
1836 Gov.	72% Dem.	28% Whig	
1836 Pres.	67% Dem.	33% Whig	
1840 Gov.	61% Dem.	39% Whig	
1840 Pres.	60% Dem.	40% Whig	
1842 Gov.	40% Dorrite	60% Law & Order	
1844 Pres.	47% Dem.	53% Whig	
1848 Gov.	50% Dem.	47% Whig	3% Free-Soil
1848 Pres.	45% Dem.	48% Whig	7% Free-Soil
1852 Pres.	63% Dem.	37% Whig	
1855[a] Lt. Gov.	29% Dem.	7% Whig	63% Know-Nothing
1856 Pres.	44% Dem.	56% Rep.	
1860 Pres.	45% Dem.	55% Rep.	

a. The lieutenant governor's race for 1855 was chosen because in all other statewide contests
either the Democrats or the Whigs ran a fusion ticket with a Know-Nothing candidate, thereby
obscuring true party preferences.

SOURCE: *Providence Journal.*

Bibliography

Unpublished Sources

American Antiquarian Society
        Henry Comstock Papers
        Samuel Smith Account Book

American Baptist Historical Society
        Six-Principle Baptist Church of Smithfield and Glocester, Misc. Records

Andover–Newton Theological School
        Isaac Backus Papers

Glocester Heritage Society
        Jesse Potter Account Book
        Potter and Knight Copybook
        Samuel Potter, Jr., Account Book

John Carter Brown Library (Brown University)
        Brown Family Papers

John Hay Library (Brown University)
        Baptist Collection
        Solomon Drowne Collection
        Theodore Foster Account Book
        William W. Knight Account Book
        George W. Potter Account Book
        Providence and Norwich Turnpike Society Documents
        Rhode Island Domestic Missionary Society Documents
        Rhode Island Six-Principle Baptist Association Minutes
        Rider Collection
        Jonah Titus Account Book

New York Historical Society
        Leonard Ensworth Account Book, 1795–1799

Old Sturbridge Village Research Library
        Freeman Jones Account Book
        Perez Peck Papers

Rhode Island Historical Society
        Ephraim Abbott Journal
        Jacob Adolphus Account Book
        Almy & Brown Co. Papers
        Lydia Angell Papers
        Nehemiah Atwood Account Book
        Baptist Yearly Meetings (Six-Principle Baptist Association)
        Burrillville Town Tax Valuations, 1821, 1822
        Butler Family Papers
        Coventry Town Papers
        Cranston Town Tax List, 1787
        Solomon Drowne Papers
        First Baptist Church of Providence Records
        Theodore Foster Papers
        Foster Town Tax Lists, 1821, 1822
        General Six-Principle Baptist Archives
        Glocester Town Tax Lists, 1821, 1822
        Elisha Mathewson Papers
        Rhode Island Quarterly Meeting, Elders Conference
        Rhode Island Quarterly Meeting Minutes (Freewill Baptists)
        Scituate Town Papers
        Second Foster Freewill Baptist Church Records
        Asa and Samuel Steere Account Book
        Warwick Town Tax Valuations, 1821, 1822
        William and John Waterman Account Book
        Western R.I. Quarterly Meeting Minutes (Freewill Baptists)

Rhode Island State Archives
        Charters granted by the General Assembly
        Coventry Town Tax List, 1798
        Petitions to the General Assembly
        Reports to the General Assembly

Town Records (located in town clerks' offices)
        Burrillville Town Meeting Minutes
        Burrillville Town Probate Records
        Coventry Town Meeting Minutes
        Coventry Town Probate Records
        Foster Town Meeting Minutes
        Foster Town Probate Records
        Glocester Town Meeting Minutes
        Glocester Town Probate Records
        Glocester Town Tax Valuation, 1778

Scituate Town Meeting Minutes
Scituate Town Probate Records
Scituate Town Tax Valuation, 1842

Church Records and Privately Owned Manuscripts
Foster Center Christian Church (in possession of Margery I. Matthews of Foster, R.I.)
Foster Town Tax Lists, 1781, 1787, 1798 and Foster Total Abstinence Society Records (in possession of Margery I. Matthews)
Glocester Freewill Baptist Church (in possession of Mrs. Clifford W. Brown of Providence, R.I.)
Hiram Salisbury Daybook (typescript copy in possession of Edna Kent of Chepachet, R.I.)
North Foster Freewill Baptist Church (in possession of church)
Rice City Christian Church (in possession of Audrey Hall, church secretary)
Warwick and Coventry Christian Church (in possession of Audrey Hall)

Maps

Davenport, Isaac. Revised by Theodore Foster. *Plan of the Town of Foster, by Conjecture from the Best Information.* 1799, RIHS MSS, vol. 8, 9.
Map of Scituate. n.d. RIHS MS, 1414.
Stevens, James. *Topographical Map of the State of Rhode Island and Providence Plantations.* Newport, 1831.
Walling, Henry F. *Map of the State of Rhode Island and Providence Plantations.* Providence, 1855.

Newspapers and Periodicals

Columbian Phenix, 1808–1812
Freewill Baptist Magazine, 1826–1830
Herald of Gospel Liberty, 1812–1820
Providence Gazette, 1785–1825
Providence Phoenix, 1802–1808
Rhode Island American, 1808–1829
Zion's Friend, and General Baptist Register, 1835–1836

Published Primary Sources

Annual Reports of the Rhode Island and Massachusetts General Baptists Yearly Conference, 1816–1870. Providence, Rhode Island.
Asplund, John. *The Universal Register of the Baptist Denomination in North America.* Boston, 1794; reprint New York: Arro Press, 1980.
Backus, Isaac. *The Diary of Isaac Backus.* 3 vols. Edited by William G. McLoughlin. Providence: Brown University Press, 1979.
Baptist Yearly Meeting. *Minutes of the Baptist Yearly Meeting in the Ancient Order of the Six Principles of the Doctrine of Christ, 1816–1854.* Providence: H.H. Brown, 1816–1854.

Beaman, Charles C. "Sketches of Scituate and Foster, R.I.," No. 3. Clippings from the *Providence Journal*. In Rider Collection, Box 343, No. 9, John Hay Library.

Cheney, M[artin]. *Circular . . . written by M. Cheney, Pastor of the Free-will Baptist Church in Olneyville*. Providence: W. Marshall, n.d.

Colby, John. *The Life, Experience, and Travels of John Colby*. Dover, N.H.: Free-will Baptist Printing Establishment, 1854.

Coventry Central Baptist Church. *Articles of Faith and Covenant of the Central Baptist Church in Coventry, R.I.* Providence: M. B. Young, 1853.

Dow, Daniel. *A Discourse in Chepachet, R.I., December 5, 1830, before the Glocester Temperance Association*. Providence: H.H. Brown, 1831.

Dwight, Timothy, *Travels in New England and New York*. 3 vols. New Haven, Conn., 1821–22.

Fearon, Henry Bradshaw. *Sketches of America*, 2d ed. London, 1818.

First Christian Church of Scituate. *Members' Manual of the First Christian Church of Scituate, Rhode Island*. Phenix, R.I.: John H. Campbell, 1878.

Foster, Sir Augustus John. *Jeffersonian America: Notes on the United States of America Collected in the Years 1805–6–7 and 11–12*. San Marino, Calif.: Huntingdon Library, 1954.

Greene, Nathaneal. *The Papers of Nathaneal Greene*. Edited by Richard K. Showman. Chapel Hill: University of North Carolina Press, 1976.

Hadfield, Joseph. *An Englishman in America, 1785, Being the Diary of Joseph Hadfield*. Edited by Douglas S. Robertson. Toronto: Hunter-Rose, 1973.

Holbrook, Jay Mack. *Rhode Island 1782 Census*. Oxford, Mass.: Holbrook Research Institute, 1979.

Hopkins, Samuel R. *A Short History of the Reformation and Establishment of the Church of Christ, or Christian Church, in Coventry, R.I., since 1812*. Providence, 1821.

Jackson, Henry. *An Account of the Churches in Rhode Island Presented at . . . the Rhode Island Baptist State Convention*. Providence, 1852.

———. *A Discourse in Commemoration of the 46th Anniversary of the Mite Society, and the 250th Anniversary of the 1st Baptist Church of America*. Providence, 1854.

Jones, David. *The Doctrine of "Laying on of Hands" Examined and Vindicated*. Philadelphia, 1786.

———. *A True History of the Laying on of Hands. . . .* Burlington, N.J., 1805.

Keach, Horace A. *Burrillville As It Was, and As It Is*. Providence: Knowles, Anthony, 1856.

Knight, Richard. *History of the General Six-Principle Baptists, in Europe and America*. Providence, 1826.

Pease, John C., and John H. Niles. *A Gazetteer of the States of Connecticut and Rhode Island*. Hartford, Conn., 1819.

Potter, Ray. *Statement of Facts Relative to the Six-Principle Church in Cranston, R.I.* Providence, 1820.

Providence Association of Mechanics and Manufacturers. *The Charter, Articles of Agreement, Bye-Laws, Rules and Regulations of the Providence Association of Mechanics and Manufacturers*. Providence, 1798.

Providence Female Tract Society. *Annual Reports, 1816–1820.* Providence, 1816–1820.

Rhode Island Anti-Slavery Society. *Proceedings of the Rhode Island Anti-Slavery Convention.* Providence: H.H. Brown, 1836.

Rhode Island Baptist State Convention. *Minutes of the Rhode Island Baptist State Convention, 1827, 1829, 1830.* Providence, 1827–1830.

Rhode Island Domestic Missionary Society. *Proceedings of the Evangelical Consociation and Missionary Society of Congregational Churches in Rhode Island for June 1834.* Providence, 1834.

Rhode Island General Assembly. *Report of the Committee Appointed by the General Assembly . . . 1809, to Inquire into the Situation of the Farmers Exchange Bank in Glocester.* Providence, 1809.

Rhode Island Quarterly Meeting of Freewill Baptists. *Minutes of the Ministers' Conference and also of the Quarterly Meeting Conference of the Rhode Island Quarterly Meeting of Freewill Baptist, held at Greeneville, R.I.* Pawtucket, R.I.: A. W. Pearce, 1851.

Scituate, Town of. *An Act for Repairing the Several Highways and Bridges within the Town of Scituate: Passed in Town Meeting, May 27, 1812.* Providence, 1812.

Second Freewill Baptist Church of Smithfield. *Covenant of the Second Freewill Baptist Church in Smithfield, R.I., Adopted February 28, 1841.* Providence, 1841.

Shirreff, Patrick. *A Tour through North America.* Edinburgh, 1835.

Stiles, Ezra. *The Literary Diary of Ezra Stiles.* Edited by Franklin Bowditch Dexter. New York, 1901.

Secondary Sources

Ahlstrom, Sydney E. *A Religious History of the American People.* New Haven, Conn.: Yale University Press, 1972.

Bailyn, Bernard. *The New England Merchants in the Seventeenth Century.* Cambridge, Mass.: Harvard University Press, 1955.

Baltzell, E. Digby. *Puritan Boston and Quaker Philadelphia: Two Protestant Ethics and the Spirit of Class Authority and Leadership.* New York: Free Press, 1979.

Barnes, Gilbert Hobbs. *The Anti-Slavery Impulse, 1830–1844.* New York: Harcourt, Brace and World, 1964.

Barron, Hal S. *Those Who Stayed Behind: Rural Society in Nineteenth-Century New England.* Cambridge: Cambridge University Press, 1984.

Baxter, Norman Allen. *History of the Freewill Baptists: A Study in New England Separatism.* Rochester, N.Y.: ABHS, 1957.

Bayles, Richard M., ed. *History of Providence County, Rhode Island.* New York: W.W. Preston, 1891.

Beamen, Charles C. "History of Foster." RIHS MSS.

Becker, Laura L. "Ministers vs. Laymen: The Singing Controversy in Puritan New England, 1720–1790." *New England Quarterly* 55 (November 1982).

Benson, Susan Porter. " 'A Union of Men and Not of Principles': The Rhode Island Antimasonic Party." Brown University, Master's thesis, 1971.

Bidwell, Percy Wells, and John I. Falconer. *History of Agriculture in the Northern United States, 1620–1860.* Washington, D.C.: Carnegie Institute of Washington, 1925.

Bining, Arthur Cecil. *Pennsylvania Iron Manufacture in the Eighteenth Century.* Harrisburg: Pennsylvania Historical and Museum Commission, n.d.

Boudinot, Elias. *Elias Boudinot's Journey to Boston in 1809.* Edited by Milton Halsey Thomas. Princeton, N.J.: Princeton University Press, 1955.

Bridenbaugh, Carl. *Fat Mutton and Liberty of Conscience: Society in Rhode Island, 1636–1690.* Providence: Brown University Press, 1974.

Brooke, John L. *The Heart of the Commonwealth: Society and Political Culutre in Worcester County, Massachusetts, 1713–1861.* New York: Cambridge University Press, 1989.

———. "To the Quiet of the People: Revolutionary Settlements and Civil Unrest in Western Massachusetts, 1774–1789." *William and Mary Quarterly* 46 (July 1989): 425–62.

Bushman, Richard L. *From Puritan to Yankee: Character and the Social Order in Connecticut, 1690–1765.* Cambridge, Mass.: Harvard University Press, 1967.

Caldwell, S. L. *History of the First Baptist Church in Providence, 1639–1877.* Providence, 1877.

Caroll, Charles. *Public Education in Rhode Island.* Providence: E.L. Freeman Company, 1918.

Cauchon, Henry F., Jr. "The New London Turnpike and the Rhode Island Turnpike Era." M.A.T. thesis, Brown University, 1960.

Cayton, Andrew R. L. The Frontier Republic: Ideology and Politics in the Ohio Country. Kent, Ohio: Kent State University Press, 1986.

Clark, Christopher. "Household Economy, Market Exchange, and the Rise of Capitalism in the Connecticut Valley, 1800–1860." *Journal of Social History* 13 (Winter 1979): 169–89.

———. "The Household Mode of Production—A Comment." *Radical History Review* 18 (Fall 1978): 166–71.

———. *The Roots of Rural Capitalism: Western Massachusetts, 1780–1860.* Ithaca, N.Y.: Cornell University Press, 1990.

———. "Taking Stock of the Nineteenth-Century Store: A Re-Evaluation." Paper presented at the annual convention of the Organization of American Historians, Minneapolis, April 1985.

Clemens, Paul G. E., and Lucy Simler. "Rural Labor and the Farm Household in Chester County, Pennsylvania, 1750–1820." In *Work and Labor in Early America,* 106–43. Edited by Stephen Innes. Chapel Hill: University of North Carolina Press, 1988.

Cole, Arthur Harrison. *Wholesale Commodity Prices in the United States, 1700–1861.* Cambridge, Mass.: Harvard University Press, 1938.

Cole, J. R. History of Washington and Kent Counties. New York: W. W. Preston, 1889.

Coleman, Peter J. *The Transformation of Rhode Island, 1790–1860.* Providence, R.I.: Brown University Press, 1963.

Conley, Patrick T. *Democracy in Decline: Rhode Island's Constitutional Development, 1776–1841.* Providence: Rhode Island Historical Society, 1977.

Cook, Edward. *Fathers of the Towns: Leadership and Community Structure in Eighteenth-Century New England.* Baltimore: Johns Hopkins University Press, 1976.

Cooper, Carolyn, and Patrick Malone. "The Mechanical Woodworker in Early 19th-

Century New England as a Spin-off from Textile Industrialization." Paper presented at the Old Sturbridge Village Colloquium on Early New England Society and Culture, March 1990.

Cornell, Saul. "An Aristocracy Assailed: The Ideology of Backcountry Anti-Federalism." *Journal of American History* 76 (March 1990): 1148–72.

Cott, Nancy F. "Divorce and the Changing Status of Women in Eighteenth-Century Massachusetts." *William and Mary Quarterly* 33 (October 1976): 586–614.

Cray, Robert E., Jr. *Paupers and Poor Relief in New York City and Rural Environs, 1700–1830.* Philadelphia: Temple University Press, 1988.

Creech, Margaret. *Three Centuries of Poor Law Administration: A Study of Legislation in Rhode Island.* Chicago: University of Chicago Press, 1936.

Cremin, Lawrence A. *The American Common School: An Historic Conception.* New York; Columbia University Teachers College, Bureau of Publications, 1951.

Cremin, Lawrence A. *American Education: The National Experience, 1783–1876.* New York: Harper and Row, 1980.

Cross, Whitney. *The Burned-Over District: The Social and Intellectual History of Enthusiastic Religion in Western New York, 1800–1850.* New York: Harper and Row, 1965.

Danhof, Charles. *Change in Agriculture: The Northern United States, 1820–1870.* Cambridge, Mass.: Harvard University Press, 1969.

Daniels, Bruce C. *Dissent and Conformity on Narragansett Bay: The Colonial Rhode Island Town.* Middletown, Conn.: Wesleyan University Press, 1983.

Demos, John. *A Little Commonwealth: Family Life in Plymouth Colony.* New York: Oxford University Press, 1970.

Ditz, Toby L. *Property and Kinship: Inheritance in Early Connecticut, 1750–1820.* Princeton, N.J.: Princeton University Press, 1986.

Dorr, Henry C. *The Planting and Growth of Providence.* Providence, 1882.

Drowne, William. "Sketch of the Life of Solomon Drowne, M.D." RIHS MSS, n.d.

Dublin, Thomas. "Women and Outwork in a Nineteenth-Century New Hampshire Town: Fitzwilliam, New Hampshire, 1830–1850." In *The Countryside in the Age of Capitalist Transformation: Essays in the Social History of Rural America.* Edited by Steven Hahn and Jonathan Prude. Chapel Hill, N.C.: University of North Carolina Press, 1985, 51–70.

Edwards, Morgan. "Materials for a History of the Baptists in Rhode Island." RIHS *Collections,* VI (1867): 313–15.

Ellis, David Meldwyn. *Landlords and Farmers in the Hudson–Mohawk Region, 1790–1850.* Ithaca, N.Y.: Cornell University Press, 1946.

Fenstermaker, J. Van. *The Development of American Commercial Banking, 1782–1837.* Kent, Ohio: Kent State University Press, 1963.

Field, Edward. *State of Rhode Island and Providence Plantations: A History.* 3 vols. Boston: Mason, 1902.

Fitz, Rev. William. *An Historical Sketch of the Public Schools of Burrillville.* Providence, 1876.

Fowler, Gail Barbara. "Rhode Island Handloom Weavers and the Effects of Technological Change, 1780–1840." Ph.D. dissertation, University of Pennsylvania, 1984.

————. "Rice City: An Evaluation of the Evidence." Master's thesis, Brown University, 1977.

Garrison, Winfred Ernest. *An American Religious Movement: A Brief History of the Disciples of Christ.* St. Louis: Christian Board of Publication, 1948.

Gaustad, Edwin Scott. "Baptists in Seventeenth-Century England." Master's thesis, Brown University, 1948.

Gettleman, Marvin. *The Dorr Rebellion.* New York: Random House, 1973.

Gilkeson, John S., Jr. *Middle-Class Providence, 1820–1940.* Princeton, N.J.: Princeton University Press, 1986.

Greene, Welcome Arnold. *Providence Plantations for 250 Years.* 2 vols. Providence, 1886.

Griffin, Clifford S. *Their Brothers' Keepers: Moral Stewardship in the United States, 1800–1865.* New Brunswick, N.J.: Rutgers University Press, 1960.

Gross, Robert A. "Culture and Cultivation: Agriculture and Society in Thoreau's Concord." *Journal of American History* 69 (June 1982): 42–61.

————. *The Minutemen and Their World.* New York: Hill and Wang, 1976.

Guild, Reuben Aldridge. *Early History of Brown University, Including the Life, Times, and Correspondence of President Manning, 1756–1791.* Providence: Snow and Farnham, 1896.

Gura, Philip F. *A Glimpse of Sion's Glory: Puritan Radicalism in New England, 1620–1660.* Middletown, Conn.: Wesleyan University Press, 1984.

Hahn, Steven. *The Roots of Southern Populism: Yeoman Farmers and the Transformation of the Georgia Upcountry, 1850–1880.* New York: Oxford University Press, 1983.

Hammond, Bray. *Banks and Politics in America: From the Revolution to the Civil War.* Princeton, N.J.: Princeton University Press, 1957.

Hampel, Robert L. *Temperance and Prohibition in Massachusetts.* Ann Arbor, Mich.: UMI Research Press, 1982.

Handlin, Oscar. *Boston's Immigrants.* New York: Atheneum, 1976.

Harpin, Mathias P. *Prophets in the Wilderness: A History of Coventry, R.I.* Oneco, Conn.: Harpin's Connecticut Almanac, 1973.

Hatch, Nathan O. "The Christian Movement and the Demand for a Theology of the People." *Journal of American History* 67 (December 1980): 545–67.

————. *The Democratization of American Christianity.* New Haven, Conn.: Yale University Press, 1989.

Heale, M. J. "Humanitarianism in the Early Republic: The Moral Reformers of New York, 1776–1826." *Journal of American Studies* 2 (October 1968): 161–76.

Hedges, James B. *The Browns of Providence Plantations: Colonial Years.* Cambridge, Mass.: Harvard University Press, 1952.

Henretta, James A. "Families and Farms: *Mentalité* in America." *William and Mary Quarterly* 35 (January 1978): 3–32.

"History of the John H. Place Family Homestead and Adjoining Farms." RIHS Misc. MSS.

Holmes, Richard. *Communities in Transition: Bedford and Lincoln, Massachusetts, 1729–1850.* Ann Arbor, Mich.: UMI Research Press, 1980.

Isaac, Rhys. *The Transformation of Virginia, 1740–1790.* Chapel Hill: University of North Carolina Press, 1982.

James, Sidney V. *Colonial Rhode Island: A History*. New York: Charles Scribner's Sons, 1975.

Jensen, Joan M. "Cloth, Butter and Boarders: Women's Household Production for the Market." *Review of Radical Political Economics* 12 (Summer 1980): 14–24.

———. *Loosening the Bonds: Mid-Atlantic Farm Women, 1750–1850*. New Haven, Conn.: Yale University Press, 1986.

Jensen, Merrill. *The New Nation: A History of the United States during the Confederation, 1781–1789*. New York: Alfred A Knopf, 1950.

Johnson, Curtis D. *Islands of Holiness: Rural Religion in Upstate New York, 1790–1860*. Ithaca, N.Y.: Cornell University Press, 1989.

Johnson, Paul E. *A Shopkeeper's Millennium: Society and Revivals in Rochester, New York, 1815–1847*. New York: Hill and Wang, 1978.

Kaminski, John P. "Political Sacrifice and Demise—John Collins and Jonathan J. Hazard, 1786–1790." *Rhode Island History* 35 (August 1976): 91–98.

Katz, Michael B. *The Irony of Early School Reform*. Boston: Beacon Press, 1970.

Knights, Peter R. "Population Turnover, Persistence, and Residential Mobility in Boston, 1830–1860." In *Nineteenth-Century Cities: Essays in the New Urban History*, edited by Stephen Thernstrom and Richard Sennett. New Haven, Conn.: Yale University Press, 1969.

Kulik, Gary. "The Beginnings of the Industrial Revolution in America: Pawtucket, R.I., 1672–1829." Ph.D. dissertation, Brown University, 1980.

———. "Dams, Fish, and Farmers: Defense of Public Rights in Eighteenth-Century Rhode Island." In *The Countryside in the Age of Capitalist Transformation: Essays in the Social History of Rural America*, edited by Stephen Hahn and Jonathan Prude. Chapel Hill: University of North Carolina Press, 1985, 25–50.

Lamoureaux, Naomi R. "Banks, Kinship and Economic Development: The New England Case." *Journal of Economic History* 46 (September 1986): 647–67.

Larkin, Jack. "From 'Country Mediocrity' to 'Rural Improvement': Transforming the Slovenly Countryside in Central Massachusetts, 1775–1840." Paper presented at the Boston Area Seminar in Early American History, April 18, 1991.

———. *The Reshaping of Everyday Life*. New York: Harper and Row, 1988.

Lemon, James T. *The Best Poor Men's Country: A Geographical Study of Early Southeastern Pennsylvania*. New York: W.W. Norton, 1972.

Lindstrom, Diane. *Economic Development in the Philadelphia Region, 1810–1850*. New York: Columbia University Press, 1978.

Lockridge, Kenneth. "Land, Population and the Evolution of New England Society, 1630–1790." *Past and Present* 39 (April 1968): 62–80.

Lovejoy, David. S. *Rhode Island Politics and the American Revolution, 1760–1776*. Providence: Brown University Press, 1958.

Main, Jackson Turner. *Political Parties before the Constitution*. Chapel Hill: University of North Carolina Press, 1973.

———. *The Social Structure of Revolutionary America*. Princeton, N.J.: Princeton University Press, 1965.

Marini, Stephen A. *Radical Sects of Revolutionary New England*. Cambridge, Mass.: Harvard University Press, 1982.

Matthews, Margery I., Virginia I. Benson, and Arthur E. Wilson. *Churches of Foster: A History of Religious Life in Rural Rhode Island.* Foster, R.I.: North Foster Baptist Church, 1978.

McCoy, Drew. *The Elusive Republic: Political Economy in Jeffersonian America.* Chapel Hill: University of North Carolina Press, 1980.

McDonald, Forrest, and Grady McWhiney. "The South from Self-Sufficiency to Peonage: An Interpretation." *American Historical Review* 85 (December 1980): 1095–1118.

McLoughlin, William G. *New England Dissent, 1630–1833: The Baptists and the Separation of Church and State.* 2 vols. Cambridge, Mass.: Harvard University Press, 1971.

Merrill, Michael. "Cash Is Good to Eat: Self-Sufficiency and Exchange in the Rural Economy of the United States." *Radical History Review* 15 (Winter 1977): 42–71.

Modell, John. "Mobility and Industrialization: Countryside and City in Nineteenth-Century Rhode Island." In *Essays from the Lowell Conference on Industrial History, 1980 and 1981,* edited by Robert Weible, Oliver Ford, and Paul Marion. Lowell, Mass.: Lowell Conference on Industrial History, 1981, 86–109.

Mohanty, Gail Fowler. "Rhode Island Handloom Weavers: A Probate Perspective." In *Early American Probate Inventories,* 86–96. The Dublin Seminar for New England Folklife, Annual Proceedings, 1987.

Mohl, Raymond. *Poverty in New York, 1783–1825.* New York, 1971.

De Miranda, Francisco. *New Democracy in America: Travels, 1783–84.* Translated by Judson P. Wood, edited by John S. Ezell. Norman: University of Oklahoma Press, 1963.

Morris, Richard B. *Studies in the History of American Law.* 2d ed. New York: Octagon Books, 1964.

Niemcewicz, Julian Ursyn. *Under Their Vine and Fig Tree: Travels through America in 1797–1799.* Translated and edited by Metchie J. E. Budka. New Jersey Historical Society Collections, vol. 14. Elizabeth, N.J.: Grassman Publishing Company, 1965.

Norton, Joseph Michael. "The Rhode Island Federalist Party: 1785–1815." Ph.D. dissertation, St. John's University, 1975.

Parkinson, Richard. *A Tour in America, in 1798, 1799 and 1800.* London, 1805.

Perry, Elizabeth A. *A Brief History of the Town of Glocester, Rhode Island. . . .* Providence, 1886.

Polishook, Irwin H. *Rhode Island and the Union, 1774–1795.* Evanston, Ill.: Northwestern University Press, 1969.

Prude, Jonathan. *The Coming of the Industrial Order: Town and Factory Life in Rural Massachusetts, 1810–1860.* Cambridge: Cambridge University Press, 1983.

Pruitt, Bettye Hobbs. "Self-Sufficiency and the Agricultural Economy of Eighteenth-Century Massachusetts." *William and Mary Quarterly* 41 (1984): 335–64.

———. *Historical and Architectural Resources of Burrillville, Rhode Island: A Preliminary Report.* Providence, 1982.

———. *Historic and Architectural Resources of Glocester, Rhode Island: A Preliminary Report.* Providence, 1980.

————. *Preliminary Survey Report: Town of Coventry.* Providence, 1978.

Rhode Island Historical Preservation Commission. *Foster, Rhode Island: Statewide Historical Preservation Report P-F-1.* Providence, 1982.

————. *Historic and Architectural Resources of Scituate, Rhode Island: A Preliminary Report.* Providence, 1980.

Rorabaugh, W. J. *The Alcoholic Republic: An American Tradition.* New York: Oxford University Press, 1979.

Roth, Randolph A. *The Democratic Dilemma: Religion, Reform, and the Social Order in the Connecticut River Valley of Vermont, 1791–1850.* Cambridge: Cambridge University Press, 1987.

Rothenberg, Winifred B. "The Emergence of a Capital Market in Rural Massachusetts, 1730–1838." *Journal of Economic History* 45 (December 1985): 781–808.

————. "The Market and Massachusetts Farmers, 1750–1855." *Journal of Economic History* 41 (June 1981): 283–314.

————. "A Price Index for Rural Massachusetts, 1750–1855." *Journal of Economic History* 39 (Decmeber 1979): 975–1001.

Rothman, David J. *The Discovery of the Asylum: Social Order and Disorder in the New Republic.* Boston: Little, Brown, 1971.

Russell, C. Allyn. "Rhode Island Baptists, 1825–1831." *Rhode Island History* 28 (1969): 35–48.

Russell, Howard S. *A Long Deep Furrow: Three Centuries of Farming in New England.* Hanover, N.H.: University Press of New England, 1976.

Ryan, Mary P. *Cradle of the Middle Class: The Family in Oneida County, New York, 1790–1865.* Cambridge: Cambridge University Press, 1981.

Ryan, Rev. T. E. *Burrillville, R.I. and the Catholic Church.* Harrisville, R.I., 1925.

Schantz, Mark S. "Missionaries and Mills: Religion in The Rhode Island Countryside." Paper presented at the Annual Meeting of the Society for Historians of the Early American Republic, 1987.

Schlebecker, John T. "Agricultural Markets and Marketing in the North, 1774–1779." *Agricultural History* 50 (June 1976): 21–36.

Shammas, Carole. "How Self-Sufficient Was Early America?" *Journal of Interdisciplinary History* 13 (1982–1983): 247–72.

Shorter, Edward. *The Making of the Modern Family.* New York: Basic Books, 1975.

Slaughter, Thomas P. *The Whiskey Rebellion: Frontier Epilogue to the American Revolution.* New York: Oxford University Press, 1986.

Smith, Daniel Scott. "Parental Power and Marriage Patterns." *Journal of Marriage and the Family* 35 (August 1973): 419–28.

Stewart, Rev. I. D. *The History of the Freewill Baptists.* Dover, N.H.: Freewill Baptist Printing Establishment, 1862.

Stone, Lawrence. *The Family, Sex and Marriage in England, 1500–1800.* New York: Harper and Row, 1977.

Sweet, Edward Francis. "The Origins of the Democratic Party in Rhode Island, 1824–1836." Ph.D. dissertation, Fordham University, 1971.

Szatmary, David P. *Shays' Rebellion: The Making of an Agrarian Insurrection.* Amherst: University of Massachusetts Press, 1980.

Taylor, Alan. *Liberty Men and Great Proprietors: The Revolutionary Settlement on the Maine Frontier, 1760–1820.* Chapel Hill: University of North Carolina Press, 1990.

Taylor, Philip E. "The Turnpike Era in New England." Ph.D. dissertation, Yale University, 1934.

Thomas, John L. "Romantic Reform in America." *American Quarterly* 17 (Winter 1965): 656–81.

Thompson, E. P. "The Moral Economy of the English Crowd in the Eighteenth Century." *Past and Present* 50 (February 1971): 76–136.

Tryon, Rolla Milton. *Household Manufactures in the United States, 1640–1860: A Study in Industrial History.* Chicago: University of Chicago Press, 1917.

Tyler, Alice Felt. *Freedom's Ferment: Phases of American Social History from the Colonial Period to the Outbreak of the Civil War.* Reprint. New York: Harper and Row, 1962.

Tyrrell, Ian. *Sobering Up: From Temperance to Prohibition in Antebellum America.* Westport, Conn.: Greenwood Press, 1979.

Ulrich, Laura Thatcher. "Martha Ballard and Her Girls: Women's Work in Eighteenth-Century Maine." In *Work and Labor in Early America,* edited by Stephen Innes. Chapel Hill: University of North Carolina Press, 1988.

Underwood, A. C. *A History of the English Baptists.* London: Baptist Union Publishing Department, 1947.

Waciega, Lisa Wilson. "A 'Man of Business': The Widow of Means in Southeastern Pennsylvania, 1750–1850." *William and Mary Quarterly* 44 (January 1987): 40–64.

Walters, Ronald G. *American Reformers, 1815–1860.* New York: Hill and Wang, 1978.

Whipple, Anna M. *Historical Facts and Stray Thoughts from the Old Elder Ballou Meeting House.* Woonsocket, R.I.: Charles E. Cook, 1897.

Wood, Gordon S. "Evangelical America and Early Mormonism." *New York History* 61 (October 1980): 359–86.

Works Projects Administration. *Inventory of the Church Archives of Rhode Island: Baptist.* Providence, 1941.

Zuckerman, B. Michael. "The Political Economy of Industrial Rhode Island, 1790–1860." Ph.D. dissertation, Brown University, 1981.

Index